GASPING
for
AIR

The Stranglehold of
Narcissistic Abuse

DANA S. DIAZ

Delaney's Heart Publications

Copyright © 2023 by Dana S. Diaz

ISBN (Paperback): 979-8-9881155-0-2
ISBN (eBook): 979-8-9881155-1-9

Cover design by Aaxel Author Services and Deividas Jablonskis
Interior design by Aaxel Author Services
Author Photo: Jenny Taylor Boudoir Photography

This book is designed for educational and entertainment purposes only. You should not rely on this information as a substitute for, nor does it replace, professional medical advice, diagnosis, or treatment. If you have any concerns or questions about your health, you should always consult with a physician or other health-care professional. Do not disregard, avoid or delay obtaining medical or health related advice from your health-care professional because of something you may have read in this book. The use of any information provided in this book is solely at your own risk. The author shall not be held liable or responsible to any person or entity with respect to any loss or incidental or consequential damages caused, or alleged to have been caused, directly or indirectly, by the information contained herein.

Printed in the United States of America

To my grandma, who withstood spousal abuses no person should ever have to endure but taught me boundless compassion and love for others despite it all.

*T*he first time I heard Crystal Gayle's ballad "Don't It Make My Brown Eyes Blue," something about it resonated deep within my soul. The lyrics perfectly expressed the conflict between desperately wanting love from someone and resolving oneself to the sadness of their rejection. It's like whomever wrote the song knew I struggled with the same feelings about my mother and stepfather. They emotionally, physically and verbally battered me, then negated my experiences altogether. Still, I wanted their love more than anything in the world. For I was only seven.

My mother would never love me, though, as long as I stood between her and my stepfather. He could never love me because I wouldn't submit to his manipulation and control. I couldn't understand why my mother chose to stay with him, nor why she allowed him to put a divide between us. All I knew was I'd never allow a man to wield that kind of power over me.

With no way out of the situation until I was older, I learned to keep my mouth shut to avoid the bruises, hand marks, and emotional scars disobedience earned me. I relied on moody melodies and expressive lyrics to help me cope with my circumstances instead. Whether singing with the radio in the car, performing in front of the mirror in my bedroom, or quietly enjoying whatever tapes my Walkman played through foam headphones, I always had music to validate and console me. I applied certain songs to situations, and sometimes to people, almost like a secret with myself.

It all started with Crystal Gayle's ballad, which I still sing and now see for the forewarning it was.

I

"I Knew You Were Trouble"

On a gloomy November afternoon in 1995, a dark blond twenty-something walked into the apartment complex office where I worked full time as a leasing agent.

In his black leather jacket, blue jeans, and T-shirt, he looked like he'd watched too many episodes of *Beverly Hills 90210*. He even mimicked the disinterested expression that Dylan, one of the show's main characters, was known for, adding to the impression that even he thought he was too cool. Only he wasn't. His scrawny body held disproportionately broad shoulders, which made him look muscular, but the dumpy diaper butt of his jeans proved the lack of muscle and tone in the rest of his body. I could get over that, though. I tended towards bad boys.

"Welcome to Maple Lake!" I said, batting my eyelashes with a bit of exaggeration. Then I fanned myself with my hand. "It's hot in here, isn't it?" What a stupid thing to say!

I'd just come out of a three-year relationship with a man I lived with and thought I was going to marry. But when he told me he put a deposit on an engagement ring, I got scared and talked him out of our relationship altogether. As a college sophomore, I wasn't ready to be a wife and mother of all the children he wanted right away. I wasn't even sure I wanted kids at all! Plus, he was openly unfaithful, and I wasn't willing to tolerate a marriage in which I wasn't enough. It was a messy break-up that left me feeling desperate for someone to belong to. It almost didn't even matter who.

Bad Boy ignored my flirting and got right to the point. "Yeah, I'm looking for a cheap studio or one-bedroom apartment."

1

"Okay, we're running a special right now, so you can actually get a one-bedroom for the price of a studio." My voice shook a little as I started my well-rehearsed sales pitch.

"I just want whatever is cheapest."

"You might as well take a one-bedroom then, but I'll let you take a look at a studio too, so you can decide," I said. He shrugged his shoulders indecisively, which I took as agreement with the decision I'd already made for him.

As I reviewed our inventory list for available units, Bad Boy stood directly in front of my desk with his hands in his jean pockets. His slightly extended hip gave away his impatience, which made me nervous, so it took me a little longer to focus. I never did well under pressure.

After pinpointing two available apartments in the same building, I circled them on a map of the complex and wrote the apartment numbers on top of the paper. "When you leave the office, go straight back to the pond we call a lake." I paused so he could chuckle at my lame joke like everyone else did. He looked at me blankly, though, so I proceeded. "Park on the lake side of the building. Once you go in, the studio is on the third floor, and the one-bedroom is on the garden level. I just moved into the third floor of that building, and the lake view is really pretty from up there. Most people prefer that, but we can select a unit in any building if you choose to rent here."

His brows scrunched when I handed him the map. "You're gonna just let me go and look by myself?"

Most people appreciated the ability to view the apartments on their own, so his offended tone sounded more like my failure to serve him, and I refused to acquiesce to some arrogant stranger to whom I owed nothing. "Yeah, just bring the keys back to me when you're done." I walked to the nearby key cabinet and returned a minute later. "Here you go!" I said with a fake smile, handing him the two sets of keys.

He glared at me as he left, clearly miffed I wasn't going out in the cold to gratify his sense of entitlement. I rolled my eyes behind his back.

Fifteen minutes later, he returned and firmly set the keys down in front of me.

"What did you think?" I asked cheerily, hoping to kill him with kindness.

"Eh, I don't know," he replied, brushing me off. Then he turned and walked out.

Good riddance, I thought. I didn't want to deal with some jackass who dismissed me like I was nothing and nobody anyway.

So I was surprised when he showed up a week later to fill out an apartment application.

"I didn't think you were interested in the apartment!" I said while I took photocopies of his driver's license and paycheck stubs. I noticed his name on his license—Darren. His mother must've watched the TV show *Bewitched*.

"I'm looking for the cheapest place I can find, and this is it," he explained. "I'm trying to save money to buy a condo in the next year."

"Wow! Well, good for you!" I returned to my desk and handed his license back to him. "That's a hell of a last name, by the way! How do you pronounce that?" His disapproving glower told me I'd hit a nerve. My voice quivered as I hurried to change the subject. "You wanted to take that one-bedroom apartment you saw, right? It's bigger than the studio and not much more cost-wise." Not that I wanted this jerk living near me.

"Yep," he snipped.

I'd have normally sat at my desk to calculate a new tenant's move-in-amount, but I remained standing to do so because Bad Boy didn't show any intention of sitting. It was still hard to focus, though, with him standing over me impatiently, so I bowed my head to avoid facing the overwhelming tension. I just wanted to hurry him, and the feelings he evoked in me, out the door.

"Okay, here's your move-in cost," I said as I pushed the itemized list across the desk towards him. "You'll pay the security deposit, pro-rated rent for the rest of the month, then the first full month as well. Your total is at the bottom."

He snatched the paper and walked out.

"Call Me Maybe"

*T*he week before Thanksgiving, Darren returned to sign his lease and pick up the keys to his new apartment.

"Happy moving day!" I said when he approached my desk.

"Yeah, it's not too bad out there today." He looked back towards the entrance door, referencing the sunshine coming in through the glass side panels.

My eyes widened as I reached for his file. "No, it's not, is it?" It felt unnatural to exchange pleasantries with someone who was usually standoffish. I preferred it, though, so I played nice too. "All I need is one signature and your check for the move-in amount, and you'll be on your way!"

"Cool." Darren took the pen I offered, signed where I pointed, and then took a pre-written check out of his pocket and placed it on my desk.

"All right, the apartment is all yours!" I smiled as I dangled the keys in front of him.

"Awesome, thanks." He smiled as he took the keys out of my hand.

I looked at him a little too long, trying to figure out where this sudden kindness, which I hadn't thought him capable of, had come from.

"That's all, right?" He distracted me out of my thoughts. That's when I noticed the greenish tint in the way the sun reflected off the light brown in his eyes. It's like I was seeing him in a whole new light.

"Oh! Yeah!" I stumbled through my words for a second, in a rush to make up for my awkwardness. "I just ... um ... I just moved into the same building. Exactly two floors above your apartment, actually. So if you need anything or have any questions or issues, feel free to knock on my door!"

4

"Okay . . ." He stared at me suspiciously for a couple seconds before he turned to leave. Then, just before the door closed behind him, I caught him glancing back at me once more.

A week later, I called to follow up on his move-in, as I did with all new lessees. He didn't answer for several rings. "Hello?" His voice was low. I looked at the office clock to make sure I hadn't woken him, but it was almost lunchtime.

"Hi, Darren! How's everything going?"

"Fine." I was glad to hear a TV blaring in the background. That meant I hadn't wakened him as I thought I might have when he answered. Still, I could tell by his short tone that I was disrupting his day.

"Okay, just let me know if you need anything! You can call me here at the office or knock on my door. Remember, I'm two floors above you in 310!" I closed my eyes and cringed as the words came out. I already told him where I lived, and the repetition made me sound desperate! I mean, I was desperate. I just didn't want to come off as desperate. Especially to him! It's not like I had some intense attraction to him or anything. Despite the one instance on his move-in day, he was a jerk and I wanted no part of him.

"Okay, thanks," Darren said, then hung up, saving me from further embarrassment.

A week after that, I returned from hanging out at a friend's house to find a piece of notebook paper rolled up between my doorknob and the door jamb. I looked around, wondering who'd left it, as if whoever did would be lurking in the hallway, waiting and watching for my reaction. Of course, the hallway was empty and quiet.

So I opened the paper and read the note. *If you get home before midnight, come down and see me. — Darren.*

My heart began to race. I was excited and confused at the same time! Since becoming single, I'd been waiting for someone—anyone—to express interest in me, but no one had yet. Even at the university I attended, with thousands of potential boyfriends passing me in the hallways between classes, no one looked at me twice! I was starting to think there was something wrong with me.

Based on our unpleasant interactions thus far, I'd have never guessed Darren wanted any part of me either. He was my only prospect, however, so I wouldn't let the opportunity pass me by. I wasn't sure if he was single, though. His gossipy neighbor across the hall told us girls in the office that Darren had a fiancée helping him move in. If that were true, why would he be inviting me to his apartment in the middle of the night?

Speaking of time, I looked at my watch and saw it was almost midnight. In that split second, my curiosity decided I should go find out what Darren's deal was. So I threw my purse into my apartment and frantically ran down the two flights of stairs before I turned into a pumpkin.

Out of breath from running, I knocked on Darren's door and told myself to act cool. I didn't want to come off eager. Still, I patted my fuzzy hair down, flipped it off my shoulders, then straightened my posture in preparation for Darren to open the door to me.

When he did, the stench of beer immediately answered my question about why he'd invited me over. His eyes were open too widely too. He didn't look like either of the two Darrens I'd met before, which made me think twice about entering this stranger's apartment.

Darren looked at me questionably too. I wondered why, then looked down at myself to see I was still wearing the long dark green plaid, flannel nightgown I'd been too lazy to change out of when my friend called me to come over earlier. It was more like a moo-moo a grandma would wear, though Darren's drunken state was even less appealing, so I figured we were even.

"Come on in!" He stepped back to allow me entrance. I did so with sloth-like caution, unsure of whether I was with entitled Darren, happy Darren, or a potentially engaged Darren.

The apartment was like mine and all the others in the complex. Plain white walls surrounded the living room. The dark bedroom would look the same. The kitchen and bathroom, which could be seen from where I stood, contained dark brown cabinets and a mixture of avocado green appliances and pear yellow counters reminiscent of the 1970s. Scratchy Berber carpet completed the extent of what $450 per month could afford.

Nearly a dozen empty pizza boxes were strewn about near the plastic garbage can at the end of the galley kitchen. An equal amount of empty beer cans lined the counters. Blankets and pillows lay scattered on the floor between the black leather couch and TV in the living room, and a red milk crate served as a side table. Only a single man would live this way, I noted.

The disarray made me slightly uncomfortable too. I'd grown up in a wealthy neighborhood north of Chicago, in a very small but tidy and well-kept duplex, where everything was in its exact place, including the temperature on the thermostat. I wasn't haughty, though, so I encouraged myself to remain open-minded to Darren. He was only twenty-one, I recalled from the birth year on his driver's license.

Plus, all the diamond engagement ring commercials and billboards meant to motivate men to buy shiny baubles for Christmas reminded me I wasn't anyone's "someone special" anymore. I wanted to be someone's "forever" more than anything, minus the cheating and baby-making my ex would have subjected me to.

"Have you ever seen this movie *Tombstone?*" Darren pointed to the TV. Then he sat on the couch. "It's my favorite movie!"

"No," I said as I made myself comfortable on the opposite end of the couch. I pulled my knees up and laid my legs sideways, then pulled my nightgown down over them to keep warm. "I was surprised to get your note. I thought you were engaged," I said to let Darren know right away that I wouldn't be someone's side interest.

He laughed and took a sip of beer before responding. "Oh, her? No!" He obviously knew who I was referring to. "I had a crush on her in high school, but she didn't give me the time of day. Then I ran into her a few months ago, and she was all over me! She said she couldn't believe how good-looking I was now, compared to back then. It pissed me off she was so superficial, so I led her on! Slept with her, took her out a few times, told her I loved her and we would be together forever. But after I moved in here, I dropped her. Stopped returning her calls, stopped seeing her . . . now she can feel what it's like to be treated like shit!"

It bothered me that he could intentionally hurt someone, justify it, and then show no remorse. I mean, how could someone like that ever be trusted? At the same time, I appreciated his complete honesty. Not everyone would openly admit to their shitty behavior.

While I pondered on whether this knowledge about him would be an issue for me, Darren took another sip of his beer. I watched his cheeks expand and his lips pucker outward, chalking up his strange behavior to drunkenness. Then, all of a sudden, he spewed the beer at me like a fountain. The cold beer dripped down my lashes and cheeks, then made its way down to the chest of my pajamas. My mouth fell open in shock. I'd been spit on by a boy in high school who called me a "dog" as we passed in the hallway, and the insult felt was similar.

I looked down at my damp lap, and even more beer dripped off the hair framing my face. Why would Darren do this to me when he'd been the one to invite me here? Didn't guys usually want to impress girls they were interested in? Or had I read the whole situation wrong, and he'd brought me here to humiliate me for my lack of servitude to him when we'd first met at the office? I looked at Darren with sad eyes, hoping for an apology, or at least an explanation, but he just laughed.

Then he raised his beer can to his lips again. I turned my face, expecting another spew, but he swallowed the beer this time, then chuckled. This was amusing to him? I looked at him with squinty-eyed scorn this time. I'd been treated like shit my whole life, and I wasn't about to let this guy disrespect me like this for no reason.

Then I reminded myself a drunk loser like him wasn't worth it. I needed to dry off anyway. I hated being wet almost as much as I hated being cold, and I was crawling out of my skin feeling both.

I looked down to assess whether I could move without spilling the small puddle of beer in the lap of my nightgown onto Darren's couch and carpet. Although he didn't deserve the respect he didn't give to me, I wouldn't lower my character to that of someone with such little regard for others.

Suddenly, another large splash of beer soaked my hair and pajamas even more. I tasted some of its bitterness as it dripped into my open mouth. I blinked a few times before rubbing my eyes to see clearly, though all I saw was Darren laughing at me.

What the hell was wrong with him? I'd known he was a jerk, so why was I here? Better yet, why was I *still* here? Because I was lonely, I reminded myself. I wasn't lonely enough to endure this, though.

The overwhelming discomfort of the cold beer making my skin tacky as it dried made me forget about everything except how cold and sticky I was. My hair was probably crunchy and needed washing. I just wanted to go upstairs to my apartment, take a hot shower, and forget this whole night ever happened.

Without thinking, I pulled my nightgown off over my head. It wasn't until I saw Darren gawking at me with lustful eyes that I realized I had inappropriately disrobed and stood before him in only my green satin panties. In open-mouthed horror at my own actions, I held my balled-up nightgown in front of my breasts and thought to make a swift run up to my apartment as I was. No one would see me in the hallways at this hour anyway.

Before I could move towards the door, Darren pounced on me like a savage beast who refused to let his prey escape. He grabbed my breasts, then placed his hands on my flat rear end while pressing his hard groin into my front.

I should have been repulsed. I wanted to be. Despite my low self-esteem, even I knew I deserved better than to be spit on with beer and grabbed at like a whore. I couldn't expect someone I barely liked, and who didn't seem to have any particular favor towards me, to treat me any better, though. He was drunk and knew I lived upstairs and probably just wanted to get laid! How could I expect any different when I was the one who'd shown up in response to a middle-of-the-night invitation and bared my near-naked body to him without thinking about the consequences? So this wasn't his fault. It was mine.

Did that mean I wanted to have sex with him? No. Nor was he so good-looking that I could justify sex for the score. He looked like Matthew Perry from the TV show Friends, except with badly bleached blond hair and dead brown eyes. Not to mention, I'd never had sex with someone I just met. Hell, I barely had experience at all! But before I could stop it or consent to it, I was lying on the carpet with him on top of me.

He pressed his face uncomfortably close to mine. When our noses touched, I cringed and instinctively tried to back away. The carpeted floor under my head reminded me I had nowhere to go. Darren pressed his forehead to mine while unbuttoning his jeans, grinning without regard for my discomfort. So I closed my eyes and resolved myself to the imminent fornication.

This was what I wanted, right? For a man to want me? I wished I didn't need a man's attention to feel worthy and validated, but I couldn't help it, and I didn't want to fight it either. Darren was here, and he wanted me. Even if just sexually, and even if just for tonight, his eagerness to touch me in certain places and feel me all over fulfilled the need I had to be desired. So I let him have his way with me.

After pulling my panties down, he went at me like a fifteen-year-old boy getting it for the first time. Part of me wanted to feel violated, yet Darren's enjoyment of my body empowered me and gave me a higher sense of myself. To think my outward appearance was perceived to be so beautiful that it could make a man wild with passion, that his body could respond to mine on a purely physical level, was profound. That feeling almost made the encounter enjoyable.

When he was finished, I reached for my nightgown, which lay on the floor next to us. Although still damp and smelling of rotted hops and barley, it was like a security blanket which would protect me from my naiveté.

"You wanna stay over?" Darren flipped the lights off, obviously assuming I would.

The invitation caught me off guard. I had no intention of spending the night with him, nor could I understand how I went from a one-night stand to someone he wanted to wake up to so quickly. Who was I to judge, though? I'd just engaged in an act I neither wanted nor refused. So I reluctantly accepted, figuring I had nothing to lose at this point.

While I settled into the make-shift bed of blankets on the floor near the couch, thankful for the dry and warm cover, Darren turned his stereo on. I recognized the melancholy sounds of the Cure's "Lovesong" and tried not to hold his taste of music against him. As a classically trained violist who'd played in two junior symphonic orchestras through high school, I'd have preferred the dark but soothing sounds of The Phantom of the Opera soundtrack.

Although the lights were off now, the full moon shined enough light into the long window on the one wall for me to see Darren retrieve a plastic cup hidden at the side of the couch. He inserted himself within the blankets next to me, then spit into his cup. I crinkled my nose. My ex chewed tobacco and I thought it was disgusting.

"Yeah, it's a bad habit." He must have seen the revulsion on my moonlit face as I unconsciously stared up at him. "I know I need to quit, but it relaxes me so I can fall asleep."

I appreciated people who were self-aware. I just hadn't expected it from an arrogant ass who'd spit beer in my face just a short time before. "I guess we all have our issues. As long as you don't smoke, though. I can't handle people smoking around me."

Silence.

"You smoke too?"

"Just when I drink a lot." I wondered what he considered "a lot" since I'd just seen him completely drunk, and it'd seemed like any other night for him. At least he appeared to be sobering now.

"What?" Darren got defensive about my silence.

"I've never smoked. Not that I'm better than anyone else. Just that cigarette smoke makes me cough. I can't handle it," I told him.

"You gonna tell me you don't drink either?" Darren snickered.

"I don't go out to bars, if that's what you mean. I'm not old enough anyway."

"How old *are* you?" He sounded panicked and slid away from me slightly.

"Nineteen, but I'll be twenty at the end of the month," I replied, eagerly aging myself out of my teens. "My birthday is two days after Christmas!"

I felt his chest heave and retract. "Shit, I thought you were gonna tell me you're underage!" He spit into his cup again. "I thought you were older."

"Like how old?" The high pitch of my voice expressed my offense. Most people thought I looked much younger than I was! I'd often been told I looked like Bruce Willis's daughter in the movie *Die Hard*!

"At least twenty-four, but that navy blue uniform of yours makes you look like you're in your thirties," he told me, then used a high-pitched voice to imitate me. "You wanna rent an apartment?"

"Oh, is that how I sound?" I chided with a chuckle. Then I playfully smacked him on the chest. As we giggled like school kids, I was surprised at how comfortable we were with each other in this moment, considering how repulsed I'd been with our physical interaction just a short time before.

Darren was friendly now, funny, and open—such a stark contrast to the standoffish, unsociable jerk I'd met at the office, and the unmannerly frat boy I'd sat on the couch with earlier tonight. Granted, we all have different aspects of our personality, but his were like different people altogether, and I wondered who he really was at the core. The only way to find out was to keep talking, I supposed.

"I'm just doing what I have to do to make it on my own," I said, referring to my work and my nautical uniform suit. "I walked out of my parents' house at eighteen, and I'll do whatever it takes to never have to live under their roof again."

"I moved out at eighteen too, but it's because my mom told me I had to move or pay rent. She wanted me to pay for my own food and for using their washer and dryer to do laundry!"

"That's crazy! But I *had* to leave my house. My mother never wanted me, and my stepfather never wanted to pay for what he referred to as 'another man's child,' so it was fun!" The raised inflection of my voice made my sarcasm clear. "They got married when I was seven. I was told to call my stepfather 'Dad' and tell everyone I was his biological daughter to save my mother from her own shame for having had me so young. But almost every day of my life growing up, that asshole would tell me my mother didn't love me, that I was a burden on them, that no one wanted me . . . and if I told anyone, I'd get a physical beating. I tried to tell my mother what he was doing to me, but she didn't believe me because, of course, he denied it all. He said I was making things up to get her attention. So eventually I stopped saying anything. She liked being with someone who had a house and gave her a car and all the stuff. And she wanted all that more than she wanted to protect her daughter, I guess. So here we are!" Suddenly overcome with self-pity, I cast my eyes downward.

"Your stepdad sounds like a dick," Darren said matter-of-factly, then spit into his cup again. His validation made me feel like someone was finally on my side.

"Yeah, he is. He tried to force me into submission, like he did with my mother. But I'm not like my mother. I stood up to him, called him an asshole to his face. He obviously didn't like that. And because he couldn't control me, I was a problem. And when you have a problem, you get rid of it, which is exactly what he did. Pushed me out. And my mother did nothing to stop me from leaving, so I guess me being gone solved her problems too."

"That sounds rough," Darren said.

"Yeah, I wish things had been different. I still try to have a relationship with my mother. It's strained, though. I've gone to counseling, but no amount of talking can change how my mother and stepfather feel about me or how they've treated me. So I was referred to a psychiatrist who diagnosed me with bipolar depression and put me on Prozac. I guess it's easier to numb the victim of abuse than to deal with the abusers."

"How does your real dad fit into all this? Is he around?"

"No, but not because I don't want him to be. I actually met him when I was sixteen. Turns out he lived only three miles away my whole life, but my mother didn't want me to have anything to do with him. I went behind her back and went to lunch and a movie with him anyway. We talked on the phone every night after that. Got along great! It's hard to explain, but getting to know him made me feel like I knew where I came from because we were so much alike. I didn't fit in at all with my mom and stepfather. But then my mom said my real dad called the house when I wasn't there and hit on her, so every time he called after that, she and my stepfather would argue about it, then make me feel bad for putting my mother in that position. So it was just easier to stop talking to my real dad to keep whatever peace I could in the house. Sucks though. I always wished he'd come and take me away with him."

We sat in silence for a few minutes. I knew I had a tendency to overshare, maybe because I wanted to put my least attractive qualities out there to prematurely weed out people who wouldn't want to deal with the mess they would eventually know me to be. Or maybe I assumed people wouldn't want anything to do with me if they got to know me, so I tried to get rid of them before I got too attached. Darren seemed receptive, though. I felt like he had genuine interest in me as a person, instead of the sexual conquest I'd felt like earlier, and I wanted to know more about him too.

"So, what are your parents like? Hopefully better than mine?"

"Yeah! Well, my dad is great. Not that he was around much when I was a kid. He was a foreman for the electric company, so he would get called out all the time, even on holidays. So it was just me and my mom and sister most of the time."

"Sister?" I'd always wanted a big sister—a built-in best friend to confide in and protect me from, or at least witness, the abuses that occurred in our house. Instead, I got a little brother—my mother and stepfather's child together—who was currently five years old.

"Yeah, Denise is twenty-five. Four years older than me. Denise's dad—my mom's first husband—died when Denise was a baby. Then she married my dad, and they had me," he summed up.

"Are you close with your sister?" I asked hopefully.

"Eh, she and my mom are close. I've always been the odd man out." *Just like me,* I thought. "I was dragged around to all Denise's dance classes and stuff, since my dad was busy working. I never got to do anything or have anything I wanted. Mom said we didn't have the money, but Denise got a car and a condo . . . my mom said it was because the life insurance money Denise's dad left them when he died was just for Denise. So I got the shaft."

Darren's blatant honesty about his childhood and the feelings associated with being second best made me understand him so much more. He was unfriendly because he didn't want to let people in and risk getting hurt. I, on the other hand, was overly friendly because I sought connection instead of rejection. We were both the same inside, though—hurt and lonely. Only a true black sheep could recognize another, a commonality that could create an unbreakable bond, whether as friends or something more.

I'd ponder on our future another time, though. It was well past my normal bedtime, and my eyelids were struggling to stay open. So, I sank into the crevice of Darren's armpit and closed my eyes. He pulled me in closer with his free arm.

A moment later, I heard Darren whisper, "If you treat me like a king, I'll treat you like a queen."

My eyes popped back open. I wasn't sure if that was a threat or a command. Either way, it was an odd thing to say. It's a given in any relationship that people want to be treated well, but we weren't in a relationship. Did he think we were because we just had sex? I was okay with that, if that were the case. I didn't want to be alone. Plus, if he felt so strongly about me already, I was open to seeing where this went. Still, what a strange thing to say!

I felt more tired than unsettled, though, so I'd make sense of it in the morning. For now, I closed my eyes again, hoping this was the beginning of a love story. Otherwise, I was just a whore.

"As Long as You Love Me"

A dinner date at Olive Garden, a red rose, and a playful snowball fight later, Darren invited me to his apartment to meet his parents. I wasn't prepared to meet them only a week into whatever we were, but I was glad (and surprised!) for the presumed depth of his feelings.

It was a Friday evening, and I'd just gotten off work. I had less than an hour to get ready, so I skipped showering and traded my nautical-style navy suit for black velour leggings and a long wool sweater. My fluffy white cat—who'd earned the name 'Kitty' as a result of me calling out, "Here, kitty kitty," to locate him when I'd come home from work or school—laid on the bed watching me change. He probably wondered why I wasn't cuddling with him on the sectional sofa in the living room, like I usually did at night.

Assessing myself in the mirror, I liked how the forest green sweater complimented my fair complexion and contrasting dark eyes and hair. My hair was my nemesis, though. The crazy curls could never be tamed to my liking.

With a blow dryer and oversized round bristle brush, I styled my shoulder length hair into thick waves, applied dark brown eyeliner on my lash line, touched up my black mascara, and completed the look with my signature dark red lipstick.

After one last look in the mirror, I grabbed my purse and keys, patted Kitty on the head, then rushed out the door as quickly as I'd come in. I didn't want to be late!

When Darren opened his apartment door, he was chuckling about something someone must have said before I knocked. I couldn't help but smile with him as I stepped inside. A man with a jovial round face to match his Santa Claus belly, and a skinny stick of a woman with auburn hair curled under at the bangs and shoulders, smiled back.

"Hi! I'm Dana." I waved and then extended my hand to the woman, who approached me first.

She shook my hand delicately, "Hi, Dana! I'm Jane." Darren had her eyes, I noticed, except hers shimmered in a way Darren's didn't. "I like your name."

"You do?"

"We were going to name Darren 'Dana' if he'd been a girl," she said.

"Oh, yeah, he told me about that!" I chuckled. "He said you even dressed him up as a girl for his first or second Halloween?"

Jane laughed as she instantly recalled the memory. "Yes, we did!"

"With yarn braids and everything!" Darren threw in.

I rolled my eyes and joked, "Someone was traumatized!" Then I offered my hand to the jolly man.

"Oh, come 'ere!" He pulled me in for the kind of hug that made breathing difficult. When he released me, I giggled at the childlike twinkle in his blue eyes and the silly grin he wore.

"This is my dad, Henrik," Darren said, as if excusing a child's improper behavior.

"Nice to meet you!" The warm welcome made my shoulders relax a bit. They always held my anxiety and tension.

"Nice to meet you too!"

Darren moved toward the couch then, and his parents followed suit. I settled on the carpet in front of the TV, facing them.

Henrik stood up right away. "Here, sit on the couch."

"No, I'm fine! You go ahead and sit by your son," I insisted, though I appreciated his good manners. It reassured me Darren was raised to be a gentleman, despite his behavior that first night.

He sat back down and Darren rose immediately. I thought it was because he was offering his seat to me instead, but he disappeared into the kitchen and emerged with a piece of pizza. "Want some?" he offered, a little too late for the good manners I presumed he'd been taught.

"No, I'm good," I lied. I was starving, but shy about eating in front of people. I'd been humiliated by grade school and high school classmates too many times for chewing with my mouth open at lunch. Even after dental surgeries and braces, I'd never gotten over the public scrutiny.

"Are you sure?" Jane asked as she got up and walked toward the kitchen.

Darren spoke with his mouth full. "My mom makes it from scratch! It's the best!" Then he shoved the last of his piece into his mouth before going back for another.

Jane came out of the kitchen with two paper plates full of pizza and handed one to Henrik before sitting down. "Are you sure you don't want some?" she asked me again before taking her first bite.

"Thank you, but really, I'm fine!" I smiled, though my stomach was sad watching them eat my favorite food.

Thankfully, Jane distracted me with conversation. "Darren says you go to DePaul?"

"Yeah, I'm a good Catholic girl going to Catholic University!" I joked, arms raised in jazz hands.

Jane laughed out loud. "What are you studying?"

"I started out pre-law with a minor in psychology, thinking I would be a child and family law attorney and get kids out of abusive homes, but I recently changed my major to communications with a concentration in broadcast journalism. A few of my professors recommended the change because they think I have a natural talent for writing and speaking. So, who knows? Maybe I'll be the next Barbara Walters!" I shrugged.

"Oh!" Jane seemed impressed.

Henrik placed his bare paper plate on the red crate next to the couch. "As long as you get your degree and work hard, you'll do well," he assured me in a fatherly tone that made me feel supported and encouraged.

"That's the plan!"

After an hour of light conversation about weather and Christmas trees, Jane and Henrik said their goodbyes. They didn't live too far away, but far enough that the dark drive back in slushy snow would take longer than usual.

"That went well!" I said when Darren returned from escorting his parents out to their car.

Darren wrapped his arms around my waist. I instinctively put mine around his neck. "I knew they'd love you as much as I do," he said, looking down at me with a closed-mouth smile of approval. "You love me too?"

Love? After only a week?

I knew *I* had a tendency to attach to people quickly. However, I'd been told I was unlovable by people who were supposed to love me no matter what, so how could someone who barely knew me fall in love with *me* so fast?

I wasn't going to question or risk losing it, though. If someone chose to love me, I could love them back. Love was a choice, wasn't it? And I had no reason not to give love a shot. Darren was sweet to me. He told me I was beautiful every single day. He was funny and playful. He spent every free second with me. We definitely had something between us.

He offered me everything I'd ever wanted—two supportive parents, a big sister, a stable life of smiles and laughter, approval and acceptance I didn't have elsewhere. So yes, I could love Darren and the life I foresaw with him.

"Forever!" I replied, gazing into his eyes adoringly. He smiled down at me, then pulled me in close. We were officially a couple.

"Creep"

The new No Doubt record was released the week before Christmas, so I stopped to buy it on the way home from work one night. I didn't usually like the music Darren listened to, but the funky sounds of this new group intrigued me from the first time I'd heard them on the grunge rock radio station Darren listened to. I loved the honesty and boldness in the lyrics and Gwen Stefani's raw execution of them.

"Look what I got!" I dangled the compact disc back and forth in my raised hand as I entered Darren's apartment. I was like a cat bringing a fat mouse home to its owner for approval.

Darren smiled as I brushed past him and plopped down on his couch without removing the long black leather coat I wore over my work suit. Then he stood over me and watched my pink, frozen fingers wrestle with the plastic wrapped too tightly around the little surprise. When I finally ripped the packaging off, I presented the CD to him with both hands and a big, red-lipped smile.

Instead of the delight I'd expected, Darren's face morphed into some seething alter ego. Like a switch had been flipped, he scowled at me with narrowed eyes and lips curled under clenched teeth.

I tilted my head and squinted up at Darren, trying to figure how a CD could cause my new boyfriend, who'd sweetly caressed my cheek with the back of his hand while we watched TV the night before, to look down on me contemptuously, as if I'd committed some unforgivable offense. I couldn't make sense of it.

He didn't say anything, and as confused as I was, I didn't know what to say either. So neither of us spoke. We just held our stares like two cowboys in the Wild West waiting for the other to draw his weapon.

Suddenly, Darren moved with swift determination towards the colorfully lit Christmas tree in the corner of the living room. My shoulders tensed as I watched him snatch a small square gift from among the few others. He violently tore off the red ribbon and Santa Claus wrapping paper and flung the paper back at the tree. Then he whipped the small square across the room at me.

It spun through the air like a frisbee, heading straight for my face. I closed my eyes and ducked, then re-opened them when the sound of the object hitting the couch alerted me that I'd been spared. Laying on the couch was the same No Doubt CD I held in my hands.

I looked back up at Darren, hoping he could rationalize the inequity of his very hostile reaction to the general meaninglessness of the CD at the center of all this.

As if answering my thoughts, he explained, "Yeah, I already bought it for you for Christmas! So you wasted my fucking money!"

Shocked at his nasty tone and unwarranted accusation, I stood up to defend myself, so we could be as eye to eye as my short stature would allow. "Well, how was I supposed to know you bought it for me?"

"Well, why the fuck would you buy yourself *anything* so close to Christmas?" he shouted back.

"Because I thought we would like to listen to it together! That's why! It's not even a big deal, though—the one you bought is still in its packaging, so I can use my receipt to return it and get your fifteen dollars back."

Darren moved toward me aggressively. I instinctively leaned back to avoid his affront, then consciously straightened up. I'd been hit enough times in my life to know when it was coming, but I wouldn't give any man the satisfaction of cowering to his power play. If he wanted to hit me, I'd stare straight into his eyes while he did.

I was relieved when Darren veered to my right instead and seized the CD from the couch next to me. He'd just meant to intimidate me, I noted, which was intentionally mean and something I refused to tolerate.

Then he tore the plastic wrap off it, like a child who hadn't gotten his way. "Can't return it now!" His immaturity was altogether shocking and repulsive.

"Why would you do that, Darren? Now we can't return either one!"

"Yeah, and you're getting one less Christmas present too!"

"What, you're punishing me for buying a CD? Jesus Christ!" When I fled my childhood home, I swore I'd never let another man abuse me ever again. So, I stormed out, taking my CD with me.

As disappointed as I was that Darren had displayed a level of irrational anger I probably couldn't get past, I wasn't heartbroken. I was emotionless actually, as I marched up to my apartment with resolve that I'd rather be alone than be with someone who behaved so erratically.

I rather enjoyed the solitude of the night too. In the short time I'd been with Darren, I'd forgotten how much I liked sitting on the couch with my Kitty, watching a show I actually liked, and eating a good old bowl of macaroni and cheese. It's like I'd already lost myself in doing everything Darren wanted to do and how he wanted to do it. So I wasn't at all upset that he didn't call or come knocking on my door with an apology. I think I needed a little break. Maybe we both did.

When I returned to my apartment after school the next evening, I was surprised to see Darren sitting on my floral sectional watching TV. We'd exchanged keys shortly after that first night a couple weeks before, but we'd had no contact since I stormed out of his apartment, and therefore no resolution, which I felt made his presence a bit inappropriate.

"Hey . . ." I drew out the greeting. I wasn't sure what to say, since I didn't know where we stood.

"Hey, babe! How was school?" He took a swig from his bottle of Miller Lite.

Babe? I felt like I was in some alternate universe where everything was the opposite of what I thought it was. I even paused for a moment to remind myself of what happened to make sure I wasn't missing something in the seeming normalcy.

We obviously needed to have a conversation. I just wished I'd had some notice to prepare what I wanted to say. Regardless, I put my black backpack on the upholstered seat of the nearest dining room chair, and set my keys on the cherry wood table before rounding the sectional and sitting on the edge of the cushion next to the light-hearted Dr. Jekyll.

I looked at him for some indication of what he was thinking, but his poker face was entranced with the TV, as if I weren't even there.

Then, without removing his eyes from the screen, he put his arm around my shoulders and pulled me into a snuggle. Was this his way of expressing he didn't want to talk about it? Or was he sorry but couldn't express it without sacrificing his machismo or something?

After completing final exams for four classes that day, my brain was too fried to figure it out or provoke Darren out of his peaceable demeanor and into an argument, discussion or break-up. I just wanted dinner and rest.

I had a tendency to overthink anyway. He'd probably just had a bad day. We all have bad days. So I took his good mood as an apology and left well enough alone.

"It Don't Matter"

month later, Darren and I were living together.

It was the end of January 1996 and a management change at work had left me unemployed. I was given only three days to vacate the free apartment I'd been allowed with my position, so Darren insisted I move in with him until I secured a new job and hopefully another free apartment.

Despite the upset of the CD incident, I agreed. We'd been getting along just fine, so I was reassured I'd been right to dismiss the issue as a bad day. There was no way I could find another place to live without income anyway, and I refused to return to my childhood home.

Playing house suited us well! We got into a regular routine in which we both held up some certain end of the bargain. Darren woke up, dressed and walked out the door to work every morning to make the money that paid the bills, while I took time having my coffee and watching the morning news before heading out to school. I'd clean the apartment, do laundry, study, and write papers on days off from school, so I could cater to Darren when he returned home from work in the evening. I'd cook something edible for dinner, and we'd watch certain TV shows together, speculating and debating about what outrageous acts the different characters on Melrose Place would do next, or who would be pairing up with whom on the next episode of 90210. It was an equitable and enjoyable partnership that carried into the bedroom most nights.

One night, a month and a half later, Darren took a call from the couch in the living room. I could hear his end of the conversation from the other side of the wall, where I was studying in the bedroom.

"Oh, hey, Denise! Yeah, she just moved in a couple weeks ago . . ." My ears perked up immediately at the reference to me. "I know . . . yeah . . . I get it, but I wasn't going to let her be homeless . . . I knew it wouldn't go over well with Grandma, since we're not married and all, but . . . yes, I know Mom doesn't agree with this either. Dad came over and made up some excuse about why Mom didn't come with, but me and Dana knew it was because she was pissed we moved in together. It really hurt Dana's feelings, since Mom liked her just fine before . . . yeah, I get it, Denise, but how do you think Dana feels? I don't even see what the big deal is anyway. Didn't you just go on a cruise with Brad? And *you're* not married!"

I appreciated Darren defending me, but it was hard to stand by and listen to him take the brunt of what had been our decision. I guess the abused little girl inside me was sensitive to others being bullied and pushed around too. Plus, how could I not take the attack personally? Denise didn't even know me, yet she obviously thought whatever influence she had over Darren would compel him to throw me out on the streets to satisfy the family's conservative values.

So, although there was really nothing I could do or say to change the situation, I walked out into the living room and stood near Darren with my arms crossed as a show of solidarity.

"Well, I don't know what to say! I guess everyone's gonna have to get used to it because she's here!" Darren rolled his eyes and nodded his head side to side as Denise presumably railed on him for his assertion. "I'm glad you guys made it back from your cruise at least . . . yeah, we're going . . . we'll see you there then . . . okay . . . yep . . . bye."

"What was that about?"

Darren's shoulders heaved in concordance with the long sigh he let out. "My sister just got back from a cruise she went on with her boyfriend, Brad, and she heard from Mom that you moved in. I guess Mom and Grandma weren't happy with her going on a cruise because her and Brad aren't married, so they're really not happy with you moving in. And if they're not happy, Denise isn't happy, and when Denise isn't happy, everyone's gonna hear about it." He leaned back onto the couch and resumed watching TV, clearly unbothered by the scolding. It was a big deal to me, though!

"First your mom, now your sister," I said sadly. "And I haven't even met Denise yet!"

"Don't worry about it," Darren replied, waving a hand in the air dismissively. "They'll get over it once they have something else to gossip about. Denise is always starting drama anyway."

"You sure this isn't going to be a thing? We've got that dinner at your parents' house with Denise, and then Easter." I'd been looking forward to meeting Denise, but the judgment conveyed in this phone call gave me a sudden case of anxiety. I tended to steer clear of people who took issue with me.

"It'll be fine," Darren said with an unconcern meant to reassure me.

"You sure?"

"I promise." Darren stood up and kissed me on the forehead. Then, with his hands on my shoulders, he looked directly into my eyes and said, "It doesn't matter what anyone else thinks anyway. It's you and me against the world, right?"

Nobody had ever defended me like he'd just done with his sister. That was enough for me to justify trusting him. "Yeah, forever."

"Sister Golden Hair"

We walked up to Jane and Henrik's modest ranch home hand in hand. The early dusk sky cast a pastel shadow onto the big bay window overlooking the front yard and reflected the golden hue of the cornfields from across the narrow road. Geese statues dressed in Easter aprons and bunny ears greeted us at the front door. I couldn't help but snicker. The whole scene was as wholesome and "country" as Darren had described.

Jane opened the front door before we could knock. "Hi, guys!" She must have seen us through the front window. Suddenly nervous about how I'd be received, I tightened my grip on Darren's hand.

He released it to accept Jane's quick hug, then stepped inside to shake Henrik's hand. I heard Henrik say, "Hello, son!"

I remained in the open doorway like a lost puppy. Jane smiled and patted my back. "How are you doing?"

I was thankful for the politeness after all the hoopla over our living situation. "I'm good. How are you?"

"Good!" Jane responded as Henrik came over to me, wearing that toothy little grin that made him look like a child up to no good. Without warning, he squeezed me so hard I lost my breath for a moment! I laughed at his enthusiasm when he released me. "And how are you?" His arm remained around my shoulders.

"Good!" I smiled at his warmth, while looking around curiously.

The white color scheme of the living room, meant to look fresh and bright, was exhausted between the simple furniture and tasteful lamps and décor. A built-in bookcase consuming an entire wall caught my attention, though. Its straight, boring lines held meticulously chosen knick-knacks and framed photos, placed in careful symmetry.

In a quick scan, I immediately recognized a slightly younger Darren in an eight-by-ten on the very top shelf to the right. His hair was thick and combed off to the side like a middle-aged man in the '80s. He wore a dark, collared shirt, and his hand was positioned under his chin as if in deep thought. His eyes looked off into the distance, like the models in Calvin Klein ads, and the uneven brows and openness of the eyes gave an expression as equally awkward as the half attempt at a smile.

Jane saw me looking at it. "That's Darren's high school graduation photo." Then she pointed to an eight-by-ten on the same shelf on the opposite side. "And that's Denise's high school graduation photo!"

"Oh!" Tit for tat. I guess it was better to have a fair mother than one who outright favored one child over another as in my family.

With her perfectly curled blonde hair teased at the bang, and her perfectly proportionate big blue eyes, Denise reminded me of Blair from *The Facts of Life*. She was definitely the popular girl who seemed to have it all. It was such a stark contrast from the insecurity portrayed in Darren's photo.

I approached the bookcase to examine the smaller photos I couldn't see from where we stood. Junior high and middle school photos of Darren filled the middle shelves. He wore a sports jersey and held a basketball in one, which surprised me. Darren didn't care for sports, and his scrawny arms didn't give the impression he had any athletic ability either. There was that thick hair combed sideways again too! I'd never imagined the persnickety guy I knew now, who strategically placed his gelled hair, leaving the house without product in his hair, never mind the crooked tooth grin he sported!

The remaining photos displayed a happy child with a 1970s bowl haircut, living a normal life of birthday parties, holidays, and family vacations. He wore a big, genuine smile in one picture, where he sat in front of a lit birthday cake. He was laughing hard in another, at a husky man doing a handstand with his head in a bucket. I wondered if that was Henrik! I smiled for a moment, as if the joy expressed in that moment were contagious after all the time that had passed.

Then it occurred to me that Darren lacked that same joy now. I looked back up at his high school graduation picture for comparison. Aside from the lack of enthusiasm in his smile, there was something about his eyes. They had a slight down-turned shape that naturally gave him a sorrowful expression. However, there was a blankness in them, like he was lost or at least devoid of the joy he'd expressed in his younger years. I wondered what happened to make him so sad. He told me he'd always felt left out—that his dad was always working, and his mom and sister were inseparable—but I felt like there was more, like something else had destroyed his spirit. Hopefully, he'd open up to me about it someday.

"Well, I better get back downstairs to Denise and Brad," I heard Jane tell Darren. I looked back to see her disappear through a nearby doorway. So Denise had been in the basement this whole time? I'd seen an unfamiliar sports car in the driveway with her initials on the license plate, but I'd been so wrapped up in psychoanalyzing Darren's old photos that I'd forgotten she was supposed to be here at all!

"You wanna join us downstairs?" Henrik extended his arm out towards me.

Knowing Denise couldn't be bothered to come up and greet us made me a bit trepidatious about going downstairs to meet her. I started to walk over to Henrik anyway. It wasn't like I could avoid the imminent meeting.

"I was going to give her the grand tour first!" Darren intervened.

"All right, come down when you're done then!" Henrik squeezed my shoulder before heading downstairs.

I looked at Darren. He put both arms up and said, "Well, this is the living room."

"Obviously," I chuckled. Then I followed him into the adjacent dining room.

"This is the dining room, and then the kitchen is back here." He walked as he talked.

Then we backtracked to the hallway near the living room, where three bedrooms and a bathroom completed the two-minute tour. I barely glanced in each room before he motioned with his hands for me to descend the stairs to the basement, which were in that same hallway.

"After you!"

"Okay!" I giggled nervously.

The basement looked like the set of *That '70s Show*, with all the wood paneling and baby food greens and oranges adorning it. Yet, it was clearly where parties were held, as indicated by the set up.

To the left were small tables and chairs, on which various board games were stacked, including Racko and Connect Four. The boxes were extremely worn. I guessed Darren and Denise had played those frequently as children.

Henrik stood behind the bar in the corner, which featured hundreds of stacked beer cans in its clear, L-shaped base. I imagined he was very proud of his unique creation, and I wondered if it had been the inspiration for the stacks of beer cans I'd seen in Darren's kitchen that first night.

Straight ahead of us was a long rusty orange and brown sofa on which Jane sat. A dark-haired man with an eerie likeness to Lou Ferigno sat in one of the two chairs facing the dark coffee table in front of Jane and perpendicular to the sofa she sat upon. Crouched by the coffee table was a long-haired blonde, pointing to pictures in an open photo album. "This was the first port we stopped at . . ." Even from the back, I recognized that perfectly curled blonde hair as Denise's.

The Hulk noticed me and Darren and stood to greet us. "Hey, guys!"

"How're you doing, man?" Darren walked over and shook the Hulk's hand. Then he put his hand on my back to guide me forward. "Brad, this is my girlfriend, Dana."

"Hi! Nice to meet you," I said as we shook hands. Despite his tall stature and thick build, his gentle voice and kind eyes expressed tremendous warmth. I immediately liked him.

"Hey, Denise," Darren greeted, interrupting her photo narration, on his way to sit in the chair opposite Brad.

"Hey." She glanced up at him briefly, then continued explaining whatever photo she'd been showing to Jane, as if I weren't even there. It hurt that she couldn't offer me the slightest courtesy.

Her rudeness seemed hypocritical, after the reproach she purported onto Darren for the social impropriety of living in so-called sin. I was equally shocked by everyone else's tolerance of her poor manners too. At the very least, Darren should have introduced me after saying hello to her.

Dumbfounded as to what to do, I looked to Darren for direction. He motioned for me to sit at the end of the couch Jane sat on, nearest to where he'd just sat in the chair. So I did. I sat quietly like everyone else, listening to Denise showcase the photos from the cruise she and Brad had been on. I quickly surmised that Denise was that one dominant person in every family who ruled the roost. Which was exactly why I needed to be in her good graces.

"And this was at the last port we stopped at. That's where Brad bought the engagement ring." She was engaged? That was big news! Did Darren know about this, I wondered? I looked to him for a reaction, but Jane's distracted me.

"Ooooh!" The elongated exaggeration was a bit dramatic.

"I was so nervous going back to the boat with it because of how big it is!" Denise held her hand out for everyone to verify its tremendous size and sparkle. "You hear about tourists being robbed and killed for their money or jewelry. And if you knew what Brad paid for this . . .We thought it would be a little cheaper on the islands, but . . ." She shot Jane a look with overly widened eyes to impress exactly how expensive her ring was. We all saw it on her finger. It was hard to miss, as were the repeated insinuations about its worth. Jane admired her daughter's diamond, regardless.

"Want another beer, Brad?" Henrik called out from the bar.

"Yeah, I'll take one!"

"How 'bout you, Darren?"

"Yes, please!" Darren walked over to the bar, and Brad joined them. They remained there, chatting about man stuff, leaving me with the two women who took issue with Darren and I living together.

Then Jane got up. "I have to go check on dinner." I watched her disappear up the stairs. I looked back to Denise, hoping she would have the decency to finally introduce herself. Instead, she looked all around, as if looking for an escape.

I attempted to relieve us both of the awkwardness. "What islands did you go to? On your cruise."

Without looking at me, Denise closed the photo album and said, "It was a cruise, so we stopped at several ports." Then she glanced behind her, to where the men stood at the bar.

I got the hint that she didn't want to converse with me, but I ramble when I'm nervous. "My family's from Puerto Rico, so . . ." I wasn't sure where

I was going with this, other than Puerto Rico being an island, but I had to come up with something quickly, so I didn't sound as stupid as I was already beginning to. "I just wondered. I'm sure every island is beautiful in its own way. I mean, palm trees, beaches ... can't go wrong, right?" I laughed at my oxymoron, though I just sounded like a moron, full stop.

So I couldn't blame her for leaving me with, "I'm going to go see if Mom needs help."

I relaxed a bit when she went upstairs, and I peeked into the photo album she'd left on the coffee table to pass the time. Most were scenic photos that could have been any tropical destination anywhere in the world. I didn't see any pictures of her and Brad, though. I guessed she didn't trust any passersby to hold her camera long enough to take pictures of the two of them together.

Just a few minutes later, Jane announced dinner from the top of the stairs. Brad and Darren started up immediately, so I jumped off the sofa to catch up. Henrik waited at the bottom of the stairs with his arm extended to allow me to go before him. "Ready for supper?"

"Uh, huh!" I smiled at Henrik's attentiveness to me. Few men in my life ever showed me the slightest consideration—Darren being a case in point. He was already seated at the dining table when Henrik and I entered the room. Henrik led me to the seat next to Darren, then took his place at the head of the table.

"Looks good, Mom!" Henrik said as Jane put down the last of the serving bowls.

"Yeah, Mom!" Darren cat-tailed, then dug into the bowl nearest to him.

As food was passed and eaten, and passed around again, Denise's wedding was the talk of the table.

"Have you told your parents, Brad?" Jane asked.

"Yeah! They're excited!"

"Yeah, his mom wants me to use the cake topper from their wedding," Denise chuckled.

"Well, that's nice!" Jane thought everything was nice.

"Maybe she'll let you wear her wedding dress too!" Darren joked. "And her super sexy granny panties for your wedding night!"

"Darren!" Jane burst out laughing in her attempt to scold her son, while Brad said, "Alright, alright."

Denise smirked. "Yeah, just what I want."

I smiled shyly at the amusing banter but had nothing to contribute to the conversation otherwise. I'd never planned a wedding or any similar event, and I didn't know the family well enough to converse about anything else in their lives. Anyway, I was selfishly stuck on how blatantly Denise ignored me. I was sensitive to it, since that had been my mother and stepfather's method of communicating their disapproval of me.

So when we got in the car to leave, I couldn't hold it in anymore. "What happened in there?"

"What's that supposed to mean?" Darren seemed to take offense.

"Your sister! No introduction. Not even a hello or goodbye. It's like I wasn't even there!"

"Who cares?" Darren's dismissive tone irked me.

"*I* do, actually. We're together, and I expected you to make me feel a little more comfortable in there than you did. I mean, your mom was fine tonight, but Denise . . . I don't take well to people who pretend I don't exist. Especially when they don't even know me!"

"She was just caught up in all her engagement stuff. It's not like it was personal."

"Of course it was! After that phone call? It was totally personal!"

"Why do you want her to like you so much anyway? She doesn't even like *me*!" Darren said.

"Because!" I didn't want to admit how much I'd built up the idea of Denise and I being sisters in my head. That sounded creepy! So I crossed my arms and looked out the window instead.

After a few minutes, Darren put his hand on my thigh. "Just give it time, Dana. Denise doesn't know you, but you don't know her either. Denise is all about Denise. She's used to being the best, having the most, and getting everything she wants. Dad sees it, Mom plays into it, and I . . . well, I just stay out of her way so she doesn't beat me up like she used to when we were kids."

Darren looked at me to see if his attempt to make me laugh had worked. I allowed a slight smirk to my lips when I turned to face him. I wasn't really mad at him anyway.

"Tell me you've never looked at Brad and almost called him 'The Hulk,'" I said.

Darren threw his head back and laughed.

"Love Is a Battlefield"

I thought my relationship with Darren was solid, until Darren worked more than he was home. He'd work late, or say he was grabbing dinner with co-workers. I wasn't bothered by his absence at first. I made use of the alone time to write papers for school and study for exams. But when I found myself eating dinner and watching Darren's TV shows alone too many nights in a row, my sense of abandonment was triggered.

Was this because his family didn't support us living together? Had they been pressuring him to be done with me? Or had I done something wrong? Worse yet, had he found someone else?

Overthinking turned into worrying, and worry turned into panic. When he didn't come home after work, I'd use every excuse to page him, probably seeming needy. I guess I was. I needed reassurance that he was being faithful and that he still loved me as much as he said he did. He wouldn't respond, though, and I'd fall asleep before he returned. I even went to bed in sexy nighties occasionally, thinking he'd wake me for sex when he came home, but I'd awaken in the morning to find him sleeping, sometimes on the couch instead of the bed. I felt like a shiny new toy that had been tossed aside with all the other toys he'd lost interest in.

Then one evening, he did come home after work. His pager beeped as soon as he rushed in, and he avoided eye contact on his way to the bedroom. I got up from the couch, where I'd been reading a book for school, and followed him to see what his hurry was about. He was rifling through clothes in the closet.

"Are you going somewhere?" I asked. His pager went off again. "And who keeps paging you? Is it that girl from work again?"

When we'd first gotten together, his pager had beeped constantly. He said he had to respond because it was for work, even though it was after work hours. He later admitted it was a girl from his work who was interested in him.

"You're not twenty-one yet," Darren snipped back like a sarcastic teenager, "and I shouldn't have to sit around here because you can't go out to bars!"

"But we're together! You should want to do things *with* me, not without me!" I complained. "Sometimes you're gone all night, into the wee hours of the morning, and I have no idea where you are or who you're even with!"

I threw my arms up and stuck my neck out a bit, awaiting a response. Instead of giving me one, Darren stomped out of the bedroom. I followed him out to the living room and watched him settle on the couch and turn on the TV. Then he crossed his arms and stared at the screen with a pout on his face.

I crossed my arms too. "What happened to the big rush to find clothes? Not going anywhere now?"

Darren didn't respond. He didn't even flinch. He just stared at the TV.

My entire body tensed, and I could feel a dull pain in my shoulders, as they collected my escalating emotions and held onto them tightly. I breathed in deeply through my nose and then relaxed my shoulders with the simultaneous release of breath. When that didn't help, I retreated to the bedroom to remove myself from the situation before I said or did anything outrageous to force him to pay me attention.

"I'm just out having fun!" I heard him holler.

The pussy couldn't take jabs until I was out of the room, huh? Well, he was going to have to grow a sack and talk shit to my face because I wasn't going to play games with him.

I marched back into the living room and yelled, "While you're out *'having fun,'* I'm lying in that bed"—I pointed to the bed for effect—"waiting for you to come home, worried about whether or not you'll even make it back okay! Because I know how much you drink, and I actually care about you! I'm not sure why, because you clearly don't give a shit about me, but I do! Do you know how that feels? Do you ever stop to think about me? Ever?"

"Fuck you!" he said, his tone as malicious as his gaze. It wasn't the first time he'd spoken to me like that, but the intensity of his loathing was in such extreme opposition to the sweet words he spoke when things were good between us. He could be so affectionate and attentive, but then so mean and hurtful. I was starting to think this "passionate" relationship he claimed we had was really an excuse for the erratic behavior he demonstrated from time to time.

I met his hateful stare, looking for something—anything—of the funny and understanding guy I connected with that first night in his apartment. Instead, I saw the cold, tense bad boy who'd walked into the office expecting subservience. He sat with his arms crossed, obstinate and choosing to withhold love from me. The rejection caused tears to well up in my eyes, but I retreated to the bedroom again before he could see me weakened by emotion.

Just as I'd sat at the corner desk, the bedroom door slammed shut at my back. I turned to see it was off kilter in the broken jamb. What an ass! I got up and tried the doorknob, but the door was stuck. I felt like an animal who'd been caught in a trap with no way out. My breaths quickened, and my eyes frantically sought escape.

"Darren, let me out!" I pounded on the door with my fist, at the same fast pace with which my heart pounded.

The wall between the bedroom and the living room was paper thin, so I heard the soft crunch of the leather couch. The sound of the TV became louder then. Had he gotten the remote to turn up the volume and tune me out?

"Darren!" I pounded on the door harder. "Let me out of here!"

I pulled on the knob with all my strength, certain I could dislodge the cheap flimsy thing, but it didn't budge. I kicked, I yanked, I tried to pull and push one way then the other to loosen it from the jamb, but nothing worked.

"Darren, seriously! Let me out!"

I pounded on the door with my palm, then listened for any indication of movement. Nothing.

Although my tears implied vulnerability, I was full of rage towards this callous man. He would learn, just as my stepfather did, that I was a force to be reckoned with and wouldn't back down to any man. If he wanted to play with fire, I'd burn this whole fucking building down.

I scanned the room with cat-like precision, looking for a weapon. An old hockey stick leaned against the wall in the corner. Instinct told me to grab it. Holding the stick with both hands on the shaft, I repeatedly pummeled the butt end of it into the wall between the bedroom and living room until it broke through the other side.

"What the fuck?!" Through the hole I'd effected, I saw the look of shock on Darren's face when he saw the stick poking out from where his head had just been against the wall. I felt victorious that I'd had the combination of gall and strength to return his violent outburst with one more atrocious. I just wished that butt end had bashed him in the head when it burst through the wall, like he deserved.

I pulled the stick back in preparation for the next blow, but Darren grabbed the other end and yanked it towards him. Still holding onto my end of the stick, my whole body slammed into the wall. I hit my head before I let go. That hurt!

"Let me out of here, mother fucker!" I threatened as I pounded the wall with my reddening palm. Then I grabbed the stick and shook it in an attempt to loosen it from his grasp and hammer it into him more accurately this time. He moved, though, and I couldn't see where he went.

My head whipped to the left when I heard noise on the other side of the bedroom door again. I stood stiller than the dead to listen. It sounded like Darren was finally prying the door open, so I remained vigilant, grasping the hockey stick firmly, ready to make him pay for turning me into this crazed mess.

Before long, the hacked-up door swung open, hanging crookedly off its hinges. Darren stood in the doorway, a crowbar in hand, staring at me with contempt. I stared back, prepared to strike. Neither of us had words for the moment, nor for the situation, and probably not for the relationship either. We just stood there with our weapons, waiting for the other to make a move.

After what seemed like forever, I called his bluff. I broke the stare and placed the hockey stick back in the corner of the bedroom where I'd found it. Then I brushed past Darren and his crowbar, took my textbook from the couch where I'd left it, and plopped down on the living room floor. I'd show him I wasn't scared of him! I had an assignment to read anyway; I didn't have time for his bullshit.

Instead of running off to his work girlfriend as I expected he would, Darren grabbed a beer from the refrigerator, sat down on the couch, and continued to watch TV.

There was no commentary or conversation tonight, however. He was pouting, and I was reminding myself I'd never be with someone I didn't feel safe with. I had no place to go, though. I was stuck.

"You've Really Got a Hold on Me"

I finally secured employment at a high-rise apartment building in a nearby suburb in late spring. I'd spoken to management about a free or discounted apartment but had to wait until one became available. I didn't tell Darren, though. I was afraid he'd overreact and kick me out of his place before then. It was better to acquiesce to keep the peace for the time being. So we went about our lives, even attending his family's Mother's Day brunch and other get-togethers as if nothing were amiss.

On a Sunday evening, Darren decided we should re-organize the garage where we stored furniture and boxes that didn't fit into his apartment, to make space for a motorcycle he bought with a new credit card I'd secured jointly with him to help build his credit. I figured it was a good opportunity for me to take stock of what I had to furnish my new apartment with anyway.

"I should have found myself an Asian woman like Kurt did. Those Asian women are submissive like women should be," Darren proclaimed.

"What? Because I'm not putting boxes exactly where you think they should go?" I snidely defended. The degradation hardly matched the task at hand.

"Maybe if you listened to me once in a while!" Darren yelled back, then returned his attention to organizing boxes and furniture the way *he* thought best. I ignored his demand for servitude and opted to stay out of his way instead of arguing.

While poking around, I discovered a box I didn't recognize. I opened one of the top flaps to peek inside and saw unrecognizable papers, pictures and cards. Must be Darren's. Curiosity got the best of me, so I looked over my shoulder to make sure Darren wasn't paying attention, then turned back so I could snoop.

On top of the pile was a white piece of notebook paper, folded in half twice. It was quite worn, which made me wonder whether it was that old or if it contained something Darren was compelled to read often.

I discreetly opened the folds. The bubbly cursive, hand-written in black ink on the blue-lined paper, clearly indicated a younger girl was the author. I looked to the bottom of the long letter, where the name "Julie" confirmed my suspicion.

I held my breath for a moment. Early on, I'd asked Darren about previous relationships. That's when he told me about Julie. He spoke of her so fondly, I couldn't be sure he was even over her. I was almost jealous! He spoke even more about how much her parents loved him, comparing their adoration of him to the lack of favor he received from my mother and stepfather. When I asked what happened to end their relationship, though, he shut down. Refused to discuss it. Clearly, she was the one that got away. I had to know why.

I looked over my shoulder again, which made me look as guilty as I felt, but Darren was still busy moving things around, so I quickly and inconspicuously read the letter.

I'm so sorry I made you mad. I'll never do it again. I promise. I love you too much to let this come between us. Please let me make it up to you with pizza for dinner. Please!

I scanned the rest of the letter for any indication of why she groveled for forgiveness, but nothing was revealed. It was probably something stupid. I mean, the guy had just barked at me over how I was arranging boxes! Most of his gripes were over nonsensical things, like Kitty pawing at the empty water bowl for a drink. He micro-managed everything!

Scuffling sounds behind me forewarned of Darren's nearness, so I quickly folded the letter and stuffed it back in the box.

I wished I'd learned something more about him, or them as a couple. Then again, I couldn't compare my relationship with him to hers. I was nothing like this spineless girl. Granted, I couldn't bear how he punished me with silence, but I'd leave him before ever groveling for his attention and affection.

"My next girlfriend is going to be fat and ugly. She'll worship me and listen when I tell her what to do," Darren mumbled loud enough for me to hear.

I rolled my eyes, secretly wishing he *would* find another girl to demean with passive-aggressive digs. Then I got back to organizing boxes.

By summer, I was promoted to leasing supervisor and finally granted the discounted apartment I'd requested. So on a slow afternoon at work, I closed the office to briefly walk through it. I already knew the floor plan and finishes well, but knowing this one would be mine added a whole other level of excitement.

Brighter days were ahead, I thought as I raised my face towards the warm sun and breathed in the fresh scent of cut grass and fragrant lilies lining the walkway towards the other building. I could definitely see myself living here, walking this same path between work and home every day.

I entered the three-story, light brick building and turned the key in the knob of my first-floor apartment. It was dark, so I crossed through the living room to open the vertical blinds. I preferred the natural light that poured into the room. Kitty would like this too, I thought as I appreciated the courtyard view outside the sliding glass doors to the patio.

The galley kitchen and bathroom were nothing special. They featured the same plain ivory counters, appliances, and cabinets with oak trim, commonly found in suburban apartments and condos.

I quickly surveyed the large bedroom, then returned to the living room. The building was quiet, I noticed. This was important to me because our current neighbors gathered on the lawn right outside our garden apartment window, drinking and carrying on noisily almost every night, preventing me from studying and sleeping. Darren joined them whenever he was around. I'd never been a party girl, though, so this serene environment fit my lifestyle more.

I just had to figure out how to tell Darren I'd be moving out. Although we'd agreed I would move in until I found a position that provided me an apartment of my own, and despite us not getting along, he wouldn't take well to the perceived rejection. My shoulders tensed just thinking about how he'd take personal offense to my independence. It had to be done, though. I just hoped he'd let me go without issue.

I rushed home after work, eager to get the talk over with, even though I never knew when to expect Darren anymore. He walked in a few minutes after I did.

"Hey!" I greeted him.

"Hey," he responded flatly. He took a beer from the refrigerator and sat on the couch to watch TV. It was evident he didn't want to be stuck in the apartment, or perhaps stuck there with me, but that was neither here nor there after what I had to share with him.

I sat on the other end of the couch facing him. I had déjà vu thinking about how we'd sat exactly like this the night we became "us," and here I was about to end it in the same manner.

"Management is finally giving me a one-bedroom apartment, and I was able to take a look at it today!" The elevated inflection in my tone lamely expressed the positive spin I was trying to put on this.

Darren looked at me, then focused down on his beer can. He flicked the tab with one finger, indicating displeasure, but I forged ahead anyway, doing my best to tread lightly.

"It's perfect for me and Kitty, and the price is right."

He didn't respond, which made me even more anxious than I already was. My armpits were moistening as a result. I hoped I wasn't exuding body odor like I sometimes did.

"So I told them I'd take it," I blurted out. In my mind, I was cringing with my eyes closed, awaiting the backlash.

Darren crossed his arms and leaned away from me. I learned in one of my basic psychology courses that physical distance equated to emotional distance. He was once again taking his love away from me, which would have hurt more if I wanted to stay.

Since I had nothing to lose now, I asserted, "Kitty and I will be out of your hair by the end of the month."

I could tell by Darren's reddening face that he was about to blow. My body tensed as I awaited the explosion.

"If you move out, we're done," he said in a low growl.

His words were welcome compared to the violent outburst I'd envisioned in my mind, though it struck me as odd that he would be so angry when his poor treatment of me and constant commentary about how I wasn't this or that implied my failure to meet his expectations.

At this point, however, there was no point arguing. I wanted things to be peaceable until my actual move. So, I attempted to soften the blow. "There's no reason we can't date! You can come over whenever you want, and I can come down here. It's not like it's that far. And maybe the space is what we need to get along better!"

No response.

"My moving in wasn't permanent, Darren. You knew I was looking for another job with an apartment included."

"Well, you did move in," he said, raising his voice, "and you can't move in with someone and then move out and expect to stay together."

"We've only known each other for, like, six months! And it's not going very well."

Darren pressed his lips together so firmly I could almost hear his teeth grinding. His nose scrunched and his shoulders heaved as he huffed through his nose heavily.

"You knew I was looking for a job with an apartment," I repeated, expecting him to take some responsibility for this decision.

Instead, he glared at me, then went to the bedroom and slammed the door behind him.

Confused by my guilty feelings, I sat in silence. I knew I hadn't done anything wrong, but maybe I'd been so caught up in the excitement of this new life I'd been imagining for myself that I hadn't stopped to wonder if Darren had had a change of heart. Maybe his extreme emotions equated to how much he loved me. Maybe he wanted me to stay here with him but didn't know how to tell me. Darren often admitted he wasn't good with words.

I went into the bedroom to see if he'd talk to me more calmly about his feelings. He lay face down in his pillow, looking completely dejected. I felt terrible for having done this to him. He did love me, didn't he?

I laid on the bed next to him and gently ran my fingers up and down his back. "I'm sorry," I whispered to his listless body, "I won't go. Okay?"

He turned to face me, and I saw the tears in his eyes. His frown and quivering lips reminded me of a toddler afraid to lose his mother's love.

"I'm so sorry," I apologized again, then reassured, "I'm not going anywhere."

He caressed my cheek ever so gently with the back of his hand. His sad eyes told me how much he loved me, even if his words and actions didn't.

I realized I must love him more than I thought too, otherwise hurting him couldn't have hurt me so much.

So when Darren asked, "You and me against the world?" I responded, "Forever."

"Crazy on You"

I loved the funny and lighthearted persona Darren presented around his family. He'd do things like stick his finger up his nose just as a picture was taken. He grabbed my butt when no one was looking. He'd raise up his knee and kick back in a repeat motion, thereby "cranking" out his farts. It was gross, but it always made me burst into laughter.

Fortunately, Jane always seemed to have a reason to gather us together, whether it be a holiday, birthday dinner, barbecue, chili supper, or potluck of some sort. So I got to spend plenty of time over the summer with the Darren I loved more than the one I hated.

Jane always planned games and activities too. She'd have us compete as individuals, couples, or girls against boys. We might have to accomplish some task before the other team, or answer trivia questions correctly. Sometimes we'd play cards or a board game to see who'd win, or race cotton balls across a table by blowing through a straw. No matter what we did, we did it together, and the positive interaction strengthened the bonds between all of us. It shaped us as a family and had the side effect of making me feel like I belonged. Even Denise was friendlier with me.

"Hello?" I'd started answering Darren's—I mean "our"—apartment phone.

"Hi, Dana! It's Denise."

"Oh, hi! What's going on?" I settled into the sofa to take the call. It was a Saturday morning, and I didn't have to leave for work for another hour.

"Just seeing if you guys wanted to come over to my condo next Friday after work. I'm having a few of our cousins over. I don't know if you met

46

Mitch and Becky yet, but they're bringing their wedding video for us to see."

She didn't have to ask me twice! "Yeah! We'll be there! I'll have to check with Darren to make sure, but I get out of summer school at three, so I can make it for sure!"

"Okay, just let me know. You have my number?"

I checked on the piece of paper Darren had written his important phone numbers on and saw her number right under Jane and Henrik's. "Yeah."

"Okay, we'll see you guys Friday hopefully!"

"Yeah!" Then to keep her, I asked, "How's your wedding planning coming along?"

"Good! We did set a date—it's going to be next April."

"Spring wedding!" I sing-songed in excitement. "Have you been dress shopping or anything yet?" She hadn't, but I heard about favors and centerpieces. She had a lot of ideas, and I was glad she'd finally opened up to me, about the wedding and in general.

I was excited to go to her condo that Friday, though motion sickness from being in rush hour traffic too long prevented me from enjoying the time. Darren didn't help either. Being there reignited his desire to own real estate, though I suspected keeping up with his sister was the true culprit.

Keeping him happy kept peace between us, though, so we spent the rest of the summer of 1996 looking at advertisements for townhouses in a prestigious nearby suburb. With our combined incomes, he thought we could afford to buy something that I thought a bit too rich for our current situation. I was still in school full time, and although I was working full time too, I couldn't be sure of what I'd be doing after graduation. However, the permanence of buying a house together proved Darren's intentions to remain with me for the forever he promised, and I wanted that forever more than anything in the world. So, I went along with it. Granting his wish effectively granted mine as well.

Perhaps a bit eager, we made an offer on the first home we toured. Unfortunately, the sellers wanted a larger down payment than we could come up with, so we didn't get the house. When I told Darren the news after work that day, he sat motionless and silent in the dark dining room.

He didn't like being told he couldn't have something he wanted.

I stood at the head of the table silently, afraid to misspeak. His chest puffed and retracted largely with every inhale and exhale from his nose, since his tight-lipped scowl disallowed air flow at all. He was seething, and his unpredictable temperament made me uneasy. I held my breath within my stiffened body as I waited for his response, like a terrified child counting the seconds between thunder and lightning to determine how close danger was.

Suddenly, Darren rose and slammed the chair against the table so hard it bounced off the edge then fell backward into the kitchen.

"Darren!" I instinctively reprimanded, as if he were my poorly behaved child.

"Don't fucking talk to me right now!" He took a beer from the refrigerator and walked out. I watched out the window as he tore out of the parking lot in his Smurf-blue Toyota sports car, screeching his tires for effect. A long exhale escaped my mouth then. I couldn't help but feel relieved that I was free of his fury for now, though I expected him back once he'd cooled off or drunk himself into forgetting about the house altogether.

I enjoyed time alone anyway. I needed a break from Darren's intense energy once in a while. So I went about my evening, completing homework assignments for my classes, studying for a test, and picking up around the apartment. When I became too tired to wait up for him, I went to bed. I figured he'd be back soon enough anyway, since he had to work in the morning.

Worry prevented sleep, though. I knew he was drinking and obviously driving. So I woke almost every hour on the hour. Every time I saw Darren's side of the bed still empty, my troubled mind became even more worried about his safety.

Around 2 a.m., I couldn't lay in bed anymore. I had to do something. I went out to the living room to check if his car was out in the parking lot. It wouldn't have surprised me if he was so mad he'd decided to sleep in the car instead of coming in. But before I got to the window, I stumbled on a bunch of blankets.

Although I knew I hadn't left them on the floor earlier, I bent down to pick them up. They were immovable! I felt along the length of them, to see if they were stuck on something, and realized they were tucked under a body. Darren? It had to be! I hadn't heard him come in, but then again, I was so tired I'd probably slept deeply for the intermittent periods I was able to.

I had to get him to bed before he woke up and blamed me for letting him sleep on the floor. He never took responsibility for his actions or poor decisions; everything was somehow my fault.

So I placed my hand on what I thought was his shoulder and lightly shook it. "Darren," I whispered.

No response. No movement.

I patted the blanket upward to where I suspected his head was. I couldn't feel any skin or hair, just blanket. He seemed to be tightly swaddled like a mummy in burial wrap.

"Darren?" Still no response and no movement.

I felt around again until I came upon the roundness of his head, and I tugged at the blanket until I felt hair and skin. My hands continued to pat his head until I felt the soft protrusion of his thin lips. "Darren," I said in a normal tone.

Nothing.

"Darren, wake up. Let's go to bed," I demanded in a louder tone.

Still nothing. My breathing quickened as panic arose within me. Had he suffocated himself under the blanket? Was he dead?

"Darren!" I raised my voice sharply.

He continued to lay there, silent and unmoving.

"Darren!" I screamed so loudly the whole building likely heard me through the paper-thin walls and ceilings. "Darren! This isn't funny! *Wake up!*"

Still nothing. I held my face in my hands and cried for a moment. Feeling panicked and crazed all at the same time, I was crawling out of my skin, hoping to escape this nightmare.

"Darren!" I screamed through pained lungs.

When he still didn't move, I kicked and kicked his lifeless body, harder each time. I couldn't accept that he was dead on our living room floor! "Darren! Oh my god! Darren, WAKE UP!"

"What the fuck, Dana?" I finally heard.

"Darren?" I was so relieved that I didn't even care about the reproach in his tone. "Oh, thank God!" I cried and fell to my knees beside him. He jerked his shoulder away when I put my hand on it, and then pulled the blanket back over his head.

"Darren?" I grabbed at the top of the blanket to pull it back down, but Darren gripped it so firmly it wouldn't budge.

"Leave me the fuck alone!"

I ignored his rude request and continued to pull at the blankets. "Darren? Why are you doing this?"

"Fuck, Dana! Leave me alone!" he shouted again, placing heavy emphasis on every word to impress upon me how serious he was.

"Darren? What's going on?"

Silence. Why wouldn't he talk to me?

Frustrated and feeling completely out of control, I stood up and kicked him in the side again. It seemed to be the only way to provoke a reaction from him. "Darren, get up!"

But he remained still and silent. God, I hated him! But that didn't mean I wanted him dead!

Triggered by feelings of rejection and abandonment, my emotions escalated to a level at which I had no ability to process them. I felt completely out of control! Having nowhere to run and nowhere to turn, I ran back into the bedroom and sobbed into my pillow. "Why are you doing this? What did I do? God, help me, please!"

Although the hopelessness in my heart begged for mercy, neither the pillow, Darren, nor God consoled me with a response. The sound of my agonizing sobs pained my broken heart even more, and I drowned in the tears of self-pity until eventually falling asleep.

When I awoke later that morning, I walked to the kitchen for a much-needed cup of coffee. I hoped the liquid caffeine would relieve my throbbing head, or at least that its warmth would soothe my scratchy throat.

I peeked into the living room first, hoping Darren was awake and as eager as I was to resolve what had happened. I didn't like the person he sometimes was, nor the person he turned me into as a result.

Darren was gone, though. Ruffled blankets on the floor were all that remained in his place. It hurt that he would leave without waking me to make things right, or at least reassure me we would talk later. It's like he didn't even care.

I went through the motions of the day without thinking or feeling. It was all I could do to function somewhat normally until I could get back to Darren. Although I swore I wouldn't grovel for Darren's affection like Julie had done in that note she'd written to him, I understood now that she'd felt lost without him, because that was how I felt now.

I hurried home that afternoon, anxiously awaiting him. When he came home, however, he refused to look at me or talk to me. He made dinner for one, then planted himself on the sofa and watched TV. Although the lack of interaction made me feel more isolated than I already did, I gave him the space he wanted. I stayed in the bedroom and studied, then slept alone in the bed while he slept on the living room floor again. As much as I wanted to resolve things, I knew it was best to wait until we were both ready to talk.

This went on for two more days. I went to work and school like a zombie, walking through life without purpose or emotions. It was like serving Darren had become my sole purpose, my whole identity, and I didn't know what to do without him.

There was no one to talk to about things either. I didn't have much communication with the couple friends I'd managed to keep after high school, so I wouldn't randomly bother them with problems about a guy they didn't even know about. It wasn't professional to whine to my co-workers either. Darren was the person I talked to. He was my one friend. Without him, I was alone.

Finally, on the third day after that awful night, Darren came home from work with a complacent, closed-mouth expression, and held out one arm. I eagerly threw both of my arms around his waist and pressed my head against his broad chest. I held onto him so tightly, like I'd never let him go. Then I closed my eyes and took a deep breath. He held me close for a long moment, then kissed me on the forehead before settling on the couch with a beer and the TV remote.

Desperate to hold onto his affection, I snuggled into him on the couch. I pulled up my knees, settling into the crevice of his armpit in fetal position.

He gladly received me, holding me with his free arm.

I looked up at him, like a small child seeking a parent's reassurance. Darren didn't even glance down at me, though. I didn't understand his avoidance. Did he regret what he'd done and was too prideful to acknowledge it? Did he feel sorrow for intentionally dissociating from me? Did he have any empathy for the pain I'd endured—first thinking he was dead and then being discarded by him for God-knows-what? I didn't want to re-open the wound so soon after being back in his good graces, though, so I opted for positive reinforcement—a psychological technique I'd studied in one of my psychology classes. "I wish things could always be like this. Calm. And good. You know?"

He took another sip of his beer and responded, "Yeah. We just have a love-hate relationship. But I wouldn't get so angry if I didn't love you so much."

My mother always said my stepfather's anger was a reflection of how much he cared. Too bad I never felt the love she'd insisted he felt, nor comfort in the excuse for the hatred.

"Push"

I sometimes wondered what Darren's family would think if they knew how he treated me behind closed doors. Would they be surprised? Ashamed? Would they even care? I thought about confiding in Denise about it all, since we'd gotten to the point of talking a few times a week. I decided against it, though, on the off chance she'd be offended at the accusations against her brother or tattle to Darren about what I'd said. It was better to keep things light for now. She was about to get married after all!

The calendar was full of pre-wedding festivities, so Darren and I shared plenty of good time together with his family. We attended a luncheon to meet Brad's parents, then we met his whole family. There were gatherings to discuss wedding details, and then the bridal shower and bachelorette party. Before we knew it, Denise's wedding day was here!

April 12, 1997, was a cloudy, rainy day, but spirits were bright in the ornately decorated church Brad's family belonged to. Family and friends filled the pews, chattering about the weather and the occasion. There were so many people that I had to climb over some to fulfill the important task of pinning the grandmas and grandpas and readers with their boutonnieres. Perhaps a minor assignment in the scheme of the event, but it was a big deal to me. It meant I was important enough to Denise that she wanted to include me in her wedding in some way. I couldn't have felt more special.

Darren was a groomsman in the wedding, so I took a seat at the outside end of the second pew on Denise's side. I felt bad assuming such a close position, compared to some of the elderly people who sat in the back rows, but I justified it with having to record the wedding on Brad's brother's camcorder. Although they had a professional videographer present, Brad's brother asked me to take a second video. I fiddled with the large device, until the organ music indicated it was time to heave it onto my shoulder.

As I watched Henrik walk Denise down the aisle, I was glad to have the bulkiness of the device covering half my face. I didn't want anyone to see the sadness suddenly overwhelming me. Not that they'd be looking at me anyway. Denise was stunning in her poofy-shouldered, white lace, full-skirted gown.

Seeing all these people here—the numerous bridesmaids and groomsmen at the altar, the proud parents—reminded me I'd never have this kind of love in my life. I didn't even know more than a friend or two whom I could scrounge up to stand next to me at the altar, let alone this many people! I didn't have a proud father to walk me down the aisle, nor would I ever face a groom who looked at me with the adoration Brad looked upon Denise with. Darren had looked at me like that for the first couple weeks of our relationship, but I wasn't even sure he liked me now. I think he liked what I could do for him more.

Our relationship was a two-way street, however, so although he was wrong to mistreat me the way he sometimes did, succumbing to him to keep the peace didn't command the respect I wanted and felt I deserved. And without respect, how could I expect him not to mess around with girls at bars, like he sometimes bragged about when he came home drunk and forgot who he was talking to?

That was my fault too, though. I'd failed to keep his interest. Compared to Denise, who looked like a Barbie doll, my unruly curls and hand-me-down clothing made me feel slapped together on a good day. I'd gained weight since starting college too—I was up twenty pounds! If I paid more attention to my appearance, maybe Darren would pay more attention to me instead of looking to other women for whatever I wasn't giving him. I mean, I wished I was enough on my own, but . . .

I stopped myself mid-thought. It was selfish of me to have a pity party for one in the midst of the most important day of Denise's life thus far. So I consciously refocused my attention to the present moment and did my best to capture this most sacred declaration of love.

After a ceremony that seemed long even for this Catholic girl, the church echoed with the sound of everyone clapping and cheering as Denise and Brad recessed down the aisle as husband and wife. The wedding party followed behind, and then the pews eventually emptied as well. I hung back to let everyone else make their way out, so by the time I got outside to throw rice at the newlyweds, I'd lost sight of Darren in the dense crowd.

After Denise and Brad were pelted with rice, they released two white doves. Everyone clapped and cheered again, as the birds flew up into the gray sky. They seemed confused, whirling this way and that, until they decided any way was fine as long as they flew together. A smile came across my lips at the thought of how simple love can be.

Denise and Brad climbed into an old black sedan and were driven away. The crowd dissipated shortly after. I stood in front of the church, waiting to catch a glimpse of where Darren was or hoping he'd come looking for me, but I found myself alone in the light drizzle instead.

"You okay?" I heard a familiar male voice ask from behind me. I turned to see Henrik and mustered a half smile for him. He put his hand on my back.

"Yeah!" I lied. "I guess I should get to the reception hall?"

"I imagine that's where everyone's headed! Let me walk you to the car."

"Thank you," I said, trying to keep my smile in place. With his arm around my shoulder, we walked towards the lone car remaining in the parking lot.

Henrik opened the car door and waited for me to start it. "You know how to get there?"

"Yeah, I have directions."

"Drive safely then! I'll see you there!" Then he closed the door, careful not to catch my long dress in it. He waved as I reversed out of the parking spot, then the rear-view mirror showed him remaining until he couldn't see my vehicle anymore.

I was the first to arrive at the reception hall, or perhaps the only one not sitting at whatever bar everyone else was having cocktails at, so I walked around the massive room to pass time. I admired the wooden dove centerpieces on the guest tables, as well as the wooden mailbox for guests to place cards inside of. It was decorated with artificial ivy and little yellow birds. The amount of time it must have taken for Jane and Henrik to handcraft and paint these wood creations was indicative of how much they loved Denise. I hope she knew how lucky she was.

I was admiring the swan ice sculpture Denise had spoken of when Henrik came into the room. I smiled as I watched him take a cookie from a tray on the sweets table. Like a kid sneaking sweets before dinner, he giggled as he stuffed the cookie into his mouth. I walked over to him, chuckling at his youthfulness. He handed me a cookie, then took another for himself, and we stuffed them into our mouths before anyone could discover our crime. Then I pulled my camera from my shoulder to take a picture of him, but he grabbed it out of my hand, pulled me close, and took a selfie of us instead. We laughed at the big goofy smiles we made.

The bridal party entered the room then, minus Brad and Denise. I spotted Darren right away and waved, but he was talking and laughing with the maid of honor—a short, attractive, skinny blonde. Jealousy stirred in me, though I wouldn't have been so sensitive if I hadn't been neglected all day. So I left Henrik to eat another cookie on his own and walked over to Darren and his blonde interest.

"Hey," I said, interrupting what looked like flirting.

"Hey," he returned without the enthusiasm he'd shown the blonde just a second before.

Henrik came up behind us. "You want me to take a picture of the two of you?"

"Yes, please!" I wasn't sure when I'd pin Darren down again, and I wanted a picture of us all dressed up in our formal attire. I'd searched long and hard for the right dress for the occasion and had chosen an elegant, pale pink gown from Von Maur. It had a sleeveless satin tank top which flowed into floor-length tulle, and a bow-shaped silver brooch at one shoulder. Simple. Unlike me. "How about in front of the ice sculpture over there?" I pointed. Darren obliged, then quickly left me to myself again. His attention was clearly elsewhere.

Crowds were starting to pile in anyway, so I took a seat at my assigned table with some of Darren's cousins. I was friendly with most of them, but still felt like the odd man out during dinner. They and their significant others belonged to the same Lutheran church that all their intertwined families had been part of for generations. So I sat quietly and listened to them gossip about people and things that were unfamiliar to me, until the dimmed lights signaled all to be quiet for speeches and the newlyweds' first dance together. Then the DJ opened the dance floor to the guests, and everyone disbursed into the blur of bright flashing multicolored lights.

I sat and waited for Darren to seek me out, but after several minutes of feeling strangely alone in the midst of this celebration, I went in search of him. He wasn't at the head table nor the bar. I checked the lobby unsuccessfully, then stopped in the restroom. When I walked back into the reception hall, the DJ summoned guests to line either side of the dance floor and dance down the middle one couple at a time. It looked fun, but I knew better than to think Darren would go up with me. He'd walked out of my cousin's wedding in Florida the year before because I was dancing without him, though I was only doing so because he didn't like to dance!

So, I was stunned when I saw Darren dancing down the middle of the dance floor with the blonde maid of honor he'd been laughing with earlier! He had to be kidding me! He'd barely acknowledged me today. It's like I wasn't even there! And when did he start dancing at weddings? When the blonde he wanted to fuck asked him to?

Tears welled up in my eyes. I felt rejected, jealous, and like my anger would uncontrollably erupt at any moment. It took every bit of self-discipline to restrain the whirlwind of emotions overwhelming me while I waited for Darren to come off the dance floor. When he did, he walked away from the blonde to a far-off table where his childhood friends sat. I marched his way to demand an explanation for his behavior.

"Hey," I greeted Darren's friends. I stood behind Darren and placed my hand on his shoulder. He glanced up at me, then returned to his conversation.

"Darren," I said loudly and with sternness. I refused to let him ignore me anymore. I didn't even care that everyone at the table was staring at us now. Darren looked back up at me with thin eyes. "Can I talk to you privately?"

"Excuse me a minute," he said with a grimace meant to express his annoyance with me. A couple of his friends responded with knowing looks and raised browswhich made me wonder what he said to them about me when I wasn't around.

Before I could think too much about it, Darren grabbed my hand too aggressively and hurriedly led me out of the reception room. We went through the lobby, towards the exit doors. Once outside and out of hearing range, he growled, "What do you want?"

Tears welled up in my eyes and my bottom lip quivered. I hadn't meant to anger him. I just wanted him to acknowledge me! Not like this, though.

Since I didn't respond with words, Darren grabbed my hand again and walked me up the side of the building next to the parking lot. I nearly stumbled trying to keep up with his quick pace. When he finally stopped, he threw my hand down and screamed in my face, "What the fuck do you want?" I closed my eyes when his spit hit my face.

Love, maybe? Some attention? Consideration? But I was too scared to ask him for anything! Instead, defeat made me drop my face into my trembling hands and sob.

"Wah, wah," he whined, pretending to cry like a baby.

Mocking my sadness was hurtful. Intentionally hurtful. "Why are you doing this to me? What did I do?" I cried, throwing my arms out.

"What did you do?" he yelled, then repeated even louder, "What did you *do?*" Did *he* even know what I'd done?

All of a sudden, he shoved me back into the brick exterior of the building with both hands, and my head bounced slightly off the hard surface. I immediately put my hand on the back of my head where it hurt and looked up at Darren with open-mouthed shock. He huffed at me out of his nose and started walking back towards the entrance to the building.

"Darren!" I called out. He neither stopped nor turned back to me, so I yelled louder, "Darren!" He kept going, so I started jogging towards him in my satin heels, careful not to slip on the moist concrete.

Just as I caught up to him, he whipped around and screamed in my face again. "WHAT?"

"I'm going home," I threatened. "You obviously don't want me here."

"I don't give a fuck what you do!" he yelled, then continued into the building.

I didn't really want to leave. I wanted him to tell me to stay. I wanted him to tell me he loved me too. And maybe, just maybe, apologize for throwing me up against the building. So I chased after him, but lost him in the crowds of people in the lobby.

His aunt stopped me before I re-entered the reception. "Are you okay,

Dana?"

"No!" I couldn't hide it. My tearful face was smeared with mascara, and some of my hair had fallen from the low bun it had been pulled back into. "Darren . . ." I started to tattle, then stopped. She probably wouldn't believe me, Darren would deny it, and I would be deemed a liar who created drama at Denise's wedding. "I just have to find Darren," I corrected, then left her with a bewildered expression.

Back in the flashing lights of the otherwise dark reception, I wandered all around searching for Darren but couldn't find him anywhere. Like a lost puppy searching for the safety and security of its owner, I stood at the edge of the dance floor with the sorrowful expression of a bloodhound.

"Dana?" I heard a female voice say from behind me. I turned to see Denise, who had the same look of concern I'd seen in their aunt's face. "What's wrong?"

It was her wedding day; she shouldn't have to deal with our dysfunction. So, I told a white lie, "I'm just trying to find Darren."

"What's going on? Is everything okay?"

Crap! She'd noticed my forlorn expression, and maybe even my teary red eyes. Her wedding reception wasn't the place to confess her brother was an abusive jerk. So I lied. "Oh, nothing! I mean, I'm fine! Just really tired. And my eyes are sensitive to light. So I'm going to go, but I wanted to make sure Darren had a ride and say goodbye to you guys first."

"No! You're not going anywhere!"

"I have to work tomorrow anyway, so I really should . . ."

"Just stay. Please," Denise insisted, then glanced around, as if looking for help with something—that something being me. A cousin and his wife, both of whom I'd met at the get-together at Denise's condo, stood nearby. "Will you stay with her?" I was grateful when they nodded in agreement, so Denise could return to her reception. I hated being a bother to her, especially tonight.

The cousin came up next to me and put his arm around my shoulders. "Whatever it is, it'll be okay." His wife, who stood on his other side, smiled at me, then held up her beer in a sort of salutation, before guzzling a good part of it down.

I gave them a weak half-smile and remained at the edge of the dance floor with them, numbly watching everyone else have fun until the DJ announced the last dance of the night. Then I collected my purse and camera from where I'd been seated for dinner and left.

I was almost to my car in the parking lot when I heard rapid footsteps behind me.

"Hey!"

I turned to see Darren. I was too tired, physically and emotionally, to go on this roller coaster ride with him, so I opted to pull a "Darren" and not acknowledge *him* for once.

I unlocked the car doors with my key fob and stared straight ahead as we both climbed into the car. When I turned the ignition, he leaned forward to look me directly in the face, but when he realized I wouldn't return eye contact, he leaned back and fell asleep. No words were spoken the whole ride home, nor when we returned home.

The sound of my alarm going off the next morning made my head pound. I pressed the button to turn it off, then turned to where Darren normally lay next to me, hoping the night before was a night*mare*. Darren snored loudly, and his open mouth emitted the repulsive smell of rotting hops and barley.

I held my breath as I got out of bed, then went downstairs to the kitchen to make the cup of coffee I desperately needed to rid me of this nasty headache. It felt sour going down, though. Recalling the horrors of the night before had also given me a stomach-ache I couldn't shake.

I dreaded the thought of going to work feeling like this. I mean, I could probably withstand the physical upset, but I was certain I couldn't hide my emotional distress well enough to engage with the public in a professional manner. I told myself not to compromise my responsible character and strong work ethic over a quarrel with Darren, but I had to. I needed to deal with Darren anyway. I couldn't function until things were right between us. So, after I made the very uncomfortable call to my office to let them know I wouldn't be coming in that day, I sat on the couch with my coffee, disappointed for letting my relationship affect my job.

Just then, the phone rang. Afraid it was my boss calling me back, I let it ring until it finally went to voicemail. Hearing the phone ring and ring gave me a little cruel satisfaction anyway, knowing it would awaken the drunk bastard.

A minute later, Darren stumbled down the stairs with the receiver to his ear and sat on the couch next to me. "Oh, hey, Denise . . . Yeah, everything's all right. Why? . . . Oh, she's right here. She *seems* fine . . . Yeah, I'll tell her . . . Sorry about that. We didn't mean to upset anyone. I just act stupid sometimes . . . yeah . . . well, have fun on your honeymoon! We'll talk to you later . . . Bye."

My knees were pulled up close to my chest, symbolically serving as defense against this perpetrator. I gripped my mug of hot coffee, which could serve as a security blanket or a weapon, depending on Darren's next move.

"That was Denise," he explained, as if I didn't know already. "She just said she hopes you're okay."

"Well, I'm not. Not after last night." The soft rasp of my voice was the result of crying so much the night before—another reason I couldn't possibly answer phones and cater to people at work all day.

"I'm sorry, babe. I know I do stupid shit sometimes," Darren admitted with the same words he'd just used with his sister. Then he wrapped both arms around me, almost spilling my precious coffee. "You still love me?"

I hesitated. I didn't want to say it if I didn't mean it, and I couldn't let him think it was okay to hurt me like he did and then apologize it away. But then I looked at him, with his pleading eyes and that sweet smirk of regret, and thought, who was I kidding? Was I going to let all this go over a drunken shove? It's not like he'd hit me. Granted, he'd raised his hand to me before, but he'd stopped himself from striking me when I'd cowered away from him! He hadn't really wanted to hurt me!

I dropped my shoulders, sighed, and caved. "Forever," I said, though "for now" would have been more honest.

"Torn"

Denise called me at work one mid-summer afternoon. "Hey! How's it going?"

"Work is crazy! Renting apartments left and right! What's up with you? You at work?"

"Yeah. That's actually why I'm calling. We have a raffle every week, for plane tickets on flights that aren't fully booked. And I won this week, so I'm wondering if you'd want to go to Las Vegas with me next weekend. Southwest is covering our flight *and* our hotel there, so it's all expenses paid!"

I wanted to jump up and down and clap my hands and scream, but I had to maintain professional composure. "Are you kidding? Yes!" Then I lowered my voice so my co-workers couldn't hear, "I don't know if I can get off work, though. I'd have to find someone to cover for me, which is nearly impossible around here because no one wants to work weekends but me. I hate to say it, but it's probably not going to happen. Let me see what I can do, though!"

"I knew it was a long shot. I just thought I'd ask because no one else can go either," Denise said.

"What do you mean no one else can go? Did you get more than two tickets?" A girl's trip would be so much fun!

"No, but I already asked a few other people before calling you, and none of them can go either," Denise answered honestly, without regard for how it would make me feel to know I hadn't been her first choice. It sounded more like I was her last resort, which didn't feel too good at all, actually. But at least I was a consideration, I reminded myself. Where Denise was concerned, that was good enough for me!

"You know what, Denise? Let's do it. Let's go to Vegas, just you and me."

"What about your work? Are they going to be okay with you taking the time off?"

"I don't know! But they're going to have to figure it out, I guess, because I'll be in Vegas with you!"

Denise giggled at my boldness. "Okay! I'll let you get back to work and call you later with the details."

"Sounds good! And thanks for inviting me. I'm so excited!"

Days later, we were on the plane to Vegas.

Up to now, our conversations and interactions had been wedding-related or family gossip. I'd been waiting for an opportunity for us to get to know each other on a more personal level. I wanted that true sister relationship with her, the kind where you could say anything and know she'll back you up or give you advice, but where you don't need to say anything because she already knows what you're thinking—like having a built-in best friend. The only way to get there was to share everything. So I did what I always do when I've befriended someone new, and told Denise every detail of my life from birth to present, leaving nothing out.

I'd hoped for Denise's sympathy when I told her about how I'd grown up in an abusive home. Yet, she wore the same open-mouthed expression of horror Jane did when I'd first told her about my past. I guessed they were partial to polite society, where things like teenage pregnancy and being strangled weren't to be discussed so freely.

After Denise uncomfortably looked at the people sitting around us, paranoid they might have heard any part of my pitiful monologue, I finally took the hint. I turned the tables, hoping she would reciprocate with some insight on her life. "Darren said you guys had it a little rough growing up too. It's so hard to believe! Your parents are, like, Beaver Cleaver nice!"

Denise looked at me with a bewildered expression. "What are you talking about? Darren and I didn't have a bad childhood." Now I was confused too!

"Maybe I misunderstood Darren then," I back-peddled, not wanting to upset Denise so soon into the trip. "It's just that he talked about being alone a lot, in a kind of neglectful way." Her piercing stare made me nervous, and nerves made me ramble. "I don't know. I think he just felt left out a lot. You and your mom were always doing girl stuff together, and Darren didn't like being dragged to your dance classes and whatever other activities you were involved in. He probably just missed having that same attention from his dad. He said your dad worked a lot and when he was home, he'd tell Darren to go outside. Like your dad just wanted to be rid of him, so he could smoke and drink with his buddies. It's hard to believe Henrik did any of that, though! Maybe Darren just felt like he didn't get the attention you were getting?"

"Well, Dad was gone a lot, but that was his job." Denise fumbled with her carry-on bag for some gum, then sat back up and looked straight ahead.

It was interesting to me that she had no defense of Jane's favoritism towards her, and the resulting exclusion Darren felt. Was she unaware of her status as the Golden Child? Maybe she'd been so caught up in the role, it hadn't occurred to her Darren had had a different experience than she did. Either way, I didn't like how she invalidated Darren's perspective. It reminded me of how my mother had constantly invalidated my experiences with her husband's abuse. I felt a sudden urge to protect Darren, while also wanting to make sense of the resentment and anger he held onto.

He had his issues with Jane for glorifying Denise, with Henrik for being absent, but he had a particular obsession to keep up with Denise. He wanted what she had. Not in a jealous way, but in the sense that he wanted to be held in the same esteem as she was by their parents. He saw how she achieved it, so logic told him to do the same to get the same result.

For example, he wanted a condo because he saw how proud Jane and Henrik were of Denise when she'd bought real estate right out of college. Denise bought a nice sports car right out of school too, which explained why Darren permitted himself to drive my brand new, fully equipped sedan instead of his older, cheaper sports car. He spent all his money buying a very expensive desktop computer and maxed out our joint credit card on name brand clothing and various other wants, as if new and expensive "things" made him feel important enough for his parents to value him more for obtaining them.

It was all an illusion, though. We couldn't afford these things. We had to cut back on expenses and sell some of the furniture I had in storage to make our minimum monthly payments.

I couldn't help but think the perfect-family facade Jane and Henrik put on was an illusion too—one Denise played into to keep up appearances. Something more was going on, though, to make Darren feel so inferior to Denise. I had to find out what it was.

"Darren said he'd find your mom crying by herself a lot, so I guess she was going through some stuff and taking it out on him?"

"I don't know what Darren's talking about," Denise refuted.

"It's just weird to me that you two had such different experiences. I mean, your parents seem perfect! But Darren said your mom would scream at him if he used the bathroom in the middle of the night? That he had to pee in the corner of his room to avoid getting in trouble? I can't imagine your mother doing that, but . . . he gave me the impression he had a tough time growing up. It's kinda how we connected."

"None of that ever happened," Denise snipped. She sounded like my mother.

I decided to let it go and let her believe her childhood was the rainbows and butterflies she believed it was. Upsetting her was no way to develop the close relationship I wanted.

I didn't know what I was supposed to believe, though. Denise had no reason to lie to me, but I'd caught Darren half-asleep, peeing in the corner of the bedroom at night, on more than one occasion.

Hoping to get rid of the awkward tension I'd created, I changed the subject. "So what's the plan for Vegas? Food? Shows?"

It took a few minutes to shake the tension, but we managed to get back on track and had a great trip. We walked up and down the strip with our three-foot margaritas, lay poolside at the MGM Grand Hotel admiring the "pool boys" bringing us more drinks than we needed, and gambled until we had more cash in our purses than we'd brought with us!

By the time we returned home, Denise was my confidante, my best friend, and finally, my sister. She probably didn't feel the same about me, but I was okay with having a one-sided relationship with her. I wanted a sister however I could have one.

"Dick"

By winter of 1997, Denise and Brad were building a house, so, of course, we had to keep up.

Darren took a side job repairing electronics, and I took a data entry position with flexibility to work whenever I could. We saved our extra earnings, until we had enough for a small down payment.

We looked at a few homes with a realtor, but there weren't many options in our limited price range. What we did see either required a lot more work to update than we could afford or were in neighborhoods we didn't care for. So we looked at new construction deals in our area and found an affordable ranch duplex in a new development. We fell in love with the model home, which featured two bedrooms, one and a half bathrooms, an office with sliding glass doors to a huge yard, and a vaulted and open kitchen and living room. It was more than enough space for the two of us, and we were excited to be able to select all the cabinets and fixtures ourselves. It was exactly the price we were looking to spend, so we signed a contract with the builder and each contributed half the down payment.

We invited Jane and Henrik to meet us at the site to see the foundation and partially constructed framework for the first time. It was freezing cold, and the ground was covered in a thin layer of crunchy white snow. The overcast sky did nothing to diminish our spirits, though. We were very proud to be building our first home at twenty-one and twenty-three years old, respectively.

"It's really coming along!" Jane's widened eyes took in the sight from the curb where they'd parked their small SUV.

"I know!" I said as I walked over to greet them with hugs and cheek kisses. "I still can't believe this is happening!"

Henrik wore his toothy grin. He put one arm around Darren and they started walking towards the framework. "Let's take a look at this, son!" Jane and I followed behind.

While Henrik and Darren inspected the quality of the materials and craftsmanship, I did my best to show Jane how the rooms were laid out. I already planned where our furniture would be placed and had ideas for paint colors and décor.

"You must be very excited!" Jane commented as we stepped over the framing to exit the structure.

"I am! It's just hard to believe we didn't have enough money for the town house we wanted before, but another lender was willing to give us a loan to build with less money down! It makes no sense!" I turned back to see Darren and Henrik walking behind us. They were discussing construction timelines, as we were promised a spring move-in date. "Whaddya think, Dad?" I'd started referring to him that way, at his insistence.

"You did good," Henrik approved. He caught up to me and squeezed me from the side. I grinned in delight, feeling the rare sense of pride my own parents denied me.

My mother and stepfather knocked down my achievements like a bad habit. It's like I wasn't allowed to succeed or accomplish anything worthy of notice, because it didn't fit into their grand scheme of making me look like a delinquent. I was supposed to fail, to be emotional and to make bad decisions, so they felt justified treating me like a child while simultaneously expressing to others how difficult it was for them to parent a difficult daughter. This house was no different.

"You and Darren haven't known each other long enough to own a house together," my mother judged when I shared the progress on the house the following week. She had no life other than working and shopping, so I sometimes tagged along with her after school, hoping for some loving bond to develop between us in a Walmart. "So if things don't work out between the two of you, you'll be left with the burden of the mortgage and real estate taxes *and* the costs of maintaining the house. Have you thought about *that?*" She always talked down to me as if I were incompetent and stupid. I also couldn't ignore the assumption I'd be left. She hadn't wanted me and assumed no one else did either.

"No, but . . ." I started to defend, but she interrupted.

"You need to think about these things before getting yourself involved with someone else financially. If that mortgage doesn't get paid or gets paid late, both of your credit scores will be affected." She sounded just like her husband sometimes.

I usually contradicted anything they said just for the sake of rejecting their disapproval of everything I did. But as much as I hated to admit it, my mother was right. Darren and I needed to have a talk about buying this house as an unmarried couple.

We were driving to Denise's condo on Christmas Day, when I decided to bring up the matter. "I was thinking about the house and everything"—I paused to turn the volume down on the radio—"and I guess I need to know what you're thinking. Like, do you think you'll marry me at some point, or . . . ?"

I looked over at Darren to gauge his nonverbal reaction, but his blank face told me nothing. He looked from the rear-view mirror to the side mirror, trying to navigate through the busy intersection.

"I mean, do you think it's a good idea to buy this house together? People normally get married, *then* buy a house, then have babies . . . We're kind of doing everything backwards."

I looked at Darren for a response. A comment, opinion, even an inquiry as to where I was going with all this would have been welcome. But he said nothing.

So, I stopped beating around the bush. "We'll be married someday, right?"

"I don't know," he responded like a snarky teenager.

I needed more reassurance than that. "It's just that I was talking to my mom about it, and I guess I need to make sure we're on the same page before we buy this house, as far as marriage and money and everything.

You know?"

The furrowed brows and pursed lips of Mr. Hyde appeared where Darren had been. I immediately stopped my nervous rambling and held my breath.

"So you don't want to buy the house with me now? Is that it? I knew your parents didn't like me!" Darren shouted.

My fear was instantly replaced with anger at his attempt to avoid the subject of marriage. "This has nothing to do with my parents, Darren! And shit, they don't even like *me*!" I argued. "But we should've thought this through before getting into a situation where our credit is combined and our financial futures are reliant on each other! It's not like we have a great relationship or anything! So I need to know if we're headed towards marriage or if we're just two people randomly buying a house together. I mean, what if we broke up? You gonna kick me out of the house, or am I gonna have to ask *you* to leave? Does the person moving out have to keep paying half the mortgage and bills? Because neither of us can afford this place on our own! Same thing if something, God forbid, happens to one of us. What then? There's a lot more to consider than just buying a house together."

"Cancel the contract then!" Darren's overreaction frustrated me.

"I don't want to cancel the contract! I just want reassurance that you're buying this house with me because you want to be with me long-term, and that this isn't just about you finally owning real estate! Why is that so hard for you to understand?"

I stared at him, waiting for a response. He clasped his lips tightly, like a two-year-old refusing to speak to his mother.

I rolled my eyes and sighed. Then I prodded, "Do you see a future with me or not, Darren? Do you want to marry me eventually or are we just seeing where this goes and hoping it goes at all?"

"I don't know! I can't guarantee anything!" he hollered. "Fuck! If you don't want the house, just cancel it! Never mind, I'll lose the ten-thousand-dollar down payment—just do whatever you want! As long as Dana's happy!"

"Why do you have to go to such extremes? And what are you talking about, losing ten thousand dollars? We each put five thousand towards that down payment, so I stand to lose just as much as you do! But I never said I wanted to cancel the house, so I don't even know why we're arguing about this!"

"Maybe *I* don't want the fucking house now. We'll just keep renting and throwing our money away instead."

I rolled my eyes at his passive-aggression, then turned and looked out the window at the gloomy day. There was no point in arguing with someone who couldn't be reasonable.

How did he turn the tables on me anyway? And how I was to blame for an irrational decision he made out of anger? What were we even arguing about? Marriage? Money? The house? I was more irritated than confused, though, because he was so difficult to communicate with! Maybe I needed to consider *that* before jumping into anything with *him*!

Hoping he'd calm down and rethink his responses, I looked over at Darren once more. His clenched jaw indicated he was still stewing, so I kept quiet and laid my head back upon the headrest. I should have known better than to ruin Christmas with my selfish need for reassurance. I was disappointed in myself for upsetting Darren, in us as a dysfunctional couple, in Darren as a boyfriend . . . I wondered if he ever felt fault for the chaotic dynamic between us, or if he really felt I was to blame for everything that didn't go the way he wanted it to. I'd never know, because Darren wouldn't talk to me the rest of the drive nor on the walk up to Denise's condo from the parking lot.

But when Jane answered the door at Denise's, Darren boisterously bellowed, "Ho, ho, ho! Merry Christmas!" Then he walked in with the jolliest smile, leaving his alter ego outside with me.

My mouth dropped open in amazement at how quickly he could flip the switch.

Jane put her hand on my shoulder with a look of concern on her face. "Are you okay, Dana?"

"Yeah," I replied, smiling complacently, "I just have a headache." This was my go-to excuse.

Denise offered me ibuprofen, and eventually I acclimated to the festivity around me—just not as quickly as Darren did. It was fine, though. We had a nice Christmas and pretended the argument had never happened.

A month later, the builder called to inform us it was time to pick out cabinets. Although Darren and I had previously decided on oak, I called him right away from the car to confirm.

"You never fucking listen to me!" he yelled from the other end. "I told you to cancel!"

I bowed my head and closed my eyes. Then I took a deep breath and tried to reason with him. "I know, Darren. But you and I both know you don't really want that. Can we just talk about this?"

"No! I'm fucking done with that house! So call them and tell them to cancel it!" he ordered, then hung up.

Even though I vehemently disagreed with Darren's order to cancel the house, I called the builder back to get it over with. It made me sick to my stomach when they reminded me we'd lose the down payment, and sicker when I told them to proceed with canceling.

When I returned home that evening, I holed up in the bedroom to avoid Darren. I had nothing to say to him after what I felt was an immature overreaction.

He ignored me too. He stayed in the living room watching TV by himself, and he didn't even attempt to speak to me until a few nights later.

"My parents are pretty pissed at you," Darren threw out during a commercial break. I was only watching the latest episode of *90210* with him because I wanted to see how something from the previous week played out in this week's episode.

"About what?" I came out of the kitchen with our dinner plates and handed one to him.

"For causing me to lose all my money!" he said, as if I were stupid.

Realizing this was about the house, I pointed out, "But I lost the same amount you did. And I'm not the one who wanted to cancel."

"Well, they're not happy about what you did. My dad especially."

What had I even done? Better yet, what the hell had Darren told his parents I'd done? He knew I loved his dad, so why would he want to compromise that relationship?

I looked at Darren, expecting he'd elaborate. When he didn't, I realized

I couldn't handle the truth anyway. I was devastated that, according to Darren, Henrik took issue with me. He'd been the one person in that family who'd accepted and loved me from day one, without judgment. I lowered my head at the thought of Henrik thinking less of me now, and tried not to cry while I ate my dinner. Darren, on the other hand, watched TV and ate his dinner, completely unaffected by my angst.

When our lease ended in the spring of 1998, we moved into yet another apartment with another special move-in rate. I liked this new apartment because it had a vaulted two-story foyer, and the deck off the living room faced a quiet wooded area where I sat with my coffee almost every morning, thinking about life and what lay ahead for me. I was about to graduate from DePaul University and had been promoted to manager of an exclusive apartment development in a wealthy suburb north of us.

Even Henrik and Jane had called to congratulate me on the new position. We never spoke of the house fiasco, so I assumed it had blown over like everything eventually does, because they treated me like one of the family again.

Everything was falling into place, it seemed, except for my relationship with Darren. He was often gone with friends to bars, parties, or on boats or motorcycle rides. None of that was my cup of tea anyway, which was more reason why Darren and I weren't happy together.

One night, he even returned home from a party, drunk and stupid enough to tell me a girl he knew had given him a hand job. "And she said she's never seen such a big dick before!" he bragged.

Neither have I, Darren.

"Tell Me Why"

In June of 1998, I stood in an alphabetically ordered line-up with hundreds of other red- and-blue-gowned twenty-somethings, waiting to enter our college graduation ceremony. Despite all the jubilant noise around me, I felt invisible and out of place; I just wanted it to be over.

Going to college hadn't been the climactic finale to growing up that I'd expected. I'd always heard people talk about their "college buddies," wild frat parties, and overcrowded beaches on spring break. I'd had none of those experiences. Having to work the five days a week I wasn't in school didn't exactly allow for social time, plus Darren's jealousy would've never allowed for time spent doing anything without him anyway. Only he had that luxury.

I blamed my stepfather, though. I wanted to go to beauty school, but he said that wasn't "real school" and being a make-up artist wasn't a "real job." That was rich coming from a man who hadn't made it past sixth grade. Status and money were everything to him, though, so I hit him where it hurt by earning my acceptance into a very expensive university, from which I was now graduating.

My dismal mood, however, was really about Darren. He'd given me the silent treatment all morning, from the second I opened my eyes. I'd done nothing to provoke him, and continued to do nothing other than breathe, to avoid upsetting him even more.

During the two-hour drive to the ceremony venue, I kept looking over at him, hoping he'd give me the slightest clue as to what bothered him so much that his bad mood was ruining my college graduation day. But he never acknowledged me. Not once. It was like I didn't even exist!

So instead of feeling the pride and joy I should have felt on my college graduation day, I felt lost and afraid because I'd been abandoned by yet another person who said they loved me.

I didn't realize how long I'd been standing there pitying myself until "Pomp and Circumstance" began to play and everyone around me began to move. I moved with them, but I went through the ceremony like a zombie. Other than walking across the stage to receive my diploma, I recall nothing significant.

When the ceremony was over, we were ushered out to the rear of the huge stadium, where thousands of attendees excitedly awaited their beloved graduate. I searched the crowd for Darren, hoping he'd honor our commitment to meet my mother and stepfather at my grandma's apartment in Chicago for dinner and cake. I couldn't be so sure, though, and wouldn't have been shocked if he'd just left me there.

To my surprise, I spotted Darren right away. Our eyes locked, but where I'd hoped for an expression of pride, I saw unmistakable hatred. I responded with the sorrowful look of a hound dog, pleading for its owner's approval. Darren turned his back to me and walked away instead.

I knew he saw me, so why wasn't he waiting? I didn't have time to wonder, though; I needed to catch up to him. I moved as swiftly as I could towards him, despite being elbowed and pushed and blocked by everyone else trying to get to their loved ones.

By the time I'd reached the parking lot, Darren had already gotten in the car. The car slightly rumbled as soon as he closed his door, which meant he'd started the ignition too. I ran as best as I could in my high heels and practically jumped into the passenger's seat before he could leave me behind. Then Darren tore out of the parking lot, screeching the tires so everyone would know his mood.

As soon as we were on the road, he yelled, "You think you're better than everyone now? Just because you have a college degree? Well, you're not! You're no better than anyone else!"

I looked over at his reddened face. That's what this was about? I'd shamed him by earning a higher degree than he had, and now I was required to disregard feelings of pride and achievement in exchange for suffering under his feelings of inferiority? In what cruel world was someone made to feel bad for one of their greatest accomplishments in life? Frustrated that nothing I did was ever good enough, I hid my face in my hands and cried.

I expected Darren to put his hand on mine, maybe apologize for ruining my special day, or console me in any way at all, but he didn't. He didn't look at me either. His stone face focused straight ahead, like the road was more important than my broken heart. Despite all the bad times we'd had, it was this moment in which I realized that he really, truly didn't care about me.

So I remained silent too. There was nothing to say anyway. I wasn't going to convince someone to care about me. I shouldn't need to.

A little while later, we pulled up to my grandma's brick apartment building in the city. I was thankful Darren had at least had the decency to bring me here, but I had no intention of staying long. I was in no mood to celebrate after the emotional torment he put me through all day.

All I wanted was to see my great-grandma, who had taken care of me as a mother would, before my mother got married and took me away. She lived here with my grandma and uncle, and I didn't get to see her very often because she wasn't in good enough health to ever leave the apartment.

Inside the tiny entrance to the building, I rang the bell to announce our arrival, then waited to be buzzed in. Darren followed behind me as we began our ascent of the three flights of stairs to the top-floor apartment. Half way up, I heard my Uncle Juni yell, "Dana's here!" I looked up and saw him waiting for us on the landing above, then quickly wiped away the tears I'd cried in the car.

"Hi, Juni!" I called up, trying to act as normal as possible. Darren didn't like me letting on to anyone that he'd upset me.

"Hi, Dana. Hi, Darren." Juni looked down shyly when we finally made it up. He led us into the apartment then, and called out, "Ma, Dana's here!"

"Daaana!" My grandma always drew out the first syllable of my name. "Congratulations!" she over-enunciated as she came to greet us.

"Thank you, Grandma!" I bent slightly to give her a big hug.

"Hi, Grandma!" Darren said cheerily as he gave her his one-arm side hug. It sounded as unnatural as my grandma's returning side hug looked.

We entered the adjacent dining room then, where my mother, stepfather, and little brother, Jonathan, were seated at the large cherry wood table which took up the entirety of the room. Darren sat at the head at the far end, away from everyone else. He was probably sulking because no one else had said hello to him. They hadn't said hello to me either, though. My mother was always doing my stepfather's bidding, and my stepfather only paid attention to Jonathan, who was wriggling his body all around and pulling the ends of his mouth outward with his fingers. He was only eight and had to be the center of attention at all times.

My grandma sat near Jonathan and laughed with my stepfather and Juni.

"Jonathan!" my mother weakly scolded. She was laughing too, so Jonathan continued acting like a clown.

I'd been told long ago I would never be part of their family, so I passed through the room quietly. I just wanted to see my great-grandma anyway.

She was in her wooden rocking chair in the bedroom she shared with Juni, just off the dining room. "Hi, Gram!" My heart filled with joy at the sight of her.

Through her thick, round glasses, she smiled up at me with a toothless grin that told me her teeth were probably sitting on the bathroom sink, and I could see her eyes twinkle with the same delight as mine.

"What're you watching, Gram? A Spanish soap opera?" I sat on the edge of her twin bed, next to the arm of her rocking chair.

"Sí!" She patted the tiny lap of her short rotund body with both hands. "Ven acá!"

"I'm getting too big to be rocked in your lap, don't you think? I mean, I want to, but I don't want to crush you!"

"You won't crush me!" she said before switching back to Spanish. "Pero está bien. Entonces, ¿qué pasa?"

I should've known she'd see right through to my heart. She knew me too well. "Nothing," I said with down-turned eyes. I glanced up when I heard an uproar of laughter from the dining room. Then I spoke lowly, "Just, you know, me and Darren."

She didn't know what had happened, obviously, but she always had some wisdom to share. "Remember what I told you about your 'father'?" She pointed towards my stepfather sitting in the dining room, then looked back at me very intently. "When a man raises his voice to you, be quiet." She put her finger to her pursed lips. "That way, when you finally speak up one day, he'll hear you."

I nodded. It actually made perfect sense to me. Lord knows I talked too much and rambled sometimes. There was no way for Darren to determine the importance of everything I said, when I voiced every thought that ran through my head. I needed to be more selective about what I wanted him to hear.

"I love you, Gram."

She kissed her palm, then put her hand on my forehead. That made me smile. Then I yawned.

"I'm going to see if Darren can take me home now."

"You tired?"

"Yeah, it's been a long day, and we have a long drive back." I stood from the bed and bent down to hug Gram goodbye.

Juni saw from where he stood in the dining room. "You leaving, Dana?"

"We haven't eaten!" my grandma worried out loud as I emerged from Gram's bedroom.

"I'm sorry! I'm tired and my head hurts. I just want to go home."

Darren stood from his chair and pushed it back into the table. I never had to ask him twice when it came to leaving the few of my family gatherings we attended.

"But Daaana," Grandma said, starting to put on the pressure, "you cannot leave without eating!"

"We got cake!" Juni enticed.

I raised my brows at Juni's fat belly. "I think the cake will be eaten just fine without my help!"

Darren offered a handshake to my stepfather. "See ya, man." Then he gave my mother a half-assed, one-arm hug.

Grandma continued her attempt to sway me. "Daaana! You cannot go! We have food!"

I went to hug her. "I know, Grandma. I appreciate it, but there'll be more for you now." I squeezed her tight.

"Noooo!" Grandma persisted. "Staaaay! Eeeeat! She motioned towards the table, but I kept moving towards the door.

"I love you, Grandma! Thank you so much for all this! I promise I'll stay longer next time, okay?"

"But Daaana!"

I had a hard time walking away from her, but Darren was holding the door open, and I didn't want to risk angering him any more by holding him up.

Back in the car, no words were spoken. Darren focused on driving, and I stared out my passenger window wishing to see the sunset from somewhere else.

When we got back to our apartment over an hour later, I used a headache to excuse myself to an early bedtime. I just wanted the day to be over . . . and maybe my relationship with Darren too. I didn't want to be with someone who intentionally diminished my greatest achievements. He should have been proud of me today! We should have been happy! But we weren't. We never were.

The next morning, I awoke in bed alone, which immediately triggered all the feelings I'd gone to sleep with the night before. Everything in me told me to walk away, that this wasn't right. But I couldn't just walk away from the time I'd invested with Darren, nor the family I'd finally found in his. I couldn't take the way he treated me, though! I needed to know if he even wanted to be with me, or if we were indeed done as I suspected.

I reached for the corded phone on my bedside table and called his cell. "Hello?"

"Hey," I said softly.

"Hey." He sounded dismal.

"I was just hoping we could talk . . . about us . . . soon?"

"Yeah, I'll be home around dinnertime. We can do it then."

"Okay. I'll see you then." I hoped he heard the sadness in my voice.

"Yep. Bye." He hung up.

I closed my eyes and exhaled out my nose.

The darkness outside seemed to seep through the sliding glass doors and into our poorly lit living room where Darren sat on his black couch. I leaned back against the breakfast bar, facing Darren with my arms crossed. His grimace told me I was wasting his TV-watching time—an indication he didn't care in the slightest. So I got right to business.

"Our lease ends at the end of April next year. They're raising rent by a few hundred dollars a month, so it doesn't make sense to stay here and overpay. But here's the thing—I don't know how to say it, so I'm just going to say it—I think we need to go our separate ways after this."

Darren pursed his lips. I stared at him, waiting for a response. Any response. That he loved me, that we'd move somewhere else together, that he agreed we should part, but he said nothing. His blank facial expression didn't change either. I took his lack of emotion as indifference, or perhaps even agreement, and continued. "So let's just call it what it is. You haven't invited me out to the parties you go to, on your friend's boat with his family, to friends' barbecues and things. And you come home and tell me you made out with this girl or got a hand job from that one. I don't know if I just don't do it for you anymore, or if I'm not good enough for you, or what, but it's pretty lonely sitting here by myself all the time. I go to work. I pay the bills on time. I keep this place clean. I finally graduated so I could make something better of myself. I feel like I do everything I'm supposed to, but with you, I get nothing. No thanks, no approval, nothing. Absolutely nothing. And I don't want to do this anymore."

There was a long pause. "I don't know what you want me to say," Darren said with harsh indifference.

It hurt that, after all this time, neither my words nor my feelings had any effect on him. He didn't look sad or upset; he didn't even look surprised. Had he been waiting for me to end it so he wouldn't look like the bad guy? Was that why he treated me so badly—to push *me* to be the one to end it?

"It's okay. Maybe this is just as well," I said. We had nothing in common other than his family, nor could we manage to get along unless we were with them, which was unrealistic to rely on in the long run. So maybe it was time to face the fact that Darren and I just weren't meant to be and that, consequentially, I had to give up a family that had never been mine to begin with.

"What are you saying?"

"Don't make me say it again, Darren."

"So that's it? We're done?"

"When our lease ends . . . I don't know." I shrugged my shoulders. "I guess." I'd hoped he'd promise to treat me better so we could remain together or at least apologize for his part in our demise, but he got up and walked out instead, leaving me alone. Again.

"All I Want for Christmas Is You"

A s if that conversation had never happened, we went through the motions of life as a couple. Before long, 1998 was nearly over.

"Looks like Darren is going to be Santa this year!" an uncle of mine proclaimed loudly. He snickered as he dropped a red Santa hat onto Darren's drooping head. Darren was completely unaware, though. His limp body and half-closed eyes made it obvious he'd drunk too many beers.

It was Christmas Eve—the only day of the year my mother's entire side of the family gathered, ironically in my grandma's tiny apartment. As midnight approached, we had a tradition of suiting up the drunkest person in attendance in a Santa Claus costume. "Santa" would then surprise the kids with a staged entrance, pass out gifts, and entertain the heckling adults with drunken incapacity.

So with the help of a cousin, Darren was taken into the bathroom, stuffed into a Santa suit, and sent out the back door. Soon after, he came through the front door, bellowing, "Ho, ho, ho!"

Everyone clapped and cheered noisily, "Yay! Santa's here!" Kids gasped and looked around at each other in amazement. One little cousin opened her mouth widely and put her hands on her cheeks like Macaulay Culkin famously did in the movie *Home Alone.*

"How was your trip from the North Pole, Santa?" a family friend called out over all the hoopla.

"Fantastic!" Darren replied enthusiastically. "It was a little cold though. The sleigh doesn't have heat!" One of the kids laughed a little too boisterously at the bad joke.

Still at the front door, Darren had nowhere to go. There were about forty people crammed into two rooms. Some sat on plastic-covered gold sofas in the living room. Others were privileged enough to get a seat at the dining room table. Children sat on the floor wherever they could find a spot, and most adults had to just stand against a wall or piece of furniture to be out of the way. No one minded climbing over everyone else to get to the bathroom or kitchen, though; we were accustomed to the chaos.

Drunken Santa, however, was not.

"Can we get a chair for Santa in here?" I called to those in the dining room. One of my uncles handed a chair to someone in the living room, then it was handed to me.

"Watch out!" I motioned for the kids to make space for me to set it by the tree. I'd been standing there, awaiting Santa's arrival, to assist with distributing the gifts. Darren had only been here for two Christmases prior, so he didn't know enough people to be able to give out the gifts on his own. "All right, Santa! Let's get this show on the road!" I raised my eyebrows to the kids, who were overly eager to get their presents.

Various family members helped steady Darren as he clumsily made his way to the chair. When he finally sat down, he wiped his forehead and asked, "Can someone get Santa a beer? It's been a long night already!" Everyone laughed, and a can of beer was passed from the kitchen through the dining room and into Santa's hand.

Darren opened it, took a sip, opened his mouth too widely, and exaggerated a refreshing "Aahhh" sound. All the kids giggled and looked at each other in amusement.

"Okay, Santa," I prodded, "we ready now? I think these kids have waited long enough!"

"Feels just like home," Darren commented, then pointed his thumb at me. "Mrs. Claus thinks *she's* the boss!"

Everyone laughed again, including me. Darren was good at putting on a show!

Then I handed him one gift at a time, telling him who it was for. He presented each gift with exuberance, occasional sarcasm, and even remembered to rub the fat belly of the costume every now and then.

After the last gift had been distributed, I was relieved. I was so hot I was getting dizzy. I needed to either take off the thick sweater I stupidly chose to wear, or step outside into the frigid weather to cool off. I think everyone else was feeling it too, because some of the kids started to get up and adults began to talk again.

"We're not done! I believe there is one more gift to give!" Darren announced over the increasingly loud chatter. Everybody stopped and turned their attention back to us.

What the fuck? I thought. I got on my knees to check underneath the tree one last time.

"Darren," I scolded under my breath as I stood back up, "there are no more gifts!"

"Oh, but there is, Dana!" he proclaimed. Then he got down on one knee and held out the empress-cut diamond solitaire ring I'd seen in the window of a jewelry store two years before. I'd said it was the prettiest ring I'd ever seen.

The room was dead quiet now. You could literally hear a pin drop. "No, you're not!" I blurted, then put my right hand over my mouth to prevent any other unfiltered comments from flying out. Darren gave me a discerning look of disapproval, for allowing my big mouth to ruin this romantic moment.

In my defense, a proposal was the last thing I'd expected! We'd discussed going our separate ways when our lease ended in four short months. It was a wonder we'd even made it to Christmas together! Plus, I'd finally resolved his rejection to the fact that we were just too different, and that we wanted different things in life. So what was I supposed to do with this proposal?

But he remembered the ring! All this time I thought he didn't care or didn't pay attention to me, he had been. And that was a game changer.

Darren took my left hand in his. "Will you marry me?" He raised his brows and looked at me with pleading puppy dog eyes.

Everyone's eyes were on me, and I felt the pressure. "Umm . . ." I hesitated, knowing I needed to make an instantaneous decision. I wanted to get married, and it made sense to marry the man I'd been living with for three years, but . . . Ah, fuck it. "Yes!" I cried, nodding emphatically.

Everyone cheered while Darren slipped the ring on my finger. I looked over at my gram. She didn't have her teeth in, and her thin lips curled over her gums, but her twinkling eyes told me she was happy for me. I hugged Darren as chatter and movement picked up around us.

"Let's see this ring!" a family friend called out from the crowd. I walked over to her, and she made a joke of pretending to use a magnifying glass to be able to see the diamond. It wasn't that small, though; she was always busting everyone's balls.

After showing off the ring to my grandma and an aunt, I went to the bathroom, where Darren was changing out of the Santa costume. He pulled me in by my elbow, which I didn't much care for.

"Don't go planning a wedding anytime soon," he whispered too close to my ear, still gripping me by my elbow. "We're going to have a long engagement because we're buying a house first. I've been saving money and I know you have too, so we're going to start looking at houses again after the holidays."

I raised my eyebrows at the unexpected intrusion of Mr. Hyde, though I shouldn't have been surprised how quickly he'd take away my elation about the proposal. I should've known there was a catch with *all* of this. He wanted a house, and I wanted a commitment. So he gave me the promise of what I wanted in exchange for the fulfillment of his wish, after which I'd be granted the fulfillment of mine. Tit for tat, just like his mother. There was no other way to explain how he'd gone from being indifferent about parting ways at the end of our lease, to suddenly finding me worthy of his undying devotion.

I'd have been embarrassed to get into an argument just minutes after becoming engaged, though, so I nodded in compliance. Darren looked me directly in the eyes with a stern stare before releasing my elbow to impress upon me how serious he was about this "deal" we'd just made. He didn't need to, though. I got it, loud and clear.

With a drooped head, I left him to change.

Juni saw me standing outside the bathroom door rubbing my forehead as he passed through the hallway to the kitchen. "You okay, Dana?"

"Yeah!" I nodded quickly and gave a half-smile. "Just taking it all in!" I held up my left hand to display the ring.

He smiled back and continued to the kitchen. I guess Darren wasn't the only one good at putting on a show.

Just a handful of hours later, we arrived at Denise and Brad's newly built custom home for Christmas breakfast. Light snow fell from the sky as we stood outside the red front door of the ivory brick ranch home, admiring the massive poinsettias and evergreen garland adorning the entry.

When the door sprung open, Denise, Brad, Jane and Henrik cheered out, "Merry Christmas!" We all laughed at their goofy surprise greeting.

Then Brad said, "Were you on Santa's 'nice' list this year?"

"I'd say so!" I extended my arm for everyone to see the engagement ring on my finger.

"I knew it!" Brad shared.

Jane grabbed my hand with both of hers, looked at my ring closely, looked up at me with open-mouthed disbelief, then looked at her son with teary eyes. "Darren!" She threw her arms around him. It was a sweet moment that almost made me cry too.

"Come on in from the cold," Henrik said as he put his hand on my shoulder to guide me in. Darren and Jane followed, and everyone chattered about how and where it had happened while we set down the gifts we'd brought and removed our coats and shoes.

"Merry Christmas, honey," Henrik said, squeezing me from the side. I smiled back at him. Despite some of the hiccups with Darren and his mom and sister, knowing I'd be one of them soon enough was the best gift Darren could have ever given me.

"Friday I'm in Love"

Four months later, we closed on our first house—a five-year-old, tri-level home in a suburban subdivision. Denise and Brad came over that evening to see it.

"Welcome to our new home!" I made a dramatic show of extending out my arm when I opened the door to them.

Denise smiled as she entered the formal living room. She looked up at the vaulted ceilings and then to the bay window to her left. "Very nice, guys!" She nodded in approval.

Brad came in right behind her and immediately shook Darren's hand. "Congratulations!"

"Thanks, man!" Darren responded with a puffy chest and rolled back shoulders. He wore home ownership well.

"You want the grand tour?" I offered in a lame attempt to sound fancy.

"Yeah!" Denise spoke for both of them.

After walking them through the empty rooms on the first three levels, Darren and Brad went down to the fourth level—a sub-basement Darren wanted to finish as an extra living area. He'd been toying with the idea of making it a work-out room for me. I suspected he wanted Brad's input on the project.

Denise and I went back to the main level kitchen and chatted.

"Whaddya think?" I asked as I leaned back against the counters. "It's not the custom home you guys built, but . . ."

"You guys did good! It's more than enough room for you two. Then maybe another one or two after you get married . . ." she insinuated with raised brows and a close-mouthed grin.

"Whoa! Let's not get ahead of ourselves! We just bought the place and we're not getting married for another year!"

Denise giggled. "Just sayin'!"

"Yeah, yeah," I jokingly dismissed with a smile.

"So did you guys look at a lot of houses before picking this one?"

"No, this was actually the only house we looked at."

"Really?"

"Yeah. Darren saw it and wanted it. He would have probably liked anything we saw, though. He just wanted a house. But when he found out we qualified for the loan, even though it was double our original budget, that was it!" I shrugged.

"You like it, though, don't you?" She suddenly seemed concerned.

"It's a nice house," I obliged. "Not necessarily what I would've wanted, but I'm not picky. And Darren is happy." There was no polite way of telling her that her brother had to have his way, and that I'd learned to serve his needs to avoid conflict. I suspected Brad could relate.

Darren and Brad came up the stairs to rejoin us. "I heard my name up here! You talking about me?" Darren smiled and put his arm around my shoulders.

"Yep, talking all kinds of crap about you," I joked back with a wink and a smile. Denise cracked up at our sarcastic banter.

I noticed Brad had disappeared into our dark living room, so I moved out of Darren's hold and walked to where Brad was examining the vaulted ceilings. Darren and Denise followed.

"I'd offer you guys a seat, but . . ." I smiled and shrugged at the emptiness of the room.

"When are you moving all your stuff in?" Denise asked as she sat on the carpet with her back against the wall. We all did the same.

"I don't know." I looked to Darren for a firmer answer.

"Soon. Our lease is up at the end of the month, and we'll have to clean the apartment between work and moving in here, before turning in the keys there," he said.

"We still won't have nearly enough furniture for this place anyway. My mother said she might be getting rid of a sofa, so maybe we'll put it in here.

Otherwise, it'll have to remain empty until we can afford new furniture."

"Has she seen the house yet?" Denise wondered.

I chuckled before answering, "My mother and stepfather have only been to one apartment I've lived in since moving out five years ago. Oh, wait. My mother came to an apartment I shared with my ex once too. But to answer your question, no. My stepfather can't be bothered with anything that has to do with me, and my mother's vision is so bad she relies on him to drive her anywhere outside of the ten-minute radius of their house and the office they own. I'm sure she'll make it over eventually, though." My head dropped, and I fumbled with my fingers.

Uncomfortable silence swept over all of us. I was immediately disappointed in myself for dampening the mood with my family dysfunction. That hadn't been my intent. I'd just forgotten how direct and honest I could be, and that polite people didn't discuss their family problems so openly.

Darren dispelled the discomfort by blurting out, "How 'bout them Bears?"

I looked up at him and couldn't help but smile at the almost inappropriate and abrupt subject change. It wasn't even football season! Then I looked at Denise to gauge her reaction. She was looking at me with tightly pressed lips, as if unsure whether it was okay to laugh, but when she saw me smiling, we both burst out laughing.

"So what were we talking about? Furniture?" I asked, recovering the conversation with an exaggerated smile.

We sat for a while after that, discussing appliances, basements, and the wedding. Although a normal night in the scheme of life, it was one that made me feel more enmeshed with this family. I didn't need my mother present; I had Jane and Denise. I didn't even need Darren to be funny and loving all the time. He just showed me he had my back. And in this tit-for-tat dynamic of ours, Darren's short fuse and demanding nature was a small price to pay in exchange for his sister and parents who cared about and accepted me into their family, and who would be my family through marriage soon enough. That's all I'd ever wanted anyway.

So when Jane called a couple days later to find out when she and Henrik could come see our new house, I shared, "I'm going to ask Denise to be my matron of honor!"

"Oh my gosh, she's going to pee her pants!" Jane squealed in delight.

She might have too! Denise announced she was pregnant with her first child not long after accepting my invitation to stand beside me at the altar. The pregnancy didn't hinder her wedding duties either. She called often to share ideas, like the floral centerpieces she'd seen Martha Stewart handcraft on a TV show. She recorded another show in which a gentleman demonstrated how to make artificial flower bouquets and invited me over to watch it. She accompanied me to bridal salons to look at bridesmaid dresses, and even coerced me into buying a wedding veil I had no intention of wearing. I just got so caught up in the excitement of the moment with my soon-to-be sister, that I went with it to make her happy.

I also did it to ease the tension of refusing to change my wedding colors. She thought I should have the bridesmaids wear navy blue instead of black, because blue looked better with her blonde hair and blue eyes and would also be more consistent with the nautical nature of the cruise ship wedding.

Although I was grateful to Denise for her input and for simply being there throughout the whole process, I still wanted the wedding I envisioned. So I had to be careful to reject her ideas in a respectful way, because without her, I'd have been alone.

I'd always imagined having at least my mother to plan the day with me, to have the sentimental moment when we found "the" dress and she told me what a beautiful bride I would be. But my mother could barely be bothered to listen when I'd tell her about some wedding detail I'd arranged. I'd have gladly had one or both of my grandmas serve in her place, and they would have done so without hesitation, but Grandma worked at a nearby hospital and Gram wasn't easily mobile nor comfortable leaving the apartment with her incontinence.

Even Darren let me have free rein with the wedding, which was unusual considering how much he had to control me and everything around him for the sake of appearances. It was like he was letting me do what I wanted with the wedding since I let him do what he wanted with the house. It didn't matter, though. We were both getting something we wanted, and we were both pretty happy!

I could tell because Darren was more easygoing. We joked and laughed together more. We didn't argue like we did before, nor did emotions escalate into violence. He even cooked dinner for us every night, since he got off work before I did. We'd eat while we watched our TV shows, then we'd snuggle in bed and fall asleep to reruns of *M*A*S*H*.

His efforts to be kind and considerate—combined with extravagant Christmas gifts, birthday cake when Christmas made everyone forget I'd been born, and fine jewelry and chocolates on Valentine's Day—made me feel loved like never before. Everything was perfect.

"Never Again"

$\mathcal{D}$ enise gave birth to her son, Mason, on March 1, 2000. He was our first nephew, Jane and Henrik's first grandchild, and, in essence, a very big deal to all of us. We visited with him as often as we could, while also preparing for our upcoming nuptials. The summer flew by, and before we knew it, it was late August.

"Ready for bed?" I asked Darren groggily. I switched off the bright kitchen lights and started towards the stairs. I wanted to be well-rested for our wedding shower the next afternoon.

"No. I'm going back to the bar to get my motorcycle before someone steals it," he told me as he took his truck keys off the kitchen counter and stumbled towards the front door. There was no way I was going to let him go, though. He'd just gotten a ride home from that bar, from the friend he'd been with, because he'd been too drunk to drive himself.

"What're you gonna do, drive your truck to the bar and drive your motorcycle back? That makes no sense. I'll take you back for the motorcycle in the morning. Nobody's going to steal it."

Darren reached for the doorknob anyway.

"Darren, seriously! Let's go to bed!" I couldn't consciously let him drive drunk. I'd never forgive myself if something happened to him, or if some random person was hurt or killed due to my negligence.

Darren swung open the front door so hard it bounced off the wooden rail behind it.

I stepped towards him and tried to grab the keys out of his hand, but he raised them high above his head, like a bully on a playground who'd just stolen something from an incomparably smaller school mate. I stood on my tiptoes and clawed his arms. We danced in a half circle, then he stepped back a few feet towards the kitchen to get away from me.

"Darren, this isn't funny! Give me the keys!" I held my hand out, like the mother of a defiant child.

"No!" he yelled. He stepped onto the living room carpet to bypass me to the door. I grunted as I used the full force of my body to physically hold him back, but he was too strong. He pushed me off with little effort, and I stumbled backwards onto the ceramic tile which led towards the door.

That push triggered anger in my heart and adrenaline through my blood. I charged at him with all my might, but even drunk, his stiffened body was too strong for me to stop. He knew it too and went for the door again. I immediately dropped to the tile floor and wrapped my arms around his ankles. It was silly to think the weight of my tiny body could stop him, but I had to try. He freed one foot from my grasp right away. I hung onto the other leg for dear life and cried as he limped forward, dragging me across the cold stone.

When he reached the door, he shook his leg and foot violently. I held on fiercely, even though my skinny elbows hit the hard floor repeatedly. My head took a few knocks of his leg too. I suddenly realized my physical ability mismatched my will power, and I was only hurting myself by letting this continue.

I resorted to begging, hoping to appeal to whatever part of his heart might remember he loved me. "Darren, stop! You're hurting me!"

"Get the fuck off me then!" He shook me loose with one last jerk of his leg. Or maybe my subconscious had given up, hoping fate would make the decision which would relieve us both of this tumult we held onto.

From the tile floor, I watched out the storm door as Darren recklessly reversed out of our garage in his truck. I cried harder as he drove away— not because I was concerned or scared for him, but because every time I thought things were going well, he'd do something to destroy it. I wouldn't leave him, though. I just needed Dr. Jekyll to choose to overpower Mr. Hyde more often, especially since I knew he was capable of being good and moral and kind.

But for now, I was too tired to think or feel anything more than I already was. So, with sloth-like slowness, I stood up, closed the front door, and held my bruised elbow as I ascended the stairs. I swaddled myself in bed and wept softly, until the warmth and comfort of the heavy blanket soothed me into sleep.

The shrill ring of the telephone on my nightstand startled me awake. Without glasses or contacts, the neon numbers on the bedside clock were blurry. I knew it was late, though, which meant something was wrong. *Darren.* I turned towards his side of the bed. It was empty. *Oh my god, Darren!*

My heart pounded as I grabbed the corded phone. "Hello?"

"Is this Dana?" I heard sirens in the background.

"Yes," I said with shortness of breath. Had I manifested my darkest wish?

"This is the Naperville Police Department. Darren gave us this number to notify you that he was in an accident and will be transported to Edward's Hospital."

My heart practically stopped. I think I stopped breathing too. For a moment, my whole world froze.

After my brain processed the words I'd just heard, I took a deep breath, put my free hand on my forehead, and closed my eyes. Then I realized I hadn't asked the obvious question. "Is he okay?"

"We can't provide any more information at this time. Immediate family can contact the hospital for updates on his condition after he's been examined."

"I'm his fiancée. Can you tell me—"

"I'm sorry, ma'am. We can only provide information to family," the officer interrupted.

"Okay, I'll come to the hospital then." I hung up and threw on the clothes I'd worn earlier. I ran down to the kitchen and grabbed my keys off the counter, then thought to inform Jane and Henrik of the situation before I left.

Jane answered the call in a tired murmur. "Hello?"

"It's me. I'm sorry for calling so late. But . . . Darren's been in an accident." I started crying, suddenly overwhelmed by the gravity of the situation.

"What happened?"

"I don't know! They won't tell me anything!" I sobbed in frustration. "They just said he was in an accident and that they're taking him to Edwards Hospital, but they won't tell me how he is because I'm not family! He gave them my name and number, though, so at least I know he's conscious."

"Okay, then I'm going to hang up with you and call the hospital," she said almost too calmly. I wasn't sure if the calm was a motherly tactic for my benefit, or if she was really that unreactive. I was grateful nonetheless; I was panicked enough for all of us.

"Okay." I inhaled deeply and exhaled through my nose. Then I wiped the tears from under my eyes. "I'm heading there now, but will you please call my cell phone and let me know what they say?"

"I will, Dana. It's going to be okay." I nodded my head up and down, as if trying to convince myself of the same.

"All right, I'll wait to hear from you then."

"Okay, drive safely."

The hospital parking lot was barren except for a lone police car. The emergency room was just as deserted.

I approached the reception desk. "My fiancé, Darren, was in an accident—" I started, but before I could finish my sentence, a police officer coming out of a curtained area caught my attention.

"I'm sorry," the nurse apologized, "but he isn't allowed visitors at this time."

"Can you just tell me if he's okay?" I pleaded. I needed to know something.

"I'm sorry. We can only give information to family."

"We're going to be married in two months," I argued. "Please!"

She gestured toward the chairs in the room and said, "You're welcome to wait." For what, I wondered? But what else was I going to do? Go home and go back to sleep?

I sat in an uncomfortable vinyl chair and looked around while I waited. Everything around me was sterile white, which I thought ironic for all the blood and grief held within these walls.

My observation was interrupted by the sound of Darren's voice. It was just a murmur, and I couldn't make out the words. Then I heard his familiar laugh. My brows crinkled in confusion. I looked towards the curtained area he lay behind. A male doctor in a long white coat emerged just then, and I caught a quick glimpse of Darren handcuffed to the bed. And he was smiling! What the hell was going on in there?

"It's a miracle he's alive," I overheard the doctor tell the nurse at the reception desk. He handed her a metal clipboard and walked away. A police officer came out of the examination area and whispered to the nurse at the reception. She pointed in my direction. I stood to meet the officer as he approached me.

"Good evening, ma'am."

"What's going on? I can't get anyone to tell me anything!" I crossed my arms.

"I understand your frustration, ma'am, but we needed to have Darren examined for injuries before reading him his rights."

"His rights?" I was completely lost now.

"Yes, ma'am. Darren is being charged with disobeying a red light, speeding, failure to avoid an accident, and driving under the influence. He's just been released by the doctor, so we will be transporting him to the jail now. It'll be two hundred dollars cash for bail, if you want to meet us there."

"So he's okay?" I asked for clarification.

"Considering he was going ninety miles per hour without a helmet on when his motorcycle collided with an oncoming vehicle, then yes, he's doing well. He's a bit bruised and beat up, though."

So was I, I thought. I felt guilty for caring less for Darren's well-being than for the frustration of living with a man who behaved carelessly and recklessly more of the time than not. When the hell would he grow up? And now I had to bail him out of jail?

As soon as I got back in the car, I called Jane with the news. "I'm leaving the hospital now. They're arresting him for DUI! So I have to find an ATM and then go bail him out." Saying the words made it more real, and I started crying again. I was no longer sad, though. I was mad.

"Oh, Dana," she sighed. "I called the hospital when we got off the phone earlier. They said Darren was okay. So let's focus on that. Get him home and get some rest. You have a big day tomorrow!"

I couldn't even think about the bridal shower right now! And I couldn't believe she wasn't more upset about all this! Granted, she was the type who didn't acknowledge anything unpleasant. She always wore a smile and found something positive in every situation, but she never, and I mean never, gave into any negativity. But the shower? Really? After tonight?

"It is supposed to be a big day, but I'm having a hard time thinking about marrying someone who puts me in situations like this! I mean, when is this going to end? He's always drinking! And now he got arrested!" My tears made it difficult to see the road ahead of me.

"It's been a long night," Jane continued to reassure me. "Just get Darren home and get some sleep."

I could tell she was trying to end the call, but I needed to vent. "He's like a child, though! He has no concern for anyone but himself! Darren does what Darren wants to do, no matter what the effect on others! What if he'd been killed tonight? Or killed someone else? We don't even know if anyone else got hurt or not! All because of his stupid motorcycle?" I stopped the car in the parking lot of a bank and bowed my head into my free hand.

"You and Darren have some things to talk about, I guess," Jane advised. "Dad and I are going to go back to bed for now. If anything changes tonight, call us back. Otherwise, we'll see you tomorrow."

I appreciated Jane's neutral stance, but I needed someone to tell me what a jackass Darren was and that I'd be better off without him. I knew I couldn't expect that of his mother. No matter how well we got along, she wasn't my mother. She was Darren's. And I'd probably just made a fool of myself by saying the things I said about him. I sniffled and took a few deep breaths to regain composure. "Okay. I'll see you tomorrow."

I hung up, retrieved cash from the ATM, and drove to where I'd been told the jail was located.

I'd never been to the jail before, nor had I ever expected to have to come here. I was a pretty straight arrow and associated with other rule followers. So as I walked through the parking lot towards the one-story building in the complex of larger municipal structures, I was surprised by how full it was compared to the ghost town the ER had been. Was there a full moon causing so much unrest in the minds of beer-bellied dads and haughty soccer moms? Or had I failed to notice the criminals in our upper-middle-class suburb, disguised in suits, designer jeans and fancy cars? I looked up to the sky to check the moon. The dark of night was starting to turn into more of a navy blue, indicating sunrise and a new day to come. Unfortunately, time held me back to the night before.

The quiet outside was immediately disturbed when I entered the jail lobby. Bright fluorescent lights assaulted my eyes, and the sound of blaring TVs and noisy chatter bothered my ears. A quick scan of the place confirmed how out of place I was here. There was an older woman with long, scraggly brown hair, standing in the corner staring up at nothing, and a young, long-bearded man with a winter cap and dirty clothing on, sitting on the floor repeatedly rubbing his nose. I held my purse close as I approached the glass-enclosed reception desk.

"Name?" the deputy asked flatly.

"Mine or my fiancée's?" I honestly didn't know. This was my first time in the clink.

"Is your fiancée the one you're bailing out?" The deputy looked annoyed with me for even asking such a stupid question.

It was stupid. Of course they were asking for the jailbird's name. So I gave it to her.

She punched a few things into her computer, then said, "Two hundred dollars please. Cash only."

I handed the money over the counter. She printed a receipt, handed it to me, and said, "Please have a seat while we get him. It'll be a few minutes."

I turned and surveyed the room again, hoping to find a lone chair, away from all the shady characters. I noticed one in the back corner of the room, opposite the lady staring at nothing but furthest from where I stood. I had to step over a passed-out old man and another unsavory who was high on God-knows-what, to make my way through. As soon as I sat, I pulled my purse onto my lap and held it with both hands. I didn't trust anyone on a good day, and I couldn't trust anyone here on any day. Then again, what more could possibly go wrong right now?

I sat stiffly and hyper-vigilantly for at least an hour before I saw Darren escorted into the room by an officer. I watched the officer remove his cuffs, almost entranced by this alternate reality I felt stuck in.

Darren looked like a wreck. The short sleeve of his T-shirt was tattered at the seams, and his dirty, scuffed shorts gave away his rough night. I noticed he favored one leg as he began towards me, and I looked down to see he had only one white ankle sock on. The other foot was bare. I rushed to redirect him out the door to the parking lot, then walked ahead of him to let him know how disgusted I was that he'd put me in this situation.

I heard Darren chuckle like a little kid behind me, but I continued to the car without paying him any mind. I couldn't imagine what was so funny anyway. Neither of us had said anything. He was probably still drunk. Hopefully, the cool morning air would sober him up.

Then he laughed a second time. I whipped my head around in disapproval, to see him standing in the middle of the parking lot looking at his bare foot. He looked at the shoe he was carrying, and then back at his bare foot again.

I stopped and jutted my hip out. "Where is your other shoe?"

He shrugged. "I don't know."

His giggle annoyed me.

"You think this is funny? I can't fucking believe you! Get in the damn car!"

I got in the driver's seat and started the ignition before Darren made his way in. He laid his head back upon the headrest and began to nod off. Glad for the peace, my tired eyes focused on the road home.

When we pulled into our garage twenty minutes later, finally ending this whole fiasco, I shoved Darren's shoulder to wake him. "We're home." Then I went into the house and straight up to bed. I had no patience left to coddle him, and I couldn't care less if he remained in the car to sleep.

He made his way up a short time later, though, loudly bumping into walls and tripping over his own feet. I pretended to be asleep already, to avoid any more interaction with him. I refused to take care of a drunk, and for once in my life, I had nothing to say.

Thankfully, he plopped down onto the other side of the bed and was snoring almost instantly. So I allowed myself the rest I needed too.

"Issues"

Darren insisted on accompanying me to the bridal shower the next day, which was just as well. No one knew of the DUI except for me and Jane and Henrik, so Darren's absence at the shower would have stirred up unwelcome curiosity into our private life. I preferred to prevent the upset of it all from seeping into what was supposed to be a celebratory event in our honor.

It was pointless, though, because the second we walked into the lakefront Chicago high-rise, Darren limped on one leg a little harder. He even threw in an attention-seeking grunt. I knew he had to be in pain, but I also knew he was overacting for the attention. So I ignored him on the elevator ride to the top level of the building. I refused to pay any mind to his attempt to play victim to an accident that was his fault to begin with.

Upon exiting the elevator, I walked ahead of Darren, into the penthouse recreation room. Sunshine poured in through the floor-to-ceiling windows, and the blue sky and waters of Lake Michigan could be seen far into the horizon. I stood there taking it all in for a moment. It was breathtaking.

"Let's go say hi to your mom and Denise before we get caught up with everyone else," I told Darren. I'd seen Jane walk through a nearby door, which seemed to lead into a kitchen. I started to walk that way, and turned to make sure Darren was behind me.

"Hi!" I announced our entrance into the kitchen area. A few guests who were helping carry trays and plates out to the main area greeted me as they passed. Denise glanced up for a second, then turned her attention back to the food she was plating. That struck me as odd, but Jane distracted me before I could think any more on it.

"Hi, Dana! Happy bridal shower day!" She gave me a weak hug and then patted my shoulder.

"Thank you!" I turned away from everyone else just slightly and lowered my voice. "I just wanted to tell you I'm sorry about last night. Thank you for letting me vent, though. It's just that—"

Jane looked behind me and interrupted. "Hi, Darren! How are you feeling?" She went to give him a side hug with one arm.

"Good!" he lied.

"Good!" Jane responded with exaggerated enthusiasm. "It's a beautiful day, isn't it?"

Small talk? After what had happened? Darren's family liked things to be nice and neat, and the DUI didn't fit into their perfectly wrapped family package, but I couldn't understand how they could pretend bad things didn't happen. Then again, this wasn't the time or place to bring up the arrest. So I went along with the facade.

"Hey, Denise!" I moved towards where she was setting desserts on a tray.

"Hey," she muttered. Then she took up a tray of treats and rushed out to the main area where all the guests were gathered. I was shocked at the blatant dismissal.

A friend from work, whom people mistook to be my sister because of our dark curly hair and coordinating dark eyes, came up to me. "Hey, Natalie!" I'd asked her to be in the wedding, so she'd participated with Denise and a childhood friend I'd kept in touch with to throw the shower.

"She's been a bitch to me all morning too," Natalie muttered as she crossed her arms.

"Oh, you caught that, huh?"

"How she just ignored you? Yeah."

I turned to Natalie to whisper more discreetly. "What's with her? Did something happen?"

"Well," Natalie started, "she and I had a little disagreement before today—about the shower. She wanted to throw you something 'nicer,' like at a country club, but the rest of us couldn't afford that. So we opted to do this instead. But she picked everything, decided everything, wanted everything her way, and still wanted us all to contribute the same amount as her. I told her I'll give her what I can, but she got pissy with me and said I owed her more money."

I sighed. "I'm sorry you had to deal with that. Denise is head-strong, but she means well. She really did just want to give me the nicest shower she could. She just forgets everyone doesn't have the very fortunate life she has. You know, being able to stay at home with her new baby while her husband works his cushy, high-paying union job. Don't worry about it, though. I'll talk to her when things blow over. *If* she'll talk to me. I don't understand why she's distant with me today."

"Probably because of the accident last night." Natalie was very matter-of-fact. It was just her nature.

My eyes bulged. "You know?"

"Yeah. Sounds like they blame you too—Denise and her mom." I was stunned that it was even a topic of discussion here, and additionally that any responsibility for Darren's recklessness had been put onto me.

"What the hell did I do? I didn't get him drunk and drive him ninety miles an hour into oncoming traffic!" I defended a little too loudly. I looked around to make sure no one else had heard me.

"No, but you let him *leave* the house drunk."

"That's what they think? That it's my fault? How would they even know he *was* drunk when he left the house?"

She raised her thin eyebrows and pressed her lips together in a complacent closed-mouth expression that made me feel as sorry for myself as she seemed to be for me. "I need a cigarette. You gonna be okay?"

No, I wasn't. But what was I going to do with a room full of family and friends? "I guess I'm gonna have to pretend to be today, huh?"

Natalie shrugged and left me in my no-win situation. I suddenly wished I was a smoker so I could escape with her to decompress. Instead, I smiled for every picture requested, unwrapped all the new housewares we received as gifts, and pretended Darren and I were meant to be.

A week after the shower, I called Natalie to see if she'd resolved things with Denise.

"No," Natalie said, "and I don't think we're going to either."

"Why not? Did something else happen since the shower?" I went out the sliding glass doors to my backyard and sat in a white plastic chair to enjoy the perfectly temperate September afternoon.

"Yeah, Denise called wanting to know when I was going to give her the money she claims I owe her! I told her I wasn't giving her any more money, and, well, let's just say she didn't like that."

I sighed. I'd really hoped they'd get along better than this. "I'm sorry, Nat. I really am. I hope she wasn't too terrible to you."

"I can handle her. I just don't understand how you two are supposedly so close, when all I see is what a bitch she is to you."

I chuckled. "Tell me how you really feel!"

"Look,"—Natalie's serious tone warned me to listen—"I know she's Darren's sister and she means a lot to you, but she's not a nice person. Just be careful with her. Seriously, Dana. Because I don't think you mean as much to her as you think you do."

"Jeez, Nat! You sound like my grandma! She said almost the same exact thing to me after meeting Denise at the shower!"

"Well . . ."

"Let's just get through this wedding stuff, and I promise you'll never have to deal with Denise again. How's that?"

"That's fine, Dana, but you should know one more thing."

"Do I really want to?"

"It's not a big deal. I just want you to be aware that Denise planned your Bachelorette party without the rest of us and . . . don't tell her I told you, but she's having us go to some seafood restaurant. I guess a band is playing there that night. I tried to tell her you don't like seafood, but she said it didn't matter. We're going because the seafood relates to the theme of you getting married on a boat on the lake or something?"

"She does like to take a theme and run with it," I sighed. "I haven't been able to get through to her that the wedding doesn't have a nautical theme. We were actually going more for Old Chicago with the jazz band and classic black and white tuxedos and dresses . . ."

"Anyway," Natalie continued, "I argued with her about the seafood place, but then stopped, because she's obviously gonna have it there no matter what anyone else says and no matter what you want. So just make sure to eat before we leave. And hopefully the rest of the night goes okay."

"I gotcha. Just know I appreciate all you're doing for me, and all you're tolerating. I didn't realize Denise would be this difficult."

"It's okay. I'll return the favor when I get married!"

After I hung up with Natalie, I called Denise. I hadn't heard from her since the shower, and I'd hoped to clear the air about Darren's DUI, since I suspected it to be the root of her hostility towards me there. But Denise didn't answer. She was probably busy with the baby.

I tried her again the following week but didn't get an answer then either. I was starting to wonder how busy she really was with the baby, or if it was really that she was too angry to answer my call.

Then the week of the bachelorette party, I tried again. She answered!

"Hey, Denise!"

"Hey, what's going on?" I was relieved to hear her friendly tone.

"I was just calling to see how things were going with you, and to find out about Saturday. I know you told me the day and time, but I wondered what the plan was, so I could figure out what I'm wearing and everything," I hinted, hoping she'd admit what Natalie had already told me, so I could assert my preferences to her.

"Just wear something comfortable. And we're going to have food where we're going, so don't eat," she advised. "That's all I'm going to say, though. I want it to be a surprise."

"Okay!" I felt guilty that I already knew the plan, but didn't want to upset her, which was why I opted not to bring up the attitude she'd given me at the shower. "Anything else going on?" I poked, hoping she might bring it up instead.

"No. Just trying to keep the baby on a sleeping and feeding schedule. Speaking of which, he's crying, so I gotta go."

"Okay. I'll see you Saturday then!" I didn't get the resolution I'd hoped for, but I dismissed it as a combination of me overthinking and her dealing with lingering pregnancy hormones.

The night of the bachelorette party, I was near the open front door, gathering my lipstick and keys to put in my purse, when I saw Denise pull up and walk straight into our open garage. A dozen friends and cousins had already gathered in there at Darren's request. He didn't want anyone stepping on our new living room carpet.

"Your sister's here!" I called out. Darren was in the kitchen making himself something to eat for dinner.

He walked to where I was, licking his fingers. "I'm going to go say hi to Denise real quick before you guys go then."

"Okay! Tell everyone I'll be out in like five minutes."

Less than two minutes later, Darren returned with raised eyebrows. "Good luck with that group tonight!"

I chuckled as I put on my jacket. "What, are they drinking already?"

"No, but my sister's in a fucking mood!" He walked back into the kitchen to eat his dinner.

"What is with her lately?" I hoped for a reason other than blaming me for the DUI like Natalie had said.

"I don't know. Probably just hormones or lack of sleep. Anyway, try to have a good time tonight."

"That's the plan!" I said as I walked out.

I rode to the secret seafood restaurant with a business acquaintance I'd invited. It was a lively place, overly done with hanging nets and enormous open-mouthed fish. The band playing inside could be heard clearly in the crowded parking lot. I could see why Denise had chosen this place. It did look fun!

"Whaddya think?" Denise asked as our group walked in.

"It's great!" I responded as I looked around at all the ridiculously large fish décor.

Denise seemed pleased and led our group to the packed bar area, where the band was playing. It was dark except for the multicolored flashing lights on the small stage, so we stood there searching for a table, or at least a place we could all stand together without being shoved out of someone's way.

"Should we just go to the bar and order drinks?" I suggested.

"What?" Denise squinted her eyes as if it would make her hear better.

"The bar?" I tried to out-do the band's volume while making a drinking motion with my hand and a backward tilt of my head.

"Okay!" I saw Denise's mouth say.

After shoving and pushing through the crowd, we made our way to the bar, but there was only enough room for Denise to squeeze in between all the other people to talk to the bartender. The rest of us watched the band while we waited for our turn to order.

I didn't recognize any of the songs the band played, nor was it the kind of music I could dance to. It was a combination of rock and country. The music didn't bother me as much as the volume of it, though. It was too loud to carry on a conversation and was sure to give me a headache before too long.

Just then, Denise turned around with a penis-shaped shot glass full of some brownish liquid and topped with whipped cream at the head. I cracked up, and she smiled at my reaction. Then she noticed a nearby table clear and rushed to place the penis on it as a claim. We all followed behind.

Once everyone was standing around the tall table, Denise pulled a white baseball cap out of her purse and placed it on my head. The word "Bride" was embroidered in gold cursive on the front, and white tulle hung from the back. Denise pushed the penis shot in front of me then, and all the girls laughed as she took my picture with it.

Because it was too loud to talk, she demonstrated for me what she wanted me to do by holding her hands behind her back and bending down towards the table with an open mouth.

"You want me to do this shot without my hands?" I asked out loud, forgetting she couldn't hear me over the music. Denise nodded up and down and pointed to the penis while preparing her camera for another picture. "I'll choke if I try to drink all that at once, Denise!"

I looked around at all the other girls. They were smiling, laughing, and calling out at me to take the shot for their amusement. So I did. Or at least, I tried. My mouth barely covered the "tip" of the six-inch glass, so I only got as far as swallowing the whipped cream before choking on the Bailey's underneath it. I grabbed the penis glass out of my mouth with my hand and coughed a few times before sipping the same sweet drink to clear my throat. Some girls clapped and others booed, but it was all in good fun.

A couple cousins flipped through a menu on the table and looked around for a waitress. I saw one of them saying something to me, but I pointed to my ear while shaking my head, because I couldn't hear her.

Denise spoke directly into my ear, "You hungry? You want to order food?"

Despite Natalie's warning, I hadn't had time to eat between work and this party, and I was pretty hungry. So I nodded yes. Denise pulled the menu in front of me. She pointed to each appetizer, then looked at me with raised brows, to question whether I did or didn't want whatever it was. Fried calamari? No. Oysters? No. Fried shrimp? No. Mussels? No. I wasn't trying to be difficult. I just didn't like any of it.

I looked over at the two cousins across from me, and they looked like they couldn't decide what they wanted either. That's when Natalie squeezed in between me and Denise and yelled into my ear, "We're all hungry and I know you're not going to eat here, so let's just go somewhere else."

I looked at her with open-mouthed horror for even suggesting going against Denise, but before I could respond, she was in Denise's ear. Then Denise firmly shut the menu in front of us and grabbed her stuff. I cringed inside, simultaneously glad for a friend who stood up for me but worried Denise would be angered we weren't going with her plan. So when Denise marched out of the bar, we all followed.

"There's a Chili's right down the street," Natalie pointed out to everyone once in the parking lot.

"Okay, sounds good! Meet you there in a minute!" the girls all chimed in. Denise said nothing, though, and went to her car with a grimace. I hoped she'd get over it for the sake of getting along with everyone tonight.

Chili's wasn't at all busy for a Saturday night, so we were seated after the wait staff pushed together a few tables. We ordered burgers and fries, and we were all talking and joking and having a good time, except for Denise. Whatever her issue was with me clearly hadn't blown over, because every time I laughed at something that was said, Denise rolled her eyes at the cousin sitting next to her, in a judgmental way that suggested I was acting immature or something. It was hurtful, but I didn't say anything. I just wanted to have fun. But then every time I started to laugh, I'd look at her to confirm whether my observation was right. Sure enough, every time, she'd pierce me with this sharp look and then roll her eyes again for the cousin to see. Eventually, I just stopped laughing. I was so consumed with hurt, thinking it mean to do this to me on the one night that was supposed to be mine.

Natalie seemed to be tuned into my feelings from where she sat at the other end of the table. "Hey, Dana! You want to go to that club we went out to before? Where you like dancing?"

"Boogie Nights? Yes! That would be so much fun!" I responded without considering how Denise would feel. By the look of disapproval on her face, I wasn't sure anything would make her happy tonight anyway. Everyone else seemed excited to go, though, so we finished eating and went on our way.

While we waited for our drinks at the circular bar in the center of the club, Denise came up behind me and forced a white T-shirt over my head. Then she took me by my shoulders and pushed me in front of a strange man. "Suck for a buck!"

I looked down at the shirt. Denise had sewn Life Saver candies around the chest area and used fabric paint to write "Suck for a Buck" on the bottom. I looked back up to see this guy rifling through the bills in his wallet and Denise's hand out waiting for cash. That's when I realized what this was about—he was going to pay her a dollar to suck a Life Saver off the shirt near my nipple! I put my hand out to stop him from handing the cash over.

"You can make a lot of money tonight!" Denise argued.

"I don't need to make money, Denise! I just want to dance and hang out with everyone!"

Denise's face changed as fast as Darren's could. She glared at me with hatred, then yanked the shirt off me. I was so scared of her reaction that I don't even remember raising my arms to allow her to remove it, as I must have instinctively done.

"Do you know how much time I put into all this?" Denise screamed in my face, while shaking the wadded-up shirt in her fist. "I have a newborn baby, who I left home to come out tonight for you! And you can't even be grateful for everything I've done for you!"

"Denise, I am! I just don't want to—"

She cut me off. "I know you don't! You don't want anything I've done! I've spent all my time planning and trying to make sure your wedding parties are nice, but you don't care about any of it. So I'm done. Have fun doing whatever it is you guys wanna do."

Then she stormed out. Everyone in our group stopped talking and gawked at me. I don't know if they were looking for my reaction or for an explanation, but I'd been stunned into open-mouthed silence at Denise's outburst.

Natalie came to stand next to me and crossed her arms. "You okay?"

"Yeah," I reflexively responded. "I mean, no, I'm not, but . . . I don't know."

My business acquaintance and a few cousins decided to leave then, offering pitiful expressions as they said their goodbyes. Before long, it was just me, Natalie, and my childhood friend who tried to dance goofy to make me laugh. It didn't work, though. Being at odds with Denise saddened me, especially since I didn't know what I'd done to deserve her coldness to begin with. So I sat at a table by myself, with a drink I never drank, watching the other two girls enjoy their night on the dance floor.

Darren was in bed watching TV when I returned home. He looked at the bedside clock as I crawled into bed, fully clothed, completely sober, and down spirited. "What are you doing home so early?"

I snuggled up against him. "Your sister. She ruined the whole night."

"What happened?" Darren turned the volume down on the TV and gave me his full attention, while I relayed the events of the night.

"I told you she could be a bitch," Darren consoled. "Especially when she doesn't get her way. I never understood why you needed to be close with her anyway. I never was."

"She's your sister, your family," I responded. "And I thought she was mine too," I mumbled before closing my eyes to sleep off the upset.

The next morning, the phone rang. Darren answered from the bedroom, where he lay awaiting the Sunday-morning eggs and bacon I was frying up in the kitchen.

"Hi, Mom!" I heard him say. "Good! How are you and Dad doing?"

Jane called at least once a week, and I sometimes called her more than that. It was nice to be part of a family that stayed connected, I thought.

"That's not how it went, Mom!" I heard Darren defend. Jane was not the confrontational type, so my ears perked up, curious to know what had provoked this reaction. "Why would she have come home early then? . . .

No, she was completely sober! . . . Maybe Denise is hormonal or something! . . . Dana wouldn't lie about this."

This was about my bachelorette party?

"I'm sorry Denise is upset, Mom, but Dana's pretty upset too! It was *her* party, and she was the one reamed out in front of everyone because she didn't want to have strange men biting Life Savers off a shirt Denise put on her. Shouldn't that be a good thing? I don't want my soon-to-be wife wanting to do stuff like that, and neither should you!"

What the hell had Denise told her mother?

"Well, I don't know what to tell you, Mom. You know how Denise is . . . Dana was the victim here, not Denise . . . I guess we're just going to have to agree to disagree then . . . I know . . . Love you too . . . Bye, Mom." Darren came down to the kitchen a minute later. "Hey."

I was standing at the stove with a spatula in my hand, but I turned and gave him a complacent half-smile. "Hey."

"You heard all that?"

"Yeah." My head dropped. I switched the burner off, since the scrambled eggs were done anyway, and turned to face Darren.

"Don't worry about any of it, okay? My sister's always been this way, and my mom is always going to side with her," he said. Then he lifted my chin with his finger, "Anyway, it's you and me against the world, right?"

"Forever," I whispered. Then I sunk into his body and let him hold me, hoping he could fulfill the promise of forever to *me*, even if it meant being at odds with his family.

"I've Got You Under My Skin"

On October 7, 2000, I stood at the base of the stairway to the top deck of the Odyssey Cruise Ship at Navy Pier in Chicago. Despite the overcast sky and chilly wind, I felt like a princess in my sleeveless couture Cinderella ball gown.

It was exactly the dress I'd dreamed of—plain white satin with a low square neckline and full, billowy skirt that bustled in the back with pearl buttons. My curls were piled on top of my head, and the average-length tulle veil fit into the bottom of my nape with a satin-flower comb.

As a bride, I'd envisioned sentimental moments wherein my mother might tell me how beautiful I looked, and my stepfather might tell me how proud he was of me. I wasn't even sure my mother wanted to be there, though. It had taken tremendous effort just to get her to meet me at the hair salon that morning. And my stepfather could only be bothered to complain about how much he'd contributed to some of the wedding costs.

Part of me expected those meaningful moments with Jane and Henrik instead, since I was closer to them than my own parents anyway, but I'd only seen Jane when we were lining up to enter into the ceremony, and I hadn't seen Henrik at all.

Denise kept her distance too. Instead of presenting me with something old and something new, like I thought my matron of honor might do, she avoided me. She hadn't spoken to me since the bachelorette party, except to offer me her pearl bracelet to wear when I saw her in the ladies' restroom just before lining up for the procession. The moment was so meaningless, she might have well been letting me borrow a pen or some other basic item. So I declined.

Snubbed by everyone who should be close to me, I didn't feel like a bride at all. I felt unimportant and insignificant, and the intense feeling of exclusion made me doubt everything, including getting married.

What the hell am I doing? my anxiety asked when the wedding march began to play.

I'm about to marry the man who loves me, my heart answered.

But then my mind reminded my heart of all the times it had been broken—when Darren took my breakfast plate and threw the untouched eggs and bacon in the garbage because I'd upset him, how he screamed insults at me until I was curled up crying in the corner of a closet in the fetal position, how he came home from nights out without me and confessed make-out sessions and hand jobs from other women. So, really, what the hell was I doing marrying him?

Because I wanted to be with the one person who would never leave me, no matter what, and be part of the family I'd finally found a place in. And I'm a girl! I wanted the pretty dress and the diamond ring and the big party. Yet, here I was, wearing the pretty dress and the diamond ring to what was about to be the big party. The only problem with my Cinderella story was that my Prince Charming was an abusive drunk, and the sister and mother I thought I'd found turned out to be the evil stepsister and stepmother.

I looked over at my stepfather, whose arm I clung to, despite the numerous times he'd strong-armed me with it when I was just a girl. He saw the worry in my eyes and said, "If he ever does anything to hurt you, I'll kick his ass." Then he snickered.

The irony of his consolation confused me even more. In what reality did the abusive king of all narcissists suddenly defend my honor? He was no more a protective father to me than Darren was a sober and attentive partner. At least I could count on Darren to throw down for me if anyone ever threatened a hair on my head, which didn't even make sense because I didn't trust Darren not to harm *me* at some point!

This was my life, though, the precedent of which had been set by the narcissist whose arm I now held onto. The reality was I wasn't Denise. I didn't grow up with a doting mother and hardworking stepfather who'd made me feel safe, loved, and protected. I didn't have a groom who adored me so much he'd go to the ends of the earth to make me happy. I was just me. Sad, lonely, dejected me, who lived for the bits and pieces of kindnesses she was occasionally thrown, like crumbs given to birds to provide just enough nourishment to live.

That feeling of worthlessness led me up the steps and into a wedding ceremony I'd considered running from moments before. I saw Darren waiting at the end of the long aisle, sporting gel-spiked blond hair, a black tuxedo, and a kind smile. There was no doubt he mistreated me, but there was also no doubt he wanted me. He'd chosen me, above all others, to be his wife, to create a life together, to be the one waiting for him at home at the end of every day. I wasn't his burden. I wasn't his obligation. I was his by choice. The hope of that permanence disillusioned me from grim thoughts that we'd someday divorce, and it reinvigorated my desire to continue towards him.

His eyes held mine, as if knowing I needed reassurance that there was enough unity between us to warrant what we were about to do. Focusing on him calmed me as I passed by our 120 guests.

"Wow," he mouthed, one hand on his chest. He did always tell me I was beautiful. Despite the superficiality, I needed to know he appreciated something about me.

After I took my place next to Darren at the white floral arch serving as an altar of sorts, the reverend welcomed everyone. The realization of what was about to happen caused me to giggle nervously. Darren yanked one of my hands ever so slightly and scolded me with discreetly squinted eyes. I cleared my throat and listened to the reverend's opening remarks and reflections on marriage.

Then it was time to say our vows. I stared into Darren's eyes as he promised to love me in sickness and in health, for richer and for poorer, and to remain faithful to me forevermore. I wanted to believe him.

Just as the reverend asked me to recite the same vows to Darren, a massive gust of wind blew down the floral arch. The best man caught it with one hand before it hit us, then stabilized it so the ceremony could continue. A giggle escaped my lips again. Darren cocked his head sideways a bit and pursed his lips.

"I'm sorry, I'm so cold," I whispered in defense. Then I turned to the guests, feeling like I had to say something about the delay in reciting my vows back. "Everything's okay!" I think the comment was meant more for myself than for the attendees.

Darren jerked my hands a second time, then shook his head no. I wondered what I'd done wrong now, and instantly realized I'd just given everyone the impression something wasn't okay. I dropped my head shamefully. I could never do or say anything right.

Just then, Denise wrapped my off-white shawl around my shoulders. "Is that better?"

"Yes, thank you," I responded while nodding my still bowed head. There was comfort in knowing she still cared about me.

Wondering if Jane might still care for me too, I glanced to Darren's parents. Jane smiled brightly, and Henrik's slight nod and grin gave me the fatherly encouragement I needed to proceed.

I breathed in deeply, then looked back to the reverend, "Could you repeat that please?"

"Repeat after me," the reverend began. And I did—correctly and without divine interruption this time.

Finally, we were pronounced husband and wife . . . God help us.

The reception was held immediately after the ceremony, on the second deck of the ship, which cruised Lake Michigan for three hours. During that time, lunch and cocktails were served, a jazz band played everything from Sinatra to disco, and confident guests entertained us with their dance moves. I love to dance, and it *was* my wedding, so of course I joined in.

When it was time for our first dance as husband and wife, everyone dispersed, and Darren joined me at the center of the dance floor. We'd taken lessons with a choreographer, and although we were no Fred and Ginger, we were sure to impress with our routine to Frank Sinatra's "I've Got You Under My Skin." We'd practiced for weeks and knew the routine so well we should have moved with flawless automation. But when the band started playing, something was off. Our movements felt robotic and abrupt. Our feet forgot the steps we'd practiced, and the stiff detachment of Darren's body lacked the intimacy one would expect between two people who'd just been wed. I looked at Darren with an expression that asked, *What happened?* That's when he dipped me back for a dramatic surprise kiss, which was cute but more for show.

The father-daughter dance was next. I'd enviously watched so many brides be turned about the dance floor by their loving fathers; I, however, I was never going to be my stepfather's "little girl," and my biological father wasn't there at all. I'd been threatened not to invite him if I wanted my mother and stepfather to pay for any portion of this wedding, or to even come at all. I'd begrudgingly succumbed.

So, when the band played Sinatra's "I Get a Kick Out of You"—a polite choice made because no song true to my relationship with my stepfather would have been appropriate—I burst into tears. My stepfather leaned his head against mine in a seemingly compassionate gesture, implying the closeness of a father bidding farewell to his adored daughter, but it was a farce which made me cry harder. He and my mother had brainwashed me to equate pain with love and tolerate less than I deserved. It was a sick cycle I was knowingly perpetuating with Darren. It wasn't what I'd hoped love to be, but it was the only version of love I knew.

I didn't want to feel all this pain and resentment on my wedding day, though, so I blocked out my feelings, danced through the end of the song numbly, and allowed our guests to assume they'd witnessed a sentimental moment. Then I put my smile on like a fashion accessory, and prayed Darren would love me the way my parents never could. He had it in him. He just didn't let me see the vulnerable and gentle side of him very often. I think it made him feel like less of a man. He was my man, though, so we'd figure it out. I just had to find him first!

I walked through the reception area, smiling and saying polite hellos to passing guests. Jane and Henrik were at their table, being filmed for our wedding video. I heard Jane assert my place in their hearts, saying, "We finally have our daughter 'Dana'!"

"Mom didn't even have a tummy this time!" Henrik threw in, with his mischievous giggle. I couldn't help but chuckle too as I passed by. He thought his jokes were so clever!

I finally found Darren in an area behind the reception room, where the staircases to the upper and lower decks of the ship were hidden. My mouth fell open when I saw he wasn't alone. His best man's older sister hung off him, with her arms wrapped around his neck as if awaiting a kiss or romantic whispers. Darren's hands were wrapped around her waist—an area of the body which should be reserved for intimate partners only.

I shouldn't have been surprised. Although I'd never met her before today, I'd always suspected *she* was the reason I hadn't been invited on her family's boat or to celebratory dinners Darren attended without me. Perhaps she had a thing for Darren, or they had something going on behind my back. Darren denied my suspicions, of course, but wasn't shy about commenting about this skinny girl in her bikini or telling me how she flirted with him. So to find them like this, today of all days . . .

I couldn't make a scene, though. I just walked to where they were and remarked, "You're a married man now, Darren! No other women, please!" Then I whipped him in the ass with the back of my hand, as if he were my ill-behaving toddler.

"She's drunk," he said, in a sorry attempt to blame the girl. He didn't remove his hands from her waist, though. She kept her arms around his neck too, side-eyeing me like I was just supposed to walk away and let them do whatever I'd interrupted. "My mom said you didn't want to go through with the ceremony anyway," he threw in.

"What are you talking about?"

"She said you looked hesitant when you guys were lining up to walk down the aisle."

"I was concerned about whether everyone was on the boat, because I saw my pregnant cousin and her husband still standing on the dock just as the ceremony was starting!" I snarked back.

"That's not what she said, and my mom wouldn't lie about something like that." He finally pushed his friend's sister away. I was glad he was pissed off now, so he could join me in marital misery. The girl seemed to be in similar spirits as she stumbled away, making sure to give me one last glare because I'd ruined the mood.

I sighed in disgust, then walked away as well. Darren deserved to know what it felt like to be abandoned for once.

I didn't see him again until the cruise ship had docked and everyone was gone. We went back to the hotel, changed out of our wedding clothes, then went to our hotel's upscale restaurant and bar to get an early dinner. It was only 4 p.m., so we were the only patrons. It was the perfect opportunity to toast our love with some bubbly and whisper sweet words to each other. We could have gossiped about the guests and happenings at the wedding and reception. We might have discussed plans for the future and our life together. We had a different dynamic, though.

Darren leaned his chair back on its two rear legs, looking at the fancy crystal chandelier in the ceiling high above. I looked up too, hoping to see something worthy of the attention he should have been giving his new wife. Then I looked back at Darren. He was looking everywhere but at me. My head dropped. I felt completely insignificant. Still.

Unsure of what to say or do, I fidgeted with my diamond rings. It was a mindless distraction from the overwhelm of self-deprecating thoughts swirling through my mind. But devoid of the elation I expected to feel on my wedding night, all I felt was hungry and bored. Just like my husband. At least we had that in common.

"Willow"

Our marriage was anything but boring. It started with Darren losing his driver's license for six months, as a result of the DUI.

"You're going to have to quit your job so you can drive me around for work every day," Darren said to me, while I cooked dinner in the kitchen one Sunday evening.

"Wait, what?"

"You heard me. Without a license, I can't drive. And if I can't drive, I can't work. So you're going to have to drive me."

"And just give up my management position and the salary that comes with it?" I looked at him with bulged eyes and raised brows.

"You think your job is more important than mine?"

"This isn't about whose job is more important, Darren!" I raised my voice and could feel the crease between my brows intensifying with my emotions. "It's about respect. Have a little for the fact that I've worked hard for my position! Not to mention I wasn't the one who lost my license!" I poured the pot of boiling pasta into the colander in the sink and the steam swarmed my face.

"But *I'm* the man of the house. *I'm* supposed to be the breadwinner!" he cried, once again using his machismo as argument.

I turned to face him, letting my right hip lean against the edge of the counter as I crossed my arms. "You're serious, aren't you?"

"What am I supposed to do, find another job? Who the fuck is going to hire a loser who has no license?"

Exactly! Which was why I wished Darren thought more about the consequences of his actions! I shook my head in disbelief.

"I'm not even fucking hungry anymore," he said before storming out the front door to the garage presumably, though it's not like he could legally drive himself anywhere.

If it had been as simple as dropping him off and picking him up at one place, I could stay at my job and drive him to his, but Darren was a field technician, which required him to travel to multiple locations daily, within a two-hour radius of our house. Jobs like his were few and far between, and he'd just stew in anger if forced to stay home while I worked. He wouldn't have been able to handle me, or any woman, being the breadwinner.

On the other hand, I could work almost anywhere. I would also have absolutely no problem being a stay-at-home wife who cooked and cleaned all day if that were an option at some point. So, really, I had no choice. I had to resign from my managerial position and become Darren's chauffeur. Maybe spending all day together would be good for us!

Day in, day out, I drove Darren around in his clunky white work van to bowling alleys with arcades, waiting an hour or three in the discomfort of the vessel, just to drive somewhere else and do it again. It was unfulfilling, to say the least.

I missed people. The only social outlet I'd had before this was work. I'd naturally clicked with some co-workers, with whom I'd talk about Darren, life, shows we watched, and cute guys who came into the office looking for apartments. I also missed meeting people from different parts of the world. I'd enjoyed talking to them about differences in our cultures, while touring them through model apartments.

Plus, for the first time since I was twelve years old, I wasn't making money. I earned a few hundred dollars a month in my side hustle selling PartyLite brand candles and holders at home parties, but otherwise left my financial stability for dependence on a drunk with a DUI conviction and no driver's license.

Looking for the positive in this dire situation, I reminded myself that Darren and I could use this time together to improve our relationship. I was eager to talk and laugh and share and philosophize. But he drowned me out with the radio instead, telling me I talked too much.

I wallowed in self-pity as we drove, wondering how I'd gone from being an independent, self-reliant, and successful young woman to a dependent and unproductive underachiever. I'd had goals and dreams before I'd met Darren, but his life choices stifled mine. He'd squashed my desire to go back to school for my master's degree—my higher education already made him feel insecure—and here I was, again allowing his mistake to hold me back from furthering a career in real estate, which I'd shown great promise in. He was my husband, though, so I assured myself I was being a good wife by deferring to his career and ego-driven request that he be the breadwinner of the home.

Still looking for a silver lining in the clouds, I thought I could informally educate myself while he worked. I occupied my time reading books about psychology. I'd always been fascinated by the complexity of why people behave the way they do, and how to change one's mindset to change one's life. I'd even considered a career as a therapist, to help others understand themselves, though helping myself overcome my own demons was likely the root of my passion. I just wished I could have intelligent conversations about different psychological theories and healing techniques I read about, but Darren was the only person I saw anymore, and he had no interest in psychobabble.

I wished he would tell me about the anger management counseling he was required to attend as part of his DUI judgment, but he wouldn't speak of that either. I was curious to know how they counseled him and what exercises they had him perform, because after a few months of whatever they were doing, Darren's temper subsided. By the holidays, he spoke to me in a kinder tone again, and even smiled at me more often!

That's why when he told me he wanted to adopt a deaf dalmatian he'd encountered while doing his required community service, I agreed. Animals seem to bring a certain joy and childlike energy into a home, and I thought it would be good for Darren, and for us as a couple, to have a loyal companion that made us laugh while exemplifying unconditional love.

So Pepper came home with us just after Christmas, 2000. Training our deaf dog with hand signals gave me and Darren a purposeful goal to accomplish in a joint effort, which was good for our relationship. I loved taking Pepper on long walks every morning and afternoon. We both had a lot of pent up energy from sitting all day!

By spring of 2001, I was relieved of my duties as Darren's chauffeur when he retained his driver's license. Instead of returning to work in real estate, I thought I could make something more of the side hustle selling candles. The sales seminars I attended a couple times a month promised great fortune with enough time, effort, and proper execution of the sales techniques presented. So I spent my days calling customers for re-orders and a couple evenings a week displaying products in women's homes, for their friends and family to purchase. I made more money as a result, but nowhere near what I'd made in property management.

I could tell Darren was bothered by the combination of me being home and not making as much money. He'd come home from work every day, see me unwinding with a book or TV show, and comment on my "leisurely life." He'd say things like, "Must be nice to sit on the couch eating bon-bons and watching soap operas all day."

He was the one who wanted to be the breadwinner, I thought! But I switched up my schedule to keep the peace. I made calls in the morning, watched *All My Children* and *One Life to Live* in the lunch hour (sans bon-bons), read in the mid-afternoon, then worked again. That way, Darren could hear me make calls to solicit orders and book parties, and then see me place orders on the computer.

Then one summer afternoon, the sound of the front door slamming shut startled me. I was lying in bed with Pepper, reading a book. Footsteps pounding up the stairs towards the bedroom halted my breathing. Shit! Darren was home from work early!

Darren appeared in the doorway, pointed his finger at me and shouted, "You need to stop reading and start looking for a fucking job!" Then he came towards the bed so aggressively that Pepper jumped off and sought cover underneath. I was scared too, but I had no escape.

Within seconds, Darren stood over me with a hateful look on his face. He raised his right hand as high and as far back as it would go, as if revving it up for optimum force. He hadn't hit me before, but his history of angry outbursts made me question when he would cross that line, and I was certain that time was now. So I turned my head and closed my eyes rather than face the violence head on.

I waited, then heard Darren's fist pound the door instead of me. My eyes popped back open to see the door bounce off the wall and slow to half closure. I unconsciously released the breath I'd been holding, thankful the door had gotten the brunt of his anger instead of me. Still, I remained unmoving as I listened to Darren's feet pound down the stairs to the kitchen.

Pepper emerged and ran out of the bedroom with her head down and her tail between her legs. She was going to Darren, like she always did when he exhibited anger, to win back his love and affection. It reminded me of that letter I'd found from Darren's old girlfriend, Julie, wherein she groveled and begged for Darren's forgiveness for what was probably nothing. At the time I'd read it, I thought she was a spineless, insecure girl whom I was nothing like. Yet, here I was now, knowing I'd have to do the same as she and Pepper: bending to Darren's unpredictable mood shifts was the only way to appease him. So I scrambled down the stairs to the kitchen, where he was leaning both arms on the counter.

"What's going on?" I placed my hands gently, but cautiously, on his forearm and back.

He whipped around, intentionally shaking me off. "What's going *on?* You need to start making money! *That's* what's going on!"

I closed my eyes as spit hit my face. "Okay," I spoke softly, "I'll start looking for something tomorrow. I promise."

"You better! I'm not going to keep busting my ass while you sit at home doing nothing!"

"That's not fair, Darren. I quit my management position to drive *you* around when you didn't have a license, because you convinced me *your* job was more important than *mine*. Not to mention you told me you didn't like me making more money than you did last year. So don't say I do nothing when I've done *everything* for you."

"Everything?!" he yelled. "Look at this place! It's a fucking pig-sty! I go to work every day, come home and have to fix shit or mow grass, and you just sit around here living the good life off me!"

This was the good life? Being spat on, screamed at, intimidated, and plain old scared to read a book was the good life? Too bad I would have traded it all in a heart-beat for a humble and poor man who sheltered me in a tent and loved me with all his heart, all his life.

But I'd married Darren.

"Okay." I breathed deeply before reigning him in. "I understand you want me to get a job, so I'll look for one. But I can't pull a job out of my ass right this second. So what can I do right here, right now, to make this all better?"

"Okay, Dana," he mocked in a snotty, high-pitched voice, bobbling his head side to side.

"Darren, I'm trying really hard to stay calm, so please don't mock me. I've asked you before not to do that. Please just have a mature, adult conversation with me," I said, keeping what little composure I could muster.

"I'll do whatever the fuck I want!" he spit-screamed in my face. "And right now, I wanna fuckin' leave!"

He snatched his keys off the counter where he'd left them, and slammed the front door shut on his way out. I heard the clunk and grind of the garage door opening next, then the escalating hum of his newest motorcycle speeding away. A long inhale and exhale through my nose relaxed my tense shoulders. With my hands on the edge of the kitchen counter, I dropped my head, closed my eyes and took another deep breath. Then I pulled the classified section of last Sunday's newspaper out of the trash.

As much as I loved having time to work out and walk Pepper, clean and cook, decorate and read, I was bored. I saw no one and went nowhere, except when I lugged my candles and accessories around, hoping for enough sales to win whatever cash or product prizes PartyLite offered for various achievements that month.

So, in a way, Darren was right—I needed to go back to work, to a real job. I needed a reason to leave the house. More importantly, I needed to earn Darren's approval to keep peace between us. The only way to do that was to get a job making enough money to where he felt more equity in our financial contributions to the household but not so much that he felt his status as the man and breadwinner of the house was threatened. Ugh.

I scoured the job section of the paper, speed reading through ads for data entry, receptionist, and customer service, when the word "dog" caught my eye. Dog walking? It paid almost too well and was in the next town over! It sounded too good to be true, but I called right away, had an interview with the owner the next morning, and took over a five-day-a-week route shortly after.

It was the perfect job for me! I spent every day playing with and walking four-legged friends who kissed and cuddled and were excited to see me! Although I wasn't getting the human interaction I sought, the animals I cared for saved me from the loneliness and depression I tended toward. My brightened spirits and surprisingly good compensation also had the added benefit of lightening Darren's mood. So things were good again. I just hoped they'd stay this way.

"Don't Let Me Down"

*D*arren decided we should live in the country, so in April of 2002, we moved into a large, two-story custom home on an acre of land an hour outside of suburbia, in a small town of only nine hundred. Although far from everyone and everything we knew, I wanted the house the second I walked through the front door. The living room had two-story vaulted ceilings, an adjacent formal dining room where I could put my piano, and a dream kitchen with an island and built-in desk. There was an eating area which exited to a large back deck where I would listen to the soothing sounds of the stream running through the back while drinking my morning coffee.

The second floor had a master suite to die for. There was a huge walk-in closet on one side of the bedroom, and the en suite bathroom featured a glass shower, soaking tub, and two separate vanities. There were two other bedrooms and a bathroom upstairs as well, and an unfinished basement Darren planned to work on in his spare time.

A few days after moving in, I stood at the kitchen island, unpacking a box. It was a Saturday, so Darren was home and watching TV in the adjoining living room.

All of a sudden, stabbing pains assaulted my abdomen. I wrapped my arms around my stomach and cringed. I'd always had unbearably painful menstrual cramps, but these were much more intense. Something was wrong. Within seconds, I was on the floor in the fetal position, and felt wetness between my legs. I wasn't due to get my period, so what was happening to me?

"Darren!" I called out in a panic. He was barely ten feet from me. The couch was just on the other side of the opening between the kitchen and living room. "I think I need to go to the hospital!"

He slowly turned his head towards me, then looked back at the TV.

I clenched my teeth and fists simultaneously when another wave of agony washed over me. I closed my eyes until it eased enough to speak again. "Darren, please! I'm in so much pain!"

He remained focused on the TV.

With one arm on my stomach, I scooted closer towards the living room. "Darren, help me, please!" I begged. The pain was almost too much to bear.

Unmoved, physically and emotionally, Darren stared straight at his precious big screen TV.

"*Darren!*" I screamed, trying desperately to get his attention. I sounded like a crazy person even to my own ears. I was pretty sure the neighbors heard me too, so there was no way he hadn't!

But he didn't budge.

I cried harder then. Our relationship was tumultuous, but I couldn't believe Darren, or anyone with any capacity for empathy, would ignore another human being suffering! What was he gaining by being so cruel anyway? Did he want me to die so he could collect my life insurance and buy more things that would actually make him happy? We had our issues, but I hadn't thought he hated me this much!

His inaction told me he did—a realization I couldn't bear right now. My husband, who'd vowed to love and care for me, in sickness and health, was leaving me to fend for myself in a desperate time of need. I didn't know if the emotional pain or physical pain was worse, but knew I had to take care of myself like I always had.

So I scooted back towards the desk and felt around for the phone. I stared at Darren while dialing the number to the nearby hospital, expecting him to suddenly acknowledge the situation and decide to care for me, but he didn't. So when there was an answer on the other end, I whimpered, "I'm in so much pain! I'm cramping and I think I'm bleeding!"

"Would you like me to send an ambulance, ma'am?" The hospital receptionist had a calm and soothing voice, perfectly fit for her position.

"No." I rested my forehead on my knees and cried softly. Medical bills made Darren angry, and I couldn't risk upsetting him any more right now.

Plus, if an ambulance brought me to the hospital, everyone would question why Darren hadn't, and I couldn't tell the truth. I couldn't ever say anything that would present Darren in a negative light. Darren would likely tell everyone *he'd* called for the ambulance himself anyway. Because he's such a concerned and attentive husband.

"Can I get an appointment with a doctor instead?" That would only cost twenty dollars with our insurance.

"The next available appointment is Wednesday afternoon," the operator offered. I needed a doctor now, but I felt like I had no choice but to accept to maintain some level of credibility.

After I hung up the phone, I rested my head back against the desk drawers. I'd never felt so alone. I didn't have a mother or father or friends nearby to call for help. I couldn't call Jane or Denise. What would I say, with Darren sitting right there? They wouldn't believe the truth about Darren ignoring my pleas for help! He'd deny my story anyway, tell them I was crazy, then I'd be labeled a liar. Tears rushed down my cheeks at the thought. Then I started sobbing again.

The volume on the TV increased incrementally, until it completely drowned out the sound of my angst. I turned to see Darren put the remote control back on the coffee table. Was my pain disturbing his afternoon entertainment?

"Oh my god!" I shrieked at the heartless, uncompassionate bastard I'd married. The blatant rejection triggered my urge to flee, but in this condition, I could barely move!

I slid myself with one hand towards the stairway adjacent to the desk. Taking several breaks to breathe and cry and breathe through the pain again, I sidled up the stairway slowly until I reached the bathroom at the top of the stairs. That piece of shit did nothing, said nothing, and probably hoped I'd fall down the stairs, crack my head, and end it all for both of us. Fucking bastard!

Once in the bathroom, I pulled my shorts and panties down. There was blood all over, and some of it dripped onto the floor. I leveraged my weight to sit on the toilet and slumped over with my elbows on my knees.

I looked between my legs to see random spurts of blood and dark red chunks expelling into the toilet. Every time I thought it was over, more came out. Was I having a miscarriage? I wasn't sure how since I was on the pill! It almost didn't matter, though; there was nothing to do but sit with my head in my hands, until both the pain and excretions slowed to a stop.

Afterward, I moved at a snail's pace to the master bathroom, where I curled up at the bottom of the shower and let the hot water mix with my salty tears.

"Why? What did I do?" I cried over and over. But no one answered. Darren didn't check on me. God didn't speak soothing words into my heart. My guardian angel was nowhere to be found. I was indeed alone.

"I Will Follow You into the Dark"

A week later, I was driving on the tollway when my cell phone rang. "Hello?" I answered as soon as I could fish the phone out of my purse.

"Are you sitting down?" I recognized my new doctor's voice.

"Yes . . ." I responded nervously. "I'm driving."

"I got your lab results back," he said, then paused before announcing, "You're pregnant!"

What? There was no way after all that bleeding and cramping! I'd heard of women bleeding during pregnancy, but I'd practically hemorrhaged! I thought it was endometriosis or something I hadn't been diagnosed with yet. It didn't make sense!

"Are you there?"

"Oh . . . yeah," I responded, still stunned by the news.

"Oh good! Now, I want to be honest with you. Your HCG levels—that's the pregnancy hormone—are lower than they should be at this stage of the pregnancy. And taking your bleeding and cramping into consideration, we'll want to take another blood draw next week to see if the pregnancy will be viable. So take care of yourself in the meantime. And congratulations! I'll transfer you to the appointment desk now."

"Thank you," I said flatly, still trying to grasp the gravity of the news, though questioning the viability of the pregnancy didn't sound promising.

After scheduling the appointment for the next week, I took a deep breath, then tilted my neck side to side to loosen the stiff muscles.

What the hell were we going to do with a baby? Darren was very clear that he never wanted kids. That was one of the few life choices we agreed on, actually. He said he didn't want to bring a child into this awful world, full of hatred and war. I just didn't trust myself not to turn into my stone-cold mother or abusive stepfather, like they say people do. So choosing not to have kids was a safe bet for both of us.

Then again, if a baby was already growing inside of me, I was going to have it. I'd aborted a pregnancy when I was sixteen, and it was the biggest regret of my life. My boyfriend's stepfather, who had political aspirations, couldn't have a teenage pregnancy tarnish his reputation with voters, so he gave us the money to "get it taken care of". When my mother and stepfather found out, they concocted an insane plan to send me to boarding school in Europe, have the baby brought back to them after birth, and tell everyone they'd adopted it from an orphanage over there. They were serious too! As a minor, my options were limited to whatever choices my mother and stepfather made for me, and there was no way I'd let them raise my baby like they raised me. So against everything in me, I aborted the pregnancy. My boyfriend's stepfather kept his seat in the State House of Representatives, my boyfriend left me with a broken heart and reputation for being easy, my parents shamed me for all of it, and my baby (I swore it was a girl) was dead.

Things were different now, though; I was married, we had a nice house with a white picket fence, a dog and a cat. We just had to figure out how to be good, loving parents. Jane and Denise would certainly help. Both were exemplary mothers, and the extended family would support us as a family should. We were in a prime situation to bring a baby into a loving atmosphere, assuming we could get our own relationship under more stable control.

The only problem was Darren. My throat tightened just thinking about Darren's reaction to this news. He wouldn't be happy. I almost hoped he'd be so angry he'd tell me to go, to live as a single mother. Better for this baby to live life with one parent who would try to love it than with a parent who didn't want it at all!

I placed my right hand on my flat stomach. "What're we going to do, kid?" I whispered to my unborn child.

I drove along, hoping to have some epiphany about how to present this pregnancy to Darren in a way he'd accept with gladness. Yet, the longer

I thought, the more my anxiety. I decided I had to just tell him. Like, right now. I didn't want to wait until I got home, on the off chance he'd take his anger out on me. So I dialed his cell phone before I could talk myself out of telling him altogether.

Darren sounded cheery when he answered. "What's up?"

"Hey!" The inflection in my voice fell at the end of my attempt to sound as bubbly as he did, but I forged ahead anyway. "So the doctor just called with my test results, and . . . and I'm . . . well . . . I'm pregnant." There. It was out. I held my breath as I awaited his response.

Silence.

I waited. For anything—comments, questions, suggestions. I could hear the noise of traffic in the background of his phone, so I knew he was still on the line. He was driving too.

"Yeah, I know. I don't know what to say either," I prodded.

"Did you stop taking the pill to get pregnant on purpose?"

What?! "No!"

"You sure about that? Because you asked me last winter if I would ever change my mind about having kids, and now you're pregnant."

Holding Denise's first-born for the first time a couple years ago had made me momentarily rethink our decision not to have kids. I saw a clean slate in Mason's innocent face. A chance to make things right, perhaps. I thought if I had a baby and treated him as if he were the most important person in the entire world, even if just to me, he would turn out so differently than I did! He would know he was loved and exude the happiness and confidence I couldn't as a child, thereby righting the wrongs done to me. So, yes, I changed my mind for a second. But he'd said no, and that was that.

Regardless of the coincidence, I did take offense to the accusation. "What are you saying, Darren?"

"Well, you wanted a kid, and I told you I still didn't, and now you're pregnant? What am I supposed to think?"

"I swear to you, I'm just as surprised as you are."

Neither of us said anything for a couple of very long minutes.

Finally, I whispered, "What're we going to do?"

"I don't know," he said grimly. "I'll see you at home."

"Okay," I conceded, then hung up. I looked down at my stomach, placed my hand on it again, and promised, "It's going to be okay, little one."

I felt silly talking to myself. It was like I was speaking to my inner child or imaginary friend. But this wasn't imaginary. There was a human being growing inside of me! And it was kind of nice to have someone to talk to. I could get used to this! As for Darren, I still wasn't sure.

I walked into the kitchen an hour later. Darren had just removed a plate of food from the microwave, and he glared at me with disdain on the way to the couch. I started to follow him, then stopped at the end of the kitchen island and watched him instead. He sat on the couch, turned on the TV, and put forkfuls of food into his mouth, without looking at or saying one word to me. I was carrying his child in my womb, but I was still as insignificant as ever.

Tears immediately welled up in my eyes, but I retreated to the master bedroom before he could see his effect on me. Not that he would. He didn't look at me at all as I ascended the stairs before him. So I snuggled into the comfort of our bed and softly cried myself to an early sleep.

The following week, I had my blood drawn, then waited for the doctor to come into the sterile white examination room with the results.

"How're you doing today?" He smiled and put his hand out.

"Good!" I lied, standing to shake it. Then I sat and fidgeted with my fingers nervously. The doctor seemed to sense my anxiety. His head dropped just slightly, and he took on a more serious expression before he sat on the short rolling stool to face me. "Your pregnancy test came back negative this time," he said solemnly. "I'm so sorry."

My head dropped too.

"Don't beat yourself up too much about it. It just means it wasn't a viable fetus. It just didn't take."

I looked up at the doctor. His kind eyes were reassuring. But in the end, I'd failed this baby. Apparently, my uterus, like me, wasn't good enough.

"I'm going to tell the appointment desk to schedule you for a follow-up in about two weeks"—he stood to leave—"but you take your time in here. And take care of yourself too!"

After he'd closed the door, I let my tears flow freely. I wasn't sure why

I was sad; we hadn't been trying to get pregnant to begin with. I guess I'd just gotten used to "my belly," as I called the baby. It made me feel less alone to think someone was with me, that someone was listening, someone who was all mine. I had so much love to give, but Darren didn't want it, and I wouldn't give him what he wouldn't give me. So now I had nothing and no one again.

Back at home, I sat on our back deck in the hot sun, hoping the brightness would overtake the gloominess in my heart. But it didn't. It just reminded me that the world goes on despite all the sadness and heartache within it. I hunched over onto my elbows, closed my eyes, and rested my face in my hands.

Would it have been a boy with Darren's blond hair? Or a little girl with my curly brown hair? Or one of each? We did have twins in our family. What would their names have been? What would their giggles have sounded like? Would they have brought love into this loveless home? None of it mattered, because the baby wasn't meant to be. At least he or she was with Faith now, the daughter I'd aborted. My work friend Natalie had suggested I name the daughter I mourned, to make the short life she'd had inside me more real and dignified, and effectively help to heal the pain of what I'd done. I'd chosen to call her by the name of a song by Spread Eagle because the lyrics said all I'd want to say to her father if I ever saw him again.

So neither Faith nor this new baby were alone. I was, though. Guttural sobs shook my body, as I mourned babies I already loved, but would never know.

A bit later, I heard the garage door opening. Darren was home. I went inside and walked to where he entered the kitchen from the garage. I planted my face in his chest. He instinctively wrapped his free arm around me, then set his little cooler on the island to put his other arm around me as well.

"I'm not pregnant anymore, so you don't have to worry about a baby," I said.

"I'm sorry, babe." He laid his head upon mine.

I didn't buy the fake sympathy, but it didn't matter. I needed consoling, he was all I had, and it was enough.

"Baby One More Time"

"**D**enise had the baby!" I announced excitedly as I hung up the phone. "It's a girl!"

It was June 2002. Although my own wound was still very fresh, I was truly happy for Denise and couldn't wait to get to the hospital to meet our niece.

"Of course she had a girl," Darren snarked from the couch, where he was in the midst of his post-work TV watching.

I approached him with crossed arms. "Come on, Darren. This is good news!"

"How? She had the first grandchild, and now she had the first granddaughter," he griped. "She gets everything!"

I'd heard this resentment before. The simple truth of the matter was that Darren didn't like when someone had something he didn't have. As a result, he was incapable of being happy for people who he felt one-upped him, including his sister.

"Why does it matter? You don't want kids anyway."

He grimaced like an annoyed toddler. "Because it's always about Denise! She got all that money when her dad died, she was able to buy a cool car, the condo . . . Now she's the one with the grandkids too! Where does that leave me?"

This was not the selfish reaction I'd expected, but I saw an opportunity to further my own selfish agenda. "Have the first biological grandchild then!" I casually suggested.

Darren whipped his head towards me. I'd struck the intended nerve.

"She had the first grandchild, and the first female grandchild, so have the first biological grandchild," I repeated. "I know your dad raised Denise, but . . . any child we have would be your dad's only biological grandchild. I mean, I know he has a daughter out there somewhere, from his first marriage, but he'll never know any grandkids from her."

"I never thought about it that way."

"So let's do it!"

"Yeah," Darren agreed. I could tell he was struggling with whether he wanted his parent's approval more than he didn't want kids or vice versa, but I didn't want to bring attention to the issue and risk him changing his mind.

"Yeah?" I asked, looking at him with pleading eyes to confirm.

"Yeah."

I smiled and scheduled an appointment with the OB right away.

Two months later, I stood in Denise's living room holding my goddaughter, Melissa, who was sleeping through the chaos of her baptismal luncheon. I'd been honored to accept the role in my niece's life, since being excluded from the same when Denise's first child was born. She'd asked Darren to be Mason's godfather, just before our wedding, emphasizing her decision that Mason would *not* have a godmother.

"So how are you feeling?" Denise asked as she placed platters of food out.

"Good, actually! My doctor just gave me clearance to try again."

"Cleared for take-off!" Denise joked.

Jane smiled. "Oh, Dana! That's great news!" She came over to me, squeezed my arm gently, then peeked at her granddaughter.

"Yeah! We'll try to get you another one of these by your birthday next year!" I raised Melissa up for show.

"Trying is the fun part," Denise chided as she flashed a knowing look my way.

It made me happy to have the support of Darren's family again. I presumed even Darren would come around once I bore his child. Babies had magical effects on people.

So I diligently monitored my ovulation cycle, continued to exercise every day and eat healthy, cut out the little alcohol I drank, and waited for the right time to conceive. September 17th, 2002, was the night.

Darren trudged up the stairs around 9:30 p.m. He'd recently picked up a part-time gig filling vending machines in schools, after his regular job every evening.

"I'm ovulating!" I jumped up from the bed to greet him, hoping my skimpy T-shirt and panties would entice him.

"I'm too tired. I just want to go to bed." He walked around me to the master bathroom.

I followed him and sat on the counter opposite his while he brushed his teeth. "Darren, I'm not waiting another month. We have to do it tonight," I said.

"Please stop," he begged, then walked to the toilet to pee.

"No! I'm not letting you say no to this!"

"Please!" Darren raised his voice. "Just drop this shit already!"

"NO!" I removed my panties before he could pull his boxers and pants back up, then took his hand and led him to the vanity. "You don't even have to take me to bed. Just get it done here."

I pulled myself onto the counter between the wall and the sink, and rubbed Darren's man part until it was erect. "Please, Darren?"

Although his mind was reluctant, his body was willing, so he gave in, accommodating me like it was a chore.

I'd have normally been hurt that he turned away from me for those few minutes, to convey his repulsion. His constant rejection was becoming my normal, however, and a small price to pay for getting what I wanted.

Two weeks later, I rushed to the nearest Target for a pregnancy test. My period always arrived with clockwork consistency, and it was late. Although we'd only had sex that one time during my last cycle, I was sure we'd conceived.

When I got home, I went straight to the half bathroom with the box. I'd already read the instructions about a dozen times on the half-hour drive back, so I knew exactly what to do. I stood in the small confines of the blue-and-pink floral walls, staring at the small cloudy-white box on the plastic stick balancing itself, and my future, on the ledge of the pedestal sink. It took less than a minute for the lines to appear, and less than a second for the smile that followed.

I couldn't wait to tell someone, but I knew Darren had to be the first. I called him from the phone on the desk in the kitchen.

"Hello?"

I glanced at the digital clock on the microwave. "Hey! I know it's early, but what time do you think you'll be home?"

"I'm actually on my way now."

I glanced at the clock again, thinking I'd misread it the first time. He usually came home between 6 and 10 p.m., and it wasn't even 2. "Oh! Cool! I'll just see you when you get here then!"

"Why? Whaddya need?"

"Nothing!" The high pitch of my voice made me sound guilty.

"So you called for no reason?" Now Darren seemed suspicious. I didn't want to tell him on the phone, though, especially if he'd be home within the hour.

"No! I mean, yes!" I was confusing myself! "I just wanted to plan dinner, is all. See you soon!" Then I hung up before I could stumble over my words more than I already had.

An hour later, Darren walked into the kitchen from the garage. I was waiting at the kitchen island with a stupid, giddy smile on my face, like a school-girl anxious to spill a juicy secret she'd been holding onto for too long.

Darren squinted his eyes and then smirked. "What?"

I pulled a small rectangular gift from behind my back and offered it out to him.

"What's this?" He took it and looked at me for a response.

"Open it!" I was going to burst if he didn't just unwrap the damn thing!

Darren chuckled, "Okay!" He unwrapped the small gift and then squinted his eyes at me again. "*Big Daddy?* Why are you giving me this DVD?"

With my hands clasped behind my back, I pulled my shoulders up and showed all my teeth in a big cheesy smile.

He looked at the DVD again, then back at me, and his eyes widened. "Are we?"

I nodded, and Darren threw his arms around me, lifting me up off my feet. I was so relieved he was as happy as I was to be pregnant!

"I Don't Care About My Baby"

Pregnancy was difficult. I threw up several times an hour, every single day. Even water and crackers made me sick. I tried every old wives' tale—from ginger root to Coca-Cola—but my body rejected everything I consumed. I lost weight and was under a hundred pounds by the end of my first trimester.

My head pounded due to starvation, and I got dizzy and blacked out from malnutrition. The pain of vomiting so violently when I did force myself to eat was much worse, though, so I lay in bed day and night, suffering alone. My OB considered an at-home IV to keep me hydrated, but I didn't want to deal with hospital equipment. It was hard enough managing to get myself to the bathroom, or down the stairs to the kitchen to let the dog out a few times a day.

I thought Darren might suddenly honor his vows to love me in sickness and in health, since he'd been on board with getting pregnant. Instead, in the little time I saw him before bed each night, he griped about me lying around doing nothing while he exhausted himself working two jobs.

I was too weak to work. I didn't have energy to clean the house. I barely had energy to walk the ten feet from the bed to the bathroom! I stopped cooking dinner because the scents made me sick. I couldn't keep anything down anyway. So I understood why Darren felt overwhelmed with the burden of our finances and household duties, but I resented him for making me feel like I was failing him as a wife by choice.

Then one Sunday afternoon in early 2003, while watching TV together in the living room, he erupted. "You can't even run a fucking vacuum around here once in a while?"

"The doctor said vacuuming causes strain on the abdominal muscles and could cause a miscarriage," I explained. I was curled up in the oversized green leather chair, eating gummy bears I expected to come back up later.

Darren stood and threw his arms in the air. "Look at this fucking place! It's filthy! I work all fucking day, every day, and this is what I come home to? And look at you! Most wives would at least try to comb their hair and put on make-up to look good for their husbands! But you!" He marched to the kitchen without finishing his insult, to get something from the refrigerator.

Rogue tears escaped my eyes, but I wiped them away before he could see the hurt he'd caused. Seeing me cry in reaction to his harsh words tended to make him angrier.

I managed my way out of the cushy chair, retrieved the vacuum from the foyer closet, and went to work vacuuming the living room carpet.

With every push and pull, I prayed the baby would survive this simple chore. And with every thought of putting the baby at risk, bitterness rose in me. I couldn't blame Darren, though. It was my choice to take the brunt of his insecure ego, so he could feel like the powerful man he needed to. It was also my choice to do as he demanded to keep the peace, though some days I just wanted to walk away.

When Darren settled back in his spot on the sofa, he watched me and the TV like a king overlooking his kingdom, enjoying the plate of food he'd made up for himself.

After vacuuming, I put the appliance away and looked to Darren, like a lowly peasant waiting for direction. I thought to return to my comfy chair, but I was afraid to appear lazy. So I opted to sweep the hardwood floors in the dining room and kitchen instead.

I was on a Beatles kick these days and found myself singing "Eight Days a Week" while I swept. I sang loud enough for the baby to associate my voice with soothing and positivity, but low enough not to disturb Darren.

I wasn't used to doing so much, though. The extra weight of my bulging belly made the simple work strenuous, and, as a result, breathing became just as laborious. I forged through anyway, allowing the rhythm of the lyrics to pace my breath, until I heard a snap underfoot. Like a kid who'd just accidentally broken an expensive vase, I froze.

"What was that?" Darren called out.

I remained silent, hoping he'd forget about it and just watch his precious TV. Instead, he came into the dining room, saw me holding the broom, then looked down at the floor where I stood. The wooden floor vent, broken in half, gave me away.

"Are you fucking kidding me?! That's a forty-dollar floor vent!" he yelled.

"I'm sorry, Darren! I didn't do it on purpose!" Then I tried to soften things with a joke. "I guess I weigh more than I thought!"

"That's fucking awesome," he said as he walked towards the door to the garage. "Just keep breaking shit, and I'll keep working to pay for it." His passive-aggression was annoying, but it stung nonetheless. I'd been conditioned to feel deficient, so every jab was like picking at a scab until it bled. And when it bled, it just hurt.

"I Knew I Loved You"

On May 29, 2003, our son Ryder was born.

"You did good, Dana," Darren praised as he watched the nurses wash and swaddle the baby boy I'd dutifully bore him. He'd been very clear about having no desire for a daughter.

I laid upon the hospital bed limply, with my head turned toward the nurses huddled over my newborn. I hadn't seen him yet. I heard him cry, though, and that alone brought me relief. He was here, and by the sound of his lungs, he was healthy.

While the doctor tended to my afterbirth, Darren was allowed to take Ryder out to the waiting area to meet our parents and siblings. Henrik and Jane had come to the hospital soon after I was admitted, and Denise and Brad had arrived while I was in labor. My mother had not planned to come at all, but had her husband drive her and my little brother, Jonathan, to the hospital after Darren convinced her she should be there.

I was a little miffed I hadn't been offered the opportunity to hold my baby first. I was also jealous that everyone was getting to see him before I did. He was mine, after all! On the other hand, I'd hogged the baby for the nine months he grew inside me, so I guess Darren deserved to have a moment he could cherish as his own. Still, I was anxious for his return.

When Ryder was finally placed in my arms, I was in awe. I couldn't believe Darren and I had made him! I'd waited my whole life for the one who would love me and want me and need me. I'd expected that person to be the man I married, or maybe even a best friend. But it was my son. He was my family and my greatest love all in one, and I would love him like no other mother had ever loved her child.

I opened Ryder's blanket just slightly to inspect him. I wanted to know every detail of this precious angel. The tiniest fingers I'd ever seen clutched the top of the blanket. I ran my finger along his hand, then those tiny fingers wrapped around mine. His untouched skin was the softest I'd ever felt. He was so pure and so perfect. He was calm too, and I wondered if Ryder innately knew I was his mother and that he was safe in my arms.

I gazed upon my little bundle, anxious for him to open his almond-shaped eyes. I knew they'd be brown like ours. I wanted to see them anyway. I couldn't wait to know his smile and hear his giggles. He was seven pounds and ten ounces of delicate innocence, untarnished by societal expectations and worldly impositions, and I'd protect him to the ends of the earth forevermore.

A nurse came over then and guided Ryder to his first feeding. He latched onto my left breast right away. Darren and I looked at each other in amazement while listening to the rhythm of Ryder's suckling. To see human instinct in action was just as wondrous as the ability to create a human at all.

Darren bent down to observe Ryder more closely. There was a particular glint in his eye I'd never noticed before, one that expressed how happy he was. *Genuinely* happy. It made me feel like everything was going to be okay from now on.

After our quiet time with Ryder, Jane and Henrik came in to say goodbye. It was almost 10 p.m., and they'd been there most of the day. Everyone else had left immediately after seeing the baby.

While Jane hugged Darren, Henrik came bedside and put his hand on my shoulder. "Good job, *Mom!*" he commended. I smiled up at him. I loved the sound of that, and I loved that I'd made him proud even more.

Jane came to the other side of the hospital bed to take a last peek at Ryder. "How are you feeling, Dana?"

"Good! It went better than I thought, but three epidurals will make anything painless!"

"I guess!" Jane chuckled, then advised, "Get as much sleep as you can here and let us know if you need anything."

"Will do!"

Darren walked his parents out, while the nurses prepared to transport me and Ryder to a private room.

Ryder slept in the bassinet next to my bed while Darren and I shared a much-needed meal. Then the nurse wheeled Ryder away to the nursery and encouraged me to get some sleep. Darren left then too.

Two short hours later, I was awakened by bright lights and a screaming baby. I sat up to see the exasperated-looking nurse rolling Ryder to my bedside. His face was beet red. She said he'd been screaming since they'd taken him from me, and nothing soothed him. So I grabbed him up in a panic. He immediately quieted.

I loved that Ryder was instantly soothed by simply being with me. It proved that he felt the unbreakable bond I felt with him too. And I wanted him to stay with me. Always.

"I've got him," I told the nurse, who stood there in shock that I could calm Ryder in a way they couldn't.

"Are you sure? It's after midnight!"

"Yeah, we're fine." I looked down at my peaceful baby boy. "Just flip the light off on your way out, if you don't mind."

"All right," she said, and left us in the dark.

I used the switch at the side of the bed to raise us up into a reclined position, then sang the Beatles' "Tell Me Why" to my sweet boy. He seemed to be sleeping afterward, so I attempted to place him back in his bassinet. The instant I moved my hands off his swaddled body, he screamed. So I grabbed him back up and kept him in the bed with me. I was okay with that, though; he was mine, after all.

Or perhaps I was his. That baby ate, played, napped, and slept, only in my arms. Day in, day out, it was just me and my little man, tidying the house, watching Baby Einstein videos, and taking walks down our short dead-end street. I couldn't put him down for two seconds—not even to use the bathroom or shower. He wanted to be in my arms at all times. But I was fine with that. Ryder gave me the purpose, identity, and love that I didn't otherwise have.

Darren, however, was not at all happy with the way Ryder favored me. If he, or anyone, tried to hold Ryder, even for a minute, that baby screamed until he was returned to me. Darren perceived it as his son rejecting him and taking his place on my priority list. And Darren wouldn't be second to anyone—not even his own son.

One night in July 2003, I came to bed with Ryder, after rocking him to sleep with a bottle.

"Uh-uh." Darren came towards the bed from the bathroom. "You need to stop coddling that baby and put him in his crib. No more sleeping with us in our bed."

"You know he doesn't sleep in his crib, Darren. He's up every two hours to eat and get a diaper change anyway, so it's easier just to have him with me."

"Yeah, and I'm up every two hours when he cries for you!" Darren retorted. "Some of us have to actually work in the morning, you know!"

"Jesus, Darren! He's a baby! What did you *think* he was going to do?" I said snottily.

"I thought his mother was going to put him in his crib to sleep at night like every other mother does!"

"Well, I'm sorry my son won't sleep in his crib!" I bitched back, then defended, "I've tried putting him in there for naps, but he screams until I pick him up. So unless you want to hear him screaming all night, he stays with me!"

"You coddle him! *That's* why he won't sleep in his crib! Even my mom and grandma think so!"

Ouch. Were they speaking ill of my parenting behind my back?

"He's only soothed by me, Darren, because I'm the only person he's familiar with! I was alone the whole fucking pregnancy, and I'm alone all day with him now, so my voice is the only one he knows and associates with safety and comfort. And I'd rather have a baby sleep with me and feel secure, than let him scream all night and turn into the insecure woman-hater *you* are!"

Darren stood as tall as possible and pointed at the door. "Then take *your* baby and sleep somewhere else! I pay the fucking bills around here! This is *my* house! And I need some fucking sleep!"

I glared at Darren. Instead of a husband or father, I saw a jealous monster. I kept my psychoanalysis to myself, though, and took Ryder into the guest room across the hall. The master bedroom door slammed shut right behind us. Asshole!

I laid in the guest bed, holding Ryder close to my chest. Then I tucked the blanket around us, ensuring it wouldn't creep up on his little face, which was turned to the side. I was fortunate he slept very still, and that I slept lightly enough to know if he moved the slightest bit. Still, I looked him over again, to double-check that his mouth and nose weren't obstructed by the blanket nor one of those tiny hands of his. In the bright moonlight which shone through the large window, I could see his eyes were already closed.

Suddenly, I heard Darren punching his bed and screaming, "GOD-DAMN IT! Motherfucking BITCH! Fucking go fuck yourself, you fucking CUNT! You love that fucking baby more than you love me! Maybe I should just KILL MYSELF so you don't have to worry about me at all!"

I looked down at this little human lying on me peacefully, knowing he'd live a life of tumult because of my choice to love him most. Unlike my mother, however, I would choose my son over my husband a million times over before I'd ever let Darren put a division between me and Ryder.

"Don't worry, little man. It's going to be just the two of us from now on, but everything will be okay. I promise."

"Never There"

I wanted Ryder to grow up in a loving home, but that wouldn't happen unless Darren was happy, and Darren decided he wouldn't be happy unless we lived on a larger property where he could raise cows, pigs, and chickens. It wasn't the first time he'd mentioned it, though I think it wasn't so much a dream of his as it was a way to make Henrik proud for returning to the family's farming roots. Regardless, if there was any hope of creating the nurturing and cohesive family life I envisioned for us, it didn't matter to me *where* home was.

So, in March of 2004, we moved to a four-acre farm, complete with apple and pear trees, walnut trees, grape vines, and blackberry bushes. There was even a chicken coop!

"I never figured *you* to live on a farm!" Henrik said between bites of cake. We were at Denise's house for Mason's fourth birthday party, which was held the same week as the move. "You going to be okay living that far out?"

"She'll be fine." Darren waved his hand in the air dismissively as he passed through the eating area of the kitchen where we sat.

"That's pretty far out for a city girl," Henrik commented, looking to me for a response this time. "What's that, an hour from your office?"

"Yeah, it's a little far. But I'll be okay. I have my hands full with Ryder anyway."

"You sure? 'Cause you don't know anyone out there. I think Mom and I are the closest, and we're a good thirty-five or forty minutes away!"

"I'm sure. I'll be going to the office once or twice a week, though, so I'll still see people. And being back in civilization will give me an opportunity to do whatever shopping or anything else I have to do before heading back to shuck corn on my porch," I joked, then excused myself to pee while Henrik chuckled at my humor.

As I walked through the unlit angled hallway towards the bathroom at the end of it, I glanced into the brightly lit laundry room to avoid bumping into anyone coming in from the garage or up from the basement, as doors to both were inside. Seeing no one, I proceeded past the doorway but then took a step back. Something I saw among the random items piled on top of the washer and dryer caught my eye. Curiosity compelled me to snoop.

I looked directly to where I'd noticed something of interest and saw a familiar picture frame sticking out from the middle of a pile of socks, papers, plastic bags, and toys which had been carelessly tossed into this teetering tower. Was that the picture frame I'd given Denise as a gift after my wedding? After checking around to make sure no one would catch me being nosy, I moved closer to the pile and saw that it was. The word "Sister," engraved in the dusty, *empty* metal frame, demonstrated the same disregard I'd been feeling from Denise for a while now.

My lips trembled as I fought to dam the tears moistening my eyes. I always knew I cared more about Denise than she did about me, but I had to resolve myself to the decline in phone calls and the short length and superficial content of them so I could have the big sister I always wanted. I'd take that relationship any way I could.

It wasn't personal anyway, I reminded myself, as I pressed my finger to my bottom lids to absorb the accumulated tears. Denise didn't have time for anything since the kids had come along. That's partially why we didn't get together for family dinners with Jane and Henrik like we used to. We just saw each other on holidays and birthdays, and I couldn't expect a close bond to develop or sustain based on an occasional catch-up.

I never saw my own family for the same reason, and the few friends I thought I still had had stopped calling and inviting me anywhere. It was too hard to talk on the phone or go places with them without the interruption of Ryder's eating and sleeping schedule and the randomness of my work.

Life on the farm distracted me from the disconnection I felt from others. The property hadn't been occupied or maintained since the owner passed away a few years before, so there was a lot of work to do before we could settle in. Darren took a week off work to paint Ryder's room, then started on the others while I cleaned trim and doors and floors behind him. We had kitchen counters replaced, appliances delivered, and ran out for meals between. By night, the three of us slept on a mattress on the floor of what was a small in-law house behind the main house, which was unpleasant because the whole place smelled of rotten eggs from the well water. I couldn't even get myself to shower or brush my teeth in it. I missed our former house terribly, and I wondered if moving had been a mistake.

Darren simultaneously accepted the new responsibility of training other electronics technicians across the country to repair arcade games like he did. It perfectly fulfilled his egocentric need to feel important. So, without consulting me, he was off to New York for a week, leaving me with a nine-month-old baby and a farm with two houses in disarray, in an area I wasn't familiar with, near no one we knew.

A couple days after Darren left, I was unpacking boxes in Ryder's bedroom when the phone rang. "Hello?"

"Hey, babe!" I was glad to hear Darren's voice. Because of the nature of his work, I didn't bother him, and I always waited for him to check in with me instead, which wasn't often.

"Hey! How's New York?"

"Good! I'm sitting on a bench looking at the Brooklyn Bridge. It's pretty cool! And I got myself a hot dog for lunch from some street vendor. You should see this thing! It's piled with all the good stuff—onions, relish, ketchup, peppers, mustard . . . It's so good!"

Darren rarely sounded so upbeat. I almost wondered if he liked being away from us. I was admittedly a little jealous. We didn't go on vacations because we couldn't afford both them and all the things Darren liked to treat himself to. I wish I could've tagged along with him and shared the experience. I didn't want my insecurities to interfere with this rare call, though, so I matched his mood. "That's so cool you get to do that! How's everything otherwise? Work going okay?"

"Yeah!" he responded with his mouth full. "I guess they're sending me to Atlanta and then maybe Minnesota after this!"

"Oh! You're coming home first, though, right?"

"Yeah, for like two days or so. They haven't scheduled my flights yet, but I'll let you know."

"Okay." My disappointment was evident in my tone.

"You okay?"

"Yeah!" I lied. "I mean, I knew you took a national position. I guess I just didn't realize you'd be gone so much. I thought it would just be a trip here and there."

"I wasn't sure how it would work either, but they're opening new locations all over the country . . ." he gave me a long explanation of why he wouldn't be home much anymore, but the why didn't matter. All I heard was that he'd only be home a couple days now and then, basically abandoning me, Ryder, and this farm he had to have.

Over the next year, I made the best of the situation. Ryder and I spent mornings playing in his toy Room, and afternoons toddling around the farm. We picked apples and blackberries and cherries from the trees and bushes on our property. He helped me plant a vegetable garden, and we watched the plants emerge from the dirt in crooked rows. Then during mealtimes, he'd watch *Scooby-Doo* and *Tom and Jerry* cartoons while I canned jellies and preserves.

Once Ryder could walk without my assistance, we started going to the nearest McDonald's Play Place, which was thirty minutes away, so he could play with other kids in the slides and tubes. It was sweet to watch other kids tend to Ryder like big brothers and sisters, helping him climb the nets and riding down the slides with him. He liked it too. I could tell by the twinkle in his eyes when he smiled.

We also made a weekly trip to the shopping mall about forty minutes away. We'd eat breakfast at Panera, hang out with other moms and kids in the children's indoor play area, then share a smoothie while we perused the storefronts.

I'd get calls to show houses in between all our activities, in which case we'd stop what we were doing to work.

One afternoon, we stopped in at my real estate office after showing a house nearby. I had some paperwork to turn in anyway.

Paula, the British receptionist; Merrick, the managing broker's son; and another realtor were sitting at the table in the large open reception area, eating their Culver's butter burgers and french fries for lunch.

"Hi, guys!" I said as I closed the back door behind me, carrying Ryder in on my left hip.

"Well, hello!" Paula turned in her chair to face us, then put her arms out for Ryder. I set Ryder down, and he hurried toward her. She picked him up, set him on her lap, and he helped himself to one of her fries. We all giggled. "How are you today, little man? Helping Mommy show houses? We need to get you a little suit so you can be her little assistant!"

I went to file my papers as she continued to sweet-talk him, acknowledging to myself how lucky I was to have co-workers who not only supported me as a working mother, but also welcomed Ryder into our work family.

"Want another French fry?" Paula handed Ryder another as I walked back in the room and approached the table.

"Whaddya say, Ryder?" I raised my eyebrows expectantly.

Ryder looked directly into the receptionist's blue eyes and said, "Dank you." Then he stuffed the fry into his already full mouth.

"I'm going to start calling him 'French Fry-der,'" Merrick said before stuffing his oversized burger into his mouth.

"Ha, ha," I said with sarcasm. "He doesn't need to be teased about his name already. Kids at school will have enough of a field day with our last name!" It was long and German, and people seemed to short circuit when they saw all the letters.

"You want to be called French Fry-der?" Paula was still making one-way conversation with Ryder while he helped himself to her fries.

"I think he likes it! Don't you, French Fry-der?" Merrick teased some more. Then he put up his palm, and Ryder gave him a high five. "See? He likes it! Right, French Fry-der?"

The other realtor at the table, an older lady who was quiet and shy by nature, bowed her head to hide her close-mouthed smile, but I could see by the twinkle in her eyes that she was amused by the banter.

"Oh my god, you guys! You all are nuts! You ready, kid?" I looked at Ryder with raised brows again. He put his arms up for me. He knew the drill.

"You sure you don't wanna stay?" Merrick stood to offer his chair to me. "I can run back to Culver's and get you and Ryder lunch!"

"No, no," I said, waving off the kind offer before picking up Ryder and putting him on my hip. "Sit and finish your lunch. I'll grab us our usual chicken finger meal and root beer float on our way out of town. We have a long drive home anyway, and I gotta get back to pulling weeds. But thank you!"

"You don't hire that out?" Merrick asked as he sat back down.

"Not everyone here can afford to hire out, Mr. Top Producer!"

Paula giggled at my boldness. We all knew Merrick lived in a big custom-built home with his wife and two kids and had probably never pulled a weed in his life.

"So you do it all yourself, huh? And take care of your kid, and work ... You're pretty amazing!" Merrick stared at me intensely, like he noticed some value or worth in me he hadn't seen before.

Caught off guard by the compliment, I held Merrick's stare. It felt good to be noticed, except I wished it were Darren appreciating all I did, not my boss' son. Merrick's blue eyes were mesmerizing, though. But when I realized we'd been gazing at each other for too long, I tried to break up the awkwardness of the moment with humor.

I flipped my hair off my shoulder and turned my nose up, pretending to be conceited. "I try!" I joked in a haughty voice. Merrick burst out laughing, and the ladies giggled. "All right, little man," I said to Ryder, securing him on my hip. "Time to go!"

"Have fun doing your yard work, Ryder!" Paula said, as she waved goodbye. Ryder flung his little hand around in response.

"Say bye," I prompted him.

"Bye!" He continued flinging his hand.

They all waved back. "Bye, French Fry-der!" Merrick threw in.

"Oh my god, stop!" I joked as we walked to the back door. Then I glanced back to see Merrick checking me out with a discreet side eye. I scowled back at him with squinted eyes, but the smirk on my lips gave him permission to enjoy the view. Despite being married, the positive attention felt good after being invisible for so long.

Back at home, our yard-work exhausted us into the early evening, so we ate leftover noodles for dinner, then settled on the couch to watch the movie *Finding Nemo*. Before Ryder could doze off, I gave him a quick bath, then laid him down in the master bedroom upstairs. Ryder fell asleep almost instantly. He'd played outside in the fresh air most of the day.

Despite being just as tired, I couldn't sleep. It was always at night—off-duty from being a mom, and alone with my thoughts—when loneliness would consume me. I called Darren, since we hadn't heard from him in a few days.

"I'm in my work van in a restaurant parking lot, so I only have a minute," he said in place of the happy hello I would have preferred.

"Can you call after dinner then?"

"I don't know, but I gotta go. My co-workers are all inside waiting for me."

Although we were disconnected emotionally and physically, the sting of being lower than his co-workers on his priority list was painful. "Can you call in the morning then? Before work?"

"I don't have time in the morning. You know me—I get up and go."

"Well, when do you have time for us? I'm not trying to be difficult, but surely you can find a couple minutes in your day to at least talk to Ryder!"

"You don't understand my life on the road, Dana! I don't have time to sit on the phone with you guys when I'm working!"

"But you have time to sit with your co-workers for dinner?"

"I don't have time for this shit," Darren mumbled before hanging up on me.

A tear, as solitary as I felt, ran down my cheek.

Although I put on a happy face for Ryder, depression had been setting in slowly. Sometimes when he watched cartoons during his snack or at mealtimes, I curled up in the corner of the kitchen behind the island, where he couldn't see me, hid my face in my knees, and cried.

I was lonely and desperate. Desperate to hear the charm and humor Darren shared with others. Desperate for him to share in raising Ryder. Desperate for any sign he did in fact love me and want to be with me. But he gave me nothing.

On the two or three days a month he was home, I followed him around like a lost puppy, begging for attention and affection with skimpy outfits and new hairdos, but he paid no mind. He didn't speak to me. He didn't look my way. He just mowed the grass, drank beer, and watched TV. The neglect was so blatantly personal, I felt defective and unworthy.

And maybe it was me. I'd struggled with depression for years but hadn't taken antidepressants since I'd met Darren. So I made an appointment with my doctor. Maybe I needed some help to be the happy and positive girl Darren had fallen for in the beginning. For the sake of our son and our marriage, I had to try!

"How are you?" my doctor, who was also my OB, asked cheerfully when he came into the bright white exam room.

I broke down crying, then hid my face in my hands, embarrassed by my obvious instability.

He sat on the short stool and rolled to where I sat. "It's all right, Dana," he reassured. Then he rested his elbows on his knees and his chin on his clasped hands, patiently waiting for me to be ready to talk.

I raised my face slightly. "No, it's not! I can't stop crying! My husband is always gone, I live in the middle of fucking nowhere and have no friends or family nearby, and I'm raising my son by myself. I love him with all my heart, but it's not the same as having someone to talk to at the end of a tough day and hold me when I need comfort or be, you know, intimate and make me feel like a woman, not just a mom. I'm just so lonely!" I hid my face in my hands again and sobbed quietly. Voicing my feelings made them seem much more real than when they were random thoughts nagging at my brain.

"I think this is a simple case of postpartum depression," the doctor diagnosed quickly. "It's very common, so there's nothing to be ashamed of."

"How can this be postpartum?" I sniffled. "I mean, Ryder's almost two!" He seemed older only because I talked to him and treated him like

I treated any other person of any age.

The doctor handed me a tissue. "Postpartum can take up to a year or two to show up. Sometimes it lasts for years too! But I'll prescribe an antidepressant. It'll make the tough days better, and the Xanax I'll prescribe will calm you more instantly when things are a little tougher to deal with than normal."

"Okay," I whimpered, thankful for anything to restore some peace in my heart and mind.

After scribbling illegibly, the doctor handed me the prescriptions and said, "Both are safe for you to take during pregnancy, by the way. Just so you know."

"Well, I don't think that'll happen again," I grumbled. How could it when Darren wasn't home? And even when he was, we certainly weren't performing the necessary activities required for pregnancy. "But thank you for considering that."

I filled the prescriptions in the pharmacy within the medical office before heading home.

When I walked up my porch stairs, Ryder waved happily from the other side of the glass door. I smiled and waved back enthusiastically.

"How did your appointment go?" Jane asked as soon as I entered. She and Henrik, who was sitting on the couch, had stayed with Ryder while I was at my appointment, which was a rare occurrence. They'd only come over a couple times because they lived over a half hour away and refused to pay the inflated gas prices.

"Okay. Doctor says it's postpartum depression and prescribed an antidepressant."

"Oh." Jane's face dropped in disappointment. I knew she didn't believe in modern medicine. She didn't even keep ibuprofen in her house. Nor did she have a respectful perspective on mental health. I'd heard her and Denise make judgmental comments about another family member who suffered from bipolar depression, as if that person were defective.

I'd expected some credit for realizing I needed help, though, especially from a woman who'd been more of a mother to me than my own the last several years. Instead, I felt the same shame my mother had put upon me for being born to her at a young age, and being used to it didn't make it

153

any less difficult to bear.

I didn't want conflict with Jane, though, so I directed my attention towards Ryder. "You watching *Cars* with Grandma and Grandpa?"

He nodded, took my hand, and led me to the floor in front of the TV, where he'd dumped his bin of Matchbox cars. We played while I made small talk with Jane and Henrik about anything other than my mental state.

Darren called that evening. "So how was your doctor's appointment today?"

I was surprised he'd remembered. I'd mentioned the appointment in one of his hurried calls a few nights before.

Ryder was in his highchair eating dinner and watching *Scooby-Doo* cartoons, so I stepped just outside our glass doors onto the porch, to tell Darren what the doctor had said.

"God-damn it! And you're taking care of my son? I knew you were fucking crazy!" Darren yelled into the phone. My heart went from zero to sixty in a second. I hadn't expected such antipathy after he'd pretended to care just a moment before.

Darren's outbursts usually resulted in him hanging up on me, so I knew I had limited time to say anything. "Is there any way for you to come home more? Or can you just make a little more of an effort to call at least once a day?" Those little efforts would make me feel more connected to him, and thereby less lonely.

"I'm working, Dana! One of us has to make a living to support our family! It's hard enough to come home for the couple days every month! It's not even worth the driving time!"

The insult hurt me deeply, especially in the midst of this conversation about how lonely I was, but now wasn't the time to put any more emotional distance between us than what was already there by arguing the point. "I know. I get it," I appeased in a low monotone.

"No, you don't! I can't be at work and make money and have to worry about you and Ryder too!" he yelled. Then he hung up, and I started to cry.

I knew from my childhood that love and attention had to be earned, so I decided to make more of an effort to make this marriage work—not to save the train wreck of a relationship Darren and I had, but for Ryder to have his family unit intact. He deserved at least that, and I couldn't lose the family I'd found in Darren's either.

"I Feel a Sin Comin' On"

"**W**hat?!" Darren growled on the other end of the line. His blatant anger extinguished my excitement, but I forged ahead with my good news in hopes it would lighten his mood.

"I just wanted to tell you I sold three houses today!" That was quite an accomplishment for a realtor in our area, and for me personally. The resulting commissions were more than what I'd make at a regular job over several months! I thought Darren might be proud of my success!

"You bothered me at work for that?! I'm high up on a ladder working with wires! Do you realize I could've fallen by answering your call?!"

"You're right. I'm sorry. I just thought—"

"Fuck, Dana! Even my mom knew not to call my dad at work unless it was an emergency!" He was screaming so loudly that I glanced around, hoping the other realtors sitting at nearby desks didn't hear the humiliating call.

"I just—" I attempted, but the call went dead. I replaced the receiver gently to avoid attention.

As I wiped the lone tear that fell onto my cheek, I noticed an older realtor look at me pitifully over his thick-lens glasses, then share a knowing look with another older gentleman who rose from his desk and left the room. I was embarrassed by their obvious witness but thankful no one said anything.

It wasn't me Darren was angry at. We'd recently learned that the balance and vision issues Henrik had were caused by a tumor wrapped around the ventricular vein in his brain. Doctors estimated he wouldn't live through the end of the year.

Darren was devastated to lose his father too soon, and I was devastated to have the father I'd finally found torn away from me. He was half the reason Darren and I were still married! On a couple past occasions where he'd witnessed Darren talking to me harshly, he'd pulled his son aside and set him straight. Darren would come back to me apologetically and treat me like a princess for whatever short amount of time he could summon the effort to. I couldn't bother Jane and Henrik with our relationship drama now, though. I'd have to learn to deal with Darren on my own.

My thought process was interrupted when Merrick entered the large room. We all looked up anxiously, since he only emerged from his private office down the hall to retrieve one of us if there was a problem. So I shouldn't have been surprised when he looked directly at me and, with a motion of his finger, summoned me to follow him.

Merrick closed his office door behind me when I stepped inside. The room was dimly lit by the little sunshine coming in through the small window, but Merrick made no motion to switch the lights on. He came right to me and put his hands on my shoulders. Then he locked those blue eyes onto mine. "Is everything okay?"

I felt genuine concern in the intensity of his stare, which I took as permission to vent. "I'm just so lonely. Darren's never home. He doesn't call. He doesn't like when I call him. When we do communicate, he treats me like I'm a bother. It's like he doesn't care! And I'm starting not to care either! I don't even know if I want to be married to him anymore, but I didn't get married to get divorced. And I wouldn't leave him while my father-in-law is dying anyway, so I'm trying to make it work. But I can't revive a failed marriage all by myself!" I hid my face in my hands and sobbed. Darren didn't like seeing me cry, so I assumed no one did.

"Wanna know a secret?" Merrick whispered.

"What?" I sniffled and wiped my face with my hand.

"My wife and I are on the brink of divorce too. Sometimes you try the best you can, and it just doesn't work."

Merrick's empathy and validation slowed my tears to a near stop. He hadn't judged my feelings; he'd just listened. I wasn't used to feeling heard, but I also didn't trust easily. So I looked up at him with my teary brown eyes to gauge his sincerity. Something about his sympathetic expression made me feel safe.

Then he pulled me into his husky body. Despite the impropriety, I felt protected in the way his arms enveloped my small frame. This wasn't right, though; my husband should be the one comforting and consoling me.

I pulled away before I could feel anything more than I should. "I've gotta go get Ryder. Thanks for this, though," I said, shyly excusing myself. Then I gathered my things and left the office.

Considering how poorly I'd been treated by men thus far in life, it wasn't a surprise I fell hard and fast for someone who showed any care or concern for me, which Merrick continued to do.

He called me on my cell phone every day from that point on—to "check on" me, he said. Those wellness checks turned into hours of talking about our pasts, our likes and dislikes, our spouses and children, and everything in between. We had much more in common than I'd expected, given our ten-year age difference. Maybe it was because we shared the same birthday, and coincidentally shared the birthday with our mothers as well. Whatever it was, he made me feel good about myself. I was smiling again, I was laughing, I was happy.

I knew I couldn't let whatever was happening between us happen, but I didn't want to remain in my loveless life with Darren, knowing there was someone out there who did think I was funny and amazing and wanted to spend time with me! It wasn't even necessarily about Merrick—the simple fact that someone liked me exactly as I was made me realize other people could see value in me that Darren didn't. But I couldn't leave, not with Henrik dying.

"This isn't where I thought I would be in my life right now," I said, expressing my frustration to Merrick on the phone, as I drove home from showing houses one night. "I thought Darren would grow up and that his temper and anger would ease with maturity. But he's exactly the same as he was ten years ago. I don't think he'll ever change."

"You mean you don't know if he'll ever love you like you want to be loved." Merrick always understood. He just got me—or rather, we got each other. "My wife and I have struggled for years too, but at least we agree divorce is the best option for us and the kids. So I understand. I'm moving in with my dad until we figure things out. I'm going to miss my new ceiling fan though," he joked. "We just bought it, and I haven't had enough time to admire it."

Merrick always made me laugh. That was one of the things I loved about him.

Oh, shit. Love?

"Back to Where I Was"

I don't know if Merrick's laid-back view of divorce was rubbing off on me, or if I was having some epiphany about my marriage, but I was starting to think Merrick was right—sometimes things just don't work out, no matter how hard you try. And Lord knows I'd tried. The problem was I was the only one trying.

Perhaps a better word is tolerating. Or complying. Okay, submitting, though the implied degradation went against my opinion of myself as a strong-willed and independent woman. Was I even strong-willed and independent? Nothing I said or did anymore seemed to support that version of me. If I'd ever been that girl, she was long gone! Who was I, then? Oh, a tolerant, compliant, and submissive wife. I didn't like how that sounded, nor how it felt, especially when Merrick saw me so differently. He'd referred to me as amazing, productive, and intelligent.

So why was I in this marriage? My instant answer was Ryder. He deserved to be raised by two parents. But Darren wasn't around. He wasn't raising Ryder; I was. By myself. And I couldn't imagine for one second that Darren's family would banish me and Ryder if Darren and I divorced.

So maybe it would be okay. People got divorced all the time. It didn't have to be the nasty, drawn-out plight people turned it into out of vengeance. I wouldn't fight over couches and TVs and silverware. I didn't even want the farm! That was Darren's dream, so he should keep it on the off chance he was ever around to do the farming.

I would only ask for alimony and child support—a reasonable request since Darren was insistent about my primary role as a stay-at-home mother to Ryder, which limited my ability to work a nine-to-five job and earn a stable income to support us.

Thinking about divorce so much led to indecision, and my indecision led to excuses. No amount of thinking led to reasons, though. I could not find one solid reason to stay with Darren, that had to do with our relationship. So, in a moment of braveness, I picked up the phone and made an appointment with the local attorney, whom I'd worked with on a few real estate transactions. It didn't hurt to discuss my options with someone I knew and trusted.

A day later, I sat in the attorney's dark and outdated wood-paneled office, with my oblivious toddler on my lap. I shifted uncomfortably in the scratchy salmon-colored upholstered chair, though it was my anxiety really causing my discomfort. It had taken so much time to muster up the nerve to come here. I wanted to get it over with before I changed my mind.

"Hi, Dana!" The attorney walked into the office with a file in his hand and sat at the wood-laminate desk across from me. He was a short, small-framed older man with a slightly tanned complexion and dark hair of which there was little left. "What can I do for you today?"

I looked at Ryder, as if seeking approval to proceed, then mumbled, "I wanted to talk to you about getting a divorce."

"Oh," he said dismally, "I'm sorry to hear that."

"Me too."

He leaned back in his chair. "Unfortunately, I'll have to decline. I've done divorces before, but I primarily do real estate law now. Plus, I know both of you and don't want to take sides."

"I guess that's why I hoped you *would* do this for me."

"I'm sorry, Dana. I'd be happy to refer you to other attorneys in the area who can help you though," he offered.

I didn't want to make the rounds to different attorneys and start rumors in our small town. It would surely get back to Darren and there would be hell to pay if he discovered I'd consulted anyone about divorce. I just wanted to know what divorce looked like for me—like how much alimony and child support I would be entitled to, and how much I could expect from the sale of the house. Although I could have cared less about the money, I had to consider whether I could realistically raise Ryder with whatever

I was granted, before causing Darren's whole family, namely Henrik, the upset of watching Darren and I fight about every penny in court. I mean, if we were still going to fight during a divorce, I would just as soon save us all the trouble and stay married!

I looked down at Ryder for confirmation of what to do. The innocence in his face as he fumbled with his Thomas the Train figure made me feel selfish. He had no idea I was trying to alter the course of his life by dividing his family simply because I wasn't happy. Did my happiness even matter, if it were at the cost of his? Or would he be better off if I were happy, but not married to his dad? I didn't know.

"No, I'll figure things out," I finally responded. I couldn't take the chance of making the wrong decision.

"Okay. I'm sorry I can't help you, but do let me know if you change your mind. I can give you a few numbers," he offered again.

"Thanks anyway," I said, and with Ryder on my hip, I left the office and returned to a life I wasn't as ready to walk away from as I thought.

"Dirty Little Secret"

By late July, Merrick and I were inseparable. He called me every morning and every night, and I found myself needing to go to the office much more often than before. I needed to see his smile, to joke and laugh with him, to hear his Georgian southern accent talking sweet to me . . . I needed *him*.

Still, I was shocked when I came out of Ryder's bathroom one morning, and saw Merrick standing outside the glass entrance doors looking in. He looked me up and down, then smirked. The lustful desire in his eyes reminded me I was under-dressed in an old and worn navy blue DePaul T-shirt which failed to hide my pink panties.

I looked over at Ryder, who was occupied with toy cars on the living room floor. He hadn't noticed Merrick outside our door yet, and I couldn't risk him ever saying anything about Merrick being at the house with Mommy, especially when Mommy was running around in panties and a T-shirt. I had to remedy the situation fast.

I cracked open the door and stuck my head out. "What the hell are you thinking? You can't be here!"

Merrick looked me up and down again, smiling even bigger this time. "I was in the neighborhood and thought I'd stop by." His innocent tone failed to hide his true intent.

"You just happened to be in my neighborhood, an hour from where you live and work? What if Darren had been home?" I glanced back inside the house, as if Darren would just appear out of nowhere and bust us both.

Merrick smiled. He knew exactly what he was doing. He'd taken the risk of showing up unannounced, hoping my jealous husband had done the same, thereby ending my marriage and making me available to him.

"Ugh!" I sounded annoyed, though I couldn't help but smile back. Merrick's bold move demonstrated the lengths he was willing to go to have me all to himself. No one ever wanted me as much as he did.

I couldn't just let him in and play house with me and my kid, though, especially when I was so scantily dressed. "Just wait here, okay?" I closed the door and walked through the living room to the stairway. "Mommy will be right back, Ryder! Just going to get dressed!"

"Okay!" Ryder chirped back, then returned to making engine sounds while he rolled a toy car across the wood floors.

I descended the stairs a couple minutes later in a fitted tank top and hip-hugging blue jeans. Merrick was standing just inside the door now, watching Ryder play. I shot him a raised-eyebrow glare for disobeying my request to stay outside, then faked surprise for Ryder's benefit. "Oh, look who's here, Ryder!"

He glanced towards the door, where my attention was focused, saw Merrick, then went back to playing cars. I was thankful he was unfazed by Merrick's presence, but I still worried this little stunt would get me in some kind of trouble. I had to get us all out of the house fast. So I motioned for Merrick to follow me to the main floor bathroom, where we could talk out of Ryder's ear-shot, while I finished getting ready.

"What the hell are you thinking?" I took eyeliner out of a small drawer and looked to Merrick for a response before applying it to my upper lash line.

"I always wondered what you looked like without make-up," he said as he leaned on one side of the door jamb, "so I could see the beautiful girl I might be lucky enough to wake up to every morning. You don't need all that, by the way. The make-up, I mean. You're absolutely gorgeous all on your own."

I cocked my head sideways at him. My closed-mouth "Give me a break" expression was a farce, though; I loved the sweet talk. And the way he looked at me with such adoration.

"You can't do this again," I said firmly. "You know that, right?"

"I just wanted to see you at home, in your natural environment. I only see 'Work Dana,' with the dresses and heels and all. But I'd never seen you as just you, on a regular day, doing regular things. I loved it, by the way—the T-shirt and panties. Just shows how real you are. You don't pretend to be anything but what you are."

His sincere desire to know the real me, at that depth, melted my heart. It was also an affirmation that our friendship had evolved into more of a romantic relationship, which was exactly why I needed him to be more careful about when and where we spent time together. "How can I argue with such sweet intentions? But you need to understand you can't just show up here whenever you want. What if Darren had come home from a trip early? Or showed up right now? How would we explain you being here? Business? He's not stupid. Or what if my in-laws were here visiting? Not that my father-in-law can leave his medical chair now, but what if? And Ryder! I have no control over what he says to people, and I can't have him randomly saying that you've been here with us alone!"

Merrick crossed his arms and stared at me with a closed-mouth grin. Apparently, my rant amused him.

"What?"

"That's your guilt talking, you know," he stated. "You're sweet on me too, aren't you?"

I looked at him with open-mouthed surprise, ready to refute his observation.

"Come here," he said.

Despite my arguments about why he shouldn't even be at my house, I immediately went to Merrick. I was just drawn to him.

Then he wrapped his arms around my waist and pulled me close. Our mouths were barely an inch apart. I could feel his breath on my lips as I stared into his blue eyes, trying to deny the lust I felt brewing down below. Then he pulled me in closer and kissed me. It was gentle and soft and perfectly moist. I couldn't take it anymore; I pushed my tongue into his mouth and grabbed the back of his head to fully pull him in. Then I jumped back just as quickly, wiping my mouth. Merrick wiped his too.

"We can't do this here!" my sudden morality scolded us both. Then I pushed past Merrick to return to Ryder, who was still playing in the living room. "We gotta go!"

Knowing our cue to leave the house, Ryder held his arms up for me.

I put him on my hip, grabbed his prepared bag of toys and snacks, and slipped on my flip-flops by the door. Merrick held it open for me, and we fled the property before a nosy neighbor or passerby could see anything worth mentioning to anyone—that "anyone" being Darren.

"Human"

Merrick and I carried on recklessly through summer, as if our happiness together trumped the consequences of being discovered. We walked arm in arm through the mall near Jane and Henrik's house. We strolled through parks hand in hand and stole kisses between bites of food at picnic lunches. Perhaps the danger of being discovered made our romance more exciting. Or maybe we wanted someone to rat us out to our spouses, so we could avoid the confrontations ourselves. Either way, we were in love and unafraid to display our affection publicly, even in front of Ryder, who seemed perfectly comfortable with the whole situation.

Then one late August afternoon, Merrick called while Ryder was napping. "I hear water running. Are you in the shower?"

"Maybe," I flirted. "Too bad you're not in it with me!"

"What I wouldn't do . . . I wouldn't do it in your house or mine, though."

"Jeez, Merrick! I was talking about a shower, not sex!"

"You don't wanna?"

"Have sex?" I wasn't sure if Merrick was confirming my desire or asking for consent to do the one thing we hadn't done yet.

"Yeah," he said with a suddenly serious tone. "I want to make love to you so bad."

Make love? I don't think Darren had ever made love to me! "Then get another place," I insinuated.

"Maybe I will, then! Thursday night?"

"I'd have to find someone to watch Ryder . . ."

"I'll make arrangements. Just as long as you're sure . . ."

"I'm sure. Are *you* sure?"

"Oh, I'm sure!" We cracked up at his enthusiasm.

I was so caught up in the amusing banter, I failed to realize the gravity of what I'd just agreed to. I was excited that this man wanted to take things to the next level with me! In any other dating circumstance, this would have been the natural next step, I justified. Except this wasn't a normal dating situation; we were both married to other people! But on the brink of divorce, I argued with myself.

From the time I hung up on that call, my usually good morals pestered me to reconsider. It wasn't like me to be selfish or to break rules. I'd been daring in the past, doing or saying something somebody didn't believe I would, but that was just for laughs, and nobody got hurt by any of those shenanigans. Infidelity, however, would alter the course of my marriage, my life, and a lot of other lives if it were ever to become known.

It's not like this was my first opportunity with another man either. Other men had flirted with me and expressed physical desire for me, knowing I was married. So what was so different about Merrick that I was willing to risk everything? Happiness, that's what. When I was with him, I felt calm and at ease, accepted and appreciated. But was my happiness worth affecting so many lives? My gut said yes, but my sensitive heart said no.

Intellect intervened, telling me to end it with Merrick; deal with our marriages, then come together if that's what the stars had in store for our futures. But don't start a sexual relationship with a man who isn't available, when I shouldn't have made myself emotionally available to him in the first place!

I was finally happy, though—truly happy. So I selected a black lace bra and string bikini panties especially for the occasion.

On the evening of our rendezvous, Merrick asked me to meet him in a parking lot far from either of our homes and office. From there, he would drive me to the surprise location he'd arranged for our tryst.

"Hey!" He smirked when I opened the door to his SUV.

"Hey," I replied with an equally seductive, close-mouthed smile. Dressed in a low-cut, shimmery black V-neck top and tight jeans, completely inappropriate for the hundred-degree humidity, I climbed into his SUV.

"You look amazing," Merrick said as he pulled away.

"I tried!" I said with a smile and a wink.

Minutes later, we pulled into the parking lot of the Sybaris—a hotel where fantasy-style rooms are rented by the hour for sexual encounters meant to be kept secret. Secrets were only kept because people were doing things they shouldn't be doing, with people they shouldn't be doing them with, I thought. Then the significance of what I was about to do caused sudden panic to strike me.

"I'll be right back," Merrick said as he got out of the car to go check in.

"Okay," I responded with a disingenuous smile. I wasn't okay. It had been exciting to talk about it, think about it, and plan for it, but being on the brink of doing it made me realize I really *didn't* want to betray my morals any more than I already had.

So what do I do? Tell him I changed my mind? Ask him to take me back to my car? I was so confused I couldn't think straight. Then I saw Merrick walking back towards the car, and my heartbeat quickened as the panic grew. I had to make a decision quickly, but emotional overwhelm stunted my ability to do so.

Merrick opened the passenger door and extended his hand to help me out of his vehicle. His gentlemanly manners were impeccable and made me feel like a princess—a distraction which lowered my defenses and let him lead my lonesome heart into a dimly lit room.

Inside the door, he gripped my waist and pulled me close. I felt his desire for me then, which stirred my desire for the way he made me feel. With Merrick, I wasn't a mother or a wife who was unappreciated despite her dutiful service; I was a woman, valued by this man for my intellect, humor, and sensitivity. He didn't want anything *from* me. He just wanted *me*. And I wanted him too.

So, just as quickly as I'd changed my mind in the car, I changed my mind again. I closed my eyes and parted my lips to allow our tongues to entangle. Then we moved to the bed, where I let him undress me and lay me down. The pent-up tension between my thighs could hardly wait for him to finish undressing himself and climb on top of me.

He kissed me passionately, then turned me over and pulled my hips up to his. After penetrating me, I turned over to face him again. I'd envisioned Merrick looking in my eyes and whispering sweet words to me as our bodies moved synchronously. I wanted him to caress parts of my body that hadn't felt a man's touch in some time. I expected overwhelming lust to explode into multiple orgasms. Instead, he turned me back upon my knees, and sought his pleasure within me, but not with me.

The impersonal and detached nature of our encounter caught me off guard. I thought I was special, that what we had was special. So why didn't he want to look me in the eyes while we made love?

Had I been duped? Or had I longed for love so desperately that I'd deluded myself into thinking this was something more than what it really was? Darren warned me many times over the years that men who were friendly to me wanted just one thing from me. I'd taken his heed as another devaluation of my worth, but maybe he was right. I had nothing to offer a man except my body. My appearance was the only quality about me that ever drew positive attention and compliment.

Disappointment in myself for being so naïve overwhelmed me with sadness, but there was no going back now. The act was done, and my marriage would be over because I'd cheated. Lives would be altered, including Ryder's, who'd done nothing to deserve the fallout that would inevitably follow. Even the bright neon numbers on the digital clock on the side table judged me for not being home to give Ryder a bath, like I normally would at this hour.

So I was relieved when Merrick was finished.

I'd hoped he'd prove my insecurities wrong by laying upon the bed with me, cuddling and telling me how amazing it had felt to make love to me for the first time. Then, perhaps, we'd kiss and touch each other until sparks re-ignited his body to enter me again, in the more loving way I'd expected to begin with. But he went to the glass-block shower instead, and turned the water on.

"You coming in?" he called out.

I laid in the bed, naked and alone, wishing this had gone differently. It was too late for regret, though. I'd messed up.

"Hey." Merrick poked his head out of the shower. "You okay?"

"Yeah," I lied, then took my time getting up to join him for a quick rinse. I stood in the hot water numbly, while he babbled about us getting our broker's licenses and running his dad's real estate office together.

It was a quiet drive to my car afterwards. I stared out the passenger window, avoiding looking at Merrick at all. Apparently having noticed, he asked, "What's going on? You hungry?"

"Not really," I mumbled. "I just wanna get Ryder and go home."

"Let's just stop for a quick bite somewhere. Whaddya feel like?"

"Seriously, Merrick." I finally looked at him with pleading eyes. "Please just take me to my car."

"But I don't want tonight to end," he said, looking back at me with undeniable sincerity before turning into a strip mall and parking in front of a Panda Express. "Come on, let's get some dinner."

I laid my head back upon the headrest and sighed. I just wanted this whole night to be over. I needed time alone to process what I'd done, and to determine what my future held with either or neither of the two men I was caught between. I couldn't do that at a Panda Express!

Before I could protest, the passenger door opened. I looked over and saw Merrick holding his hand out to me, like a prince escorting his princess to a ball. He treated me so well, my conflicted heart didn't want to deny us the opportunity to be happy together, but my mind reminded me we couldn't be a couple. Not now and not like this, at least.

"What's wrong, little girl?" That was his nickname for me.

"I . . . I just . . ."

He reached over me to unbuckle my seat belt before helping me out of the car. Then he threw his arms up in the air and shouted, "I'm on top of the world!" He grabbed my cheeks in both hands and planted a kiss on my lips.

I cracked a smile as I closed the door to the SUV and then leaned back against it. I was glad to have made him so happy, and I'd expected to feel the same euphoria after consummating our love. Yet, I was still trying to make sense of the impersonal interaction it had turned out to be. Plus, I felt tremendous guilt for what we'd done to our spouses, and anxiety about anyone finding out. Discouraged by knowing this would have to end before we really had a chance, my smile dissipated, and my head dropped down.

Merrick touched my cheek with the back of his hand like Darren had done in the beginning of our relationship. Then he lifted my chin with his finger. "I'm going to marry you," he said as he looked into my eyes very intently.

If we weren't married to other people, if we didn't have kids who would be affected by our divorces, if his father-in-law didn't work at our real estate office and mine wasn't dying, then yes, I'd marry him too. But we had no business being in a romantic relationship to begin with, and I wouldn't delude myself with fantasy. One of us had to be realistic!

"I'm never marrying again!" I blurted out. "Let's just go get your food."

Merrick stepped back with open-mouthed surprise and stared at me like I was someone he didn't recognize. I marched towards the entrance of the fast-food joint then, my arms crossed. I felt bad for being so mean, but I was glad Merrick was offended. Maybe then he'd go home to his wife and forget about me! We were better off living our miserable lives apart, rather than ruining others' lives together.

I looked back to make sure he was following me. He was still by the vehicle with a shocked expression on his face. "Come on," I ordered him. "You want food, right?" Then I opened the door of the establishment and sat at a table like a pouting child doing something I didn't want to be doing. Merrick joined me after placing his order at the counter.

"You sure you don't want anything? I know you like the orange chicken bowl," he enticed.

"No. I just want you to eat so I can go home."

"Okay," he said, then went back up to the counter to retrieve his food.

"Is this because I said I want to marry you?" he asked when he returned to the table with his tray and sat across from me. "I thought that's where this was leading!"

With crossed arms and a stone-cold face, I watched Merrick take a bite of food. He looked sad, and I knew it was because of the shitty attitude I was giving him. I didn't want to treat him badly, but I wanted to make him hate me so he'd walk away and this whole mess we'd created could go away with him!

At the same time, I cared too much to let him think I didn't want him too. He deserved an explanation at least. "It's a lot of things, Merrick.

I mean, what the hell are we doing? We can't get married! We're already married to other people! And what happens if this gets out? We have kids to think about. Family. Your father-in-law works at our office, for God's sake! So, what, we get married and run the office together with him still working there? This is so much more than just us and what we want! There's a domino effect we have to consider here!"

"Ain't no thang but a chicken wang!" His usual laid-back response didn't lighten the mood like it usually did. I found it quite inappropriate, actually.

"Merrick . . ." My sorrowful eyes begged for him to take the situation as seriously as it should be. I didn't know what to do any more than he did, but we needed to figure out how to proceed, even if it meant moving forward separately. Not that I wanted to end things and go back to my unhappy life without him, but we couldn't keep a full-fledged relationship under the radar. We were bound to get caught sooner or later.

As if reading my mind, Merrick looked at me very intently and said, "It'll all work out, LG. I promise."

I wanted to believe him, I really did, but I was a realist who lived life with intention. I didn't leave things to chance. I couldn't stop thinking of every possible scenario that could result from the various paths which lay before us. End things with Merrick? Divorce Darren? Marry Merrick? Stay with Darren? Tell our spouses? Don't tell and keep carrying on?

As I sat quietly with my thoughts, I barely heard Merrick telling whatever story about an attractive female client he'd taken to lunch in a bad neighborhood. He continued the story on the short drive back to my car, during which I wished I could live more in the present like he did, oblivious to my conscience and the effects of my actions. But then I wouldn't be the sensitive and caring woman he loved, worrying about everyone else except myself.

As soon as he pulled up to my car, I climbed out of his. "I love you," he said.

"I know," I replied, purposely not returning the sentiment. It wasn't fair to lead him on when I had no idea where tonight would lead either of us.

I was eager to pick Ryder up from the sitter anyway and get home. Even though I normally felt imprisoned within the walls of our house, there was a strange sense of security in knowing what to expect in every second of the daily routine I had to uphold.

I couldn't sleep after what I'd done, though. The guilt was too much to bear. I'd failed my husband, my son, our family . . . My only defense was that I finally felt the love I'd always longed for. But at what cost?

I laid in bed wide awake, clinging to Ryder as if his innocence could protect us both from the consequences of my shameful sins. But the dark night knew the truth, taunting me with the promise of a dawn that threatened to bring my secret to light.

Darren could never find out though. If he did, he'd kill me.

"Bizarre Love Triangle"

My eyes popped open when I heard my phone buzz. Along with the bright sun coming through the many windows of the bedroom, the second buzz abruptly thrust me into this new day. I grabbed my cell from under my pillow before it could wake Ryder too. "Hello?"

"Good morning, gorgeous!"

I couldn't help but smile at the sweet wake-up call. I'd become accustomed to Merrick's voice being the first I heard every morning. "Morning!" I said as I stretched my free arm high above my head.

"Last night was amazing."

My mood went sour in an instant. I'd answered my morning call so reflexively, I hadn't thought about the night before just yet. I wanted to block the memory and the upset of emotions that came with it, out of my head altogether. "Merrick, we can't do that again."

"Why not? I love you, you love me. Even my pastor says it's okay," he persuaded.

"Your pastor?"

"Yeah, I talked to him about us. He knows my marriage isn't going well. My wife and I don't even sit together at church. I told him I met someone and I'm happier than I've ever been, and he said if we love each other and it feels right, then it's okay!"

"But it's not! And I'm curious about a man of God who would tell you it is!"

"Anyway, meet me for lunch today, okay?"

I huffed. I knew he'd heard me. He was just avoiding the religious debate that would ensue, because he knew he wouldn't win. It almost bothered me, though, that he showed no signs of guilt or remorse!

Merrick sensed my hesitation, "Darren's not coming home today, is he?"

"Does Darren ever come home anymore?"

"No," he answered his own question.

"Exactly."

"And you're not going to see your in-laws?"

"No." I suddenly felt guilty about that too. "My father-in-law is confined to his hospital-like chair that turns into a bed, and my mother-in-law says it upsets him that people are looking at him all pitifully when they come over to say their last goodbyes. So he doesn't really want visitors. Not even us!"

"And you're not showing houses to your sister-in-law?"

"No." Denise was pregnant with her third child and needed another bedroom for the new baby. I'd taken her and Brad through several houses, but she was very particular about what she wanted and where, and hadn't found it yet. "But the next time I do show her a house, you can't call me like you did last time!" He'd been so brazen on that call, telling me things he wanted to do to me and with me, that I had to turn down the volume on my cell phone and walk away from Denise and Brad so they couldn't accidentally overhear!

Merrick chuckled. "So you'll meet me at noon then?"

"Yeah, I'll meet you," I succumbed, but only because I was intent on setting things straight.

Of course, lunch led to making out, then another day spent kissing in the park, then another having a quickie in a vacant home Merrick had listed for sale. Caught up in the lair of Merrick's charm, I suppressed the guilt of my wrongdoings, justifying it all with deserving happiness.

After a few more weeks of carrying on like this, a call from Denise about a house she wanted to put an offer on reminded me I had a husband who had a family I couldn't risk losing. So when Merrick called to check in with me that same afternoon, I decided to set him straight. For real this time.

"We can't keep doing this," I told him in a lowered tone. Ryder was in his high chair eating lunch and watching *Finding Nemo* for the millionth time, so I walked upstairs to take the rest of the call in my office.

"What are you saying?" Merrick worried. "I want to be with you!"

I looked down to hide my smile (and my guilt). I liked hearing that from the man I was in love with, but I wanted the man I married to say those words to me. "I know, but this isn't just about you and me. We have spouses and kids! If you think about it, we wouldn't have marital problems if we gave our spouses even half the attention and effort we've given each other!" Nor if our spouses gave us what we needed too, I thought.

"I told you, I'm getting divorced," he persuaded.

"I know, but you're still married. And so am I."

"I want to be married to *you!*"

I sighed. I was getting nowhere with him. "Look, we have something between us. But the reality is that we shouldn't be doing anything we're doing. So please go deal with your marriage and let me handle mine. I know you don't want to hear this, but I will not leave Darren while his dad is dying. I can't do that to him, and I won't do that to his family."

"Listen, just meet with me at the park off 126 and we'll talk about this," he insisted.

He always wanted to talk about serious things in person, so he could make me forget about them with kisses. He *was* the best kisser.

But I wouldn't let him distract me this time. Maybe if I pushed him away, denied him the physical privileges of a husband-wife relationship, he would get the picture. "Fine, I'll pack up Ryder and be there as soon as I can."

Forty minutes later, I parked behind Merrick's Durango and rolled down my window when he walked towards my vehicle. He leaned through and kissed me so tenderly it took my breath away.

"You don't really want to end this," he said, knowing his effect on me. Then he kissed me again. Those damn kisses! Darren had never kissed me like that. Ever.

I pulled back slowly with my eyes still closed. "We can't do this," I said softly, but even I wasn't convinced of my own words.

Merrick took my left hand in his and examined my wedding bands. The empress-shaped center diamond and the twenty-five baguettes contained in the wedding and anniversary bands glimmered in the sunshine. "He must love you a lot," Merrick deduced based solely on the beauty of the three rings. My head dropped. He should've known better after all I'd confided in him. I was Darren's possession, and these rings were his claim on me, like a cat pissing on something to mark its territory.

Realizing his mistake, Merrick lifted my chin and stared into my eyes intently. "I will cherish you. I promise." Then he kissed me again, and I believed him.

"Mercy"

arren came home that same weekend, complaining once again that it was an inconvenient waste of time for him to travel back on his days off. He could have stayed out of town, for all I cared. Other than taking me to dinner that Saturday night, with the expectation of getting laid afterward, he didn't pay me any attention at all. He didn't talk to me, didn't look at me. He just watched TV, drank beers, and bitched about all the things he had to do around the house, as if I were deficient for having failed to nail loose cedar siding back onto the exterior walls and repair the leaks in the roof myself.

Darren's pissy attitude made it hard not to miss Merrick. The gentlemanly charm, his care and consideration, his humor, his affection—he was everything Darren wasn't, and everything I wished my husband to be. It was too risky to communicate with Merrick when Darren was home, though, unless I was able to escape to the liquor store by myself to buy Darren more beer.

Thankfully, Darren would be heading out of state again Monday morning. Since he expected his laundry to be done before then, I spent the Sunday morning tending to it in our basement laundry room, even though I'd have preferred to be outside with Darren and Ryder, enjoying the last of the warmth and sunshine the September day offered.

I had just pulled a load out of the dryer when my phone buzzed. I looked at my phone where it lay on the ironing board, and saw Merrick's name on my caller ID. I grabbed the phone in excitement but looked up the stairway in paranoia before I answered to make sure Darren hadn't come in from mowing grass. The humming sound of the tractor outside told me it was safe to take the call. "Hey!"

"I told my wife," Merrick muttered in a solemn tone.

My heart stopped. "Are you kidding me? We agreed to keep this quiet!"

"I know. But now we can be together," Merrick avowed.

"No, we can't! Your wife may know, but my husband doesn't! What am I supposed to do? Just pack up my kid and walk out on him? I told you I wouldn't leave him while his dad is dying!"

"Do I need to come get you?" Merrick offered, as if I was incapable of leaving my husband and home of my own accord.

"NO!" I expressed my anger too loudly, then looked up the stairs again to confirm I was still alone. "Damn it, Merrick! Does anyone else know?"

"Just a couple people at the office, and the mortgage broker . . . and my son overheard me tell my wife, but he heard the name 'Donna,' not 'Dana,' so he doesn't know it's you."

"Oh my god, Merrick! What have you done?"

How could he have betrayed me like this? He had no right to tell people about us without my consent, especially when I'd explicitly told him I wouldn't divorce Darren while Henrik was still alive. It was only a matter of time now before Darren would find out and I'd lose everything—my home, my family, maybe even my son! One person would tell another, and before long, the truth would be on my doorstep! I struggled to breathe just thinking about Darren's rageful reaction and whatever other ruinous effects Merrick's confession would have on both our lives.

"I gotta go," I blurted, then hung up. I didn't want to be around in case Merrick did decide to show up as some romantic overture to take me away. Or worse yet, if his wife decided to seek her rightful vengeance.

I was already dressed, so I ran upstairs and packed Ryder's bag with snacks and toys, put it in the car, and acted calm and cool when I went out into the yard to collect him. "Hey, kiddo! Mommy's going to take you somewhere extra special today, okay?"

"Okay!" Ryder giggled as he ran towards me with Pepper galloping alongside him. I swept him up into my arms, just as Darren pulled up next to us with the tractor and turned it off.

"I've gotta go show some houses," I said, figuring he wondered where I was going. "We'll be up in the suburbs though, so it'll probably be a while."

"All right."

"I just figured I'd get Ryder out of your hair so you can—" Darren restarted the tractor and drove off before I could finish my sentence, which was just as well. I was lying anyway.

While driving away, I did get a call to show a house about thirty miles east. I agreed to meet the customer there, then took Ryder to the nearby mall for lunch afterward. While Ryder picked at the orange chicken and rice I'd ordered for us to share in the food court, I tried calling Merrick. He didn't answer. I tried again a few minutes later, but it went straight to voicemail. After a few more failed attempts, my phone battery died altogether.

Having no way of getting a hold of anyone now, I had no idea whether Merrick was at his house dealing with an angry and devastated wife, or at my house getting pummeled by my jealous and vengeful husband. There was nothing for me to do regardless, except keep my cool for Ryder—a challenge without my Xanax—and keep us safe, which meant keeping us away from everybody.

So we stayed out until dark, banking on Darren falling asleep drunk. I didn't want to answer any questions about where we'd been or why we'd been gone all day, nor did I have the emotional energy to argue with him about the same petty crap we always fought about.

The glow of the TV was a welcome greeting that shone through our living room windows when we pulled into the driveway. The normalcy of it reassured me nothing was amiss here. I'd have surely seen signs of violent outrage if Darren had found out about the affair. Still, I walked in cautiously, holding Ryder tightly on my hip, in case I needed to make a run back to the car to escape an unanticipated attack.

As expected, Darren sat in his recliner undisturbed. He didn't look my way, nor say anything, so I didn't say anything either. I just quietly closed the door behind us, went straight down the dark hall to give Ryder a bath, then locked us in Ryder's room to prevent Darren from bursting in and bothering us in case I'd judged the situation wrongly.

Fortunately, the night passed without incident, and emotional exhaustion made me sleep so soundly I didn't even hear Darren leave before Ryder and I awoke in the morning. I was relieved to be rid of him and the tension he exuded, but anxiety about Merrick took its place. I'd charged my phone overnight, but I still hadn't heard from him. I had to go to the office later that morning to update a file, though, so hopefully I'd see Merrick then to discuss damage control.

When I pulled into the back lot of our ranch-home-turned-real-estate-office, only two vehicles were parked there. I was glad for the minimal presence; I didn't know who knew what yet, and I hoped to avoid negative attention or judgment, especially from Merrick's father-in-law. I'd even left Ryder at Jane and Henrik's, though it took some convincing to get Jane to watch him for the hour I promised to be away.

I opened the back door of the office warily, surveying the situation before entering. One realtor sat in the back corner of the room where all our desks were lined into two rows. He looked up and smiled at me, in the same fatherly way he always did. Then I saw our new receptionist wave me into the main lobby area as if the coast were clear, so I sat at the computer nearest her desk.

"Hi," I said shyly. I was suspicious she knew, by the way she'd given me the OK to enter.

"Hi, Dana!" she greeted cheerily. Then she went about her work like any other day, which put me at ease.

While the computer booted up, I looked out the big picture window that took up the full length of the back wall. It overlooked the grassy area and parking lot in the rear, where Merrick and I sometimes kicked a ball around with Ryder. Then I saw Merrick's Durango pull into the parking lot, and immediately leave. The receptionist and I looked at each other. Clearly she thought it odd too, but neither of us said anything. I'd call Merrick after I finished my work to find out what was going on.

A few minutes later, the sound of gravel crunching at a rapid rate turned our attention to the window again. An older sedan tore into the parking lot, and a six-foot something, stringy-haired brunette, dressed in athletic shorts and a dirty T-shirt, emerged. A second later, the Amazonian woman burst through the back door of the office with the snarl and nastiness of a pitbull on attack. The other realtor, and a mortgage broker who'd just walked in, rushed to forcibly hold this homely woman back.

"Run!" the realtor shouted to me.

"Now!" the mortgage broker added.

They obviously knew who she was, and obviously knew I was in danger, which meant they obviously knew.

That was Merrick's wife, wasn't it? Without another thought, I grabbed my purse and keys and high-tailed it out the front door. My heart was beating a mile a minute as I sped away in my vehicle, then stopped at a gas station down the road to puke out the door.

As I sat with my sweaty head laid back upon the headrest, my cell phone rang. It was Merrick. "What the hell was that?" I gasped, still short of breath from puking.

"Are you okay?" Merrick avoided answering me.

"No, I'm not!"

"Did she hurt you?"

"So that *was* your wife? How did she even know I was there?"

"She doesn't want me at the office with you. So when I pulled in and saw your car, I called her and told her I wasn't going in because you were there. That way, she'd know I was doing as she asked."

"So you served me up to her on a silver platter? You couldn't just wait for me to leave?" I was disgusted with him. "And why would you ask me if she hurt me? Did you think she would? And you still called her? What the fuck, Merrick?"

I pulled the phone away from my ear to cough. I was still trying to catch my breath.

"I have something else to tell you, and you're not going to like it," he said. My body stiffened. I couldn't imagine what he could tell me that equaled or outdid this mess we were already in. "This isn't the first incidence of infidelity. That's why she's so upset."

I dropped my head into my hand and attempted to rub off the tension building in my forehead. "What are you saying?"

"A while back, my wife's niece was staying over. I had too much to drink that night, and, well, I kind of touched her ... sexually ... but only because I was too drunk to realize it wasn't my wife."

My mouth fell open, but no words came out. He'd broken my trust, withheld information, and now he was excusing another sexual interaction with some lame excuse about being drunk? Bullshit he hadn't known it wasn't his wife. He'd known exactly what he was doing, just like he'd known exactly what he was doing pursuing the lonely, vulnerable, neglected and love-starved woman he recognized me to be. I'd fallen prey to an experienced hunter.

All this time, I'd thought I was special. He'd made me believe we had a connection that superseded our marriages and age difference and any other obstacle to us being together. I excused our sins on the basis that we were meant to be, even if it meant hurting other people to fulfill our fate. But I was just another notch in his belt, wasn't I? Just like I'd suspected the night we consummated our relationship, it was all a lie.

Darren had been right all along.

"The End of Everything"

I'd rather live a familiar life of misery with an asshole, than with a pussy who would save his own ass before saving mine. So I resorted to the predictability of Mom life in T-shirts, glasses and solitude. Ryder and I were busy on the farm anyway; we picked bushels of apples by day and slow-cooked homemade apple butter on the stove by night.

The real estate market trended down with the falling leaves and temperatures, so I changed my cell phone number and switched to a local real estate office where I could start fresh, without the stigma of screwing the boss' son. Darren didn't question the change, because working close to home made logical sense anyway.

With Merrick and the affair behind me, I breathed easier. I didn't worry about anyone calling or showing up. I didn't stress about Darren finding out what I'd done. I just isolated with my son and focused on creating the memories with him that I didn't have with my own mother.

We made construction-paper turkeys to decorate the glass door for Thanksgiving and wrote something we were grateful for on each of their colored feathers. We made reindeer food to sprinkle on our lawn for Christmas. We sent a letter to the North Pole, and baked cookies in the hope that Santa would come eat them all. I'd taken our simple life for granted, and I developed newfound appreciation for the quality time spent with my son.

The holidays were otherwise somber. Henrik hadn't been able to leave the confines of his recliner since June, so Thanksgiving and Christmas Eve were celebrated with a simple meal at Jane and Henrik's home. Henrik

185

couldn't eat much, though. My beloved father-in-law couldn't do anything except exist with the uncomfortable uncertainty of never knowing when his life would finally end.

Then on December 25, 2005, our house phone rang too early.

My eyes popped open, and I instinctively looked down at Ryder to see if he had awoken too. It was dark as night outside, but the glow of the Christmas tree lights across from the couch we'd slept on allowed me to see Ryder's eyes were still closed. With the weight of his body on mine, I couldn't move, but I heard the sound of Darren's voice behind the master bedroom door upstairs. Then I heard sobbing.

The mournful sound made me tearful too. It confirmed what I'd suspected to be the reason for the untimely call. Although we'd known it was coming, we weren't ready to let go of our jolly patriarch.

I wanted to run to Darren, wrap my arms around him, and feel the consolation of his arms around me as we grieved together. No matter our relationship, my heart was sensitive to suffering, and we would both suffer from this tremendous loss.

But before I could do anything, Darren burst out of the bedroom and ran down the stairs so fast he almost fell down them. Then he rushed past the couch to the door. Ryder stirred with all the commotion.

"Darren?" I looked up at him with tearful eyes.

"I gotta go! My dad—" He choked on a sob, then he slammed the door behind him.

Ryder lifted his head and looked at me with sleepy eyes.

"Merry Christmas, little man!" I said brightly, wiping tears from my eyes. I'd become an expert in instantly shifting gears for Ryder. I wanted nothing but happiness for my only child.

Just then, the Christmas tree lights flashed off and then back on. Ryder and I looked over at the tree, but nothing looked amiss—all the ornaments were in place, the gifts under the tree were intact, neither the dog nor cat were near. From where I lay, I could even see the plug firmly stuck into the outlet. Must have been a power surge, I reasoned. The chills running through my body thought otherwise.

"Is that you, Dad?" I whispered, my eyes turned upward. "If it is, I love you. Already miss you! And Merry Christmas!" New tears fell. I couldn't wipe them away fast enough.

"You sad, Mommy?" Ryder asked, wiping my face with one palm.

"Yeah. Grandpa went to Heaven and Mommy misses him," I said, even though Ryder was too young to understand what that meant. I took a deep breath and smiled. "But I'm ready to open presents! Are you?"

Ryder nodded eagerly. So I exchanged my watery eyes and sniffles for exaggerated surprise as I helped Ryder unwrap all the toys and treats "Santa" had brought for him. Then I spent the rest of the day removing them from their bulletproof packaging and installing the appropriate batteries so he could play with them all right away.

Darren called in the midst of everything.

"How's everything going over there?"

"Busy. Mom and I sat with Dad—Dad's body, before calling anyone," he choked on held-back tears.

"I'm sorry you have to go through that. And your mom too. I wish I could be there with you guys." I hoped he'd ask me to come. Even though he'd taken my vehicle, I could drive his work van over. I wouldn't infringe on their mourning without an invitation, though.

"No. Ryder doesn't need to be here and see all this." I understood but still felt excluded. The family should be together, and I thought I was family. "Anyway, they just came for him—the body, I mean. So Mom and I have a lot of calls to make. Gotta call the funeral home about his cremation, gotta call my sister . . ."

"Denise doesn't know yet?"

"No. Mom and I wanted some time before the phone started ringing. If we told Denise, you know how she is. Everyone would know, and it would have gotten a lot crazier a lot sooner." Now I didn't feel so bad about not being there. "So I'm gonna stay here with Mom today," Darren continued. "She needs me. You guys will just have to do whatever, like you normally do."

"Okay, just let me know if there's anything I *can* do from here. I'm . . ." There was nothing more to say that didn't sound stupid or cliché.

Darren broke down crying in an instant anyway. For a moment, we cried together. But later, when night descended and Darren hadn't called again or returned home, I cried alone. He'd lost his father, but he was forgetting I'd lost his father too. He'd forgotten about me altogether.

There wasn't even a seat for me with the family at Henrik's celebration of life. I watched with the rest of the crowd as Jane, Darren, Denise, Brad, and their kids mourned their loss without me. Even Ryder sat with the family, on Darren's lap. I knew then exactly where I stood with everyone, which was alone, like I always was.

"Bad Things"

The year of 2006 started off much better than previous years, mainly because Darren started coming home from work trips more often. I didn't know if he'd always had this time off and chose not to tell me, or if his travel schedule had suddenly lightened, but I was glad to see him be a more present father and husband.

He pulled Ryder on his little sled and took him on four-wheeler rides around the yard. They played cars together on the floor of the living room and watched *Scooby-Doo* while I cooked dinner. Nothing made me happier than seeing Ryder's dimples when he looked up at his dad so adoringly. I was starting to look at Darren the same way again too!

He smiled when I walked in the room. He joked with me, and we laughed together. He took me out on date nights and carried conversations with me. I wondered if Henrik's death had made him realize life was too short to waste miserably. Regardless of the reason, I was finally happy in our marriage, and Darren seemed to be too!

By summer, things had gotten even better. Farm life was in full gear. I kept busy planting, watering, and weeding the gardens while Ryder chased the tractor Darren mowed upon. Sometimes the rooster would chase after Ryder too, which made me chuckle.

Working together towards common goals and having cooperative effort from each other developed newfound respect between us. It was nice to share ideas and future plans for the farm, and for life in general. We really did want the same things, and we were finally on the same side!

Real estate in our sleepy town picked up too, and the steadier flow of income unburdened Darren of the full weight of financial responsibility. I could tell by his positive support and encouragement of my career that the unburdening had lightened him emotionally too. I also benefited by the sense of accomplishment of contributing to the household more, while primarily remaining a stay-at-home mom.

Then, on a Friday afternoon in late June, I came inside for a drink and saw the red light blinking on the phone. Ryder was busy petting the new barn kittens on the porch, so I pressed the button to listen to the new voicemail message.

"I hope your father-in-law died knowing you're a whore! I'll fucking kill you and your fucking son, you lying bitch!"

I froze. I'd heard that voice before. It was Merrick's wife. She'd called just after finding out about me and Merrick last year, to warn that she wouldn't stop calling until Darren knew everything. Fortunately, Darren hadn't been home then or any other time she'd called, and he was out of town now too.

Why was she calling after all this time, though? I understood her issue with me, though I'd argue she needed to take more issue with her husband. But threatening my son's life was crossing a line. He shouldn't suffer for my mistake!

I released the breath I hadn't realized I'd been holding, then ran to the toilet almost too late for my stomach to expunge my sins. My trembling hands could barely wipe the side of my mouth or the sweat from my brow. So I remained on my knees, slumped over, until the room stopped spinning.

When I felt okay enough to get up, I went to the kitchen for that water I'd come in for in the first place. Then I stood against the island, wondering how to handle this. I couldn't risk her calling the house again, on the off-chance Darren might be home. So do I ignore her call and hope she doesn't call again? Do I call her back and give her a piece of my mind? Do I just take her power away by confessing my infidelity to Darren? The latter was obviously the right choice, but I'd waited too long to have a loving husband and doting father to Ryder to ruin it all now!   There was no other way out of this mess, though. I couldn't think of one thing I could say to this woman that would make her leave me alone. She wouldn't believe me if I told her I didn't want Merrick. She wouldn't care if I told her how angry and violent Darren could be. She wouldn't care if Ryder grew up with divorced parents, or just one. She just wanted me to suffer like she had.

As sick as it made me to think about it, I knew I had to tell Darren. I didn't want to, but I couldn't live my life in fear, wondering when she'd resurface or what she'd say or do to achieve vengeance.

So after dropping Ryder off to my mother that Saturday afternoon, I sat on the edge of Henrik's old leather recliner, awaiting Darren's return home from Minnesota. We planned to have one of our date nights, but I couldn't go out with this dark cloud looming over me. I'd have to talk to him as soon as he got home.

Different scenarios ran through my head about how to tell Darren and how he'd react. None made the news any easier to deliver, nor any easier to hear. I rubbed my temples with my clammy hands, ignoring the pain building in my upper back. That was the least of the punishments I'd suffer, and a small price to pay for what I'd done.

Awhile later, Darren burst through the door excitedly. "Let's get naked!"

I looked at him, tears welling in my eyes, knowing this was the last time I'd see this wonderful new husband I hadn't had enough time with.

He got serious at the sight of me. "What's wrong? What's going on?"

I still didn't know what to say. "I did something really bad," I insinuated.

Darren sat on the couch and leaned forward to position himself face-to-face with me. He even laid out his palms in front of me as a show of support, but I couldn't consciously lay my hands in his.

"What is it, Dana? What did you do?"

I hated stalling, but I couldn't say it. "Um . . . someone was inappropriate with me."

His head jerked, as if short-circuiting. He placed his hands on his thighs, ready to spring into action and kick the ass of whomever had caused my pain. Then he looked at me intently. "Did someone touch you? *Who?*"

Although I was knowingly misleading him, I went with it to avoid saying what I knew I eventually had to confess. "Um . . . yes. Merrick. At my old office."

His chest heaved. "Where? Did he do it at the office? What happened?" Darren thought I was the innocent victim I implied. I wished I could leave it at that.

"Well . . . it wasn't just him."

"What do you mean? Did you guys kiss or something? What the fuck happened, Dana?" His eyes widened with panic. There was nowhere else to go except exactly where I didn't want to go.

I closed my eyes, exhaled out of my mouth, then said, "We hugged. And kissed. Then . . ." I paused, gulped, breathed deeply, then opened my eyes and said what would be the nail in the coffin of our marriage. "We had sex."

I looked at Darren sorrowfully, expecting him to slap me. I wouldn't have blamed him if he did.

He didn't look at me, though. His eyes moved back and forth and up and down, as if looking for answers in places where there were none. I knew the struggle to find reason, because I'd searched my mind for the same answers and came up empty too.

"How many times, Dana?" He looked me dead in the eyes. "If it was just once, I'll go beat the shit out of that bastard for doing that to you!"

I looked down at my fidgety toes. I really didn't want to answer that question.

"How many times, Dana?" Darren shifted in his seat uncomfortably, knowing he probably didn't want to hear the answer either.

I looked up at Darren and took a deep breath that made my chest and shoulders heave with the weight of the burden I was carrying in my heart. But I remained quiet. Darren's clenched teeth and deeply furrowed brow indicated a rage within him that made me nervous to tell the truth. I was truly afraid of what he might do to punish me.

"HOW MANY?" Darren screamed. "Twice? Ten? More? How many times?"

"I don't know!" I screamed back.

"What do you mean you don't know? Jesus Christ, Dana! How many times did you fuck this guy? I could get over one time, maybe two or three. But more than that? More than that means you wanted it!" He punched the couch beside him, stood up, turned around aimlessly, then sat back down.

Darren was right. I had wanted it. I'd wanted to be wanted, and Merrick had wanted me when Darren hadn't. And it had felt good! I'd been happy, I'd smiled again. So I'd allowed it. Even though everything in me had told me not to succumb to infidelity, I hadn't wanted to let go of how Merrick made me feel. But Darren couldn't handle the truth right now. So, I lied. "I didn't. I swear I didn't."

"Are you fucking kidding me?" he yelled, standing over me. "Where did you guys do it? You didn't do it in our bed, did you?"

Details of when and where could never be erased from memory, so there was no benefit to making the situation come alive in his mind any more than just knowing it happened. "It doesn't matter, Darren," was all I would share.

An exaggerated frown overtook Darren's face. His simultaneously surprised and frightened eyes begged for a reason to make sense of the tumult in his heart. His childlike vulnerability struck me as odd for someone who sought control and dominance over others. Maybe he wasn't the cruel and heartless man I knew him as. Maybe he was trying to protect this hurt little boy I saw in front of me, with the facade of a harsh bully no one would mess with, just like I was trying to soothe the abused and neglected little girl inside me by pleasing people for approval.

My heart and my eyes cried for both of us then. Darren tried to maintain his composure, but then his trembling lips gave way to heart-wrenching, open-mouthed sobs which mourned what we had finally become as a couple, and what I'd effectively torn apart. I'd never thought it would end this way.

Then, without warning, Darren grabbed my arm and forcibly pulled me down the hallway. I didn't know where he was taking me or what he would do, but I didn't resist. I deserved to be punished for what I did.

In Ryder's bedroom, Darren threw me down onto the brightly colored tractor-and-dump-truck comforter covering the small twin bed. Then he tore my shorts and panties down. Sex? I was completely confused but afraid to challenge him, so I remained still, my arms spread outward and legs hanging off the bottom corner of the bed. Darren unbuttoned his jeans while he knelt on the bed between my legs and entered me.

He placed his elbows on either side of my head so I couldn't move, then went at me hard. Spit spewed as he grunted with every forceful thrust. I couldn't turn my head away, so I closed my eyes instead as he roughed up my lifeless little body.

When he'd finished marking his territory, he stood, zipped his pants, and demanded, "Get your clothes on and get the fuck out of my house."

Then he left the room.

I lay there a few minutes, sprawled out half naked, just as he'd left me. I didn't know how to process what had just happened. He needed to feel powerful and in control of me, I knew. But to do what he did where I read to our son every night, and where our innocent son played every day? How could I see this room as a safe place after this? Or had that been his intention—to put a stain on the one person and place that remained unscathed through the tumult of our life? Either way, involving Ryder in this in any way sickened me.

Feelings of shame, disgust, regret, guilt, sadness, and revulsion took turns with my psyche until I decided to feel nothing at all. I zoned out. Numbed my mind. When my thoughts calmed, I re-dressed and quietly gathered my things.

As I approached the door to leave, I turned to Darren and whispered, "I'm going now."

He sat in his dad's chair and stared at the TV. He didn't acknowledge my goodbye. He didn't even flinch. So I took my purse and keys from the coat rack and opened the door. I turned back once more, half expecting Darren to tell me to stay, but he didn't. So I left.

Then I drove the hour and a half to my mother's house, where Ryder was. Despite the abuse I endured as a child, I was mature enough to understand the abuse was specific to me, for being the physical manifestation of the teenage pregnancy my mother was ashamed of. My mother and stepfather were, in fact, better grandparents to Ryder than they were parents to me.

"Please don't ask any questions," I said as I walked through the door and past my mother.

Her home was the last place I wanted to be, but I needed my son. He was the only person who truly loved me, and the only one who made me feel safe. So I went straight to the room Ryder slept in and held him closely, as if holding on to any remaining innocence left in my world.

"Talk Is Cheap"

One night at my mother's turned into two weeks. I told Ryder it was a long sleepover at Grandma and Grandpa's, like a vacation. He was only three, so he neither opposed nor questioned the extended stay, perhaps because it was a change of scenery and a break from our routine. So he played with his toys on the living room floor every day while I read whatever books Barnes and Noble offered about recovering from infidelity. When my mother and stepfather came home from work, they took turns amusing their only grandchild, and I'd take a long walk alone to try to get a hold of Darren. Every call went about the same.

"How're things going?" I'd try to spur conversation.

"Fine."

"Dog doing okay without us there during the day?"

"Yep."

"How's Kitty? I've had him since I was nineteen. He must be wondering where I disappeared to!"

Silence.

"Ryder misses you! You want me to have him call you later?"

"He's the only reason I'm even having this conversation. Otherwise, I'd have thrown your cheating ass out. But no, I'm not ready to talk to him."

That was rich coming from Darren, after all the times *he'd* fooled around on *me*. But I wanted to come back home. "I know. For what it's worth, I'm sorry. I—" The dial tone stopped me mid-sentence.

Still, I called every evening like clockwork. At some point, he had to talk to me about what I did, or at least let me know whether or not he wanted to stay married.

I was adamant that we try to make it work. Maybe I needed to redeem myself after my mistake, or maybe I wasn't ready to admit failure by getting divorced, but by God, I would not give up without a fight.

Then one night, Darren surprised me. "You and Ryder can come home, but only if you agree to marriage counseling."

I don't believe for a second that rehashing the issues that tore a couple apart will restore the good will needed to save the relationship. In fact, I think counseling does the exact opposite. But Ryder and I needed to get back to some normalcy, and I'd do anything for my son. "Okay. I'll look online for someone in our area and make an appointment."

"I'm doing this for Ryder," Darren clarified. "If it were just you and me, I'd be done. I just want to make sure you know that."

"I understand." I understood his intentional and constant reminder of where I ranked with him, which was lower than low. I was scum of the earth for what I'd done, which was interesting considering all the transgressions he'd committed towards me in the past. But I supposed we'd work that all out in counseling.

Our first session with the marriage counselor was just a few days later. Darren and I sat several feet apart, facing this averagely attractive and slim brunette, whose kind eyes assessed us from behind her thin round glasses. She dressed conservatively and sat with her legs crossed in a high-backed, floral-upholstered chair.

The room was the same as every other counselor's office: a small lamp on a side table cast a calming golden glow on the neutrally painted walls, and we sat in the midst of plants and wooden bookshelves full of books about the psychology of family dynamics and other issues which caused marital and family demise.

"What couple do you know who you feel you are most similar to?" she began.

Darren and I simultaneously answered, "Uncle Jose and Aunt Leila!"

We looked at each other, surprised we'd agreed on something, then I looked back to the counselor to explain. "That's my uncle and his wife.

They fight *all* the time. Like, screaming insults at each other at the tops of their lungs."

"Yeah, it's not a good situation," Darren added.

"Okay! Acknowledging what your relationship looks like is a good start," the counselor encouraged. "So then, what brings you here?"

Of course, Darren started with my affair, knowing he'd gain the counselor's sympathy right off the bat. Then he told her I'd been diagnosed with bipolar depression, as if that justified his position as the forever victim of the mean and moody wife he made me out to be. He seemed satisfied when we left, though, since the counselor had believed everything he said and seemed to sympathize with his plight.

Our second session was a week later. The counselor dove right into the affair. "How do you feel about what she did, Darren?"

He wiped invisible tears and sniffled. After a delay for effect, he responded, "I'm devastated." He dropped his head, put his hand on his forehead to hide his eyes, then sobbed. At least that's what it sounded like.

The counselor looked at me expectantly. A wife who wanted to save her marriage would have apologized profusely for the betrayal, then consoled and reassured her husband that she loved him and that it would never happen again. Instead, I sat stone-faced. I'd already apologized. Every single day, I'd apologized. I was truly sorry too. But I refused to coddle Darren when he was playing the victim. I was a victim too, but no one stopped to ask me about all the horrible things he said and did to me that made me vulnerable to the charm of another man. Darren and the counselor were busy making me feel like the villain in this marriage, and it took every ounce of self-discipline to sit there and listen to all the bullshit without defending myself.

"You seem indifferent towards Darren's devastation," the counselor said.

"There's no excuse for what I did," I admitted. "It was wrong and I wish I'd handled my marriage instead of seeking my needs outside of it. But it's hard to have a relationship with someone who's not there. I mean, he works out of state mostly, and he won't even call home except maybe once every few days for a couple minutes!"

"So communication is an issue?" She was pulling a trick from Psych 101: repeating what she heard me say.

"It's not an issue. It's non-existent!" I snapped. Darren instantly stopped his show of crying. Funny how eliciting my rudeness could appease him.

"What do *you* think about the communication between you and Dana?" The counselor asked, inviting Darren back into the conversation.

"It could be better." He always said the right things to the right people.

"Let's talk about communication, then," the counselor said as she handed us each a paper titled "Fair Fighting". She proceeded to read us the instructions for resolving conflict, giving us examples of how to speak respectfully instead of reacting, and telling us to actively listen to each other without interruption. Then we made appointments for our next few sessions.

I highly doubted either of us would stop screaming at each other to check the sheet for nicer verbiage, but I put the papers on the refrigerator to give the appearance that I gave a shit. Plus, it was easier to follow an instruction sheet than get a divorce. At some point, though, one of us threw the papers in the garbage, which was just as well. We never referred to them anyway.

We kept going to counseling for the sake of keeping our family unit together, but by the end of the year, little else was resolved. I thought it a waste of time and money to hear him bitch about things like laundry. Apparently, he never had clean socks. And the house was tidy but not clean, which he didn't understand because I was home all day with Ryder. I was a failure as a wife, and I think he expected the counselor to cure me into a happy marriage.

"The dog is always pawing her water bowl because *no one* ever fills it!" Darren complained, clearly referring to *me* as "no one."

"Have you considered purchasing a large self-watering bowl for the dog?" The counselor suggested.

No, he hadn't, but *I* rushed out to buy one at her suggestion. I wished I could laugh at the ridiculousness of spending thousands of dollars for marriage counseling so a water bowl could suppress Darren's anger, but it wasn't funny.

When we arrived for what would be our last session, the counselor had a video camera pointed toward our chairs. We looked at each other with raised brows, so she explained. "I set this up so we can review your body language and tone of voice when you communicate with each other here. Sometimes seeing yourself from a different perspective will help you to understand how the other perceives you."

"Okay." We smiled for the camera awkwardly. I never even liked my picture being taken, let alone a camera recording me.

"How are things going at home?" the counselor began. She looked back and forth, waiting for one of us to respond. Neither of us seemed to know how to act with the camera recording, so we remained quiet, hoping the other would answer.

Darren finally spoke. "I don't think she loves me anymore." Then he hung his head.

I looked at him quizzically. Was he seriously putting on a show for the camera now?

"How does it make you feel to hear that?" the counselor asked me.

The pressure had built up. I exploded. "How does it make me feel? I don't know. Indifferent? Maybe a little pissed off that I have done everything he's asked, let him buy everything he's ever wanted, lived the life he chose for me, and now I have to sit here and listen to how I've failed him because his fucking socks aren't white enough! Darren has told me many times he doesn't like me and that I'm no fun. One of his so-called friends even told me Darren hates me, then hit on me after that, even asked me how I shaved my pubic hair. Not the kinda guy I wanted to believe, but Darren hasn't done anything to prove him wrong! Up until recently, he rarely came home on his days off, ignored me when he was home, and treated me like shit on the rare occasion he decided to grace me with the slightest attention. Add onto that all the times he's gone out with friends and come home to tell me he made out with someone in a bar, or got told he had a big dick by a chick he allowed to give him a hand job—oh, wait, that happened twice! Two women have given my husband hand jobs! So how am I supposed to feel? Please tell me, because I think I've been pretty fucking tolerant!"

"Well, maybe if you weren't such a fucking bitch all the time!" Darren's head turned towards me, slowly, like the possessed little girl in the movie

The Exorcist.

The counselor's eyes and mouth widened at once. I was sorry she had to hear such vulgar language, but I couldn't help feel satisfaction that our true dynamic had finally been revealed.

"Dana, would you please have a seat in the waiting area?" she firmly ordered. I gladly left her with the lovely Mr. Hyde.

From the brightly lit waiting area just outside her office, I could hear her discipline, "You may *not* speak to your wife like that. The hostility in your tone of voice, as well as your word choice, is unproductive to the counseling process."

"Well, she's a fucking bitch, and you're finally seeing her for who she is!" Darren yelled to spin things around. "And I'll talk to her however I want! Nobody tells me how to speak to my own fucking wife!"

"Do not use that kind of language in this office, Darren," the counselor scolded.

"*You* don't get to tell me what I can or can't say *either*!" Darren shouted before storming out. The office door bounced off the wall so hard it closed itself. I briefly caught a glimpse of the counselor sitting in her chair with her mouth open before I chased after him.

He was already climbing into his work van when I caught up with him in the parking lot.

"I'm never fucking coming back here, so you and your fucking counselor can enjoy your time together," he declared, referring to the upcoming sessions we'd already scheduled. "I'm not the one who needs the fucking help anyway, you bipolar bitch!"

"I'm so sorry I'm not perfect like you, Darren!" I lashed back. "Maybe I'm not even bipolar! Maybe I just married an asshole!"

Darren slammed his door and screeched his tires, tearing out of the parking lot. I didn't even care, though. Nor did I care that he was already locked away in the master bedroom when I returned home with Ryder an hour later. Nor when we awoke to find him already gone on a business trip the next morning.

He was done with counseling, and I was done taking his shit.

"Basket Case"

A major storm hit the Midwest in January 2007. Ryder and I were snowed in for weeks. Every day, I'd awaken with the hope of sunshine to melt enough snow for us to at least pull our SUV out of the garage. But every day, I'd awaken to the same dull blue sky and see the snow-laden branches of all the evergreens surrounding our property weighed down like my mood. It was like living in the movie *The Shining*.

It was still and quiet, all day and all night. No cars passed on the impassable roads. Not one animal print could be seen on the snow-covered ground. Even the house was quiet because the phone rarely rang. I had no friends or family I talked to with any regularity anymore.

So every day was exactly the same as the one before. I built LEGO houses for Ryder, so Pepper could destroy the hours of work with a single step. We watched the same *Tom and Jerry* and *Scooby-Doo* videos over and over. I'd jog around our kitchen island to get rid of excess energy, and Ryder thought it was fun to chase after me. I'd do anything to prevent myself from painting "REDRUM" all over our walls!

We'd been pretty isolated since my admission to infidelity. I practically stopped showing houses, because every time I did, I was accused of screwing someone. Same if I went to the office. Darren had turned into my prison warden, even timing my trips to the store to get cat food. It was my fault, though. I obviously couldn't be trusted around anyone with a penis.

So, despite the lack of improvement in our relationship, I was happy when Darren called in the midst of a six-week business trip to California. He was my only contact with the outside world.

"Lenny and I are on a beach getting tattoos! The weather here is perfect!" he bragged.

"Whaddya mean you're getting tattoos?" Darren was so particular about his professional appearance, always making sure his shirt was tucked and every hair was in place to impress others. I couldn't understand how tattoos fit into that image.

"We're just hanging out on the beach having a few beers and decided to get them!"

Jealous he was kicking back on a beach while I was cooped up with an energetic toddler, I jabbed, "I didn't realize we had money to spend on tattoos. I haven't had a real estate sale in months!" "Where the fuck did all our money go?" Darren accused.

"What are you talking about? *You're* the one out there drinking and getting tattoos! I couldn't spend money if I wanted to! The last time I was able to leave the house, our debit card was rejected for a three-dollar charge at the post office!" It had been humiliating to hold up the line of impatient people while rummaging for coins in my purse with Ryder on my left hip. The cashier ended up paying the balance for me to prevent any more upset in the line behind me.

Silence on the other end told me I was out of line for snapping back, so I took a deep breath and attempted to engage in conversation. "Dare I ask what kind of tattoo you got?"

"A thorny vine around my ankle!"

The lack of meaning and symbolism in this tattoo he "had" to have annoyed me. "That's great. You don't call for how many days, and when you do, you tell me you spent money we don't have on a fucking tattoo because you're drunk on a beach and just felt like getting one? Must be nice to be you." I said, using one of his own lines on him.

"You're always such a fucking bitch! *That's* why I don't call you!"

I moved into the bathroom and closed the door so Ryder wouldn't hear me from the living room. He was occupied with toy tractors and a movie anyway.

"Maybe I'm a bitch because my husband never calls me and when he does, he doesn't even ask how his wife and son are doing!"

"It's hard to give a shit about you when you're such a cunt!"

"Then don't call me anymore, you fucking drunk!" I hung up, then curled into a ball on the floor by the tub. I was lonely enough without the constant arguing to remind me he wasn't happy either.

The phone rang and rang, then stopped, then rang and rang again, then stopped. I knew it was Darren, so I didn't answer. Everything I had to say to him had all been said before. We just went in circles, and I didn't have the emotional stamina for another go-round right now.

"Mom! Open the door!" Ryder knocked. I'd left him too long, I knew, but I didn't want him to see me anxious or upset.

"I'm coming, cutie pie! Mommy just needs a minute!" I called out in a fake, high-pitched voice. I heard the pitter-patter of his little feet returning to the living room, but knew he would give me exactly a minute, if even.

So I splashed water on my face, rubbed off my smeared mascara, then went to the living room to watch *Chicken Little* with my little man. Although we'd seen it over and over, Ryder looked at me as he burst into laughter at the same scenes every single time. His exaggerated joy was infectious, and it made me burst into laughter with him. Then, while the credits rolled, we sang and danced to "Don't Go Breaking My Heart" with the characters on the screen. Ryder's version of dancing was jumping up and down on the brown leather sofa, while I held his hands for safety and bounced from side to side with him. I had to be careful when I sang, though, because if I sang Elton John's parts, Ryder would correct me, "Just the girl parts, Mommy!"

We ended our night in a bubble bath. I got in with him, wearing my red triangle bikini, and sat at the back of the tub watching him play with little foam cars and draw on the shower walls with bath crayons.

"Hand me the shampoo bottle, would you?" I pointed to the corner ledge behind Ryder. He took the bottle, unscrewed the cap, and handed the bottle to me. "Thank you, little man!"

While I poured shampoo into my palm, Ryder flipped up the top of the cap he'd kept and set it on my head. "You look like a toilet, Mommy!"

He cracked me up. "Well, thanks, I guess!"

"When is Daddy going to sleep over again?" he asked. I abruptly went quiet and stared at Ryder with a crinkled brow. "I like when he sleeps at our house," Ryder added matter-of-factly.

His innocent perception of what was really neglect and abandonment left me speechless. I thought I occupied his time enough to prevent notice of his absent parent, and that I loved him enough that it didn't matter Darren was gone so much. I wondered where his mind was, that he would bring up his dad in the midst of a funny moment.

"Um, I don't know, sweetie. Soon."

Then, just as quickly as he'd saddened, Ryder was back to making engine noises while moving a foam car across the top of the bath water.

Ryder fell asleep as soon as I laid him in the master bed with me. I was still wound up from the call with Darren, so I turned on a mindless TV show to distract me from my thoughts.

Then the phone rang. It was too late for a casual call. It was probably Darren. I didn't want a continuation of our previous call, but I couldn't let the phone wake Ryder either.

"Are you okay, Dana?" Jane asked as soon as I answered.

What a weird thing to ask! Plus, I was surprised to hear her voice on the line at all at this hour. "Yeah, why? Are *you* okay?"

"I'm fine. I just wanted to make sure *you* were because Darren called and asked me to come to your house to check on you. I thought it was a strange thing to ask, but he said you were upset earlier, and he couldn't get a hold of you to make sure you were okay. You know I don't like driving at night, though, so I thought to call instead."

What kind of game was Darren playing, lying to his mother like that? "I'm sorry he involved you in our argument, but I'm fine," I reassured her. "Ryder and I are in bed. He's already asleep."

"Well, you *sound* fine," she commented, "so I won't keep you. Get some rest, and call if you need anything!"

"Will do, and same goes for you!"

When I hung up, I was livid he'd given Jane the impression I needed a wellness check. Was he trying to set me up to look unstable? I wouldn't put it past him to file for divorce, then fight me for custody of Ryder, using my mental health diagnoses to make me appear like an unfit parent.

I would never let that happen, though. Ryder was all I had in this world, so Darren would have to kill me before I'd ever let him take my baby away from me.

"Without Me"

D arren returned home in March of 2007, significantly colder and more aloof with me. Only Ryder deserved his dad's time and affection, and Darren made that much more of a show of ignoring me to demonstrate how little I meant to him in comparison to our son. He'd greet Ryder with enthusiastic smiles, then glare at me with hateful disdain. He'd pack Ryder in the car to go for ice cream but leave me behind without a word. He kissed Ryder goodbye when he left for work or wherever, but I didn't even warrant a glance. It was making me mad. Crazy mad.

On a Saturday afternoon, I was in the kitchen preparing a snack for Ryder. Darren walked past me to leave. He didn't say a word or look my way. So when he put his hand on the doorknob, I asked, "Do you even care about me?"

He turned to face me. "I refuse to argue with you," he said arrogantly, as if suddenly so mature. Then he opened the door to leave.

"Why are you doing this?!" I shrieked, rushing to force the door closed with both hands. I wouldn't let him escape me without explanation.

He stared at me with such indifference, then looked over at Ryder who played on the floor in front of the TV, non-verbally implying what an unfit mother I was to fight in front of our son. I'd have normally moved the fight elsewhere, but he'd driven me to wild emotion I couldn't control.

"*Answer me!*" I screamed. My lungs pained under the strain.

Darren looked right through me. I was invisible and non-existent to him. Me—his wife, the mother of his child. I was nothing and nobody, except an occasional roll in the sack.

Triggered by childhood memories of neglect, my breaths quickened into the pant of a dog on a hot summer day. I looked back and forth and all around me, looking for a way out—out of this situation, out of my body, out of this life. Overwhelmed with feelings of blatant rejection, I needed Darren to put soothing arms around me and tell me he loved me, or at least that everything would be okay. But he didn't. He just stood there, staring at me hatefully.

I had to do something drastic to get Darren's attention. Something completely insane he couldn't ignore. Intellect tried to dissuade me, but I was desperate for soothing, acknowledgment, even an argument! Or maybe I just needed a Xanax to calm myself instead . . . Wait, that was it!

I grabbed my bottle of Xanax out of the kitchen cupboard. I poured most of the pills into my cupped hand and held it up to Darren's face. "I'm going to take all of these! Is that what you want? Do you want me to die?"

He looked down at me reproachfully. My sorrowful eyes pleaded for the tiniest gesture of care or concern, but he remained unmoved.

So I threw the pills towards my mouth, allowing some to be ingested. Then I panicked. I couldn't be sure how many pills I'd swallowed. I hadn't meant to swallow any! I just wanted Darren to care enough to stop me from swallowing them at all! But he hadn't. Jesus Christ, which one of us was more fucked up?!

With fearful eyes, I looked to Darren for help. He looked down at the pills scattered about the floor around us instead. Then he walked over to Ryder, picked him up, and carried him outside.

He abandoned me. Left the pills to do his dirty work for him. Had that been his intention? To make me so desperate for his attention that I would do something stupid to get it? He couldn't be that cruel, could he? I mean, he'd been in the past, but I thought we were past that! Or maybe we weren't, and that's what this was all about. He wanted me dead, as retribution for the affair.

I didn't have time to make sense of things, though. I didn't know what effect the pills would have and when. I needed Darren to help me, or get help for me, to purge them from my body before irreversible consequences occurred.

I walked out to the porch and saw Darren pushing Ryder on the swing set behind the house. He smiled at Ryder, as if it were just another day, completely ignoring the fact that he'd seen me swallow too many prescription pills. Triggered by his lack of concern for me, I ran to my vehicle, hoping he would see me and ask where I was going. But he didn't.

I knew I should go back into the house and try to purge the pills myself, but anger demanded that I follow through with my attention-seeking tantrum. I threw the Explorer in reverse and accelerated at high speed down the two-hundred-foot gravel driveway. Before turning out onto the road, I screeched to a stop and looked in my rear-view mirror. Darren wasn't running after my vehicle to stop me like I wanted him to. He'd called my bluff. We both knew I wasn't leaving without Ryder. And as I reversed to return the vehicle to the garage, I knew he'd have more reason to call me crazy now too.

"Why don't you give a fuck about me? Huh?" I yelled out on my way back to the house. I really wanted to know, actually, but Darren ignored me. Ryder didn't look my way either. He was so enthralled with his father's attention, I wondered whether I meant anything to *him*! Maybe I was nothing to everyone. Was I that hard to love?

Dejected and depressed, I went into the house and sat in the corner of my kitchen floor. The thump of my body against the lazy susan reminded me how tired I was, emotionally and physically. I didn't want to do this anymore—fighting, feeling, acting crazy. I just wanted to walk away. Why I wouldn't was beyond me. I'd stayed for Darren's family before, but Ryder was the only reason now—a reason that was starting to sound like an excuse for my fear of the unknown.

I couldn't think anymore, though. My brain was getting fuzzy, and my drowsy eyes weren't helping. They were too tired to even produce tears. I could feel my body becoming limp. I was strangely calm, staring into space, thinking nothing, and better yet, feeling nothing. My breathing slowed. Maybe I would fall into eternal sleep and be freed of my earthly pain. Maybe I should have driven into the river, like that deranged mother in the news had done with her children. Wait. Children. Mother. Ryder!

Regaining some sense of myself for a moment, I crawled about the floor and tried to pick up the pills I'd spilled. I'd have never forgiven myself if Ryder got a hold of one. My body wouldn't move as quickly as I would have liked, but it was all I could do to salvage the little bit of energy remaining in my over-medicated body.

Darren walked in then. I looked up at him with sad, tearful eyes that begged for sympathy. I noticed he didn't have Ryder with him. Thank God! I didn't want my son to see me like this. Where was he anyway? Not that I could go get him in this condition. My strength was escaping me quickly.

"Please help me," I whimpered.

Darren reached for my hand. Relieved he was finally exhibiting some care for me, I took it and used it to try to leverage myself up. My legs were like jelly underneath me, so I struggled. Then Darren took my other hand and pulled. What was he doing? Suddenly fearful, I squirmed to release his grip, but couldn't. He dragged me down the hall, into the bathroom, and shook my hand free. As the top half of my body clunked onto the floor, Darren closed the door to the bathroom. I heard the door to the house close after that.

My strong will wanted to get up and run far away from here, but my body was too weak to move. I was going to die here, on the bathroom floor, as alone as I'd felt in this world until Ryder was born, and it was all my fault.

I envisioned Darren playing the sad widower of a mentally unstable wife who was so depressed she'd taken her own life. He'd thrive in others' pity and glorification of raising Ryder alone, telling them how he loved me but couldn't save me from my own demons.

I wouldn't give him the satisfaction, though. Ryder was my life, and I wasn't ready to leave him. However, right now I couldn't do anything but stare at the base of the toilet and pray. It was the last thing I saw before one solitary tear dripped down my cheek and my eyes closed.

Then my eyes popped open. I was alive! I could barely make out the dark knots in the pine wood ceiling, though, as the descending dusk darkened the house. Hours must have gone by.

Groggy and disoriented, I rolled over and got up on my knees. My back was stiff from laying on the hard floor, so I took my time to stand, using the bathroom counter for leverage. The shadows in the mirror reflected a curly mess of tangled hair and bloodshot eyes. I looked like I'd fought my way through the depths of hell. But I was composed now, and ready to be Ryder's mother again. I just needed to find him.

After a deep breath and a crack of the back, I emerged from the bathroom to see Darren and Ryder on the living room sofa watching cartoons. Neither looked my way. I stood at the edge of the hallway, where it opened into the shared living room and kitchen area, and waited to be noticed. It was as if I didn't exist, like I was watching their lives without me play out before my eyes. It made me wonder whether I was really there, or if I was a ghost looking in on my family after . . . I couldn't even think about that. I was here. I'd survived taking a few too many pills. And Darren was just an asshole.

Anyway, I was thankful to see Ryder safe at home, where he should be. I'd half expected to have to go in search of the two, then fight with Darren to get Ryder back from him. I had neither the mental nor physical energy for either.

The buzz of my phone distracted me then. I took it from the kitchen counter to see who it was. I wasn't exactly in the mood to talk to anyone, especially my mother, whose name was shown on the caller ID. It was strange of her to call, unless it was something important, so I decided to answer. I walked past Darren and Ryder and slouched into Henrik's old recliner first, hunkering down for my mother's endless rambling. "Hello?"

"We're on our way to your house to get you, Dane. We can take you to a hospital or to our house for a while . . ." The rushed panic in her voice caught me off guard. She'd never been concerned about me *before*. All the times I'd needed my mother, she was indifferent to me. So what suddenly changed? And what the hell was she talking about? Coming to get me? Taking me to a hospital? "Darren said you tried to overdose on some pills! Why would you do that? Why would you try to commit suicide when I just buried my brother a month ago? How could you do this to me?"

Thankful I hadn't inconvenienced my mother with my death, I looked over at Darren with complete disgust. The mother fucker had left me for dead, and called the one person who might hate me more than he did. Un-fucking-believable.

"I don't know what's going on or what you were told," I lied, "but I'm perfectly fine. I don't need you to come here. I don't need a hospital—"

"You need help, Dane! We just want to get you somewhere where—"

Anger pushed the bounds of my patience. She only cared about me when there was an opportunity to present herself as a good mother. When had she ever called and asked, "Are you okay, Dana? Do you need to talk about anything, Dana? How are you feeling, Dana?" She never stopped to think about me for one god-damn second, so I refused to entertain her bullshit concern now.

"I'm not gonna say this again, Mom. Do not come here. I'm not leaving my house. I'm not leaving my son. And I don't need you or your damn help!" I glanced Darren's way again. He remained entranced with the TV, still acting like he couldn't see or hear me, even though I knew he could. Amazing how he could cause such chaos and then sit back without any remorse or concern.

"We're already on the way, Dane," my mother persisted. "Darren said you need help and—"

"Stop with the help crap! You don't even know what's happened here today, but you just assume it's *me* who needs help? Why is it always me? Your husband abuses me, I'm lying for attention. My husband mistreats me, I'm the one who's crazy. Jesus Christ, Mom! When the fuck are you ever going to be on my side? You haven't even asked me what my side is!" I took a few deep breaths to calm myself, taking note that Darren was still ignoring me. "I seriously need you to stop, Mom. I'm fine. Ryder's fine. Everything's fine. I'm not going anywhere with anyone. I'm staying here, in my house, with my son. I absolutely will not leave Ryder."

"We'll bring Ryder if Darren will let us, but we're coming for you!"

She always pushed. "What don't you understand? *I am not coming with you*! And after everything that's happened today, I just want to be left alone for fuck's sake!"

"We just want to get you the help you need."

"Like you helped me by strangling me and throwing me down half a flight of stairs when I was sixteen? Then locked me up in a mental institution after I reported the abuse to the police? Thanks, but I'm good, Mom."

I ended the call, knowing I had a better chance of sanity with the motherfucker who'd left me for dead, who, of course, was still staring at the TV. His lack of humanity repulsed me.

Like I said, I wouldn't leave Ryder. My only options were to leave with my son or return to my normal routine. But because Darren had involved my mother and stepfather, who'd now attest to my incompetence to care for Ryder after whatever they were told happened today, I really had only one choice.

So, without a word, I took Ryder for his nighttime bath. Then we went to bed. And like all the other bad days and nights, I prayed I was doing the right thing by staying in a loveless marriage for the sake of my son. I just hoped I would survive this loving sacrifice.

"You Oughta Know"

They say if you always do what you've always done, you'll always get what you always got. I decided to test this psychological theory by doing something different in my marriage. If the theory proved correct, Darren's reaction to me would change as a consequence, hopefully for the better. We both knew I wasn't leaving, but I wasn't going to live in misery either.

I figured I'd start by being nice, to insert some basic courtesy into our relationship. No fighting, no cussing and insulting—although I'd argue the point that I only engaged on that level to defend myself against the same. And since the best quality Darren saw in me was my appearance, I'd make myself irresistible too. He'd commented too many times on my lack of effort to look good for him.

My experiment started when Darren arrived home from a business trip the day before Mother's Day, 2007. I walked out to meet him at his van, wearing my best Stepford-wife smile. My red-stained lips matched the red accents on my fitted yellow top. A padded bra made my bosom look big and buoyant for B-cups. I completed the look with very short white shorts and white lace wedges. They accentuated my newly toned and tanned legs. I'd been walking at least five miles a day in the early summer sun, strolling Ryder along the back roads, and it showed.

"Hi! How was your drive?"

Darren climbed out of his van and slid by me, contorting his body to avoid touch. He was dressed in khaki pants and a tucked-in polo shirt, which struck me as odd for his long ride home from Minnesota. Maybe he had a work meeting before leaving, I thought. But that didn't explain the avoidance. I wanted to keep the mood light, though, so I made myself useful by going to the back of his van for his bags.

"I got 'em," he said, averting his eyes. Avoidance meant guilt. What was he guilty of? I wondered as I followed him into the house.

Before I caught up to him, he locked himself in the main floor bathroom. *Maybe he wants to change out of his work clothes*, I thought. So I took the garbage out while I waited.

Just as I turned from closing the gate to the garbage enclosure, Darren appeared behind me. I jumped and shrieked, then chuckled at my exaggerated startle. Darren wasn't laughing with me like he usually did, though. I looked at him inquisitively, wondering why not.

Keep things light and happy, I reminded myself! So I smiled and moved towards him, attempting to give him a proper greeting of a hug and kiss, but he stepped away. Rejecting affection now too? It was usually the other way around!

"You *are* a good mother," Darren said. The emphasis on the "are" was pointed to make me aware of what I was not, which was a good wife.

Then he handed me a small white daisy he must have picked from our yard on his way to startle me. I hesitantly took the flower, as if accepting it was like sealing some sort of deal, though I had no idea what I was consenting to.

His strange behavior was worrisome. His refusal of my touch and affection were more so, since he often complained that I neither initiated nor granted him the sex he craved. So I tested him. "You wanna . . . ?"

"Nooo," he prolonged. "I had a long drive. Was hoping to just chill and have a few beers." Then he started walking back towards the house. Now I was suspicious. He'd never refused sex. But if he wasn't getting it from me . . .

I followed Darren into the house. "I don't think we have any, but I can go get you some!" I offered eagerly. Normally, I'd be put off by his drinking, but perhaps the alcohol would tell me what was really going on with him.

Darren opened the refrigerator to confirm the beer inventory. None, just as I'd said. "Yeah, if you don't mind." He walked past me to his dad's chair and sat with the remote.

"Not at all! I'll be back in a few." Maybe my servitude would do the double duty of instilling some good faith between us, so I was off to the liquor store to buy him some beer.

While I was there, the older male cashier gave me an obvious and appreciative once-over. I smiled, glad someone had noticed my effort to look sexy.

The customer ahead of me in line looked back to see who the cashier was checking out. Then he said, "That your beer?"

"No, sir. It's for my husband," I responded.

The man looked at the cashier and commented, "I sure wish I had an old lady who looked like her!" He looked back at me, then back to the cashier. "And brought me beer to boot!" They chuckled while I smiled at the compliment. It confirmed for me that I'd succeeded in making myself attractive enough to warrant special attention. Why Darren wasn't taking the bait was still a mystery, though.

He was watching TV when I returned. I opened a beer and handed it to him, then plopped on the couch playfully and crossed my lean legs to draw attention to them. "So whatcha wanna do tonight?" I asked, batting my eyelashes flirtatiously.

"I just wanna watch TV," he murmured.

I stared at him for a moment, then dropped my head in defeat and looked at my fidgety fingers instead. I normally didn't give up so easily, but I could only give so much effort in return for so much rejection. So I walked up the stairs to the bedroom, hoping he'd at least notice me leaving. I even paused at the top step to look at him, to no avail. I took the hint and went to bed, despite the early hour and despite my hunger for dinner.

I awoke in the wee hours of the morning to find myself alone in bed. The living room TV blared, so I went to check if Darren was still up. From the railing overlooking the living room, I saw Darren sleeping in the recliner, holding a can of beer. He must have fallen asleep by accident, I excused. But reason told the truth—Darren just didn't want to sleep with me. I went back to bed, wondering why he hung on if he didn't want me, unless it was to prolong my suffering for what I'd done.

Later that morning, the bright sun woke me with the promise of a beautiful Mother's Day. I immediately looked to Darren's side of the bed. It was still empty. The emotional and now physical distance between us immediately dispelled my hope for a better day and a better relationship. I begrudgingly got out of bed and went in search of the man who was supposed to glorify me for birthing and raising his only child.

Fully dressed in a name-brand polo shirt and pressed khakis, Darren came out of the bathroom just as I reached the kitchen. "Morning!" I said cheerily.

Darren walked towards the door without saying a word. He smelled of a cologne I didn't recognize. "Are you going somewhere?" I glanced at the clock to confirm it was too early to leave. We had plans to pick up Ryder from my mother in a few hours, and then meet Jane and Denise and her clan at Portillo's for lunch.

"Goodbye, Dana," he said in a cryptic monotone. Then he turned the doorknob.

The perceived exclusion triggered me. "Why are you acting like this? Why are you doing this to me?"

Darren didn't answer. He glared at me for a second and then walked out. My breaths shortened as I watched him drive away. Then a dull pain imposed itself in my chest. I took deep breaths until I felt well enough to make my morning coffee. I needed the familiar structure of my routine to stabilize my emotions.

Despite their dissociation from me, I knew Jane and Denise would ask why Ryder and I hadn't come with Darren as expected. I wondered how he'd respond. Would he tell them the truth? That he left without me? Abandoned me? Or would he tell them some story, like I was depressed or suicidal again, to make me look unstable? Sudden gumption made me call him to demand an explanation for his behavior. But, like the coward he was, he didn't answer.

I had half a mind to show up to Portillo's anyway, but ruining Jane and Denise's Mother's Day wouldn't make me feel any better, nor would it do anything to mend the division between us. So after I picked up Ryder from my mother, I stopped at the McDonald's Play Place Ryder and I frequented, hoping to salvage our Mother's Day with lunch and some play time with other children, but it was a ghost town. All the children and mothers and families were celebrating the day as they should, which wasn't at McDonald's. So we went home.

For Ryder, it was a normal day of playing tractors, watching cartoons, and reading a bedtime story before bed. For me, the day was emotionally torturous. Being excluded from my husband's life and from his family plans was an intentionally hurtful slight I couldn't forgive. There was nothing I could do, though, except continue through the motions of life for Ryder.

When Darren didn't return home or answer my calls before we went to bed, my overwhelming feelings of abandonment and exclusion worsened, preventing sleep. So I lay there instead, listening for any sign my husband had come home to me after all. But he didn't.

"Happy Mother's Day," I whispered to myself before finally closing my eyes, though it hadn't been a happy day at all.

The next morning, I set up Ryder with breakfast and a cartoon, then called my missing husband.

"Hello," he mumbled in a very quiet and low tone after several rings. He must have been debating whether or not to answer.

"Is there someone else?" I blurted. Nothing else made sense at this point.

When he didn't answer, I repeated the question, louder and slower this time. "Darren, is there someone else?"

There was a long pause, then a reluctant, "No."

His hesitation gave away his lie. "You owe me the fucking truth, Darren. Is there someone else? I'm not going to ask you again!" I yelled.

Another long pause, followed by a low, "Yes," confirmed my suspicion. Then Darren hung up.

I ran into Ryder's bedroom and screamed into the pillow on his bed. Then I fell onto the bed and cried hysterically, still holding the phone that had been the messenger of devastation. Anger got me back up on my feet, but anxiety made me keel over and crouch back down on the floor. Physical pain would have been more tolerable than the emotional turmoil of rejection and betrayal. I screamed into the pillow again before standing back up resolutely, composing myself enough to be half of a mother to Ryder that day.

I knew this was Darren's revenge on me for my mistake. He wanted me to hurt the same way I'd hurt him. Most people would say he was justified in doing that, but inflicting pain upon someone intentionally, especially when you know the depth of that pain, is just plain cruel. So after my tears had dried up, my pain morphed into equally intense anger. We were going to deal with our relationship once and for all. I wouldn't live in limbo anymore.

I called Darren over and over, to the point of harassment. He wouldn't answer. He wouldn't respond to text messages either. I persisted until he finally answered my call over a week later. I didn't waste time with polite greetings either. "So what's going to happen now? You just going to avoid me and Ryder? Just toss us aside like garbage? I mean, if you want out, just fucking leave."

"I'm gonna stay with my mom until we figure things out with the house," he said. "I guess we need to put it up for sale. And the rental too."

I huffed in disbelief. He *had* to have this farm. He *had* to have the three-acre farmette next door when it had gone up for sale just six short months after we'd moved in. And now it was all dispensable? "So now Ryder and I have to move because you stuck your dick in some random chick? And I have to tell our renter, who pays us a year's rent in cash, up front, that he has to move too? That's great, Darren! Guess you just like to screw everybody, don't you?" I was being snarky and sarcastic, but I didn't give a fuck.

"You're much prettier," he offered as consolation.

"Are you fucking kidding me?" This wasn't a beauty contest! These were people's lives! The fact that he could completely disregard the consequences of his choices astonished me.

"She wants you to know she's really sorry for this too. She divorced her husband for cheating on her, so she knows what it feels like."

"Are you serious right now?" I yelled. "Tell her she could stick her hypocritical apology up her lying fucking ass! Or maybe you could, since you're the one sticking it to her these days!"

Darren remained unusually low-key. "I'll always take care of you, Dana. But I'm young enough to get married again and have more kids, so I just want to move on without too much issue."

"Wow! Marriage and kids already? Either this has been going on a lot longer than I thought, or you're moving as fast with her as you did with me!"

"I didn't mean for this to happen."

"Bullshit, Darren. You've been threatening to divorce me for as long as we've been married. I don't do something you expect me to do, divorce. I say the wrong thing, divorce. I don't say anything, divorce. I can't fucking win with you! It's fine, though. Neither of us has been happy for a long time."

"Just talk to an attorney," he nudged. "She said it's not as bad as people think it is."

"Who? Your girlfriend? So now I'm taking legal advice from her? You know what? If you want out, you call the damn attorney!" I said. Then I hung up. And called an attorney.

I was advised to sell one or both houses before filing, so I put them both up for sale the next day. I didn't really want to sell them, nor did I have any intention of being the one to file for divorce. I just wanted to call Darren's bluff.

"Bad Blood"

T he rental house sold within a week, to a younger couple from the suburbs. Of course, Darren left it to me to tell our renter he had to move. He'd moved there just two years before, after divorcing his wife. So, because of the circumstances, he understood and cooperated with moving so quickly. I gave him back his rent money for the remaining portion of the year, as well as additional money to help with moving costs, figuring he shouldn't have to pay for Darren's self-proclaimed mid-life crisis.

I was paying for it for all of us anyway. Darren had made me drop off clothes for him at his mother's, then dropped off the face of the earth. He didn't call. He didn't answer our calls. He didn't text. He didn't come to the house—not even to see Ryder. I was just fortunate Ryder was used to his dad not being around, so it didn't faze him.

It affected me, though. I was wired from my abusive childhood to believe there was something inherently wrong with me if someone abandoned me. In my head, Darren's rejection of me was a reflection of some quality or qualities I exhibited, which made me unlovable. So what was it about me that was so insufferable he had to leave? The only thing I could come up with was that I was crazy. Other than beautiful, he'd always called me "crazy."

And maybe I was! I'd been through enough harrowing experiences in my life to warrant mental and emotional deficiency. My racing thoughts crippled my ability to work and sometimes to be a mother. I would get so worked up just thinking about Darren's dismissal of me that I'd get short of breath and have chest pains. Headaches and stomach aches plagued me too, though stress had done that to me since childhood. So I decided to seek help. If nothing else, Ryder deserved a better and healthier version of me, especially if it was just going to be him and me from now on.

"You're having panic attacks," a psychiatrist told me after asking some preliminary questions. He was a tall and equally wide southeastern European man, with longer dark hair parted to one side. Black-framed glasses to match his full beard gave him the distinguished look of a college professor at a prestigious university. Yet, his moniker "Dr. George"—used in place of his very ethnic name—made him seem humble and approachable. "During times of high stress, your body pumps cortisol—a stress hormone—into your bloodstream, sending you into 'fight or flight' mode. This causes that panicky feeling you described. Have you noticed any patterns around your stress? Like certain people or places?"

I could've made a list, but I started with, "Well, my husband recently moved out."

"That'll do it!" he chuckled.

"Yeah, things have always been touch and go with him unfortunately." I told him of the affairs, counseling, the Xanax incident, and now Darren moving out. He asked how I felt during those life events, as opposed to uneventful days.

"I have happy moments. With my son mostly. We sing and dance, and play and read and watch movies . . ." I smiled at the thought. "But when I'm sad or upset, I'm *really* sad or upset. I feel things so deeply, like they're an offense to the core of my being. And sometimes there's so many emotions whirling around in my brain that I get overwhelmed trying to process them all."

"What happens then?"

"It's like my brain freezes up! I can't think straight. I can't make a decision. I can't distinguish one thought or emotion from another. I lose focus altogether. The overwhelm sends me into a panic. I can't breathe. Then I cry out of frustration!"

"Wow," he replied, "I thought this was a simple case of the divorce blues, but there's a lot more going on here. Has anyone ever told you you're bipolar?"

"Yes, actually. A psychiatrist diagnosed me with Bipolar Depression when I was nineteen and put me on Prozac. Then my OB diagnosed me with postpartum depression after my son was born, and he prescribed Zoloft. I take Xanax for anxiety too."

"Okay," Dr. George stalled as he wrote in his notepad. "You seem to have more of the downward spirals than the highs associated with other forms of bipolar disorder, so I believe that's an accurate assessment. I'm going to prescribe Seroquel. It's a mood stabilizer used to calm the nerves in the brain. You'll notice fewer ups and downs within a few weeks. And it'll curb these panic attacks as well as those other symptoms, by steadying your moods. Just remember to take it at night, because it will make you sleepy."

"Okay," I agreed, willing to try anything to temporarily numb my emotional pain.

After he entered my new prescription in his computer, he leaned back in his office chair. His elbows sat upon the armrests, and he turned a pen in circles between his fingers. "From what you described, it sounds like your husband exhibits the more classic symptoms of bipolar disorder— impulsiveness, infidelity, careless spending of money. Has he ever been diagnosed with any mental health illnesses?"

"No. Based on their disappointment in me when I was diagnosed with postpartum depression, it's fair to say his family thinks mental illness is shameful. So of course none of them have issues."

"Okay." He nodded, then joked, "It's just that your relationship reminds me of Kurt Cobain and Courtney Love. You know, the lead singer of the '90s grunge band Nirvana and his wife?"

Yeah, and one of them is dead, supposedly at the cause of the other, I thought to myself.

I looked down at my fumbling fingers while the doctor spoke again. "Are you open to counseling? You might benefit from talking to someone."

"I don't believe in counseling, honestly. I don't think it's beneficial to re-hash traumatic events and negative feelings, especially when my body physically responds to it all. Plus, talking about stuff doesn't change anything. It just brings it to the forefront of thought, which evokes the feelings I'm trying to stifle. So, no," I responded.

"Sounds like post-traumatic stress. Do you at least have someone you *can* talk to if you wanted to vent? Someone you trust?"

"Yeah," I said, as if trying to convince myself. "My neighbor Stacy has actually been really helpful."

"You've known her a long time?"

"No, but it feels like I have! We owned the property next to us—Darren *had* to have it. We had a perfect renter in there too. But when Darren moved out, we sold the place to Stacy and her husband. They have a little girl about Ryder's age, and the kids play together all the time now. So Stacy and I have been spending a lot of time together as a result. As a matter of fact, Ryder is there now. Stacy offered to watch him so I didn't have to bring him here with me."

"Okay, that's good," the doctor said. "I just want to make sure you have an outlet for your upsets and frustrations."

"Yeah, definitely. Stacy gets me in a way most people don't. I can confide in her and she validates my feelings or gives me an alternate perspective to think on. And it's good to know I have someone nearby who's keeping an eye out for me and Ryder. Makes me feel less alone."

Dr. George stood up from his chair, indicating the appointment was over. As he walked me out of his cozy, book-filled office, he advised, "I want you to think about your life, Dana. The medication will help, but sometimes a lifestyle change is a better option. Think about your marriage, what you want your life to look like, and make adjustments where necessary."

I nodded. "I understand." What I understood was that he thought I should divorce Darren. And he was right. I shouldn't be with someone I had to take medication to be with! However, I was resolute in my decision to hold out for Darren to file for divorce. Despite my affair and our unhappy marriage, I'd chosen to stay. If he chose not to, then *he* could pull the trigger. I was done cleaning up his messes.

After filling the prescriptions Dr. George provided, I returned home to see Darren's white work van parked in front of the garage. Then I saw Darren, and immediately tensed. He was sitting on the steps up to our porch with his elbows on his knees, tapping his foot impatiently. He didn't like waiting. I hadn't expected him, though, nor did I know what had prompted this visit. It had been a few weeks since he'd been to the house. He was "too busy working"—code for screwing his girlfriend, I guessed.

I parked my Explorer in the middle bay of the garage and walked out to the wide concrete pad separating the three-thousand square foot structure from the house. "Hey," I said apathetically.

"Mommy!" I turned to see Ryder running towards me from Stacy's house, with a giddy smile on his face.

"Ryder!" I matched his enthusiasm and squatted to receive him with open arms. He turned towards the open garage instead and emerged seconds later on his motorized John Deere Gator. He drove that toy tractor in circles between the house and garage for hours each day.

As I stood back up, chuckling at how Ryder had left me hanging, I waved at Stacy. She was standing in her side yard, with her daughter Ashlynn on her hip, from where she'd watched Ryder return home. After she'd waved back, I walked towards the house where Darren waited.

"You know he's been asking for you," I said.

Darren bypassed polite talk. "So what did the doctor say?"

So that's what this was about! Jane must've told him where I'd gone. I'd asked her to watch Ryder while I went to the appointment, but she'd declined, saying she didn't want to be involved in the issues between me and Darren. In other words, she was siding with her son, who'd probably convinced her he was justified in leaving because I'm a cheater and had mental problems.

"He prescribed something for bipolar depression. It's supposed to help even out my moods."

Darren rubbed his forehead, then threw his baseball cap down and yelled, "Fuck!"

I instinctively jumped back.

He continued, "That means Ryder can have your fucked-up head. That's genetic, you know!"

My fear instantly switched to anger. "You're mad because Ryder might have a genetic predisposition towards depression?"

"Yeah! Our son could be fucked up because of YOU!" He pointed his finger at my face.

"I'm not 'fucked up,' Darren. I'm sad," I asserted. "And you're acting like I purposely infected Ryder with some disease, which just adds insult to injury!"

"Well, no one wants their kid to be fucked up!"

I looked back to check on Ryder, thankful the obnoxiously loud hum of his motorized toy muffled this unpleasant interaction, which would likely affect him more than my contribution to his genetic make-up. He seemed unfazed.

"Would you please stop calling our son 'fucked up'?" I said as I turned back to Darren. "And thanks for your support, by the way."

"Crazy bitch," he jabbed, then walked to his van, got in, and slammed the door as hard as he could for effect.

I rushed over to where Ryder was and stood in front of his Gator to make sure Darren didn't run him over when he tore out of the driveway. Then us two crazies watched Darren leave. Again. He was getting good at that.

"Who Can It Be Now?"

ot long after, I was startled awake by the sound of our keyless
electronic door lock beeping in the middle of the night. Someone
was entering a code to gain entry. No one but me and Darren
knew the code, so when I heard the lock disengage, my heart stopped.

The month before, a couple in their eighties, who lived just two roads
over, had been pummeled to death with a shovel while they slept. The
suspected intruder had supposedly been caught. But here I was alone with
Ryder and no way to save us from the same awful fate, if perhaps they'd
gotten the wrong guy.

I heard footsteps, then froze in fear as they came up the stairs. Oh
my god! Who was in my house? I had to do something! I quietly crept
out of bed and moved towards the door. Then I went back to get Ryder,
figuring I'd rather try to escape with him than attempt to fight an intruder
without a weapon. But it was too late. The bedroom door flung open, and
the light switched on.

My eyes blinked as they adjusted to the sudden brightness. "Darren?"
I exhaled and my body relaxed, until the familiar scowl of Mr. Hyde put
me back on alert. "What are you doing?"

Darren moved past me and snatched Ryder out of bed. My slow
reflexes couldn't keep up with him as he hurried back down the stairs.
Ryder screamed and reached out for me.

"Darren!" I screamed as I ran after them. "Give me back my son!!"

The large square coffee table in the middle of the living room blocked
Darren's direct path to the door, allowing me to catch up. I grabbed Ryder

at the armpits, but Darren moved backward, forcibly releasing my hold. Then he moved around the table towards the door.

"Darren!" I grabbed for Ryder again, but Darren maneuvered himself out of my reach.

"Mommy!" Ryder screamed with tearful eyes and outstretched arms.

"Oh my god, Darren! What are you doing?" I grabbed for Ryder again, getting hold of him this time.

"I'm taking him far away from your crazy ass, and you're never going to see either of us again, you fucking cunt!" Darren jerked Ryder out of my hold.

He was within a couple feet of the door with my son—my life—in his hands. I couldn't let him leave, but what could I possibly do? I was small, and Darren's strength easily overpowered me. I had to think quickly. So I threw myself down on the wood floor and wrapped my arms as tightly as I could around his ankles. I'd been here once before, on the night of Darren's DUI, but I wouldn't let go this time. I'd bite his ankles if I had to—anything to stop him from escaping with Ryder.

Darren tried to shake me off, so I leveraged my legs up off the floor and wrapped them around his feet to restrain him with more strength than my arms could manage on their own.

"You're not taking my son!" I screamed.

He kicked harder and finally twisted one of his feet out of my grasp. Then he opened the door and stepped forward with his free foot, limping onto the porch while the splintered edges of the worn wood floor scraped my knees. I held on firmly despite the pain.

"Darren, please!" I begged. "Give me back my baby!"

He tried to move forward again, but I weighed myself down with enough adrenaline and strong will that he couldn't take one step further, despite his persistence. We were at a standstill.

"Mommy!" Ryder screamed again. I looked up helplessly, unable to reach for him without letting go of Darren's ankles. I couldn't take that risk.

"It's okay, sweetie," I lied in what I thought was calm compared to the hysterical crying we were both noisily disturbing the quiet summer night with.

Then Darren held Ryder up in front of him, so they were face to face.

"You want your fucking mother?" His spit flew onto Ryder's face. "Have the fucking whore, then!"

Darren practically threw Ryder down to me. I snatched my baby back and pulled him close. Then I locked us in the house, as Darren recklessly sped out of our driveway.

"Mommy's got you, baby," I said as I leaned against the back of the couch and slid down to the floor.

With his head on my shoulder, Ryder and I sobbed together, until he fell asleep. Then I walked back up to the bedroom, locked the door behind me, and lay on the bed with Ryder in my arms. I couldn't be sure Darren wouldn't return, so I couldn't sleep, and I wouldn't let Ryder go. I lay in silent vigil instead, until sunrise dictated the start of a new day.

"What Am I To You"

arren and I did what we did best after a bad encounter—we pretended like it never happened. I couldn't forget, though. His erratic behavior made me nervous, and I couldn't be sure we wouldn't be one of those families found dead in a car somewhere, victims of a murder-suicide. I had to reign Darren in before he caused irrevocable harm.

I thought of the saying, "Keep your friends close and your enemies closer." Although my husband shouldn't be my enemy, he was, and I had to end this war between us to ensure mine and Ryder's safety. But what could I possibly do to get close to Darren again? He shut me out the second his girlfriend had interrupted our marriage.

When I didn't have an answer to a question, I deferred to Google. I typed "how to get my husband back" into the search bar of my laptop. I came across an article that explained the correlation between physical intimacy and emotional connection. We definitely lacked both. So, although he'd rejected my offer of sex the day before Mother's Day, maybe I needed to try again, but harder this time, and hope it would make him feel enough of a connection to me to end all this nonsense. It was wrong to use sex to manipulate, I knew, but losing my son to a ruthless wreck who'd tried to steal my baby away from me was worse.

I called Darren right away, figuring there was no time like the present to enact my new approach. As usual, he didn't answer, so I left a voicemail. "Hey. I know things haven't been great between us, but I also know neither of us wants it to be this way. So can we call a truce? Can we just try to get along for Ryder's sake, at least? He really misses you. And he's not the only one. Would be nice for you to stop by sometime. Maybe have dinner with us. Just think about it. You know where we are."

Darren showed up that afternoon. Ryder had fallen asleep in his high chair, so I put my finger to my lips and led Darren by the hand down the hall to Ryder's bedroom. "Thanks for coming," I whispered as I closed the bedroom door. "How have you been?" I stroked his arm gently.

Darren stood still, looking down at me with a combination of confusion and pleasant surprise. Then he cocked his head sideways and squinted his eyes.

"I know," I dropped my head shamefully. "You want to know what caused this change in me. This change of heart." I looked back up at him. "I just want things to be good between us again." I brushed my hand between his legs. His manhood twitched, so I took the positive response as a signal to proceed.

I slowly stood on my tiptoes, letting my body slide up his, until our lips met. He seemed to lean down to meet me, then pushed me away just as we were about to kiss. I remained cool. "Darren," I said longingly. I put my hand back where it had been, and the hardness gave me the permission his mind wouldn't to proceed. So I went in for that kiss again. He didn't stop me this time. He allowed my tongue in, then moved me to the bed and lay me down. We disrobed like two teenagers eager to have each other before Mom and Dad got home. It had been a while, so the quickness of the tryst felt much the same.

Darren smiled after, but then regretted it. "I'm sorry. I shouldn't have done that with you."

"Why not?" I got up to dress alongside him. "You're my husband and I'm your wife. You're allowed to do that with me."

"But it's not fair to . . ."

"To who? Your girlfriend?"

"Yeah." He dropped his head.

"Well, I'm not planning on telling her. Are you?"

He looked up at me with raised brows. I knew I was shocking him, but I also knew I was getting to him.

"Look." I crossed my arms. "Regardless of what you're doing, I'm a woman with needs. And you didn't like me getting those needs met outside our marriage, so unless you're suddenly okay with that, you're it." Hoping the hidden threat triggered his need to possess me, I left the room.

Ryder had awakened, so I immediately switched to Mommy mode. "Hey, little man!" I chimed in my high-pitched baby-talk voice. "Look who's here!" I turned to make sure Darren had followed me back out to the living room.

"Daddy!" Ryder eagerly raised both arms up for Darren to lift him out of his chair. Then they rolled Matchbox cars across the floor and over furniture while I cleaned up the kitchen from lunch. It amazed me how children could forgive and forget without question. I wished I could do the same.

Darren returned regularly after that, under the premise of seeing Ryder, but then he'd pull me away to a bedroom at any opportunity to be alone. The more sex we had, the nicer Darren was to me, and thereby the easier it was for me to be nice to him. Even though this had been psychological (and sexual) warfare on my part, the result was proving hopeful for the future of our marriage!

So when Darren told me he'd leased an apartment a half hour away, I was stunned. I'd thought I almost had him back, that it was only a matter of time before he'd move back in the house with us and move forward with our marriage. I didn't want to cause conflict, though, so I kept my feelings to myself and carried on with an agreeable attitude and positive support for whatever he wanted to do. I even helped him pack up the moving truck he brought to the house to take away whatever extra furnishings me and Ryder wouldn't miss. But then he told me of his plan to use home equity from our house to purchase a cheap fixer-upper even further away! He intended to live in the apartment while remodeling the house he'd bought, so he obviously wasn't coming home as I'd expected. Yet, he hadn't called an attorney either.

He barely called after that. Visits dwindled again too, as did the physical nature of them. Nothing had happened to explain why he was pulling away, and the mixed signals frustrated me. If I wasn't his wife, or his lover, then I needed to know why I was still here.

"What are we, Darren? Are we married? Are we getting divorced? I mean, we'd been having sex, while you were probably getting your jollies off your girlfriend too. Now you have an apartment and a house . . . what am I supposed to make of all this?" I pressed when I finally got him on the phone one afternoon.

"I don't know," he muttered from the other end.

"Well, you better figure it out because I'm tired of living in limbo! I'm your wife, but I feel like the babysitter you're screwing on the side, and I'm not okay with that! So either shit or get off the pot. Be my husband and move back home, or call an attorney and go marry your frickin' girlfriend! I don't even care anymore! Just make a damn decision!"

He hung up. Coward!

I lay in the pitch dark that night, ruminating about all the awful insults, hostile expressions, and physical threats Darren had burdened me with over the years. The thoughts replayed in my mind until I was so nauseous and clammy, I was sure I'd be sick. I didn't want to move and risk waking Ryder, who was sprawled out next to me in peaceful sleep. So I removed the thick comforter to cool off, hoping for relief.

The intense pressure building in my chest made me squirm uncomfortably, so I inhaled and exhaled at an even pace to relax and reset my body. But when I felt a strong pain under my left armpit, I got scared. I knew the signs of a heart attack.

I tried not to panic, but my throat tightened, making it hard to breathe. I'd been born with a heart murmur and experienced arrhythmia now and then, so my worry was valid. I put my right hand on my breastbone to check the pace at which my heart was beating. It was pounding, but in even intervals. Still, I wasn't reassured. If Ryder weren't asleep next to me, I'd have rushed to the emergency room.

After several deep breaths in my nose and out my mouth, my mind calmed, and my heartbeat slowed. I was tired and wanted to succumb to sleep, but I was too afraid to let my heavy lids close. What if this was a heart attack, and I had another one while I slept? I wouldn't let Ryder wake up to a dead mother! Nor could I leave him in this world with an incompetent drunk of a father. So I forced myself to lay still and awake, watching the bedside clock challenge my patience until morning came. I'd never been so glad to see the sun rise.

After Ryder awoke, I called the medical center and explained what had happened overnight. I felt fine now, but the nurse told me to come in for an EKG anyway, as soon as I could get there. I immediately packed up Ryder, figuring it was best not to take chances with my heart.

"Your EKG results are normal," the female doctor reported to me in her Indian accent. She stood in front of where I sat in an exam room with Ryder on my lap. "What you described was probably a panic attack resulting from some anxiety you have."

"I've had panic attacks before, but this was different," I insisted.

"I'm sure it felt that way, but without any evidence, we have to believe it's anxiety."

"So that's it, then?"

"I'm afraid we have no reason to justify further testing," she maintained. "I suggest you go home and get some rest."

I was tired and would have loved nothing more, but I couldn't shake this sudden fear of death, especially when I was the only one in the house with Ryder, and no one ever came to the house to know if either of us were okay. So I called Darren as soon as we returned home, to let him know what was going on.

It went straight to voicemail, so I left a message. "Just in case something happens, I wanted you to know I was at the doctor this morning. I thought I was having a heart attack last night, so they wanted me in for an EKG first thing. They said it's normal now, but there's no way to detect anything unless I'm hooked up to a machine while it's occurring. So I guess I just have to hope it really *was* a panic attack like the doctor said. Anyway, no need to call back. Just wanted to keep you in the loop."

Darren called back a few minutes later. "I got your message. If that happens again, please call me. We have our issues, but I don't want you to die." I wasn't sure I believed him, but regardless, I was grateful he'd responded.

A couple days later, he showed up at the house. I sat on the porch steps, where I'd been watching Ryder play in the mulch with toy tractors.

Darren walked up to me with the same sweet eyes he'd displayed the night he'd first told me he loved me. "I'm coming home," he said.

I'd waited half the year to hear those words, so I should have been thrilled! But the unrest in my heart told me something different. I'd gotten used to life without Darren. There was less tension in his absence. I was more at ease without having to worry about what I said and did and how Darren would overreact to it all. I was starting to feel better about myself without his constant judgment and name-calling. I had a friend in Stacy, and I was even starting to make friends with some of the moms from Ryder's pre-school. Some of them were on their way for the jewelry party I was hosting at our house that same afternoon.

Was I still lonely? Yes! I wanted a husband to come home to me and Ryder at the end of every day, to love us and share life with. But was having that worth the degradation and dysfunction that always crept into our dynamic?

"Aren't you going to say something?" Darren's agitated tone triggered my automatic response to appease him to avoid conflict.

"Yeah! Um, I'm just surprised is all! But yeah, that's great!" I mustered a close-mouthed smile.

Darren put his hands on his hips, pressed his lips together tightly, then looked away. I braced myself when he looked back to me.

"Fuck, Dana! I expected you to be a little more excited about this! Isn't this what you want?"

"Yeah! Of course!" I backpedaled. "I'm just ... you know ... processing it! I didn't think you were coming back after you bought that fixer-upper, so this is just ... unexpected!"

He huffed out of his nose. He expected fireworks and a parade, and my unenthusiastic response hadn't sufficed.

"I'm very happy!" I tried to convince him—and myself. "You coming back tonight?"

Darren's shoulders relaxed. "Yeah, I'm going to go get a change of clothes from the apartment. I'll be back later." He looked at Ryder playing beside us. Then he looked at me with disappointed eyes and that tight-lipped complacency. "See ya."

"Okay!" I tried to sound a little more excited as he walked to his van and drove away. It was all a farce, though. I knew it. He knew it. Yet, here we were, about to give it another go.

"Same Old Love"

*It's like he's mourning the break-up with his girlfriend, or the single life I let him have for a while there," I confided in Stacy. We stood on my porch, while Ryder and Ashlynn drove their matching motorized gators in circles between the house and garage. It was a late afternoon in late fall, and Stacy had come to fetch Ashlynn for dinner.

"He mopes around here all sad, with his head hung, shuffling his feet, like he wants me to feel sorry for him or something," I continued. "But how am I supposed to feel bad for him? I mean, he cheated on me, made sure I knew it . . . Did I ever tell you about the time he cranked that new version of the song 'Girlfriend' in his van? It was blatantly obvious he did it for my benefit! Then he said he was moving home, but he *clearly* doesn't want to be here. He hasn't even brought back all his clothes and the few random things he took with him to his mom's and then to his apartment—which he's still renting, by the way. I don't even know if he's given his landlord notice yet!"

"He probably *is* mourning his girlfriend, which is good because that means they actually broke up! But you'll have to deal with it if having him home is what you want. He probably watched you do the same thing after *you* cheated on *him*!" Stacy was a straight-shooter. I appreciated that about her, even when it hurt to get shot.

"Yeah, but I was mourning short-lived happiness, which I'd *chosen* to end in favor of my marriage. *He's* mourning the death of being able to have his cake and eat it too. No other man gets to screw his wife *and* his mistress. At least not when his *wife* knows and consents to it!"

Darren drove up just then. Stacy raised her eyebrows over the rim of her glasses. "Well, I'll be next door if you need me. And remember—I have a gun and I know how to use it!" Her laugh was an infectious cackle as bold and distinct as the red of her straight, shoulder-length hair. I couldn't help but chuckle too.

Stacy gathered Ashlynn and proceeded across the acre of grass between our houses. Darren barely acknowledged her as they passed. She returned the discourtesy.

"You're awful chummy with our new neighbor," Darren commented as he walked past me and into the house.

I put Ryder on my hip and followed Darren in. "Yeah, I like her. Is that a problem?" I put Ryder down in the living room and turned on the TV, hoping to distract him from the impending argument.

"Not at all! I'm sure her husband likes you too, walking around in your short-shorts and bikini top!" he said, referring to what I wore outside during the summer while playing with Ryder or doing yard work. Then he sat in his dad's recliner.

"What are you insinuating?" I crossed my arms while I awaited his response.

"Nothing, Dana!" he replied in a snide, high pitch meant to mock me.

"So when are you giving up your apartment?" I poked just to piss him off.

"That new friend of yours give you a backbone?" Darren got up and walked toward me with pursed lips, then pointed his finger in my face. I instinctively leaned back while he spit-screamed, "Don't forget who made you! You were *nothing* when I met you! *I* built you up and gave you confidence and self-esteem. *I'm* the one who made you successful. *I'm* the one who paid for this house and gave you this life. So, if you wanna act like this, go to your new fucking friend's house and stay over there. I'm sure her husband or one of his friends will fuck you. That's what you want, isn't it? You want some trailer trash piece of shit fucking you instead of me? That's why you walk around with your tits and ass hanging out?"

"Yep! Sure is! But don't worry, I'll check with you to get clearance on my wardrobe the next time I go out in the fucking yard."

Darren hadn't expected my bold retort. He glared at me, then made his way towards the door.

"Where are *you* going?" I asked.

Darren ignored me, put his shoes on and walked out.

I ran out the door after him. "Darren! Where are you going?"

"Back to my apartment!" he yelled, then got in his van and backed out of his spot recklessly.

"Married men don't have apartments!" I screamed at him from the middle of the driveway. He sped away, and his tires kicked up gravel around me. I looked over at Stacy's property to see if they'd witnessed this. Lord knows we'd given them some entertainment in the short time they'd lived there.

Then I went back in the house and locked *all* the locks so Darren couldn't get back in while we slept. We now had a deadbolt on the top of the entry door. I'd begged Darren to install it after he'd tried to steal Ryder from me in the middle of the night, claiming I was worried for our safety after that double homicide nearby. Then I threw out the keys, so it could only be unlocked manually, from *inside* the house.

The next evening, I was standing at the kitchen island cubing chicken when Darren walked in and proclaimed, "I'm giving up the apartment and permanently moving back here."

The consistent inconsistency between his words and actions made me suspicious of his true intentions, so I simply replied, "Okay," and went about making dinner.

"That's it?"

I looked up from what I was doing and saw him still standing at the door expectantly. "What do you want me to say, Darren?"

He threw his arms up. "I don't know! Maybe come give me a hug? Act like you're happy?"

I couldn't ride the emotional roller coaster with him anymore. "You were already back, and you left again. So I'm sorry if I'm not throwing you a fucking party," I said with a blank expression, then returned my attention to dinner.

"What the fuck?" Darren yelled. Ryder turned away from his cartoons and Matchbox cars to see what his dad was angry about, but he returned to them just as quickly. It saddened me that tension and anger were so commonplace in our home that he was as unfazed as I was.

"You were so sweet when I first came back home!" Darren continued. "But now you're the same bitch I left in the first place!"

"I know. I'm insufferable," I agreed in a monotone voice, without taking my eyes off the food I was preparing.

"You're such a fucking cunt!" he screamed and then stormed out to the garage.

Ryder and I went about our evening—eating dinner, bathing, and going to bed—as if it were just another night that Daddy was away on a work trip. I wasn't going to chase after a grown man acting like a child, nor make any effort to give Darren the soothing kindness he refused to give me.

In the middle of the night, however, I heard Darren come in. I'd been awake, as I was most nights now, since my distrust of Darren disallowed the feelings of safety I needed to rest. The familiar sounds of Darren bumping into walls and doors on his way to the main floor bathroom told me he'd soothed himself with alcohol again. I just hoped he didn't wake Ryder this time. Ryder was sleeping in his own room by himself now, at Darren's insistence, and it was directly across the hall from the bathroom.

I cringed when the bathroom door banged shut. Then I heard Darren slam the toilet lid down, and the bathroom door bounce off the wall. It pissed me off that he had no consideration for us, or at least for our son. Then my body tensed when I heard Darren stumble towards the stairs.

Stomp, stomp, thud, knock, knock, thud, thud, thud. "Fuck!" Darren shouted. He'd fallen on the stairs again. It was a wonder Ryder slept through the ruckus.

When Darren finally found his way into our bed, I pretended to be asleep. I didn't want to engage with the drunk. I even positioned myself on the far edge of my side of the bed, so we wouldn't touch. We had separate blankets too, because I didn't even want to share something that simple with him. I was only there because I'd gotten tired of hearing that "a wife should sleep in the same bed as her husband." It's not that I didn't want to lie in the arms of the man I'd married; I just didn't want to lie in his.

"Glycerine"

I was married to a miserable drunk who thought I was a cheating whore, but neither of us would give up on the sham of a marriage we sustained by avoiding each other altogether.

Darren would wake up (eventually) and either go to work or lock himself in the master bedroom to sleep off his hangover or bad mood. He'd come down at night to eat dinner, then settle into his dad's recliner to drink beers and watch TV while Ryder and I slept all night. I had no idea how his paychecks didn't reflect the amount of time he took off work, but I didn't dare ask. That would require talking to him, which I tried not to do, since it usually resulted in an argument.

Ryder and I maintained the same routine we'd always had, regardless of whether or not Darren decided to go to work. I'd have my morning coffee while Ryder and I played in the toy room. Then Ryder would play with Ashlynn if she wandered over or go to pre-school on the couple days a week he was registered. We'd have lunch after, then do chores and errands until dinner. Our busy life exhausted us by bath time, but we still snuggled in bed to read a book every night—Ryder's favorites being about tractors and race cars.

I should have been more bothered that Darren and I were living separate lives, especially when I'd stayed with him primarily to ensure Ryder grew up with both parents in the same house. However, seeing as how we disagreed on most everything, I was glad to raise Ryder the way I wanted to, without having to consult Darren on every little decision along the way. I knew I couldn't immerse myself in my mom role without Darren, though, since it was his income that primarily paid the bills. So despite him exhibiting behaviors I'd rather Ryder didn't see, I credited Darren for at least providing for our family.

Then, in the summer of 2008, I was standing in the middle of the cereal aisle in Walmart with a cart full of groceries when my cell phone rang.

"I have some bad news," Darren said dimly.

"What? What's going on?"

"I was demoted . . . and my salary was reduced to what it was before the promotion."

I froze. "What do you mean? How much of a reduction are we talking?"

"Almost thirty thousand a year," he mumbled.

My mouth dropped open. I'm pretty sure my heart stopped too. "That's almost three thousand dollars a month, Darren! How are we supposed to pay our bills making that much less every month?" I didn't even care that other shoppers overheard and were staring. "How did this even happen?"

"Well, with everything going on with us, they said I wasn't performing to their standards. I missed a lot of work, you know." Yeah, I knew.

All those days he'd lain in bed instead of going to work suddenly made sense. However, I didn't miss his attempt to project blame onto me for this. An attorney I spoke with while Darren was running around with his girlfriend warned me that many men intentionally lose their jobs or sources of income to weasel their way out of alimony and child support. I just didn't think Darren would actually do that, after promising to take care of me and Ryder no matter what happened.

"What are we going to do? I hardly sell houses anymore. We've got all these bills . . ." I rambled.

"Maybe you need to get a *real* job."

"What's that supposed to mean?" The validity of my real estate career wasn't the issue, but I wouldn't let him get away with the insult. "You know, you're the one who wanted to be the breadwinner, because you're the *man* and all. And you're the one who wanted me to stay home with Ryder instead of work. And you're also the one spending more than you earn. So don't try to blame me for our financial problems when I'm the one always fixing them!"

"Fuck, Dana! Why can't you ever be a good wife who just says 'yes, sir' when I ask you for some fucking help!"

My eyes widened. "I'm not a good wife? Have I not let you put us into major debt buying motorcycles and four-wheelers and houses? Even when we couldn't afford what you wanted, you always went out and bought whatever it was anyway. Did I protest? Or tell you you couldn't have something? No, I didn't, Darren. I even let you have a fucking girlfriend for God's sake! So I'm not going to stand here and listen to you tell me I'm not a good wife when I have tolerated more than my fair share of your shit!" I looked around again, though I was so riled up I didn't care who heard me, including Ryder. He sat in the seat of the cart in front of me, more interested in the pouch of crunchy snacks I'd allowed him than the upset tone of the call.

"This is what I'm talking about!" Darren responded. "You bitch about everything—every fucking thing—but you don't support me!"

"Now I'm not supportive?" He had some nerve attacking *me* when *he* was the loser who'd gotten demoted. "If you want a supportive wife, why don't you try being a better husband? Yelling, 'Why can't you be normal like my mother and sister and just have babies,' after I tell you I think I miscarried again isn't what *I* call being a good husband!"

"Why do you always have to bring up shit from the past?" Darren's defensiveness was his way of avoiding accountability. However, bringing up issues we hadn't resolved wasn't going to fix the current problem.

"You're right. We obviously have to sit down and figure this out—together. I'll see you tonight."

"Yep," he said, then hung up.

"We" didn't figure anything out that night. Darren drank beers and watched TV while I added up the insurmountable amount of mortgage and credit card debt Darren had accumulated, panicking about how we would ever repay it. He wanted to erase it with bankruptcy, but I refused to sacrifice the high credit rating I'd worked hard to maintain.

We had to lower our monthly obligations, though, so I made the decision to sell Darren's fixer-upper, thereby unburdening us from the second mortgage he'd taken against our farm to pay for the house and its renovations. Although we sold the house in a reasonable time frame, it was valued at half the amount Darren had invested in it. So I had to make arrangements with the bank to pay off the $60,000 difference between what we'd gotten for it and what we owed. It was my fault, though, because according to him, I "mismanaged our money."

He also accused me of "stealing" *his* paychecks. Yes, to pay the mortgages, and utility bills, car payments, insurance . . . our financial situation had nothing to do with the hundreds of dollars a month spent on alcohol, not to mention the chewing tobacco and gas and parts for his four-wheelers and dirt bikes.

Instead of arguing with him, which was pointless, I focused my energy on making ends meet. I rummaged through drawers and closets, looking for anything of value. Whether five dollars or fifty, if we didn't need it, I packed it up and sold it on eBay. Every little bit added up, and I mustered enough money to pay some small bill every month.

I started looking through grocery ads, planning meals around sales and coupons. It was almost a game to see how much I could buy if I worked it just right. My biggest accomplishment was getting $114 worth of groceries for only $14 out of pocket! You'd have thought I'd won the lottery by the way I bragged about it to anyone who'd listen!

I wasn't above doing anything to make ends meet. I babysat some kids here and there, sold off all my PartyLite candles and holders, had garage sales . . . I would lay awake at night figuring how the next bill due would get paid and then enact my plan.

Meanwhile, Darren made no effort to help our situation. He still got drunk most nights, slept all day, missed work more than his employer was probably aware, and stuck me with keeping us afloat. I'd never felt so much contempt for another human being.

"All You Ever Do Is Bring Me Down"

I wouldn't leave Darren, though. It was fall of 2008 and Ryder had just entered kindergarten. I wouldn't displace my son just as his life was starting to take shape.

Life was bearable, for a while anyway, mainly because we were busy running Ryder to tee-ball practices and baking cookies and cupcakes to share at games. Ryder made new friends on the field and at school, and we, in turn, made friends with the parents. It wasn't long before we were an exclusive clique.

We'd all barbecue together. We went to minor league baseball games together. We gathered the kids for sleepovers and trips to water parks and museums. We went to carnivals and drive-in movies with each other. Eventually, we got together at one of the families' homes to watch football every Sunday too. It was good to see Ryder's giddy smile as he ran around with his little buddies. It even made me happy to see Darren joking and laughing and enjoying life again.

So I didn't mind when Darren started going out to bars with some of the dads in our friend group, until I caught him leaving the house in the middle of the night. He got up out of bed, dressed, and left! He thought I was sleeping when he snuck out, but I watched from an upstairs window as he got into a strange car with someone I didn't recognize. I couldn't even tell if it was a man or woman from where I stood. But a man who leaves the house in the middle of the night without telling anyone is up to no good, so the details didn't matter anyway.

After it had happened a few times, I knew the rumors I'd heard from the other moms must be true. It wasn't like Darren had never messed around with women at bars before. I'd just hoped all that was behind us. Still, I was hurt that Darren publicly paraded his disrespect to me and our marriage around our small town. But I didn't let on to anyone that I was bothered. I dismissed the rumors, laughing them off as gossip, and put on the air that we were a happy couple raising our only child. I'd heard another couple in our group was involved in their own cheating scandal anyway, so the attention turned onto them soon enough.

Then one afternoon in early 2009, I was helping one of my mom friends clean up after hosting another get-together. "You really outdid yourself this time, Tara!" I commended. "Everything was so good!" I scraped a plate into the garbage, then put it in the soapy sink water for her.

"Thanks!" she replied as she did the same. "Just too bad Darren couldn't make it."

"Yeah . . . he had to work." Or so he said. It was a Sunday.

"That's okay. We like you better when he's not around anyway," Tara's husband, Ryan, commented as he passed through. Tara and I both stopped what we were doing and looked at each other, before Tara shot Ryan the look of death, like he wasn't supposed to say that out loud.

The deprecating remark surprised me too, considering what quick friends Darren and Ryan had become when they'd initially met at tee-ball practice.

"What?" Ryan responded to Tara's glare. She rolled her eyes, then continued washing dishes.

Ryan took his last swig of truth serum before throwing the beer bottle away. Then he pointed at me. "You're a lot more fun when he's not here to tell you what to do and what to say. You loosen up!" Ryan said before reaching into the refrigerator for another beer.

"Sorry about that," Tara said to me.

"It's okay." I leaned against the counter by the sink and crossed my arms. "Darren and I definitely have our issues. Every couple does. I just didn't realize anyone saw past the 'happy family' facade."

"Oh, we *all* see it!" Ryan declared on his way out.

Although I'd thought we'd done a better job of hiding our dysfunction, I was almost glad others could see past the show we'd apparently failed to perform. It confirmed that my perspective wasn't as skewed as Darren's dual personalities sometimes made me think it was.

No matter where we went or what we did, I always felt like I had to subdue myself, because Darren treated me like a naughty child who had no sense of proper social etiquette. When I joked at a wedding, he scolded me for being drunk. When I danced at another, he pulled me by my arm to a place he thought no one could see or hear him to tell me not to move so provocatively. If I smiled at someone, I was fucking them. If I laughed at a joke, I was flirting. He even chastised me once for taking too long getting drinks at a wedding. He didn't believe that the line had been as long as I'd said. According to him, I was screwing someone in a coat closet.

Eventually, I tired of explaining myself and just surrendered to Darren's unspoken rules. I sat silently at parties and events. I didn't talk to anyone. I didn't laugh at any jokes. I didn't dance. I didn't get drinks. I quit drinking alcohol altogether, actually. But withdrawing didn't help my cause either, because Darren said I was being rude. I couldn't win!

So I stopped interacting at all. I declined invitations and stopped going most places, including next door to Stacy's. I still saw Stacy most days, when she came by to retrieve Ashlynn for dinner or to go somewhere, but after I'd disengaged from our usual chat sessions enough times, she started sending her husband over for Ashlynn instead. I felt bad dissociating from her without explanation, but it was easier than fighting with my jealous and judgmental husband about who I was friends with or arguing with Stacy's domineering feminist persuasions to resist my husband's control.

The fact was I let Darren control me. I didn't like it, nor did I think it was right, but it was what I felt I had to do to keep the peace in our home and keep our dysfunctional family together. If that meant no friends or family out of his fear they'd influence me against him, then I would focus on my son and my work. I had Darren's debt to pay down anyway.

I barely had income anymore, though. Real estate in our sleepy town wasn't worth as much as where I'd worked before, and there were more realtors per square foot than there were houses to sell. So I took a job watching two babies for a while, until the baby's grandma offered me a corporate job with a better and more consistent income.

As the communications director for a Touching Hearts at Home franchise, which provided caregivers for the elderly and disabled, I gave presentations about the benefits of our services to social workers and medical staff at hospitals, rehabilitation centers and nursing homes. Office sales escalated to a million per year within a year and a half, and I was published for the first time on the Alzheimer's Hope website. I was still home every day to get Ryder on and off the school bus too. I felt like Superwoman, like I could do everything!

By night, however, Darren's inattention made me feel like I was nothing, and that nothing I did was noteworthy. It's like the more I accomplished outside our house, the more insignificant he wanted me to feel at home. I'd become so depressed and irritable due to Darren's neglect and disregard that a slight criticism at work triggered me to quit without notice and storm out of the building. It wasn't what I wanted, and I cried for days after in regret, disappointed that I'd allowed Darren's treatment of me to influence such a self-sabotaging overreaction. It just made me resent him more.

Fortunately, my mom friend Tara, who owned a cleaning service, hired me to cover for her while she recovered from shoulder surgery. My proficiency at cleaning, combined with the reliable and trustworthy reputation I quickly developed, increased business to the point that I was able to buy Tara out of the business altogether by spring of 2011. Business continued to skyrocket, and soon I had a waiting list for service and a cleaning crew I'd hired to help me. I was making sustainable income that could restore the financial independence I'd had before marrying Darren, and knowing I could potentially support me and Ryder on my own was a game changer.

On the way to a cleaning job one summer afternoon, a cute and well-maintained ranch home for sale caught my eye. I got to thinking about what life would look like there, for just me and Ryder. I could see him running through the acre yard with Pepper while I planted flowers along the walkway to the porch. I envisioned birthday parties on the back deck, with colorful balloons tied to the rails. I could see Kitty sitting in the big bay window, watching the birds fly from tree to tree. Most notably, however,

I felt like I could live in peace there. It was a fantasy that begged me to consider whether buying a house was a viable option at all, so I calculated the mortgage payment in my head. Then I calculated it on paper as soon as I could, to confirm what I'd come up with. Even without the promise of child support, I was surprised I could easily afford the monthly payment!

All the reasons that kept me in my miserable marriage attempted to deter the possibilities that suddenly lay before me. They were no longer valid, though. This house was in the same town, close to our current home. Ryder could remain in the same school with his new friends. I'd already lost Darren's family whom I'd been so afraid to risk losing before.

So, without one solid reason to deny myself, and my son, the possibility of a peaceful and happy life, it was no longer a matter of "if" I would leave anymore, but "when."

"Ain't No Rest for the Wicked"

I put my earnings in a checking account, separate from the one Darren reluctantly allowed me to hold jointly with him. So he had no idea how much I was making. He saw how much I worked, however, and assumed we had more money to spend.

He bought a truck on eBay, using my PayPal password saved on my laptop to access the bank accounts tied to it. By the time I'd found out, it was too late to cancel the transaction, because the truck was already in transport from Florida. It turned out to be a lemon beyond repair, so it went to the scrapyard, along with the $11,000 it had cost.

He still "needed" a truck, suddenly claiming he couldn't drive his work van for personal use. I didn't know where Darren had gotten the money for the truck he bought next, but at least it started. Unfortunately, it needed more work than he'd expected, and he didn't have the money to put into it, so it sat in the driveway unmoved and unused.

Then he bought a Repsol motorcycle with the last $10,000 of our home equity and sold it three weeks later for only $5,000. He didn't return that $5,000 to our home equity, though. He even kept the leather jacket he'd bought to match the crotch rocket, though it hung in the closet, unworn, for years after.

I finally sat down between Darren and the TV one night. "I made a list of all our bills and balances, Darren, and I don't know if you realize this, but we're almost a hundred thousand in debt. That's without the mortgages."

"Let's just file for bankruptcy," he suggested with a cavalier attitude.

"No! I've worked way too hard for my good credit score and I'm not letting that go to shit because you refuse to stop spending money!"

"Everybody else works the system," he defended without removing his eyes from the TV screen, "so why can't I? Why do you think I steal cash out of the token machines at work?" His casual admission shocked me, though his lack of morals shouldn't surprise me anymore.

"Are you serious right now?"

"Well, *you* never give me any money."

"You're right! I don't! I can't give you money I don't have!" I lied. Really, I *wouldn't* give him my money because I knew he'd blow it!

"We never have *any* money, though!" he yelled back.

"Because you spend it all!" I yelled louder. "You've literally exhausted every financial resource we have to buy beer and trucks! And now I see you've used my social security number to get credit cards that you've run up too!" He didn't know I'd seen the statements for those new cards in our email. The truth sure shut him up, though! He stared at the TV with a pout on his face and his arms crossed. "Don't worry. I'll figure it out like I always fucking do!" I vented out loud, then walked away.

I worried about Ryder overhearing the limitless arguments about money. Although he never wanted for anything, I didn't want him to think we had any less than anyone else. We should have actually been pretty well off with what Darren and I earned, but we couldn't be when one of us saved and the other spent exponentially more.

I refused to allow Darren's financial drain to affect Ryder's life, so I socked away my cash tips for whatever my son might need. When he was bullied and the school did nothing to change the circumstances, I worked harder to afford the hefty tuition of the private Catholic school in the next town over. Ryder became self-conscious there, about wearing the hand-me-downs he'd always worn, on days when uniforms were excused in lieu of street clothes. He wanted to have the same name-brand shoes and clothing the richer kids donned, but we were just making ends meet as it was. I had to get creative to make sure he wore whatever would make him fit in with the new crowd. I'd have done anything to prevent him from being picked on again.

That's when I discovered Goodwill. I shopped there regularly—not because we were poor, but because we could buy more Nike and Under

Armour shorts and shirts for the same amount just one would cost brand new. Darren balked at the idea of his son wearing gently used clothing, but Ryder was thrilled with the bags full of name-brand gear I'd bring him! After I explained how I'd been able to buy him so much of it, he started shopping there with me too!

Then one afternoon, Ryder came home from school almost too excited. "I got you something, Mom!" He rummaged through his backpack and handed me a stack of wrinkled coupons. "My teacher threw them in the garbage, so I pulled them out for you!"

I smiled. I was a proud mama. I was just sad that he made more effort to help with household finances than his grown-ass father did.

"Because Of You"

*D*espite always pretending everything was normal and fine, I worried about how Ryder interpreted Darren's treatment of me. Darren held me to very rigid standards, which I called "rules," and followed by choice.

The rules changed at Darren's convenience. Sometimes following them was wrong. Other times he'd make up new rules as we went, to achieve some selfish end. Sometimes I didn't even know if *he* knew the rules he'd already established through my own trials and errors, so I had to read between the lines to know what was expected of me.

"You're too loud!" he bellowed while I talked to a new mom friend on the phone one evening. "Go outside if you have to be on the phone!" Rule noted—no talking on the phone in the house.

But if I took a call on our porch, he'd come out and snark, "Why can't you take this call in the house? You fucking whoever's on the phone?" I was embarrassed the potential customer on the other end of the call had heard that, so I just stopped talking on the phone altogether when Darren was around.

"You should've seen Ryder with the friend he had over today," I started to tell Darren while I cooked dinner one night, "They were blowing farts on each other and—"

"Can't you see I'm watching TV?" he snapped, cutting me off.

"I was just trying to tell you a funny—"

"I can't possibly listen to every word you say, Dana. You talk way too fucking much." I shut down and mindfully noted not to speak when the

TV was on, which it always was. So I just stopped talking.

He timed me if I left the house to buy something as simple as cat litter, because I was always gone longer than he thought I should be. So I made sure to stop at the store *before* coming home after work, and didn't leave the house once there.

Dinner had to have two sides to the main dish, and he didn't like having similar meats on consecutive nights, so I started planning dinners a week in advance to ensure I didn't screw up. I even assigned certain foods to certain days to make a cute game out of it. We'd have Mexican Monday and Tortellini Tuesday, and Friday was always Pizza Night.

After years of conforming to Darren's every wish and command, Ryder began to do the same. If Darren slammed a door, Ryder would run a perimeter check for any household item affected by the impact. If Darren saw something just slightly off, he'd bitch until one of us moved it that one centimeter to the right, where it rightfully belonged in Darren's opinion.

It almost felt like Ryder was helping me appease Darren because he recognized how hard his dad was on me and wanted to prevent me from taking the brunt of Darren's burden. That wasn't my son's responsibility, though, nor the intent of my choice to submit in the first place.

Then one afternoon, Ryan came to the house to help Darren move a large armoire to my upstairs office. The stairway wall was slightly scratched in the process.

"Fuck!" Darren yelled when he noticed the marred paint. "Nobody has any respect for my house and my shit!" Then he walked out, slamming the door so hard the walls shook.

Ryan, Ryder and I stood frozen for a moment, though Ryder and I were more shocked that Darren had displayed his outburst so openly to someone who'd never met Mr. Hyde. Then Ryder saw a picture which had been knocked crooked when the door had slammed, and he hurried to straighten it before Darren returned.

"Somebody's got OCD!" Ryan laughed.

But watching my pre-teen son acquiesce to a narcissist wasn't funny to me, especially when it was becoming a habit, done in an effort to save me from the same.

"The Promise"

$\mathcal{E}$motions were running higher than ever by spring of 2014. We buried Denise's husband Brad, who'd dropped dead of a sudden heart attack. Darren's grandma passed two weeks after, though we'd known she'd go soon after her husband, who'd died months before. Darren forced me to put Kitty down in the midst of it all because, at nearly twenty years old, the poor thing wasn't always able to make it to his litter box in time. We were still mourning our beloved dalmatian, Pepper, who'd suffered a fatal dog bite in our front yard the summer before. All these losses within such a short timeframe made me reconsider whether Darren and I could withstand losing either each other too.

I mean, Denise's life had been ripped away from her in an instant. She lost her partner, her confidante, the person she thought she'd grow old with, and had involuntarily become a single mother to three grade-school children who now relied solely on her for the emotional and financial support she no longer had herself.

Yet here Darren and I were, alive and well, wasting precious time being petty and shitty to each other, when we could be making the most of the life we'd created. Darren had proven capable of being a good husband and partner in the past, so if he would just choose to be that man again, to recommit to me and our marriage the same way he had after Henrik died, I would gladly reciprocate by being the best wife I could be. Our relationship had never been better than it was in that short time before I'd confessed my affair to him. Even our sex life had reached new heights then.

I knew Darren hadn't forgiven me, though. He was one of those hurting people who hurt people, and he wasn't done hurting me for my indiscretion.

He confirmed my suspicion in the middle of a summer night. I was startled awake after the full force of Darren's fist punched my pillow. His knuckles had brushed my ear and landed less than an inch from my head. Then he rolled over, laying with his back to me, and resumed sleep.

I stared into dark nothingness after my eyes popped open, paralyzed and muted by terror. I lay there frozen, until the sound of my mouth gasping for air broke the trance I'd been frightened into. Even then, I remained unmoving out of fear I'd disturb the peace.

I couldn't fathom how a man could almost obliterate his wife's face and then continue sleeping as if he hadn't almost killed her. Did he even know what he'd done? He'd exerted too much force to have been unaware, in my opinion. He had no history of sleepwalking, so it wasn't that. Why was I even trying to find some reasonable explanation for the violent assault anyway? Was I so accustomed to making excuses for him, to protecting his reputation, that I'd find some validity for injuring or killing me? No! There was no excuse for what he'd done, nor any guarantee it wouldn't happen again. So I moved with sloth-like caution to the far edge of the bed and lay awake the rest of the night, contemplating my response to Darren if he happened to remember what he'd done.

There was no mention of it the next morning, but I couldn't deny my apprehension. Sleeping in the same bed with Darren felt like sleeping with the enemy. I didn't feel safe. Regardless of whether it had been conscious or not, I didn't trust him not to hurt me. I'd always known it would only be a matter of time before he struck me. I never thought it would be in my sleep, though.

I couldn't sleep elsewhere without telling Darren why, however, and telling him what he'd done would cause an argument I didn't want to have. So I continued to hang off the edge of my side, staying as far away from Darren as I could. Yet, doing so prevented sleep altogether, and I struggled to perform my physical job without sufficient sleep. Like everything else with him, I couldn't win!

After a few nights of avoidance, Darren caught on. He was so offended by the distance between us that he lined three king-sized pillows down the center of the bed. "I don't want you touching me while we sleep," he proclaimed. I didn't protest. In fact, I was glad the dividing wall of pillows had been his idea. Although done out of spite, those pillows were my only protection and the only boundary he wouldn't cross in our marriage.

I'd wasted years telling myself that staying in this marriage for Ryder was the right thing to do. But was it really worth sacrificing my well-being, safety, and security? I mean, I would do anything for my son, but what was the real benefit for Ryder to have both me and Darren in the same house? If it were anyone else asking, I'd argue that a boy needs his father in his life as a model of how to be a good husband who cares for his wife and children, and to have another male to talk to about manly things. In our situation, however, having Darren as a model of behavior was more of a disadvantage to Ryder. I just hoped Darren's drunken antics and violent tendencies dissuaded Ryder from the same.

So what was I still doing here? I wasn't even sure anymore, but we continued going through the motions day after day, month after month, until another year had gone by.

I was driving home from Thanksgiving dinner at my aunt's house in November of 2015, when, out of nowhere, Ryder commented, "I wish Dad came with us to family stuff."

"I know, kiddo, but you know your dad. He doesn't want to come because he says our side of the family doesn't like him. It's better off this way anyway, though. The few times he has come with us, he just sat by himself and got mad that we were visiting with everyone and not paying attention to him."

"Some of them don't like him, but they try to talk to him anyway! He's the one who won't talk to them!" Ryder argued.

I nodded. "I know, but it's just like when we go to Navy Pier on our own, or even when we went to LEGOLAND without him in San Diego. Your dad always has some excuse not to go places with us. And it's best not to take him anywhere he doesn't want to be."

"Just promise me one thing, Mom," Ryder said after some thought,

"Don't divorce Dad until I leave for Wyoming. He'll make our life a living Hell and I don't want to be here for it."

The blunt truth stunned me into open-mouthed silence. It's like Ryder's simple request answered an age-old riddle I'd never expected to solve.

Ryder hadn't asked "if" I was going to divorce Darren; he'd made a statement about "when" I would divorce Darren. It was presumed, spoken as if common knowledge, like he'd always known divorce was imminent. So why was *I* struggling with the thought of it?

As if his request had given me the permission I needed, I resolved myself to what I'd wanted to do all along. "I promise, Ryder."

So that was it. When Ryder graduated high school, I'd get him settled at WyoTech—the technical school he'd been eyeing since he was seven years old—then come back and divorce Darren. Having this cooperative plan in place, a strange peace settled in my heart. I was almost excited; I finally knew what the future held.

"I can't believe you'll be at WyoTech in six short years! Still planning to take the diesel mechanics program, or do you think you might switch to automotive or rat rods?"

"Definitely diesel," he affirmed. "That'll never change!"

Just like your dad, I thought.

"Come Out and Play"

"I haven't changed!" Darren shouted at me. "You're the one who's changed!"

"You're right, Darren! I grew the fuck up and you didn't!" I yelled. "You are exactly the same twenty-one-year-old I met, drinking till you're trashed every night, and thinking about nothing but yourself!"

It was 2016. Darren and I stood on opposite sides of our kitchen island in the midst of another argument about money. He'd purchased a $500 chainsaw, even though I'd told him there was less than $10 in our account after paying bills. All the checks I'd written for the bills were returned for insufficient funds as a result, and the bank charged us a couple hundred dollars in overdraft fees we couldn't afford to pay. I told him I wouldn't sit back and watch him put us in financial ruin, and he didn't like it, so the argument shifted from money to personal insult.

"You're the fucking problem, Dana! You used to be so sweet . . . and fun! But you're no fun at all now! You don't drink. All you worry about is money. You don't give a shit about me. All you care about is the king!" That was his new reference to Ryder, for my obvious favor towards him.

"You're absolutely right, Darren! I stopped drinking because someone has to be the grown up around here. I worry about money because you obviously don't. And Ryder is the king! He is my son, he comes first, and I won't apologize for that!"

I retreated to the dark quiet of the basement, where I'd been sleeping. Since finally coming to terms with the decision to divorce, I no longer felt it necessary to appease Darren by sleeping in the same bed with him or accommodating any of his demands for that matter. He didn't know of my plan to leave, but he would have been stupid not to sense the distance I was putting between us.

The basement had become my safe place anyway. No one went down there, so it was untouched by the negativity oppressing the rest of the house. It was merely a place for Ryder and his friends to spread out their sleeping bags and watch movies, and where I would escape to my craft room to make jewelry or wrap gifts.

It was cozy too. The half log exterior siding we'd chosen to finish the interior walls with created the feel of a vacation cabin, which was exactly what I was going for. It calmed me to feel like I was somewhere else, away from the farm and this life. The warm wood ceilings and floors added to the grounding sense of nature brought into the room by the log furniture and antler décor.

Variant-shaded gray stones covered the walls surrounding the seventy-inch 3-D TV and built-in beams, which served as shelving. Adorning them were framed photos of Ryder in hunting gear and old railroad lanterns, which were once part of Henrik's collection.

The other side of the built-in unit was made into a rustic dry bar which held a few bottles of champagne that had been gifted to me by customers. The dusty wine glasses sitting on the rough wooden counter near them, however, attested to the lack of celebration in our home.

Darren retaliated against my newfound peace down there. He'd startle me awake at all hours of the night by stomping around on the floors and stairs above. Other nights, he'd barge into the basement yelling about my shortcomings as a wife, as if I was supposed to feel guilty for his unhappiness and return to my previous servitude towards him. He was desperate to assert his place as man and dictator of the house and bully me back into submission, but the loss of sleep affected me more than his words.

I was so tired I could barely trudge through each day of work. The bags under my eyes gave away my drowsiness, as did the slumped shoulders I couldn't keep up any straighter than my head. Some days, I'd nod off driving from one cleaning job to another. Yet, no matter how tired I was, I was afraid to fall asleep at night, or into such a deep sleep that I wouldn't hear Darren come downstairs and hurt me before I could defend myself.

So I started putting a two-by-four under the knob inside the basement door. Then I'd sleep on the basement couch with my head facing the stairway. That way, if Darren tried to open the door, the sound of wood falling down the stairs would wake me and give me the opportunity to defend myself against whatever verbal or physical offense he'd come at me with.

I felt crazy doing this. No normal person in a normal marriage had to strategize about how to protect themselves just so they could sleep. It was so ridiculous I sometimes questioned myself about my reality. Were things really the way I saw them? Or was I so tired I couldn't think clearly? I didn't even know what was what anymore!

Just a couple nights into this new routine with the two-by-four, the loud clunking sound of it falling down the wooden stairs awoke me. I jumped off the couch faster than my reflexes normally responded and looked up the stairs to see the hazy blur of Darren standing in the doorway. Everything had happened so fast, I forgot to grab my glasses from under my pillow.

"What the fuck?!" Darren yelled.

I grabbed up the two-by-four and gripped it tightly like a baseball bat. My heart felt like it would pound right out of my chest as I stood at the base of the staircase, ready to swing. The sound of my quick, heavy breaths filled the silent pause.

"You're fucking crazy!" Darren said, then walked away, leaving the basement door halfway open.

I remained in my offensive position until I heard Darren stomp up the stairs to the second floor and firmly shut the master bedroom door. Then I ran up the basement stairs, closed the door, and replaced the two-by-four.

After I'd tucked myself back into the reclined couch, I breathed deeply to calm my pounding heart, though calm seemed like a fantasy in this house of chaos and conflict.

I'd done this to myself, though. I'd thought that if I followed all Darren's rules, did what he wanted me to do, said what he wanted me to say, that he'd love the person he'd molded me into and everything would be okay. By consuming myself in what he wanted me to be, however, I'd sacrificed who I actually was.

I wasn't just Darren's wife. I was Ryder's mother. I was a daughter, a granddaughter, an aunt, a cousin, a friend. I was a woman with my own ideas, unique talents, and aspirations Darren didn't support. There were things I wanted to do and people and places I wanted to see that Darren had no interest in. Devoid of these connections and experiences, my life wasn't even mine.

Just then, I had an epiphany. Darren wasn't the one who'd held me down all this time; I was. I'd chosen subservience. Granted, I had my reasons, but I had even more reasons to choose to free myself of the bounds I'd allowed Darren to impose on me. So I ripped off the hypothetical collar and leash, and took back ownership of my life. Darren wasn't going to like the change in me, but seeing as he didn't like who he'd turned me into either, I had nothing to lose.

"Unhappily Married"

Structure and simplicity worked best for me, so I started my journey back to myself with a new routine of walking the perimeter of our property every morning. Hearing birds chirp and breathing in the cool, fresh air of each new day brought peace to my soul and clear perspective to my otherwise cluttered mind. It was my more active method of meditating, I suppose.

Afterward, I'd go inside, make a cup of coffee, and sip on it as I walked upstairs to my office, where I checked emails and perused the internet before leaving for work, as I always have.

One morning, my sacred alone time was interrupted by a handwritten letter awaiting me on my desk. I recognized the technical-looking font as Darren's. After all the vulgar things he hadn't hesitated to call me and insult me with, I couldn't imagine what he'd opted to communicate in writing as opposed to saying directly to my face.

The notebook paper was titled "How to be a good wife," which was an insult in itself. My shoulders heaved in correlation with the big sigh I took, before reading my instructions.

*Say good morning.
*Say goodnight.
*Kiss me when you get home (on lips).
*Respond to me when I talk to you.
*Surprise me—on anything.
*Initiate sex.
*When I'm upset, show me love. Don't ignore me.

260

*Call me.
*Hold me.
*Touch me.
*Give in when we argue.
*Ask how I am.
*Get interested in MY life.

I shoved the list aside and turned to my laptop. Despite my promise to Ryder, I'd intended to look up a divorce attorney I'd spoken to before, so I could call her later that day to get more insight into the time frame and process of ending this charade. This list of instructions didn't hinder me in the slightest.

Not that it was unreasonable. Most wives in a loving marriage would naturally do all of these things for her husband, but I wasn't in a loving marriage. After all the drunken nights, neglect, violence, infidelity, verbal and emotional abuse, financial irresponsibility, disrespect, and disregard, he had some nerve asking me for anything. But then again, if these simple courtesies would appease him while I secretly planned my marital exit, I'd enact them like a list of chores.

"Good morning!" I called out from my office when Darren woke up a short time later. That had been my first instruction. I supposed I could check it off the list now.

Darren paused at the top of the stairs and looked at me suspiciously. I suppose that qualified as surprise, so I could check that off the list too.

I walked over to him then and gave him a kiss on the cheek. "Did you sleep well?" I placed my cold hand on his back—intentionally. I kissed him, touched him, and asked how he was, so check, check, and check.

He flinched, grimaced in annoyance, then replied, "Yeah."

"Good!" I responded with a smile, then returned to my office to find that attorney's phone number.

When Darren came home from work that evening, I greeted him at the door with a kiss and took his lunch cooler from his full hands. On my way back to the kitchen, I said, "Dinner's in the oven. Be about a half hour. Why don't you rest in your recliner until then? I'll get a beer for ya!"

"Okay . . ." He squinted one eye suspiciously. He was picking up on my Stepford-wife act. It's what he wanted, though, wasn't it?

So every day when he came home from work, I gave him the same quick kiss (on the lips) and catered to his every whim. I can't say I minded the much more pleasant demeanor he took on as a result, though I knew it would only last as long as I kept up mine. Tit for tat.

Then one day, Darren came in and waited at the door, holding out the lunch cooler for me to take. I remained at the kitchen island chopping vegetables, instead of rushing to kiss him and retrieve his things like I'd been.

When he realized I wasn't leaving my dinner preparations, he walked over and put the cooler on the opposite side of the island from where I stood chopping vegetables.

"Hey," I said dimly, glancing up to acknowledge him for a second.

"Hey." Darren came over to me, put his hand on my back, and leaned down with puckered lips. I offered my cheek instead. I could tell the snub caught him off guard because he just stood there staring at me.

"What?"

"What's going on with you?" Darren turned to get a beer out of the refrigerator behind me.

"Nothing at all," I said, even though my head was pounding and the one light on in the kitchen was making it worse.

"Then why are you acting like a bitch again?" said the man who was talking to his wife like an asshole again.

"What? Because I'm not coddling you?"

"Yeah! This is just like when I moved back home—you were sweet and nice and did everything for me, then you just stopped, and our marriage went to shit again!"

Because I didn't feel good, my patience with him was thin. I slammed the knife I held onto the butcher block cutting board and threw my arms up. "Jesus Christ! What do you want from me, Darren? Did it ever occur to you that maybe I don't feel up to par once in a while? That maybe *I* need some taking care of? Or am I not allowed to feel under the weather because it's inconvenient for your entitled ass?" I heard Ryder's bedroom door shut then. He was in his room playing games on his computer.

"I can never do anything right, can I?" Darren whined. His exaggeration reminded me of an angry toddler who wasn't getting his way.

"Why do you always do that? Here I am, with a fucking migraine, but you're turning things around so I feel sorry for you?" My head hurt from raising my voice. I closed my eyes and took a deep breath to relax. I didn't have it in me to argue tonight, so I made a quick decision to relent. I opened my eyes and said, "I'm sorry. I just don't feel good today." Then I carried the cutting board to the stove and used the knife to scrape the vegetables into the pot of boiling water.

When I turned to put the cutting board into the sink, Darren was behind me with his arms extended. "So you do love me?" A half-smile came across my lips as I huffed out in disbelief. It was always about him.

But I knew one word would prevent an otherwise exhausting night, so I gave in with a defeated mumble. "Forever." Then I leaned into his arms for a weak and very quick hug to placate his ego.

Although I was thankful for the near miss of an argument, I was disappointed in myself for once again compromising my sense of who I was in deference to someone who opposed everything I believed in. The only way I could think to honor myself, appease Darren, and simultaneously fulfill my promise to Ryder to stay through the next few years was to set boundaries.

I started by withdrawing from Darren physically. If he couldn't give me the love and respect of a spouse, then he wouldn't get the physical spousal privileges. I didn't want the affections to distract either of us with the artificial bond they temporarily created. So, although I occasionally star-fished to get him off my back about the lack of sex in our relationship, I wouldn't kiss him on the lips. That was too intimate, and he was a terrible tongue kisser anyway. I offered my cheek instead, like I would do with a brother or cousin.

Darren didn't think rules applied to him, though. He came home from work every day, trying to kiss me on the lips every time. After several instances of me turning my head and sticking my cheek out, he scolded, "You know I don't like when you do that."

"And I don't like being told what to do and how to do it." I snatched his coat from him and walked away.

"Car Crash"

Spring of 2016, Darren came home from work in the middle of the night, slamming the door to announce his bad mood. His lack of consideration, combined with his passive-aggressive, attention-seeking behaviors, infuriated me. I went to the kitchen to find out what his problem was and diffuse it before he woke up Ryder too.

"What's going on?" I whispered in a sleepy voice. I blinked my eyes as they adjusted to the light in the kitchen.

"I fucked up my back," he barked, as if I'd caused the injury.

"What happened?" I rubbed the crusties out of my eyes so I could see better.

"What don't you understand?" he yelled. "I fucked my back up again doing work I shouldn't fucking be doing! I shouldn't be crouched under a roller coaster car while everyone stands around watching me do everything!"

Darren had been diagnosed with two degenerative discs in his early twenties. The chiropractor had warned him against back-breaking work then, and also told him to stop riding four-wheelers and dirt bikes because the off-road terrain caused his spine trauma it wouldn't be able to withstand over time. But Darren wouldn't be told what he could and couldn't do. Plus, he tended towards situations in which people would feel sorry for him. He thrived on pity.

He wouldn't get it from me, though. I crossed my arms to warm myself against the cool air he'd brought in with him, then rationalized, "Your boss knows you have a bad back, so why would he have had you do that anyway? Especially if there were other people there who could have done it instead."

"Someone has to do the fucking work to pay the bills around here!"

I wasn't going to escalate his mood right now by pointing out the fact that he only paid half or less of the bills. I also worked very hard—cleaning houses six days a week—and paid for everything his income couldn't. "Well, when they ask you to do something you shouldn't be doing, you need to speak up."

With the most disdainful expression, Darren pushed past me and locked himself in the bathroom. I wasn't deserving of his presence, I guessed, because I'd advised him to handle his work situation like a mature adult. I didn't care, though; it was late and I was tired, so I went back upstairs to retrieve my pillow and blankets. I'd treated myself to sleeping in the master bed that night, since Darren said he'd be working overnight instead of during the day like he normally did, but now that he was home and after what had just happened, I was moving back down to the basement.

I couldn't get back to sleep while Darren was having a tantrum, though. I lay in the dark, with wide-open eyes, listening to him slamming cabinet doors shut and throwing objects around in the bathroom. He punched something too, but I couldn't determine whether it was the shower wall or the actual wall. When he finally stomped up the stairs to bed, I remained awake for a bit to make sure the quiet wasn't teasing me into thinking it was safe to close my eyes.

The next morning, I was in the kitchen making coffee when Darren stomped back down the stairs. I immediately froze in place. Not just because Darren's anger made me nervous, but because that sound triggered me back to my childhood when my stepfather would pound up or down the stairs, looking to punish me for whatever wrong he'd faulted me for.

Darren knew what he was doing too. I glared at him for cruelly exploiting my fear, and he glared back before disappearing into the bathroom to get dressed. He emerged in his work clothes a couple minutes later, slamming the door behind him as he left.

I was confused. He'd said he'd hurt his back, so where was he going? I really didn't want to engage with him so early, but my curiosity got the best of me. I followed him out to the porch, my desperately needed coffee in hand. "Where are you going?"

"Where the fuck do you think I'm going?" he hollered back before slamming his van door shut. Then he put the van in reverse so fast I jumped back in fear it would hit the porch I stood on. I looked down at my spilt coffee, then back up to see Darren accelerate forward at high speed. The tires squealed before leaving black marks on the concrete pad between the house and garage. Then the back end of the van fishtailed on the gravel and bounced off a tree. The tail-light shattered, then the van wobbled back and forth before finally settling still. Its remains lay all over the gravel and grass.

I froze again and watched as Darren jumped out of the van to assess the damage. There were multiple large dents in the side and back of it. "See what you made me do, Dana? Fuck!" He took a broken part from the ground and chucked it across the lawn.

His unpredictable anger scared me. I rushed into the house, engaged the deadbolt, then flattened against the wall to the side of the door. I listened to determine whether Ryder had been awakened by the commotion, but I only heard the quick huffs of adrenaline-induced panic coming from my mouth. It was a wonder the kid slept through this and all else that occurred here.

It was too quiet, though, and I worried about Darren's whereabouts. I moved towards the front window and peeked out to see what he was doing. After kicking a piece of wreckage out of his way, Darren got back into his van. He drove through the dewy grass, leaving black ruts behind him as he headed towards the road. Then he revved the engine and squealed the tires again before turning out. Relieved he was gone, I closed my eyes, relaxed my shoulders, and took a deep breath to recover from the rough start to my day.

I imagined Darren would have a rough day too. He would have to come up with a lie to excuse the damage to the van, especially since he'd wrecked the previous one driving home drunk a couple years before. *A deer ran out into the road*, he'd told us all, but even his mother didn't believe that story.

"Better Man"

After days of complaining of back pain, and weeks of lying on the couch because a chiropractor failed to relieve it, I couldn't decipher whether Darren was claiming to be in so much pain to get out of working, or if he really did have a serious injury. So I made an appointment for him to see an orthopedic surgeon, who discovered a herniated disc and recommended surgery as soon as they could schedule it.

"Friday the thirteenth is *not* the day to have surgery," I warned Darren.

"What do you want me to do? Lie here in pain because of your stupid superstitions?" he retorted from the living room sofa.

"Yes, actually! At least until the next available day!"

So on Friday, May 13, 2016, Darren had surgery. The orthopedic surgeon assured us Darren would walk out of the hospital feeling better than ever after the twenty-minute routine procedure. I was counting on that too. As badly as I felt breaking my promise to Ryder, I'd decided I was ready to file for divorce just before Darren had gotten hurt. I just couldn't wait five more years. But now I'd have to wait—at least until he recovered from surgery and returned to work. I'd stay married to Darren as long as I had to before allowing him to take advantage of his medical situation to gain spousal support from me.

While Darren was prepped for and taken into surgery, Jane and I sat in the expansive waiting room together. She'd insisted on being at the hospital, which I'd have welcomed in the past, but the polite small talk that comprised the little interaction we had anymore was just awkward.

"They said the surgery would only take twenty minutes," I said at the risk of telling her something she already knew. I wasn't sure what else to say.

Jane smiled and nodded in acknowledgment, then looked around. I did too—for some meaningless topic of conversation we could fill the void between us with. Then she pointed at the multicolored gardens outside the floor-to-ceiling windows. "Those flowers are so pretty. And this weather! Are flowers coming up at your house?"

"Some." I refrained from commenting about how they'd remained underground this spring, hiding from Darren. Last summer, he got mad at me and took his chainsaw to my tall fountain grass and perennial blooms. "I'm going to get a cup of coffee. Would you like one?"

"No, thank you." She raised her water bottle for show.

"Okay. I'll be right back then." I didn't know if she'd suddenly taken up coffee drinking, since I didn't know much about her at all anymore, but that Nespresso machine I'd seen when we came in had been calling out to me to make a caramel latte.

I sat back down next to Jane, blowing on the surface of my latte to cool it. "So how's Denise and the kids?" Despite Denise shutting me out, I always worried about how she and the kids were managing without Brad.

That got Jane going. The proud grandma filled me in on Mason's basketball season and marching band activities, the plays Melissa had seen and upcoming shows she'd attend, and the foods Caleb, Denise's youngest, recently introduced into his very allergic diet. I was glad for the update but sad for the distance between us all now. I knew nothing of Denise's life, and in turn, Jane and Denise didn't know much about ours. I had been the link between us all before, oversharing in phone calls and visits. Their only connection to us now was through the short phone calls to Darren's cell phone, inviting us to a holiday or birthday party. Otherwise, it was exactly as Darren had always said—Jane and Denise stuck together, and we were on the outside. It was heartbreaking, but I nodded and smiled on cue, happy to have some semblance of what used to be.

As time passed into an hour, then two hours, beyond the expected completion of Darren's surgery, I started to worry. I couldn't imagine what was taking so long, unless something had gone wrong, which would have been just my luck.

Finally, after two and a half long hours, the surgeon finally came through the door. He walked over with a tense expression.

"How's he doing, Doc?" I stood to meet him, nervous to know what was wrong.

"Not too good. There was a complication." He paused. "Every disc in the spine has one nerve root to it. Darren, unfortunately, has a second root to the herniated disc, which is extremely rare. I didn't see it until we were in there—it wasn't on the MRI. So in order to relieve the herniated disc, I had to cut away at the second nerve root, and I really pissed it off."

"What does that mean for Darren?" A large gulp cleared my restricted throat for the deep breath I expected to need after he answered.

"Well, I've only seen this once before, so we'll have to wait and see what kind of recovery he has."

"We'll see" wasn't good enough for me. I needed to know how much longer I had to remain married to this man before I could file for divorce. "How long do you think his recovery will be?"

"It's hard to say. Could be a few weeks. Maybe a few months. Maybe more . . . You can come back and see him whenever you're ready." He walked away then.

I dropped my head, knowing Darren would milk his prognosis for as long as he could, when movement behind me distracted me from my self-pity. Jane was busy collecting her purse and sweater and water bottle, apparently anxious to see her son. I grabbed up my things too, then we went back to the recovery room to assess the situation.

Darren slept upon the hospital bed in the dimly lit room, so we entered quietly. Jane stopped at the foot of the bed and gripped her purse and sweater tightly, as if they were her security blanket. I'd have normally given her comfort, but our dynamic these last several years relieved me of any obligation to soothe. She'd never been receptive to affection anyway.

I put my purse down on the metal chair at the bedside and approached Darren slowly, careful not to wake him. But then a nurse came through the door and disrupted the quiet, causing Darren to stir uncomfortably.

"We went ahead and filled his prescriptions here in the hospital, so you don't have to make a stop on your way home," she said as she handed me a couple small white paper bags with the red Walgreens logo.

"Okay, thank you." I took the bags and inspected the contents.

Gabapentin and Tramadol—those were some hard hitters.

"He's in pretty bad shape," the nurse commented. "I'm surprised they're not keeping him overnight."

"Overnight?" I wished out loud.

"Yes," the nurse responded, "he should really be monitored overnight in the condition he's in, but the doctor instructed us to release him. It's probably going to be a rough night for him, though. And you too." I didn't need the warning. I already knew he'd exaggerate his condition to milk me for all the attention and pity he could.

Just as the nurse exited, Darren groaned loudly, "I'm in so much fucking pain! This fucking sucks!" He pounded the bed with a fist while he rambled more profanities.

"I gotta get outta here," Jane blurted. Then she ran out the door! I stood still with an open mouth, stunned that she'd bailed without consoling her son or saying goodbye. I couldn't go after her either, because the nurse re-entered with a wheelchair and asked me to bring the car around.

I took my purse, then took my time getting the car, hoping the extra time with Darren would compel the nurse to convince the doctor to keep Darren after all. But to my dismay, the nurse was waiting at the curb with Darren in the wheelchair as soon as I drove the car up. He wore an exaggerated frown on his face, to complement the irritated grunts he made as she transferred his stiff body into my unaccommodating little Kia Forte.

As we drove off, I wished I could find positive words of encouragement to share with Darren. I wanted to tell him everything would be okay, that he'd heal and we'd get through this together, but it was all bullshit, so I chose to say nothing instead. He didn't say anything either, but the sharp tension said everything, so I didn't dare break the silence by turning the radio on. I'd never been so eager to get home.

Five minutes from the house, a black cat ran out into the middle of the road. I slowed the car, thinking it would move as we neared, but it sat in my path, taunting me with its stare. I love animals too much to run one over, and there was no way I'd run over a black cat on Friday the thirteenth, so I slammed on my brakes. The back end of the car fishtailed on the gravel, then came to a stop just before the cat's demise. Darren and I were propelled forward, then slammed backward. The cat casually sauntered off into the open field.

"What the fuck, Dana?!"

"I'm sorry!" I yelled back. "I wasn't going to run that cat over!"

"So you slam on your brakes right after my back surgery?! You fucking kidding me?"

I didn't respond because I was indefensible. I shouldn't have done what I did, but given the option, I'd prioritize the cat's life over Darren's pain again any day.

With a slightly bowed head, I proceeded until we pulled into the driveway a couple minutes later. Darren unbuckled his seat belt, then without warning, jumped out of the slow-moving vehicle just as I was turning to park in front of the garage.

I slammed on my brakes again and looked out the passenger door he'd left hanging open. "Darren!"

He glanced back with an exaggerated scowl, then continued to limp towards the house with clenched fists. Feeling frustration and worry all at once, I parked the car, closed the passenger door, then rushed after him, but he shook me off when I put my hands on his arm for assistance.

"I'm trying to help you, Darren!" I scolded.

"I don't need your fucking help," he bitched back, but he still allowed me to unlock the door and help him up to the bedroom. After laying him down on the bed, he banged it violently with clenched fists and screamed. "AHHHHHHH!"

His anger was nothing new, and completely warranted given the situation, but it triggered me nonetheless. I had to get out of there, away from him, and immediately. So I ran out of the room and out to my car.

While collecting my purse and Darren's medications from the back seat, emotions overcame me. I leaned against the car, fell to the ground in a crouch, with my face in my hands, and broke down crying.

Why did Darren hate me so much? What was it about me that made me so awful that I was undeserving of his love? It couldn't just be the affair, because this had started long before that. Hell, Darren's neglect was the reason I was vulnerable to Merrick in the first place! And I was sorry. I'd never been more regretful about anything in my entire life! But I tried everything to make this man happy and make our marriage work, but no one was happy and none of this was working. I couldn't live like this anymore!

"I hate my fucking life," I sobbed aloud to no one. Then I remembered my grandma telling me, "Don't you cry a tear for nobody!" She was right. I was stronger than this. But I didn't want to be strong sometimes.

For now, I had no choice. I wiped my tear-filled eyes, stood straight back up, took a deep breath, and walked back into the hell I called home to face the Devil head on.

"July"

Darren's recovery didn't go well. One of his feet went cold and numb the day after surgery, which the surgeon attributed to nerve damage. He was advised to take his medications as prescribed and give the nerve time to heal, but Darren refused both, limping around for pity instead and claiming he was disabled and couldn't go back to work. Ever.

So I worked on scheduling more cleaning jobs until I was fully booked, seven days a week, ten to twelve hours a day. It was exhausting, but I was thankful to have the ability to make up some of his lost income so quickly, as well as have an excuse not to be home. I figured I just had to keep this up until Darren was back to work anyway. Despite his assertions to the contrary, he *had* to go back to work at some point.

Then at the end of July 2016, we received a letter informing us that Darren's employer was "eliminating his position." They were canceling his employer-paid health insurance and offering an insulting $1,500 in severance pay for his seventeen years of service to the company. That wouldn't even cover a month's mortgage payment!

"What're we gonna do?" I panicked as I sat on the coffee table with the termination letter in hand, facing the cheapskate who'd also opted out of the short-term disability coverage his company had previously offered for a mere twelve dollars per month. "No job, no income, no insurance . . . I can't believe this is happening!"

"I know! My company had a fundraiser for that guy who got cancer, so his family didn't have to worry about money."

I looked at Darren in disbelief that he equated that man's situation to ours and felt slighted in comparison. "He died, Darren!"

"Yeah, and his family didn't have to worry about anything because of all the money everyone gave them!"

I wasn't even going there with him. We had to focus. "Look, we need you to have *some* kind of income. I mean, you haven't brought a paycheck home since before your surgery, and that was almost three months ago! I'm doing my best to pay the bills, but I don't know how long I can cover us on my own."

"NMFP!"

"Not my fucking problem" had become Darren's motto, and he always added a little gloat to his tone when he said it. But he was right. It never was his problem. His problems were always my problems, and I was tired of bearing the burdens of his poor choices.

"That's fine, Darren." I stood and crossed my arms. "I'll do what I always do then and take care of everything myself. By the way, has your mother called to see how you're doing?" That was a nasty poke at the fact that she hadn't called in a while. Neither had Denise. None of Darren's supposed friends or co-workers had called at all since his surgery. He didn't have anyone but me, and he needed to be reminded of that.

"No," he pouted. "No one gives a fuck about me."

Exactly, I thought, but I kept my mouth shut to let his own words sink in. Perhaps he'd reconsider taking me for granted if he realized I was the last remaining person with any sense of loyalty towards him.

After considering our financial situation, I came to the conclusion that we needed to sell some of Darren's toys. We needed the money more than we needed a boat, dirt bike, and stock car he couldn't drive, though I'd have settled for his miraculous rise from the couch with a healed back and foot. Darren opted to advertise the items for sale on Facebook Marketplace instead, probably hoping they wouldn't sell.

Within three days, however, all three were driven away by their new owners. Darren lay on the couch for days after, sulking. His selfish soul just couldn't grasp that those toys cost money to insure and maintain, and that keeping our heads above water financially needed to be a priority over pleasure right now.

"This is all your fucking fault! You're the one who wanted me to have surgery!" he yelled from the couch while I prepared his lunch in the kitchen on a Sunday afternoon. I heard Ryder's door slam shut. He couldn't stand when Darren and I argued. "Now I'm useless and can't do anything—I can't work, I can't have fun . . . What's the point in even being alive?!"

"Don't even," I defended. "I encouraged you to get to a doctor who could help you because I was tired of hearing you bitch about how much pain you were in. But *you* said you liked the surgeon, and *you* set up the surgery! And how the hell is it my fault you had another nerve root the doctor didn't know about? You want to blame someone, blame him!" I was tired of being blamed for all that was wrong in his life. "All I know is you better start helping me out because I don't know how long I can sustain us. And with my cleaning schedule so full, I don't have time to work another job either."

"*I told you, I'm never working again!*" Darren screamed. "I took care of you for seventeen years, so now it's *your* turn to take care of me!"

"You took care of me? Really? Other than the first half of my pregnancy with *our* son, I've always worked for my own money, and I've always paid what you decided was my portion of the bills. So don't even go there!"

Ryder came out of his room then and walked straight out to the garage without a word.

"That's great. See what you did, Darren?"

"Fuck you," he replied.

I opened the refrigerator and immediately got dizzy. I held onto the door handle for balance until the room stopped spinning. Then I turned back to Darren and pleaded, "Can you at least fill out the online application for Social Security Disability? You can do that from the couch, can't you?"

"What, for the twelve hundred per month they say I'm worth? I won't get it anyway," he refused.

"That's twelve hundred less I'd have to worry about busting my ass for! And if you're really disabled like you say you are, then why wouldn't you get it?" I challenged.

"I don't want to, so stop asking! Why is everything an argument with you?"

"I don't know, Darren. I don't know anything anymore," I said as I handed him his lunch plate.

I made the application for Social Security Disability on his behalf and spent the next year and a half filling out paperwork and responding to endless requests for medical records and witness statements.

Nearly two years later, in April 2018, Darren was finally granted a hearing. If they ruled in his favor, he'd receive a lump sum of benefits, retroactive to the day of his surgery. We needed it too. He still wasn't working, and I was working too much.

All he had to do was show up and answer the judge's questions. Despite his history of bad decisions, there was no way he could screw this up.

"You Lie"

One week before the hearing, I received an upsetting text message from a neighbor while I was at work. It didn't make sense to me, though. All I got out of it was that Darren had asked her for some big favor that she couldn't accommodate without risking her job.

"What the hell did you text our neighbor today?" I asked the second I walked in the door after work. Darren was lying on the couch watching *Impractical Jokers*.

"I asked if she would be a reference for me. I signed up on Home Advisor as a handyman and needed to give them ten references." Now the text made sense. His nonchalant attitude did not, however.

"You do realize your hearing with Social Security is only a week away, right?" I stood in front of him with my arms crossed.

"Yeah."

"And that our neighbor is a Social Security judge?"

"So?"

"*So?* Are you fucking kidding me?" I threw my arms in the air. "You have a hearing for Social Security Disability in less than a week and she's a Social Security judge . . . What don't you understand?" I walked to the kitchen for something to drink. I couldn't stand to look at the stupid fuck.

"I don't see what the big deal is," Darren defended. "I've done some work for her in the past."

I flipped back towards him. "You shoveled snow for her once or twice, Darren, and maybe did a couple other things I asked you to help her out with. But right now, you're claiming to be disabled and trying to get physical

277

work. Do you even know Social Security has a whole department of people who investigate applicants online? If they see you on Home Advisor, they'll deny you, and all the time I've put into this will have been for nothing! I swear you're trying to fuck it up just so you can say you were right about not getting it."

"Well, I'm not waiting a week for a judge to decide whether or not they'll give me money. I need to start making my own money now."

"*Now?* You've been lying on the couch telling everyone you're disabled for the last two years, but suddenly *now* you need to make money?"

"Well, you're not making enough to cover the bills and my expenses, so, yes, I need to make money *now*, Dana," he responded in a mocking tone.

"What expenses, Darren? Booze? Chewing tobacco? Four-wheeler or snowmobile parts? Forgive me if I'm not pulling my weight around here." I walked away in disgust.

A week later, we sat at a long laminate-top table in a sparsely furnished, white-walled room at the local Social Security Administration office, facing a large monitor on which a female judge joined us remotely. It wasn't our neighbor, though. She'd told me she'd recused herself before the case could be assigned to her.

"Shall we begin?" the judge asked. The hard rain pelting the tall windows distracted my focus, which just added to the anxiety already stirred up within me.

The administrator in the room with us dictated Darren's name and the cause for the case, which the judge repeated, then asked, "Do you have legal representation?"

Darren sat silently, so I piped up, "No, ma'am. I'm Darren's wife. I came to assist in answering any questions."

"So you have no legal representation?" She directed her question at Darren this time.

"No, ma'am," he said with a side-eye towards me.

"Well, I don't know that we should proceed, then. Most people obtain representation when they get to this point in the process." There was judgment in her raised-brow glare.

I spoke up nervously. "If I may, I have been filling out the paperwork for my husband, and I brought it all with me. I'm confident I can answer whatever questions an attorney may have answered for him."

"Are you an attorney?"

"No, ma'am."

"Do you have experience in disability law?"

"No, ma'am." I lowered my head. It was ironic to me that a disability judge would make someone feel so deficient.

"But you want to act as representative for your husband?"

"Yes, ma'am."

"And you agree to this?" she asked Darren.

"Yes, ma'am," he responded.

"All right!" she said with a know-it-all tone. "Then can you please tell me the amount of the qualified prescription cost credit he is requesting?"

What? This had nothing to do with his physical ability to work or not! Still, I scrambled through my inches-thick file of paperwork, recalling a form on which I had to list his medications and their costs.

The judge huffed impatiently. "Do you have this information or not?"

"Yes, I had a paper about his prescriptions. It's in here somewhere," I said as I rifled through the papers in a rush. The pressure wasn't helping me find the one I sought any faster.

"Do you even know what I'm asking for?"

"Yes, ma'am—the cost of his prescriptions."

She huffed impatiently and filed the paperwork in front of her. "This is ... Sir, I am going to grant you another hearing in thirty days. I expect you to leave here today and find an attorney to represent you in your case. Bring that attorney here with you for the next hearing. Do you understand?"

"Yes, ma'am," Darren responded, then threw me another sideways glance of disapproval. I didn't need help feeling badly.

Dejected and disappointed, we left without a word. Once in the car, Darren laid into me. "What the fuck happened in there?"

"I don't know! It got off track so fast!" There was no use re-hashing what we'd both witnessed, when we had little time to remedy the situation. "Just start calling attorneys today. Like now, on the half-hour ride home. Please!" I backed out of the parking space and proceeded into traffic.

"You know I don't like making phone calls," he said. Of course he didn't. That would require effort. "This was all your idea anyway."

I ignored his deflection and called attorneys for him as soon as we got home. After speaking to several who didn't have time to represent new clients, I found one who would take the case. I even emailed him all of the records pertaining to it, but Darren never called him back to secure representation for his second hearing. As a matter of fact, Darren didn't even attend the second hearing!

So instead of celebrating the benefits I'd hoped he'd been granted, my mood was funereal. Any hope I'd had for financial assistance was gone, as well as any hope to ever get out of this marriage without Darren fighting me for every penny he could suck me dry for.

He lay on the couch as always, watching some stupid show on TV while I made dinner. Then his cell phone rang.

"Oh! Hi, Mom!" I heard him answer. "Oh, I didn't go . . . No, it wasn't rescheduled or anything. They wanted me to get an attorney this time, but I didn't find one, so . . . yeah . . . and Dana told me I shouldn't bother going anyway. We both knew it was a waste of time. I wasn't gonna get the benefits. You know how our government is . . . yeah, it is a shame. We could've really used the money . . . okay . . . yeah . . . Thanks for calling, though . . . Love you too, Mom . . . Bye!"

"What was that about?" Although I'd been standing right there and heard the whole thing, I wanted Darren to admit to the lie he'd just told, because I didn't appreciate being a part of it.

"My mom just wanted to know how the hearing went."

"And you told her I didn't think you should go?"

"I tell my mom a lot of things."

I stopped what I was doing and turned towards the couch, my hand on my hip. "What's that supposed to mean?"

"Well, sometimes I tell my mom and my sister things about you that may not be true so they won't like you," he said a bit arrogantly. I was stunned—partially by his admission, but mostly because he'd spoken the truth for once.

The truth hurt too. But then it made sense of everything. I suddenly realized he'd been the cause of the division between me and Jane and Denise all along. They'd believed whatever lies Darren had told them about me. And why wouldn't they? He was their family. I wasn't. But what a cruel thing to do to the woman you married, knowing she'd been ostracized from her own family for refusing to permit mistreatment.

"You're un-fucking-believable," I muttered, then continued to make dinner silently.

"Circle the Drain"

At the end of June 2018, Ryder and his friends attended the annual town festival, which pays tribute to the town's manufacture of World War II ships, with live bands, a carnival, and a beer garden. Darren told Ryder he'd pick him at 10 p.m. When I awoke at 1 a.m. to pee, I noticed Ryder's bedroom door was still open. He never left it open when he slept, so I checked his bed. He wasn't there.

Maybe he slept over at a friend's house, I reasoned to subside my worry. But when I went back out to the living room and looked up the stairway to confirm Darren was home, I saw the master bedroom door was open too, which meant he wasn't in bed either.

I went to the window to see if the lights were on in the garage. Other than the moonlight reflecting off Darren's white truck, it was pitch black. My personal vehicle, a Toyota FJ Cruiser I'd treated myself to a few years before, was missing from its normal spot, though. I shook my head and huffed. That asshole always felt entitled to what wasn't his.

I went back to the basement to check my phone. No calls or texts. So I texted Darren and Ryder to find out where they were.

When neither responded after a few minutes, I called Darren. It went straight to voicemail. I tried Ryder next, but after several rings, his voicemail message offered no consolation. I lay down, trying to calm my worry with logical thinking, but every second that passed caused the pains in my chest to become more intense. I was starting to lose control of my breathing too, which didn't help my already pounding head.

Common sense reminded me I would have received a phone call if any of the tragic scenarios in my head had actually happened, but it was 2 a.m. and I didn't know where my kid was. I was crawling out of my skin with the discomfort of rising panic. I needed to do something other than sit around and wait. So I put my taupe-framed glasses over my watery eyes, grabbed my phone and the keys for my Kia, and ran out the door in my pajamas.

I drove to the festival in town first. No one was there. I called Darren and Ryder again. Still no answer.

My systematic mind decided to drive up and down every street of the small town and work my way outward. It was a long shot, but at least I'd feel like I was doing something proactive. Plus, it would buy time until one of them responded to me.

After an hour and a half, I still hadn't found them. I parked at the BP gas station at the four-way stop on the main drag, clinging to the hope that I would see Darren and Ryder go by on their way home. Everyone coming in and out of town drove through this intersection, including the same police car I'd already passed a few times tonight.

When the police car turned around and slowly passed the gas station a second time, I thought I should look like I'd stopped to make a call, so I wasn't suspect to some shady crime more likely to occur at this hour. I dialed Darren first, and when I got no answer, I tried Ryder again. Then I tried them both a second time. Still no answer. The third time, Ryder answered as if I were a nuisance.

"What?" he growled. He sounded just like his dad.

I was relieved to hear his voice, though. "Oh my god! Ryder, where are you?"

"We're fine," he said gruffly, then hung up.

"Ryder? Ryder?!" Why had he hung up on me? I called back, gripping my phone as if it were the lifeline to my only child, but he wouldn't answer.

Ryder, please call or text me back. I'm begging you. I just need to know where you are. Please! I texted him.

After several minutes and no response, I started to panic again. I didn't understand why Ryder wouldn't talk to me or respond to the text. He was obviously hiding something, but what? No good happens in the wee hours of the morning.

There was no doubt in my mind this all led back to Darren. He'd had a few beers before leaving the house to get Ryder, and God only knows how many more he might have had at the festival before they left.

I was more upset that Ryder was covering for him. Ryder had seen his dad drive with open alcohol, stumble around drunk at home, verbally abuse and physically threaten me. I'd always hoped he'd see the wrong in his dad's actions and refuse to enable or excuse them as I had for so many years. Instead, he implored me to never call the cops on Darren. "I don't want to be the kid whose dad ends up in jail," he'd said. I complied, though the request itself confirmed to me that even Ryder knew Darren was a criminal and opted to protect him no matter what the cost to me.

What Ryder didn't know was Darren had already been in jail—the first time for DUI, and then again for attempted breaking and entering at one of his work locations. The second little stint was chalked up to Darren setting off an alarm accidentally. That's what he told me, at least, but I couldn't be so sure after the handful of times Darren had admitted to me that he'd stolen money from coin changers and vending machines at work. I'd also paid a fine for public disturbance after Darren brawled with a man he didn't know at a gas station in the middle of a night out drinking with a friend.

These thoughts about Darren's alcohol-induced criminality motivated me to continue my search. I would not allow him to drive my son around while drunk, nor give Ryder the impression this behavior was acceptable.

I drove through the parking lots of the local bars. Tears flooded my bloodshot eyes as I turned out of the empty back lot of the last one, though I was able to clearly see the spinning red and blue lights in my rear-view mirror. I pulled aside immediately, right in front of the "Wrong Way" sign on the one-way street. *Crap!*

I rolled down my window as the officer approached my car. "What's going on this morning, ma'am?"

"I'm looking for my son," I choked out between sobs. "My husband was supposed to pick him up at the fair at ten, but they never came home."

"I wondered why you were driving around town," he said, pulling a small notebook and pen from a pocket in his protective vest. "What are your husband and son's names?"

I answered, spelling our long German surname for accuracy.

"And what is the make and model of the vehicle they're driving?"

"They're in my dark purple Toyota FJ Cruiser. It's lifted and has a white top with a roof rack. You can't miss it."

The officer pressed the button on the two-way radio near his shoulder and repeated the information I'd provided.

Suddenly, my phone rang and Darren's name came up on the caller ID on my radio. My phone was connected to the Bluetooth in my car, so the sound of the ring and the phone call came in loudly through the speakers.

"It's my husband! May I answer the call?" The officer nodded yes, so I pressed the green phone icon on my steering wheel. "Darren, where are you?"

"I saw . . . saw . . . did you . . . did you call me?" His slurred words gave away his drunkenness.

The officer got back on his radio. "Back-up requested. Suspected 23152." Fuck!

"Darren? Where are you? Are you and Ryder okay?"

"We uh . . . we're . . . we . . . we're on way . . . home."

Just then, I saw the familiar headlights of my FJ in my side mirror.

"That's them! Coming from the south!" I called out my window. One of the four officers now on the scene walked to the middle of the street and directed Darren to pull over in front of me. Darren swerved too far to the right, ran up and over the curb onto the sidewalk, then swerved too far to the left to correct his error, landing half on and half off the sidewalk before coming to a complete stop.

"Please stay in your car, ma'am," the officer instructed, then walked toward the FJ..

I watched anxiously as another officer walked up to the passenger side of the FJ with his hand on his holster. The officer on Darren's side opened the driver door, and Darren got out holding his hands up in the air. The officer then led him toward the squad cars blocking me in. The officer who'd stood by the passenger side of the FJ followed behind them. Darren walked as crooked as he'd driven, glaring at me as he passed. I didn't even care. I just wanted to see Ryder, to see with my own eyes that he was okay.

"May I check on my son?" I asked the officer out my window.

"Yes, ma'am. But please have your son remain in the vehicle," he ordered.

"Thank you," I said, and hurried over to the driver's side window of the FJ.

I stood on my tiptoes to see into the cab. Ryder sat in the passenger's seat, staring ahead blankly. He leaned his head into his hand. He wouldn't look at me.

"Are you okay, Ryder?"

"I'm fine!" he barked back, then turned to look the other way completely.

His hostility confused me. "Ryder, what's going on? Where have you been all night?"

"I told you we were fine!"

"Ryder!" I snapped back. "I've been calling and texting you both for hours! Just please tell me where you were!"

"*No!* Just fucking leave!"

"What's going on with you?" I asked with narrowed eyes. "I just wanna know where you were and what you two were doing! I'm your mother. You owe me at least that!"

"No, I don't! And if dad's arrested, I'm not coming home with you either! So just leave me alone!"

He'd never spoken to me that way before. I teetered between wanting to give him space to process his obvious anger and scolding him for treating me disrespectfully. I took enough shit from Darren; I wasn't taking it from my kid too. "You can be mad at me, Ryder, but none of this is my doing. So if something happens with your dad, you can stay at a friend's house until you cool off. But don't you talk to me like that. I love you no matter what, but you don't get to treat me like this. I've done nothing wrong here."

Ryder wouldn't take his eyes off the nothingness outside his window, nor speak to me any further. At least he was okay, I reminded myself again. That was all that mattered. So I let Ryder be, lowered myself back to the ground, and turned to see Darren failing a sobriety test.

"I had ... umm ... back surgery," I overheard him tell the officers, "and there's nerve damage in my leg and foot."

Always an excuse. The officers sensed it too. They looked at each other knowingly.

The police chief saw me and walked to where I was. "Your husband is clearly under the influence, but we're going to let him go on one condition."

"Yes?" I should have been grateful, but I was actually hoping they'd take him away in cuffs.

The police chief pointed his finger at me in emphasis. "I want you to get in your car with your husband and your son and go home. Go straight to bed. I don't want you talking about this at all tonight. You can deal with him tomorrow, after he's slept this off."

"Yes, sir." I met his stern stare so he knew I understood.

"But," he continued, "if we get a call to your residence for domestic disturbance before then, we're taking him straight to jail for DUI, no questions asked. Do you understand?"

"Yes, sir," I agreed, secretly hoping that was exactly what would happen.

The police chief walked back to Darren and read him the riot act version of what I'd just been told. Darren submissively agreed with a few "Yes, sirs," and then another officer informed Ryder to get in the Kia with us.

"Here are the keys for the other vehicle, ma'am." An officer passed them to me through the open window. "The vehicle is locked up for now. You can come back and get it tomorrow after the dust settles."

Tomorrow was already today by the time we got home. And when I returned from mass a handful of hours later, Ryder was sitting on the loveseat with his head leaned on his hand. He looked tired and irritated. I could relate. Darren sat across from him on the longer sofa, his arms crossed. His face held fury and determination. Neither spoke. I felt like I'd just walked into enemy territory.

"What's going on, guys?" I moved cautiously toward the loveseat and sat next to Ryder. He moved further towards his end of the couch, making a clear point of dissociation from me. I looked at him inquisitively, confused and hurt by his rejection.

"Are you fucking kidding me, Dana?" Darren's outburst made me turn my attention to him. "You set a trap for me!"

"What are you talking about?" I furrowed my brows at the accusation.

"What are you talking about?" Darren mocked in a high-pitched voice. "You called the cops and arranged to have them arrest me for DUI! Do you realize what would happen if I got a second one? How much it would cost? I'd go to jail! You wanna get rid of me that bad?"

I wanted to answer his hypothetical question honestly, but now wasn't the time. "Listen to yourself, Darren," I defended. "Cops don't run around conspiring with people to 'set traps.' If you'd answered your fucking phone to any of my calls or texts, none of that would have happened anyway!"

"My phone was dead! I didn't get any of your calls or texts!" Darren yelled.

"Really? Then why did you call me on your way home?"

"I plugged my phone into the car charger and saw you called!" he snapped back.

"Well, I called and texted Ryder too, so why didn't he answer me?"

We both looked at Ryder. "I told you we were fine!" he snarked, then looked at me with the same hateful disdain his father punished me with. It was jarring and I didn't understand his sudden siding with his dad. He was *my* son!

"Yes, Ryder, you told me you were fine, but I didn't know where you were, what you were doing, who you were with, and I still don't know!"

Ryder crossed his arms on his chest and looked at Darren. They were tag-teaming against me, and it was Darren's turn to get in the ring with me.

"Face it, Dana," Darren said. "You called the cops, sat here and conspired with them, then let them set a trap for me."

"You're fucking delusional, Darren!" I was sorry Ryder had to witness this, but I needed him to hear the truth and not the nonsense his father had filled his head with. "I was crying my eyes out wondering where the hell you were with my son in the middle of the night, and I made a wrong turn and got pulled over! But *you* were the one driving drunk and swerving all over the fucking road! So I'm not the bad guy here! This was all *your* doing!" I looked over at Ryder after saying that, to see if anything I said was sinking into his usually reasonable brain.

He wouldn't look at me, though. He got up and went to his room instead. Then he slammed the door shut, silently expressing the antipathy he felt towards both of us.

"See what you did, you fucking cunt?!"

I'd had it. I stood over Darren and pointed my finger in his face for once, "You did this, Darren. This was all *you*."

Darren huffed out of his nose, then got up and walked out too. Funny how quickly the cockroach fled when the truth shed light on his lies.

"The Lonely"

I'd been done with Darren so many times, yet here I was, still married to him for the sake of a son who'd betrayed me. I couldn't bear ill feelings towards Ryder, though. No child should have to choose one parent over the other, nor live in the midst of parents who are constantly in conflict. Fulfilling my promise to Ryder, however, to wait until he was out of high school to divorce Darren, was taking its toll.

Every day that passed made me more bitter and more physically ill. Several symptoms took their turn with me—headaches, sore throats of varying severity, frequent fevers, shortness of breath, dizziness, chest pains, stomach aches, idiopathic constipation. I lived with the annoyances, thinking the fast pace and long hours I worked had caught up to me, or that my daily exposure to bacteria and viruses in the numerous places I cleaned were to blame for making me sick all the time.

But neither explained why my hands and arms would numb and deaden, or why my hands pained more often. I was having difficulty holding onto anything anymore. I couldn't tear toilet paper off the roll to wipe some mornings. I couldn't grasp a dryer sheet from its box to dry our wet laundry. I couldn't even hold on to my cleaning rags at work! Every time I dropped one, I'd pick it back up just to drop it again!

It wasn't just the nuisance of my dysfunctional hands that bothered me; I was scared. I was afraid of being incompetent and at the mercy of a neglectful drunk to care for me, and I worried about being reliant upon him to pay the bills, because I knew I'd end up dead and that Darren and Ryder would be homeless. Mostly, though, I was afraid that if I couldn't work, I'd never be able to afford to get out of this marriage with custody of my son.

Then on November 3, 2018, everything came to a head.

I'd rented a cabin an hour from home for just a night, thinking I could get away and get some peace. Darren found out and decided it would be a romantic night away for the two of us instead. It wasn't what I wanted, but I knew if I didn't agree to his idea, I'd end up canceling the night away altogether. So we went.

Darren started drinking as soon as we arrived mid-afternoon, and only left the cabin to go to the main lodge for dinner with me two hours later. Before sunset, we were back in the cabin for the night, where he drank even more, became rude and belligerent, and fought with me about all the same things we always did. I went to sleep early to end my misery, leaving him to fall asleep drunk in a chair.

He awoke in the morning to pee, insulted me as I made a cup of coffee, took off on foot down the highway, returned to chastise me for not chasing after him, then sexed me roughly. I hadn't wanted it, but I didn't fight it. I didn't say anything about it either. I just showered and dressed, hoping to relieve the bruised feeling between my legs. Then I packed the car to go home.

Darren drove with the radio turned up, scrolling through Facebook and laughing at reels he watched instead of focusing on the road. I smiled and laughed at every one he shared. It was all I could do not to cry tears of self-pity for what I allowed him to get away with in our life.

"How was your trip?" Ryder asked when we returned home.

"Great!" Darren said as he settled on the couch and turned on the TV, leaving me to lug in our bags and empty the laundry out of them.

"Yeah?" Ryder looked to me for a response.

"Yeah, it was good, kiddo!" I lied with a smile.

Nothing was good, though. Darren was sick for doing what he'd done to me, and I became sicker for the same.

From that day forward, I consistently awoke at 3 a.m. It didn't matter how late I stayed up, nor how tired I was; I could not sleep past 3 a.m. But I couldn't lay there and do nothing either. It's not like I had a smartphone to play games on or scroll the internet. So I started walking laps around the basement family room to pass the time quietly. I made a game of walking until my Fitbit buzzed to alert me I'd achieved ten thousand steps. I didn't need the exercise, but it was something to do while I listened to music on my old Apple iPod.

The urgency to pee, which was another new symptom that presented the same time as the early wake-up, interrupted my morning walks to the point of extreme annoyance. I counted roughly a dozen or more trips to the toilet within my first hour awake every single morning, and then between a half to a full dozen times per hour all day long. Workdays were prolonged because of the abnormal frequency of urination. I'd peed my pants a few times too, when I'd failed to make it to the bathroom in time.

Two weeks into my body's inexplicable new patterns, I was fifteen pounds smaller. Everywhere I went, I saw the look of shock on people's faces when they saw my skeletal ninety-three-pound frame. I agreed it was a drastic change in too short of time. I also didn't think it was a coincidence that these newer symptoms and weight loss had occurred immediately after that rough incidence of unwelcome sex, but I couldn't tell people that. So I joked about the flat belly I now had without effort, and the tighter clothes I looked better in now. It wasn't funny, though. Something was very wrong with me. I just didn't know what.

I was changing into my pajamas one night when I noticed a vein protruding from my arm, as if it were overly strained. I looked at my other arm and saw every single vein and muscle fiber protruding from it as well. My arms were so pale and skinny, it was actually alarming. I turned to the mirror and moved my arms inward and outward, expecting to see something more normal in a different angle, but the mirror refused to lie.

I came out of the bathroom in a panic and held my arms out over the railing to the living room. "Is this what I look like?" I cried out.

"What?" Darren didn't even look up from the TV. He never paid me any attention. So I went back into the bathroom and closed the door.

I looked into the mirror again, examining my face this time. I turned from right to left, then left to right. My complexion had the grayish pallor a cleaning customer had recently observed. Another customer had said I looked like a truck had hit me, and she was right too! The purplish half circles under my eyes and slumped shoulders I trudged around with outwardly expressed how dead I felt inside. Considering the progression of physical symptoms, I figured it was only a matter of time before I did just drop dead. And I wasn't sure I would even mind.

I buried my face in my hands and closed my eyes tightly, as if closing off thoughts of hopelessness. I don't know how I'd let things between me and Darren get so out of hand that my physical health had deteriorated so drastically and so quickly as a result. I was withering away, and I didn't know how to stop whatever was happening.

I could go to the doctor, but doctors ordered tests that cost money we didn't have and racked up medical bills Darren wouldn't approve of, which would just create more tension at home and more pressure to work for more money. The consequential stress would make me sicker, which would put me back to where I started. So really, what could I do? Nothing. Absolutely nothing.

I rubbed my temples, took a deep breath, and straightened up. Then I looked in the mirror again and wiped the tears welling up in my eyes. "You're stronger than this," I told my reflection.

Strength was only necessary when having to endure some sort of suffering. I was indeed suffering, yet I had no choice but to endure it.

"I'm a Mess"

$\mathcal{J}$ust after the New Year of 2019, I decided to do something about my health after all. Darren had stripped me of everything he possibly could—my sense of self, my confidence, my self-esteem, my happiness, my money. I wasn't going to let go of my physical well-being too just because he thought money spent on medical bills was better spent on needless things like truck accessories and motocross shirts. He wasn't the one paying the bills anyway; I was.

So I made an appointment with Dr. George.

"What's going on?" He picked up a pen to take notes. He was the psychiatrist I'd started seeing when Darren moved out in 2007. Over the last decade, he'd proven his knack for knowing what ailed me by a description of my symptoms alone.

I relaxed into the high-backed upholstered chair which faced his paper-piled desk and sighed. "Well, all the same stuff I told you about at my yearly check-up last fall, except I feel like I'm getting worse. I've been tracking my symptoms on a spreadsheet I created, and they're occurring more frequently and with more intensity."

"I do recall you worrying about shortness of breath and chest pains, dizziness and blacking out . . ."

I interrupted with a continuation of the extensive list of ailments, adding, "Yeah, and with this winter weather, my fingers are red and swollen too. They literally hurt just sitting here." I held them up for show.

Dr. George leaned his large body slightly forward and looked down from behind his black-framed glasses to inspect the thick pink appendages.

"That's Raynaud's syndrome. It's a circulatory issue that's sometimes related to autoimmune disease. Make sure you wear gloves outside because the slightest exposure to cold can cause frostbite to set in quicker than it would for someone without Raynaud's," he said. "But all those other symptoms sound like adrenal or thyroid issues. The stiff muscles and lethargy concern me too. You should be assessed for multiple sclerosis. And I want you to see a cardiologist about your heart. The blacking out comes from your low blood pressure, but we don't want to take any chances, especially since you were born with a heart murmur and have irregular heartbeats on occasion. While you're at it, I want you to get a sleep study."

While he wrote this all down for me on multiple pages of a light blue prescription pad, I asked for clarification, "A sleep study?"

"Yes." He reclined in his leather chair and spun his pen between his fingers as he spoke. "You've had issues with breathing during sleep in the past, and that could have implications on your heart and brain activity. The sleep study monitors all of that during an overnight test they conduct at the facility, which is here in this medical complex." He pointed in its general direction with his pen, then he handed me the papers he'd written his orders on.

I looked them over, then looked back up to Dr. George. "Where would I go for an MS evaluation?"

"I'll write down the name of a neurologist I recommend for that. You might also want to see your gastroenterologist about your stomach problems. I know constipation and stomach aches have been a constant struggle for you, and you haven't had luck on any medications for either, but it wouldn't hurt to check in again." He took a minute to write these additional directives, then handed me that paper too.

"Okay," I sighed. This was turning out to be much more fuss than I'd expected.

Sensing my overwhelm, Dr. George said, "Hopefully, it's something as simple as having developed toxicity to the Seroquel you've been taking. You are still taking that, right?"

"Yeah, three hundred milligrams per night," I replied.

"You've been doing well on it too," he pondered out loud. "Why don't we cut back on it anyway? Let's say a hundred and fifty milligrams per night. Just to see if it relieves any of your symptoms. You can cut the pills you have in half."

"Okay, I can do that."

"All right, then!" He stood up to cue the end of our visit, then had an afterthought. "Have you ever been to a functional medicine doctor?"

I shook my head as I stood. "Nuh-uh. What kind of doctor is that?"

"They're doctors who look at the whole body as the interactive system it is, as opposed to specialists who focus on only one organ or system," he explained. He opened his office door to escort me through the bright white corridor to the exit. "I'm just wondering if it might be beneficial for you to consult with one, to get some insight we may not get elsewhere."

"Hmm. Worth looking into, I guess!" I said without committing. I had enough to do!

"Yes. And let me know when you have some answers! Take care now!" he said as he closed the office door behind me.

Over the next two months, I underwent an exhaustive evaluation for MS, an ultrasound on my thyroid, an echo-cardiogram, stress echo-cardiogram, wore a Holter monitor for forty-eight hours, and had blood drawn three separate times.

After all that, I was told I didn't have MS but should be tested for neuropathy, that I was "hypersensitive" to my body, suffered from major anxiety, and had low thyroid numbers but not low enough to diagnose as hypothyroidism. My heart proved to be healthy too, except for a conduction delay on the right ventricle, which was deemed a harmless defect.

So aside from being prescribed a blood pressure medication I refused to take because of the bothersome side effects I didn't need to deal with on top of everything else I suffered, the medical world offered me no resolution or reason for my malaise. I was right back to where I started.

I hadn't yet called a functional medicine doctor or sleep neurologist, though, because Darren bitched about the numerous medical bills already coming in the mail. Of course, he hadn't worried about medical costs when they'd pertained to *him*, nor had he contributed to paying them over the last couple years since his surgery. So, like a defiant teenager, I scheduled an appointment with the nearest functional medicine doctor I could find online. One more doctor's visit wouldn't make a difference in our finances anyway.

After a very thorough consultation with the FMD, wherein I repeated the same mysterious puzzle of symptoms I'd relayed to the several doctors before her, she sent me away with orders for a cortisol test, urine culture, and blood draw, all to be sent to Mayo Clinic for evaluation. Mayo was considered the world's leading medical mecca in over a dozen specialties, so to have nineteen vials of my blood sent there was a serious move which validated my concerns about the seriousness of my condition. And I was justifiably scared about the potential outcomes.

"They said it would be a month or two until the test results come back," I shared with Darren when I returned home from having my blood drawn at the hospital, "and I don't know if I can wait that long. I mean, the doctors have thrown out ideas of a pituitary gland tumor, fibromyalgia, lupus, Hashimoto's, even lymphoma!"

While I awaited the off chance of consolation, I set my travel coffee cup on the kitchen island to remove my shoes. I'd taken it with me in case the cookie they offered after the blood draw didn't do its job of preventing light-headedness, a consequence which never came.

When Darren didn't respond by the time I'd laid my shoes at the door, I looked over at the couch where he lay watching TV. He was looking at Facebook on his phone.

"Hello?" I said to get his attention, though my health alone should have warranted it.

"What?" he said without averting his eyes from his phone.

"Did you hear anything I just said?" I stood with my hands on my hips, facing the back of the couch.

He slapped his phone down onto the sofa cushion next to him. "Fuck, Dana! I can't possibly listen to every word you say!"

His annoyance with my attempt to reach out for support instantaneously escalated my self-pity. "I know. You've said that before," I said as I walked towards the stairway to go up to the bathroom. "But don't worry. I won't bother you with my talking, or my illness, or how scared I am about whatever might be wrong with me . . ."

Halfway up the stairs, I looked down at him to see if my passive-aggressive words had their intended effect. His focus on his phone gave me my answer. So, with a drooping head, I continued up the stairs, and kept the worry in my heart to myself.

"Figures"

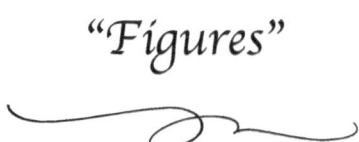

While cleaning on a Monday in late March, I received a call from my accountant. "Hi, Dana! I'm working on your taxes and had a quick question."

"Okay?"

"I'm curious about the 401K disbursement taken January first, 2018, because I don't see any indication of it on the tax planner you sent me."

"What 401K disbursement?" Darren had retained his 401K account after being let go by his employer a couple years before, but I knew nothing about him taking money out of it.

"There was a disbursement for fifty-one thousand dollars from the Vanguard account in Darren's name."

"There must be a mistake," I insisted. I hadn't seen a tax form come in the mail regarding this, nor could I imagine that amount of money coming through our bank account without me noticing. But then I remembered the $45,000 he took out of his 401K the year before, without telling me. I hadn't seen that money come through our account either.

"I don't know anything about this," I was embarrassed to admit. "Let me call Darren and call you back."

I didn't need this stress right now. I was anxious enough about the test results I was awaiting from the Mayo Clinic. So I dialed Darren immediately, hoping to straighten this out.

"Our accountant just called. It seems there was a disbursement for fifty-one thousand dollars taken from your 401K? Please tell me this is a mistake."

"I told you I took the money out the first week of January last year!" His snarky tone implied I was stupid for asking him about it. "The market was unstable and—"

"No, Darren. You didn't tell me," I cut him off. He didn't know shit about the market anyway. "Please tell me you have the money somewhere."

"No! I spent it."

"None of it's left?" I hoped for a different answer this time. I couldn't imagine what a couch potato could spend that much money on without anyone noticing! "You had to know you'd owe taxes on that money!"

"I did put some aside for taxes, but I spent that too. What do you think I used to pay for the cows and the paddocks I built for them? Anyway, that was *my* money to spend how *I* wanted!" I honestly didn't know how he'd paid for all that. I'd just been glad it wasn't with *my* money.

"Yes, I know . . . everything is yours." *Except for our problems*, I thought. "So what do you intend to do about this?"

"What do you *mean* what do I intend to do? *You're* the one who handles our taxes!"

"So *you* spend all this money, and *I* have to deal with the consequences?" I didn't wait for an answer or another insult. "Whatever. I have to call the accountant back," I said. Then I hung up. There was nothing more to say to a man who'd selfishly squandered the last remaining funds we could fall back on in an emergency. The damage had already been done anyway.

Back on with the accountant, I confirmed Darren had authorized the disbursement. "I'm really sorry for the omission on the tax planner I sent you. I wasn't trying to pull a fast one to avoid paying taxes or anything. Darren told me when he pulled the money out, but it was so long ago, I must have forgotten," I said, taking blame for the error instead of telling the shitty truth about my husband being a deceitful liar.

"All right," our accountant said with a sigh that reflected my own frustrations. "Let me enter this in my computer real quick, so it can recalculate your tax liability."

"Yeah, no problem," I said, then anxiously awaited a verdict I already knew wouldn't be in my favor.

"Okay, well," the accountant stalled. My whole body tensed at the impending doom. "The money Darren cashed out of his 401K is considered income, so you'll have to pay taxes on that. The withdrawal also disqualifies you from the government assistance you were granted for medical insurance, since it had been based on your house cleaning earnings alone, so you'll have to pay that back too. And I know you paid the predicted tax amount due for *this* year, in quarterly payments throughout the *last* year, but even after that, you owe twenty-two thousand dollars total."

"By April fifteenth?" I asked, even though I knew it was the designated deadline for filing yearly taxes in the U.S.

"Yeah."

"But that's less than a month away!"

"I can file an extension for you if you need me to."

I huffed, though it wasn't the accountant I was annoyed with. "No . . . well . . . I don't know. Let me just see what we can do and get back to you. I appreciate your time and patience with us," I said to end the call.

Then I closed my eyes and exhaled out of my mouth, to calm the intense desire to go home and beat the crap out of the piece of it likely laying on the couch without any worry in the world. Then I reopened them and worked swiftly to finish cleaning, fueled by the same adrenaline that propelled me into attack mode when I got home.

"We gotta figure out this tax bill, and we gotta figure it out now," I said to Darren as I slammed the mail on the kitchen island after work. Ryder was representing his school at a Future Farmers of America event, so I wasn't worried about him overhearing. "I mean, I just paid off the medical bills from your surgery, and now I've got all the bills for my medical stuff coming in. So you're gonna have to find a way to pay this because there's no way I can save that much in a month."

"File for bankruptcy then," Darren casually suggested from the couch.

I leaned back against the kitchen island and crossed my arms. "We've had this conversation before, Darren. I will *never* file for bankruptcy! I've worked my ass off to keep us afloat, and I'm not gonna let it be for nothing just because you don't give a shit!"

"It's not a big deal," he said with a dismissive wave of his free hand. The other was holding his phone. "Bankruptcy goes away after a few years. Everybody does it."

I went to the couch and stood over him. "It *is* a big deal, and I won't do it! It takes seven years for bankruptcy to be removed from a credit report, and in the meantime, we wouldn't be able to finance anything, like we had to for Ryder's braces or when I needed a new vehicle for work! So you need to help me figure this out!"

"Pay late, then. They just charge a penalty." His calm logic made me feel like I was overreacting, but I knew I wasn't.

"We could pay late, but the penalties are stiff! And by the time we'd have the money to pay, we'll owe quarterly payments for next year's taxes! If we get behind on those too, we'll never catch up!" Still entranced with his phone, it was like he hadn't heard me at all. "Fuck, Darren!" I stomped one foot down. "I'm tired of living like this when we make enough money not to!"

He finally put his phone down, and the hateful Mr. Hyde yelled, "Then go find yourself a rich husband, you fucking gold digger! You've been using me for my money for twenty years!"

"What money, Darren?!" I screamed, throwing my arms up. "Please tell me what fucking money I'm using you for, because I could use some of it right now!"

"The money I made working at my job!" he snapped back as he sat up.

"I used you to pay our mortgage? And our bills? And when are you going to stop throwing your seventeen years of work in my face? You do realize people typically work more than seventeen years, right? Not to mention, I've worked since I was, like, twelve years old, and you act like I just live off of you or something. I mean, aside from my pregnancy with Ryder, I *always* worked and *always* paid my fair share, as well as some of *yours*. So I don't want to hear your shit about working anymore, when *you* don't even have a fucking job!"

"You're just pissed 'cause you have to work and take care of *me* now! How fucking fair is that?" Darren yelled as he stood with clenched fists and a jutted chest meant to intimidate me.

An out-of-place grin came across my lips as I shook my head in disbelief. "It's *not* fair, Darren. *Nothing* is fucking fair around here," I said. Then I went down to the basement. Sleep was my only escape from his bullshit anymore.

"Break My Heart Myself"

~~~~~~

The functional medicine doctor called to tell me she'd received my test results from Mayo Clinic. She wouldn't tell me anything over the phone, though; I had to wait until my follow-up appointment in mid-April.

"You're autoimmune, Dana." Dr. Newport leaned forward onto her folded hands, looking at me intently. The sunshine beaming into the well-appointed bright white room reflected off her medium-length blonde hair, as if she were an angel sent to soothe my emotions upon hearing this dismal news.

I took a deep breath in and out of my mouth. I was relieved and strangely calm. Although not good news, finally knowing what was wrong meant we could move forward with a resolution.

"Your thyroid levels are low," she continued, "and your adrenals are definitely overworked, but it was your dangerously low white blood cell count that gave the indication. Your body thinks it's fighting something, but it's only fighting itself."

Jesus. I knew I was alone in this life, but even my own body had turned against me? I hung my head and closed my eyes for a second in a moment of self-pity.

After a couple strokes of her keyboard, the doctor continued, so I looked back up at her. "Your abnormally high cortisol levels are most alarming, however. Mayo thought the results were due to faulty lab work, but the re-test they performed came back just as high, demonstrating levels as high as 2,540 when they should have been in the hundreds. Even

600 to 700 is within normal range, depending on the time of day. It seems your body is mistaking the inflammation caused by the cortisol—a stress hormone—for foreign cells which need to be eradicated."

"So what do we do now?"

"We keep testing until we can determine which autoimmune diseases you suffer from. We tested you for rheumatoid arthritis, and it was negative, which confirms you have Raynaud's syndrome in your hands. You're negative for celiac disease too, but you clearly have a gluten sensitivity. We tested you for about twenty autoimmune diseases altogether." She handed me a lab report. I stared at codes and numbers which made no sense to me while she continued, "Your numbers are really close on some, but not definitive. Most of your symptoms indicate fibromyalgia, so we need to look into that or adrenal fatigue . . . could be anything. Many autoimmune diseases have similar symptoms. Some mimic other diseases. And sometimes you're just generally autoimmune. I think you fall into that latter category, or have two or three diseases simultaneously, which is also common with autoimmunity."

Another deep breath. "This isn't something we can fix, is it?"

"Unfortunately not. Autoimmunity is irreversible. It is, however, manageable." Dr. Newport sat forward in her chair and folded her hands together on her desk again. "Most doctors want to throw a pill at your symptoms, but sometimes you just need to change your lifestyle. I'd like you to start by implementing the Autoimmune Protocol Diet, which consists of organic, gluten-free, soy-free and dairy-free foods. Eliminating those toxins will relieve or eliminate some of your symptoms, particularly the inflammation which is causing you the pain and stiffness in your muscles. Mediterranean foods would benefit you most, so maybe try incorporating some of those into your meals until they become habit. I think you also need to reconsider your work. Exposing yourself to all the chemicals you use to clean is only making you sicker. You should at least start wearing a face mask and gloves, not just for cleaning, but out in public as well, to protect your compromised immune system."

She paused to let that all sink in. I used the break to bend my head side to side to stretch the muscles in my neck, which had stiffened with tension. Then I blew a breath out of my mouth and relaxed my shoulders.

When I looked at her again, Dr. Newport perceived my readiness to hear what remained of her assessment. "Stress is what did this to you, Dana. Something in your life is so stressful, it's caused the elevated amounts of cortisol to wreak havoc in your body. This didn't just happen either; it takes years of consistently high cortisol to do this kind of damage. So I want you to consider what's causing you so much stress and try to eliminate or minimize it, because all the cortisol being pumped into your bloodstream is making you very, very sick."

"You're not the first doctor to tell me to change my life," I admitted, recalling how Dr. George had told me the same.

"Then maybe it's time to heed the advice," she said with a nod of her head. I recognized the psychological trick meant to induce agreement.

"Maybe," I responded with noncommittal avoidance.

"For now, let's run some more blood tests. I want to rule out the autoimmune diseases that can be diagnosed simply. Once we have that information, we'll reconvene," she said as she neatened a stack of papers in front of her. Then she set them down and looked at me again. "I want you to download a snoring app too. Let me write down the name of it for you."

"But I don't snore. At least, I don't think I do," I said as she wrote down the name of the app and handed the paper over to me.

"But you said you think you hold your breath during sleep, because you sometimes wake up gasping for air, and that most days you wake up in the morning with a headache. I have a feeling that plays into all this somehow. The app is free, so just give it a try for a couple nights."

"All right," I promised, suddenly wondering if I should have called that sleep neurologist after all, for the sleep study Dr. George had recommended.

"Let's plan on two weeks for your follow-up, then!" she said as she stood.

I made the appointment with her secretary on my way out, then went back home to the obvious source of my stress—the man who'd done this to me and the part of my lifestyle I'd been warned twice now to change or rid of.

If Darren had gone back to work after his surgery, as I'd expected him to, I'd have divorced him in a heartbeat. But he hadn't, and the occasional bit of money he made doing odds-and-ends jobs now hardly qualified as income. Since I was now the primary breadwinner, Darren would be entitled to alimony, and I refused to give him any more of my hard-earned money than he'd already squandered. So until he earned a substantial income he could support himself with, I wasn't going anywhere. I just hoped my body could endure the potential long-haul.

"Sitting, Waiting, Wishing"

⁓

When the time came for my follow-up appointment with Dr. Newport, I got a call informing me she'd left the office to go out on her own. No one had access to her files nor my records, and it would be months until she was expected to open the doors of her new practice. So my appointment was canceled, and I had no way of knowing the results of my latest blood tests.

I felt like a hamster in a wheel, trying to run forward, but never able to escape the spot I was stuck in. The frustration of going nowhere was getting to me. I was starting to think my life would never change, no matter what I did to influence improvement.

Arguments with Darren were just as circular. He decided being a handyman wasn't for him and opted to mow lawns instead. He spent thousands of dollars we didn't have on lawn equipment without consulting me first, then berated me for not supporting his new venture when I asked how he'd make that money back charging thirty dollars per lawn.

How could I support him, though? First, he was supposedly disabled and would never work again, then he arose like Jesus and could suddenly perform physical labor, simultaneously saying he didn't have money and was thereby unable to contribute to the outrageous tax bill he'd stuck me with. I couldn't keep track of what was what with him! It was no wonder I was stressed out!

It was bad enough I'd used money I'd been secretly stashing for when I divorced Darren to pay that tax bill. It pained me to give up the only financial security I had and the only hope for a future without the bastard.

There was no other option, however, and it wasn't worth worrying about when I had a couple years to restore it.

I started sleeping in the master bedroom again too, to alleviate the nightly commentary about how a husband and wife should sleep in the same bed. I had reservations because of the near miss punch a few years before, but when Darren continuously lined pillows down the center of the bed so we didn't touch, my fear shifted into amusement at his ridiculous contradictions. At least I was laughing instead of crying.

Other than bullshit bickering, Darren and I had no relationship. We were basically roommates who were married, living our own lives but bound by a child who insisted we remain together. As such, I didn't expect anything special on Mother's Day. I actually planned to go see *The Curse of La Llorona*, a horror movie that had just been released, and invited Ryder to come with me. Aside from that, Mother's Day was going to be just another day.

I awoke around 3 a.m. as usual and stealthily sneaked into the master bathroom to pee but not flush. Flushing would wake up Darren and disturb the peace of the precious alone time I wasn't willing to sacrifice on today of all days. It was my gift to myself, I supposed. Then I went to the basement, where I turned on the TV and let Amazon Prime surprise me with whatever it thought I might like based on my previous viewing choices. Today's pick was the movie *Hell House*. I chuckled at the fitting coincidence.

I let the movie play as background noise while I walked laps for its duration. Despite my lethargy and other ailments, I maintained my active lifestyle to get my blood pumping. That was probably the only part of my true self which remained, though Darren had tried to take that away from me too.

I used to walk or jog the perimeter of our property, but the path left by my tread irritated Darren so much that he'd restricted me from doing so. I took my morning jogs to the back roads for a while but opted for the basement when speedy drivers or bad weather made it unsafe for me to be out there. Even the basement was becoming an issue. Darren said the wood-laminate floors he'd installed weren't meant to be walked on so much. It was one of the stupidest things I think he'd ever used as an argument with me, so I walked on the floors anyway.

When the Fitbit I wore on my left ankle buzzed to alert me of my ten-thousand step achievement, I turned off the TV and went up to the kitchen to make my morning coffee. My coffee and I then went up to my office. Although it was a Sunday, there were always emails to respond to, client accounts to reconcile, and bills to pay online.

I hadn't been up there long when I heard Darren groan loudly to make all aware he was awake and in the chronic pain he used as a crutch to avoid responsibility. My shoulders immediately tensed. Then I heard the bedroom door open, and his pounding feet approaching. Darren appeared in the entrance to my office seconds later.

"Good morning!" I greeted with fake cheer and a forced smile. Being polite when I could summon the self-discipline made life bearable for me and Ryder. "You're up early!"

Darren's long, grumpy face and dead, greenish-brown eyes viewed me with reproach as they always did. Still, I leaned into his body for the affection expected of me.

"Don't touch me! Your hands are cold!" he barked. I stepped away from him quickly. I should have known better than to touch his back. It contradicted the rule to hug him, but I erred on the side of affection.

Without another word, Darren turned and went down to the main floor bathroom to shower and dress. I followed him down to re-heat my coffee and to make sure I'd be rid of him for the day.

"You off to work?" I stated the obvious in the form of a question. Darren had a neon yellow shirt with his business name on it, though the so-called business wasn't even a corporation or legal entity of any sort.

"Yeah. I'll be back in time to go to that movie, though. One o'clock, right? Then maybe pizza at the Italian restaurant across from there?" He must have overheard me telling Ryder how much I craved their barbecue chicken pizza when we were making plans for the movie.

Unsure of how to tell Darren I preferred to just go with Ryder, without getting into a major fight, I succumbed. "Sounds like a plan!" I wasn't as excited as I sounded.

"All right, I'll see you later, then," he said, then walked out without wishing me a happy Mother's Day. I huffed out my nose and sipped on my hot coffee, while I watched his black trailer full of lawn equipment wobble as his white truck turned onto the road.

Ryder came out of his bedroom then.

"What's got you outta bed so early on a Sunday, kiddo?"

"I'm coming to church with you," he said as he went into the bathroom to get ready.

"Yay!" I was happy for the surprise accompaniment, and went upstairs to get ready myself. When I came back down, Ryder was in the kitchen drinking a glass of water.

"Happy Mother's Day," he mumbled, and gave me a weak one-armed hug, which was a grand gesture considering his introverted nature.

"Thank you! Happy Mother's Day to you too!"

"But I'm not a mother," Ryder said with crinkled brows.

"But I wouldn't be a mom without you!" I pointed at him with both index fingers and a cheesy smile.

"Ha, ha," Ryder responded sarcastically, though I saw him smirk out of the corner of my eye as I turned away to get my shoes. His glum mood was just tiredness, I knew. Plus, he was too cool to let me think I was funny.

We returned home from mass an hour later, with a few hours to spare before Darren would be home. I called my grandma while Ryder watched YouTube videos to pass the time.

"How's Darren and Ryder?" Grandma asked in her heavy Puerto Rican accent.

"Good! Ryder went to church with me this morning!"

"That's nice. Darren . . . *no se fue?*" she asked in her mix of Spanish and English.

"No." I paused to think of a polite excuse for him, then opted for a half truth. "He had to mow a big lawn today, so he couldn't come with us." Darren had scored a mowing job for a school, which took up the whole of every Sunday. He was glad for the money, and I was glad for the peace on the one day I could usually take off work anymore.

"My husband, your grandfather, didn't go nowhere with me either," Grandma replied, as if she saw through my excuse. "He went from work to the bar then to whomever's bed, but never nowhere with me."

"I'm sorry, Grandma," I consoled. She was at that age when a person starts repeating the same regrets and injustices, as if trying to resolve them before it's all over.

"Your grandfather was always with this one and that one. He brought *los mujeres a la casa tambien!*" she said with such emotion, like it had just happened yesterday. She continued to relay her experiences with her husband's alcoholism, abuse, and infidelities, all of which I'd heard before, but all of which made me feel like she understood my situation in a way most wouldn't.

"You're a very strong woman to have endured all that! He was not a good husband to you and you deserved better," I said, offering validation so she could heal.

About the time Darren said he would be home, I told my grandma I had to get off the call so I could be ready to go. She didn't need to know Darren didn't like me being on the phone when he was home, nor did she need to worry about anything more than she already unnecessarily did.

"Will Darren be nice to you today, *mija?*" The lament in her tone answered the question for me.

"Of course he will!" I lied to reassure her.

"Okay, *mija.* God bless you, and I love you."

"I love you too, Grandma. Have a happy Mother's Day and I'll talk to you again soon," I promised. Then I waited for Darren.

A couple hours went by without any word from him. We'd already missed the movie, and I was starving since I'd skipped lunch to save my calorie consumption for the pizza. There was no use texting Darren, though. He was mowing and wouldn't have heard or felt his phone vibrate anyway.

Finally, almost four hours after he said he'd be home, my phone buzzed. *On my way. I fucking hurt.* There was always an excuse for what was really his failing as a husband, although I wondered if he'd ruined today intentionally to punish me for . . . I couldn't keep track of all my shortcomings.

But I played along. *I'm sure you are. How about Ryder and I get pizza and bring some back to you? That way, you don't have to worry about going anywhere and can just relax when you get home.*

No way, we're goin', he insisted.

Of course, he wouldn't allow a situation which made him look like less than a perfect husband, though he had no problem drinking down his Gabapentin and Tramadol with Miller Lites until he was so trashed he'd lash out at me and Ryder for the slightest offenses. I suspected this would turn into what Ryder and I called "one of those nights".

Can't wait! I lied, then took ibuprofen for the headache I'd developed from hunger.

I was looking in the kitchen cupboard for a snack when Darren burst through the door a while later. By the time I'd turned to greet him, he was standing nose to nose with me. The hostile look on his face, stiff upper body, and trembling hands warned me to back away. But I was cornered and unable to escape. I turned my head to the side and held the edges of the black Corian countertops with both hands, bracing myself for whatever was coming.

"You're pissed, aren't you?" he screamed. "I can see the look on your face! Fuck! I can't do anything right!"

What he saw was fear and repulsion, but I didn't dare speak. I just closed my eyes and mouth to prevent his spit from spewing into them and prayed for this moment to pass quickly.

"I have chores to do, and the trailer to unload, but don't worry, I'll shower and get dressed so we can go eat, even though it makes no sense to do that since I'll have to get dirty again when we get home. But as long as *you're* happy!"

His deflection failed to make me feel guilty, but hearing Ryder slam his bedroom door shut to isolate himself from the volatile situation pissed me off. I had to use every bit of self-discipline to diffuse Darren's unreasonably elevated mood for both our sakes.

"I'm not upset at all," I said, speaking lowly and calmly. "Go ahead and get showered and dressed, and Ryder and I will take care of the chores for you. We'll go whenever you're ready. Or we can just order a pizza from town and not go at all. Whatever you want."

"NO!" He was such a bully, using his loud shout and larger size to intimidate me. Then he stomped the five feet down the hall to the bathroom and slammed the door shut. When I heard his electric razor turn on, I unconsciously released a deep breath of relief and tip-toed down the hallway to Ryder's room.

I tapped on his bedroom door lightly to alert him to my presence.

"Hey! Will you help me do the chores so your dad doesn't have to worry about them?"

"No!" he cried, raising his voice to me. "And you're not doing them either!" Paranoid that Darren might have heard all this, I looked behind me to make sure the bathroom door was still closed.

Then I turned back to Ryder and begged, "Will you please do them, then? Please? I just want to have a good night."

"No," he responded more firmly. I knew he didn't want to help his dad because of the unwarranted attack on me just before, but Ryder's vengeful mindset forgot there were consequences to Darren's anger.

"Okay," I relented. I closed his door and went to feed the animals myself.

The dreary late afternoon matched my mood, I thought as I went down the three steps off our wraparound porch. I noticed weeds growing in the gravel which curved between our big oak barn and the second house, complementing the general state of disrepair of our landscape and outbuildings.

The wet grass had soaked through my signature gray Converse shoes by the time I approached the door of the chicken coop. I always liked the red metal roof on the barn, so in a rare act of consideration, Darren had painted the door to the coop the same color. It offset the orange-colored wood stain of the exterior coop walls nicely and gave the property some color continuity.

Our Rhode Island Red chickens, which were actually brown, scurried and clucked around my feet, kicking up the bedding laid on the concrete to keep them warm. One hen occupied one of the three boxes built into the opposite wall but left her task of laying an egg to eat with the other chickens as soon as I poured grain into the skinny metal trough in the middle of the floor. Their water container was full, so I left them for the more difficult chore of feeding the larger livestock.

As I passed the fenced pig-pen, the three Duroc pigs stared at me with anticipation. They were smart and had learned that the sight of us meant food. They excitedly bounced their way into the adjacent paddock shared with the Dexter cows to await their feed. Unlike the pink and black pigs we'd raised before, this tan-colored breed had a particular enthusiasm which always made me smile.

Upon reaching the door to the metal paddock at the back corner of our property, I heard unintelligible shouting somewhere far off behind me. I turned to see Darren, clothed in the dirty pants and T-shirt he'd come home in, running at me like a defensive lineman coming in to bowl me over. His face was beet red—the color of anger.

I closed my eyes and cowered to protect myself against the expected collision. When I felt Darren push past me, however, I realized he'd only meant to scare me. My fear gave him power.

I remained frozen in that fear as he hurdled the metal rail into the pig stall. The piglets bounced around his feet with eager eyes, thinking they were about to eat, when Darren grabbed the four-foot metal trough and threw it at them. I cringed, remembering when he'd kicked our deaf dalmatian, Pepper, with the full force of his foot just for being in his path during one of his moods. She'd had an alarmed look on her face before running away with her head down. At least the piglets seemed unfazed as they scampered around to stay out of his way.

Darren retrieved the trough from where he'd just thrown it and hastily filled it with grain. Much of it fell to the ground, but the indiscriminate piglets consumed it anyway, saving me from blame for the waste.

Then Darren noticed I was still there, watching his tantrum unfold. "You want a husband who's home with you? Go find one who'll treat you better, then! Please! I can't make you happy, and I'm tired of trying! It's impossible to work and be a good husband and a good father! I can't do it! I CAN'T FUCKING DO IT!"

No, he *chose* not to do it. But the little girl in me remembered too well how anger turned into slapping, then into hands wringing my neck and throwing my little body around. I wanted to run, to hide, to leave, but anger conditioned me to remain still to avoid unwanted attention. Darren had been pushing the bounds of acceptable behaviors, so it was only a matter of time before he made contact, and I never knew when that time would come.

As if thinking for my stunted brain, my feet finally took charge and fled the scene. I instinctively ran towards the house, but Ryder had already seen and heard too much. Going into the house would be like walking into a trap anyway, and I needed an exit route just in case things got worse. I saw my car then and instantly decided it would better serve as temporary refuge.

My heart raced as I jumped into the driver's seat and locked the doors. I gasped desperately for every breath I took. Although out of breath from running, I felt like a panic attack was coming on too. They'd been coming on more frequently during the last year, in direct correlation to the compounding hatred Darren exhibited towards me.

Tears began to fall from my eyes uncontrollably as I wondered why I'd been punished with this miserable life and a body that couldn't handle it anymore.

I tried so hard to be the wife Darren wanted me to be, but he was never happy. And because he was raised with tit-for-tat ideology, he wouldn't allow me the slightest happiness either. So why was I still here? I asked the million-dollar question yet again. Then the pressure in my chest grew into a sharp pain.

I scanned the black interior of the car hopelessly. I don't even know what I was looking for. Answers? A way out of this situation? A way out of this marriage? I put my hands over my face and allowed my long curly hair to drape down and hide the pain I tried so hard to disguise with fake smiles and well-thought-out excuses. People always saw the sadness in my eyes, though. They'd noticed the bright light in them dim slowly over time, until it eventually went out altogether.

Suddenly paranoid I'd be discovered, I looked back and forth, from one side mirror to the other, then to the rear-view mirror, though I struggled to see much at all through the blur of tears. This was like combat, and I awaited the surprise attack I knew would come.

I'd been training since I was a little girl, equating upset to the emotional and physical trauma which followed. I'd learned to read people's verbal and nonverbal language, to assess the enemy and strategize for my protection. That's why I startled easily. Ever hyper-vigilant, everyone was a threat, and no one could be trusted.

I suddenly realized how pathetic I must look. A warrior couldn't look defeated when facing the enemy. So I flipped the visor down to look in the little mirror. As suspected, the windows to my sorrowful soul were muddied with smeared black mascara and smudged eyeliner. I tried to wipe the mess off my face, but even my make-up fought me today. I'd have to war with Darren looking like the hell he'd turned me into.

In the quiet solitude of my car, stone-faced and still, I laid my head back upon the headrest and took a moment to reset before the inevitable confrontation. Then Darren appeared out of nowhere, startling me when he knocked on the car window.

The hateful and violent Mr. Hyde I'd left in the cow paddock had transformed into his kinder counterpart. Standing before me with his apologetic, closed-mouth grin and upturned brows, he'd likely attempt to lure me with sweet words and romantic gestures, as he'd done in the past, but I wouldn't fall for his false promises anymore. I trusted his actions less than his words anyway, and I couldn't be sure he wasn't trying to trick me into exiting the car so he could harm me. That's why I lowered the window just slightly enough to hear whatever he wanted to say.

He didn't say anything, though. He pulled a red tulip from behind his back instead and held it up to the window as a peace offering. I recognized it as one of the few which had emerged from the ground this spring, and I was annoyed he thought it okay to pick. That flower couldn't erase his atrocious behavior, yet I felt compelled to go with the flow of these turbulent waters to avoid drowning in his undertow. I was already drowning though, in so much misery that I didn't hear the words he finally spoke. I couldn't listen to more bullshit meant to persuade me to continue living this life I didn't want to live anyway. So I rolled the window up and stared straight ahead as if he weren't still standing there.

Darren took the hint and walked away dejectedly. I knew the feeling well, but I cared less for his feelings than my own these days. His feelings, needs and demands had always come first and I was made to feel selfish for having feelings of my own because they were contradictory to his agenda and served no purpose to him. I never thought a person could be so uncaring and inconsiderate, but he'd proved me wrong.

After a couple short minutes of quietude, my rear-view mirror caught Darren and Ryder coming out of the house. Darren had changed into clean blue jeans and an old brown hoodie he practically lived in.

I knew what he was doing, and his manipulation of the situation was maddening. He'd likely told Ryder I was waiting for them in the car to go to dinner. Fulfilling my one Mother's Day wish made Darren look like a good husband, and my current mental and physical state would seem unstable to our son, who hadn't witnessed the preceding events.

So here I was, again being forced to play a role in a twisted version of reality. I had no choice, though. Like everything else in my life, I was in this mess for Ryder. So I smiled at him as he got into the back seat.

He was in good spirits, having just laughed at something Darren said to him before they got in the car. After all these years, it still amazed me how Darren could instantly alter his persona from one extreme to the other yet shame *me* for a bipolar diagnosis.

"Who's ready for some pizza?" Darren slapped his hands together, and rubbed them up and down after settling into the passenger seat. Then he smiled at me and put his left hand on my right thigh, putting on the air of an affectionate and loving husband for Ryder's benefit.

I proceeded out our gravel drive, thinking of Amy Winehouse's sultry voice singing, "What kind of fuckery is this . . ."

"Don't You Want Me?"

By the time we were seated at a table in the lowly lit Italian restaurant, the fake charm Darren had exhibited in the car was used up. He'd expected me to participate in his show, to pretend what happened hadn't, thereby covering up his mistreatment of me on a day when I should have been made to feel special. But I shut down instead. I wouldn't converse. I wouldn't laugh at jokes. I was so tired of letting him get away with unacceptable behavior, I just couldn't find it in me to get past it, regardless of the occasion.

So there we were, sitting at Mother's Day dinner, in tense silence. Ryder knew I quieted when upset, so he remained quiet too. Darren leaned back in his chair with his arms folded, glaring at me. I stared back, secretly wishing the back legs of that chair would give way and dropkick him onto the floor for me.

The cheery waitress disrupted our silent war. "Can I get some drinks for you?"

"Yeah, I'll have a Miller Lite," Darren said. Of course he had to order first.

"I'll have a Sprite," Ryder followed.

The waitress looked to me then. "I'm fine. Thank you."

"Okay!" the waitress acknowledged and returned with the drinks right away. "Are you ready to order, or do you need a few minutes?"

"We're ready," I responded. We always had the same pizza order, no matter where we went, and I didn't want to be there any longer than I had to.

After ordering, we waited for our food for what seemed like forever.

Not one of us spoke. Darren drank the first of several beers, looking all around, except at me and Ryder. It made me feel like the wallpaper was more important than us, which was probably his intent.

I looked all around too, envious of the families sitting at other tables, talking and laughing. That's how Mother's Day should be, I thought. Then I looked at Ryder regretfully, wishing I'd chosen a different life for us. He avoided eye contact to avoid inserting himself into the tense dynamic between me and Darren. Darren would have taken it as Ryder siding with me, and it wouldn't have gone over well.

When the pizzas finally arrived, Ryder and I immediately grabbed slices and took bites of the cheesy deliciousness. Darren sat with his arms crossed, however, offended that his upset hadn't suppressed our appetites.

The pacifist in me decided to give in for Ryder's sake. I put a couple pieces of pepperoni pizza on a plate and pushed it in front of Darren.

He pushed the plate back. "I'm not hungry."

I'd had it with him! We'd wasted the entire day waiting for him, then came here at his insistence, but he wasn't hungry? I wouldn't argue in a restaurant full of people, though. So I pulled cash out of my pocket and placed it on the table.

"I got it," Darren said and pushed my money back to me. I gladly took my twenties back and walked out of the restaurant. I'd been paying the price for marrying him too long already.

Outside, I stood against the brick exterior of the building and wept in the rain. I didn't understand what I'd done to deserve such animosity. Darren treated others kindly and respectfully, and everyone liked him. It was only me, who'd been a good wife to him and an even better mother to our son, who wasn't privy to his kindness.

I decided to get in the back seat of my Kia, where my sadness wouldn't be on display for everyone in our small town to witness. Then I texted Darren: *I'm in the car, but take your time and let Ryder finish his dinner.*

I leaned my head back on the headrest and watched the raindrops hit the window, to calm my heart and mind. They dripped down the glass like tears, reminding me of all the tears I'd cried over the years.

The buzz of my phone distracted me from the sadness I was settling into. *Take your son home. I'll walk,* Darren ordered. Then his own guilt followed. *I'm sorry I can't do anything right. Working my ass off. But like my last job, I can't make money and spend time with you.*

He'd been using the work argument for years, but the issue had never been his job; it was his shitty attitude towards me when he was home. He was just too egocentric to see fault within himself or feel empathy for his neglected wife. Nothing I'd ever said had any effect on his perspective, though, nor would it now, so I didn't respond.

Trying to let you be. I don't make you happy. Period, he poked.

I ignored that text too. I wouldn't engage in a war of words neither of us would win.

Darren and Ryder exited the restaurant then. They spoke heatedly for a moment before parting. Darren walked away, and Ryder came across the street to the car, got in, and started the ignition.

"Ryder! We can't just leave your dad here!" I scolded.

"If he wants to walk home, let him walk home!" Ryder yelled. The rain was falling faster now, so he turned the windshield wipers on and checked the side mirror for an opportunity to pull out into traffic.

"Ryder! Seriously!" I insisted. "We're not leaving your dad to walk fifteen miles home in the rain!"

"Then he can find his own ride home," Ryder barked back. I agreed, but I'd left Darren to walk home in the past, and he never made it home in a better mood than he'd been left! Plus, I didn't want Ryder to learn revenge from me.

"Will you at least follow your dad until he gets in the car?"

"No! If Dad wants to act like a baby and refuse to get in the car, getting home is his problem!"

I felt vindicated by the alignment of our thoughts, but I knew I had to convince Darren to get in the car immediately. Ryder never minced words, and he would drive us home no matter what I said, unless I could convince Darren to get in the car immediately.

Please come back to the car, I texted.

Why? I know you don't like me anymore.

Wait a second! He'd told me he didn't like *me* anymore, on more than a few occasions! But this wasn't the time to point out his tendency to twist things in his favor.

I'm sorry for getting so upset before. I love you. Just please come back and get in the car so we can go home.

I wasn't sorry, nor did I love him. Yet, here I was, lying to manipulate him, as he'd done to me so many times. I was no better than him now, I thought as I dropped my head in disappointment.

When I looked up again, I saw Darren walking towards the car on the opposite side of the street. "Ryder, your dad's coming back! Wait for him! Please! He's right there!" I leaned forward and pointed in Darren's direction.

Darren crossed the street after traffic had passed, and climbed in the back seat with me. Ryder tore out into traffic then, to make sure Darren knew he'd almost been left behind.

Darren looked over at me then. He was drenched. Served him right, I thought as I turned and looked out the window again. Then I felt the seat depress next to me. I looked over to see Darren smiling while he attempted to put his wet arm around me. I instinctively pulled away. Repelled by my repulsion, he moved as far to the other side of the car as possible, crossed his arms, and glared at me with disdain.

I turned away and watched the raindrops on the window again. The sound of them pelting the glass was the only sound we could hear in the tense silence, the whole drive home.

Although it was only 6 p.m., I went upstairs to the master bathroom to get ready for bed. As I lifted the top of the hamper to throw my clothes in, I noticed the last line of an article in the People magazine which lay on top: "If it doesn't feel like love, it isn't love."

Total truth. But I wanted love so badly, I'd been willing to pretend all this time.

Back in the kitchen, I took my bedtime medications. A combination of Seroquel and Clonazepam would put me to sleep within twenty minutes, and thankfully so. I was ready for this day to be over, like all the other days before it.

As I put my glass in the sink, I felt Darren's hands grip my hips and his groin press into my behind. He had to be kidding! Did he seriously think sex was even a possibility after what had transpired tonight? I wondered if he got off on conflict with me. Regardless, it wasn't going to happen.

Without a word, I stepped out of his grasp and returned the almond milk carton to the refrigerator. When I closed the door, Darren stood too close behind me, staring at me in disbelief. "Really?" he ridiculed. "You can't just let shit go for one fucking night?"

Blank-faced, I slipped away from him and went down to the basement where I slept on the reclining sofa. I unfolded the two lush comforters I left there, and placed my pink-and-red-striped sock monkey pillow on the far end so I could lay facing the stairway, just in case an unwelcome nighttime visitor wandered down.

Then I plugged my phone into the charger behind the sofa and swaddled myself in the layers of blankets. I was calmed by the way the sofa cradled my little body in its crevice. It felt like I was being held, though I wished I was being soothed by an actual person. A kind and loving husband maybe, who pained to see his sweet wife in despair. I placed a man I knew in that fantasy and drifted off to sleep.

I awoke the next morning with chest pains and one of those headaches I got after crying too much. I referred to this feeling as having an "emotional hangover." Coffee and ibuprofen usually relieved the infirmity, but I had to pee first. I stretched my arms over my head and extended my legs with pointed toes before sitting up. Then I reached for my cell phone to check the time.

There was a text from that certain someone I'd fallen asleep thinking of. *Hope you had a happy Mother's Day!* I smiled.

The next several messages were from Darren, all sent after I'd went to sleep the night before. I grimaced before even reading them.

Sorry 'bout today. I know. It's my fault. Always is, always will be. The sex thing . . . don't worry. Have zero interest in it anymore. Was just asking you tonight to make you feel better.

What was meant as punishment meant nothing. I didn't care anymore. I didn't feel anything either. Nothingness was where I survived. Was it normal to feel nothing after twenty-four years together? I wasn't sure, but I had zero interest in giving Darren another thought.

"I Told You I Was Mean"

Early September, I was invited to my sister Gia's housewarming party. She was one of two siblings from my biological father and his ex-wife, who'd just recently passed of a pulmonary embolism.

Darren didn't like Gia, however, so since *he* didn't want to go, he didn't want *me* to go either. "She reminds me too much of you when *you* were young. And why do you want to go so bad anyway? You've lived forty-some years without them! What does it matter to be part of their lives *now?*"

Aside from the hidden insult to me and my sister, Darren was partially right. Until my dad's ex-wife's funeral the month before, it had been a few years since I'd been included in a family gathering. Prior to that, it had been several years. There was no animosity between any of us. Birthday and holiday sentiments were exchanged. I was my dad's daughter, however, the result of a teenage tryst, and none of us were a constant in each other's lives, which made me optional.

The rarity of this invitation was exactly *why* I was so adamant about attending the housewarming. "Because they're my family, Darren. And my siblings just lost their mother a month ago. I won't miss any more time with them just because *you* don't want to go."

I'd shied away from family and friends for too long, either because Darren didn't like them or claimed they didn't like *him*. Really, he didn't want me to talk to anyone, because if I talked to anyone about *him*, he knew they'd influence me to leave him. People like my sister—who were well-educated, well-traveled, respectable, and trustworthy—were a particular threat to Darren's ability to control me, since their intellect and reason

322

would appeal to the same in me and motivate me to act, and he couldn't risk losing the source of his livelihood.

"Well, what time are you gonna be back, then?" Darren prepared to set a timer on me.

I huffed as I gathered my purse and an afternoon coffee for the road. "I don't know. Five or six? I mean, it's a two-hour drive each way, and I can't predict how long the party will go."

I saw Darren cross his arms and grimace when I passed the couch to put my shoes on by the door.

"So, what? I'm just supposed to sit here all night and wait for you?"

I rolled my eyes. "Yeah, I guess so," I said as I walked out, thankful to escape before he decided to come with me after all. He would have ruined what turned out to be a pleasant drive, with the windows rolled down and the radio cranked up with Cardi B music he wouldn't have tolerated.

I was one of the first guests to arrive at my sister's house. It was a beautifully renovated three-story Victorian home situated on a quiet tree-lined street in a suburb north of Chicago. I was surprised my sister and her fiancé opted for a life so far outside the busy city they'd spent their entire lives in, away from everything and everyone they knew. Gia said they'd gotten a great deal on it, though, and hoped to have and raise lots of children there once married.

After getting a tour of the never-ending number of uniquely shaped rooms, set within crammed hallways and random staircases, I floated between the modern kitchen and alternatively antique formal dining room. I introduced myself to some of Gia's friends and her fiancé's family as they arrived and waited for their own tours through the home. Then I hung around the living room where our brother, Remy, played video games.

Remy was tall and slim but sat slouched into a dark low-set sofa, wearing a T-shirt and athletic shorts. He held a game controller in his hand and focused his full attention on the TV against the wall across from him, but I attempted conversation anyway.

"Are you working now? Or going to school?"

"I work at PetSmart," he shared.

"That would be the best job! I love animals!"

"It's not that great," he murmured.

"I remember when you rode horses when you were little!" I tried to lure the shy twenty-year-old into any common ground we could converse about. "They say 'animal people' have more sensitive souls than others."

He didn't respond, and the lack of reciprocation was awkward. I tried to fill the silence with a different topic.

"So when did you dye your hair blond? It looks good on you, by the way. It's just so different from your dark hair!"

"Gia did it."

"That's cool! She did a good job!" Through the big bay window looking out to the front yard, I saw our dad walking up to the house then. "Oh, Dad's here! I'm going to go say hi." I checked the clock on the way to open the front door for him and saw Gia and her fiancé setting food out onto a long folding table near the kitchen. Just in time for dinner too. It was almost 5 p.m.

"Welcome!" I said boisterously when I opened the front door. I extended one arm outward, as if hired help ushering a guest into some magnificent mansion. My dad smirked. He was a tall Dennis Franz with Ray Liotta eyes—exactly what you'd expect a Chicago cop to look like.

"Hey, Dana! How you doin'?" he said with his coordinating Italian accent.

"Living the dream!" I said sarcastically as I gave him a hug.

"Yeah," he snickered.

He hadn't been there before either, so I led him towards the kitchen. "Gia just put food out. I think most everyone's outside, except me and Remy and a few other people who are hanging out in here." I motioned towards the adjacent dining room, which opened to the living room.

"Hi, Dad!" Gia stopped to greet him as she passed through to get something for someone. "We're eating, so help yourself!"

"I will," Dad said.

Gia turned back to me with an afterthought, "Are you able to eat any of this?" I was surprised she'd remembered the new diet I'd told her I followed and appreciated the consideration. I wasn't used to it.

"Don't worry about me, hon! You just take care of everyone else! Anyway, I've got my coffee." I raised the Hello Kitty travel cup I'd brought my salted caramel latte in.

When I set it back down on the kitchen counter, I saw a notification on my cell phone, which lay next to my pink cup. It was a text from Darren, which I neither opened nor read. I walked over to where my dad was preparing a plate of food for himself instead.

"So how you been feelin'?" he asked before taking his first bite of food.

"Good! I mean, as good as I can." I told him about the toxin-free diet I followed now. "I've actually noticed a difference in how I feel since I started eating cleaner food. Like my inflammation—it's gone down tremendously. I'm not in as much pain. I have more energy. It's just hard to believe stress and food and all the things we take for granted can cause so many health problems! But you know how that is, with your diabetes." I heard my phone buzz but ignored it.

My dad swallowed another bite of food and looked at me with crinkled brows of concern. "I don't get it. What's causing you so much stress that you're sick because of it?"

I didn't tell people about the things Darren said and did to me, never mind my dad, who was a cop. This wasn't the time or place to confess those truths anyway. "Oh, you know, life!" My phone buzzed again. I looked over at it anxiously, knowing it was probably Darren again. "Gimme a second to check my phone. Damn thing keeps buzzing, and I wanna make sure Ryder doesn't need me for something."

"Yeah, go ahead!" My dad continued eating while I scrolled through the multiple text messages I'd received.

Are you on your way home yet? Darren texted just before 5 p.m.

You still at your sister's? he texted not long after.

You said you'd be home by 5 or 6.

Can't answer me?

"Is everything okay?" My dad asked. He must have seen the serious look on my face. I always did wear my heart on my sleeve, so to speak.

"Yeah!" I smiled to offset his concern. "I just get resting bitch face when I'm trying to read text messages. You know how small these phones are. And with *my* eyes . . ." I laughed at my self-deprecation. "I just need to respond to one message real quick. I'm sorry!"

"Yeah, of course," my dad said as he brought another fork full of food to his mouth.

I'm still at Gia's. My dad just got here, so visiting with him now, I typed.

"I'm sorry, Dad," I said as I put my phone back down on the counter. It buzzed again so I took a quick peek.

You said you'd be home around 5 or 6. It's almost 6 and you have a 2-hour drive.

"One more message, Dad, then I'm yours. I swear!"

"Take your time," he said, then went to the living room to talk to Remy.

I texted Darren back for what I hoped would be the last time. *You're right. I did. But my dad didn't get here until about then and I want to talk to him some more. I'll be on my way soon!*

I felt like a dog on a retractable leash, and I knew I'd have to wrap up my visit quickly to avoid having to explain myself again. So after taking some pictures with my dad and siblings, my dad walked me to my car.

"Sorry I have to leave. Just a long drive!" I excused.

"Yeah. Well, I'm glad you came up. Drive safely and text me when you get home, Okay?"

"I will. Love you, Dad!" I watched him in my rear-view mirror as I regrettably pulled away. He waited in the street, like he always did after a visit, until he couldn't see me anymore.

I wondered how different life would be if I had been raised by a parent who actually cared about me, instead of the two who couldn't even be bothered to ask about my health this last year. I guessed I wouldn't have ended up with someone like Darren, who treated me as unworthy as I'd been raised to think I was.

Speaking of whom, I'd forgotten to text. *Leaving now.*

Will try to wait up for you, but not feeling well.

I shook my head and huffed. He wanted me home but didn't want to see me? And when was he going to stop using illness as code for drunkenness? Or was he just trying to get attention by saying he was sick? I didn't know, nor did I care. I was just pissed he'd interrupted my time with my family, especially since visits with them were so few and far between.

A few minutes later, my phone lit up again. *Going to bed. Can't take this life anymore.*

I knew there would be consequences to going somewhere other than work, which was why I never went anywhere, saw no one, and had no friends.

It was easier to live a lonely life than to deal with the guilt he burdened me with. I didn't respond, though. I turned on the radio and cranked up the volume to tune out my cynical thoughts.

I'm the worst person in the world. You and Ryder should both leave me. PLEASE DO!!!

This was all a ploy for attention, I deciphered. Yet, manipulating him with kindness was all I could do to keep him at bay and keep whatever little peace I could for myself. *I wish you could see yourself how other people see you. That's the man I fell in love with and who I get a glimpse of every now and then. If you need help, I will help. But I need taking care of now too. And I want my husband to be the one who does that.*

Thanks, but I'm more fucked up than you could understand. I'm toxic. Take our son and leave before I hurt myself.

He'd threatened suicide in the past. I'd reacted by rushing home to stop him, which was exactly what he wanted now. But I couldn't drive any faster and the boy cried wolf too many times for me to believe him anymore anyway. Instead, I secretly played out the suicide scenario in my head, only it ended with the police suspecting me of wrongdoing, based on my cold indifference to his passing.

I'm serious. Just go run and hide with Ryder! I don't want you guys to see me kill myself.

I refused to engage, and because I didn't, he finally reneged. *Going to bed.*

Thank God!

He didn't bother me after that, so I relished in the peace of the remainder of the drive, singing along to acoustic covers that calmed me and watching the colorful sunset wane into a dark horizon.

The dented wreckage of our electric pizza oven awaited me on the front porch at home. It looked like it had been thrown out the door, which I guessed was exactly what had happened.

This wasn't the first appliance Darren had destroyed. I once discovered a large butcher knife sticking out of the top of the waffle iron. Darren hadn't oiled the iron properly and the waffles had gotten stuck inside, so he stabbed it for being uncooperative. The waffle iron before that had been violently thrown to the kitchen floor for the same reason. So guess what he got for his birthday that year? Yes, a waffle iron. I was a bitch when I wanted to be.

His tantrums were getting old, though. I took a deep breath as I walked past the broken oven and into the house, where the black TV screen indicated Darren was indeed in bed. Only the dim light over the kitchen sink was on.

Ryder's bedroom door was closed, but I knew he was still awake because I'd seen the light on in his room when I drove up. So I put my purse and coffee cup on the kitchen island, then tapped on his door lightly before letting myself in. "What's going on? Are you okay?"

"I'm fine!" He stood and closed his bedroom door in my face before I could say another word. I didn't understand his animosity towards me, but I knew it had to have something to do with Darren and the pizza oven. Maybe Ryder resented me for leaving him alone with his dad in a mood. If so, I was sorry I hadn't been there for him but also glad I'd missed Darren's delirium.

Back in the kitchen, I saw shredded cheese all over the counter and floor, and an uncooked frozen pizza haphazardly folded in on itself inside the sink. I worked too hard to let perfectly good food be wasted. So after cleaning up the mess, I flattened and cooked the discarded pizza, then put it in the refrigerator. I chuckled as I imagined Darren's surprised expression when he opened the refrigerator the next morning and saw the resurrected pizza staring back at him in its full cheesy glory. I knew he'd be mad. He'd probably go crazy and chuck the pizza out the door too! But I didn't care.

I went to bed in the basement, feeling satisfied for finally entertaining my vengeful thoughts in lieu of the higher road I tried to stay on. It was time I turned the tables on Darren anyway. He'd been calling me crazy for years, but maybe I was just as much of an asshole as he was.

"Saint Nobody"

After an unusually sound sleep, I woke up the next morning refreshed and relaxed. I went through my usual routine of making coffee and walking, but more leisurely since it was Sunday and I had nowhere to go except church. Despite having all the time in the world, I lost track of it and panicked when I realized I only had twelve minutes to get dressed and get there. Of course, my clothes were in the bedroom where Darren was still sleeping.

Any other day, I would have just worn dirty clothes from the laundry basket, since they'd get dirty while I cleaned houses anyway. People probably thought I was poor or non-hygienic because I sometimes wore clothing two or three days in a row to avoid going in the bedroom and waking Darren. Not today, though. I deserved to wear clean clothing, especially to mass, so I was going in. I supposed I needed to make sure he hadn't followed through on his suicide threat anyway.

I opened the bedroom door slowly, then assessed the dark room before entering. The blinds were still down and Darren was snoring, so I tiptoed towards the closet doors to my immediate left, careful not to step on certain floorboards. I'd learned which ones creaked from failed attempts to retrieve clothes in the past. Then I manipulated the bi-fold closet doors as noiselessly as I could to take jeans and a sweatshirt from the shelves inside.

Just as I was pulling the bedroom door closed behind me, I heard Darren stir. Then I heard a soft, "Hey."

I froze and looked back. "Sorry!" I whispered. "I just needed clothes for church."

"How was your sister's thing?" he asked groggily, rubbing his eyes.

"Good! I'll see you in a bit." I turned again to creep out of the room.

"That's it? Good?" He spoke in a normal tone now.

So I did too. "I'm sorry, but I gotta go. I'm gonna be late for church."

"You spend more time at that fucking church than you do with me!" he shouted. "You fuckin' the priest or something?"

I closed the door. I had neither the patience nor the time to engage. Anyway, if he'd looked at his bedside clock, he'd have seen I was running late. It was almost like he was testing whether I'd pick him over church, which would just lead to another fight about my disloyalty to him and our marriage!

I closed myself into the master bathroom to dress as quickly as I could to get out of Dodge. I pulled on my jeans and threw my dark pink sweatshirt over my head, but the sound of the bedroom door opening told me it was too late.

The bathroom door burst open and bounced off the linen closet door knob behind it. Darren stood in the doorway with his broad shoulders, puffed chest, and mean face. "You always say you want me to talk to you, so then I try to talk, and you leave?"

There was no way out, so I cowered away from him slightly, unsure of his next move. "I just needed to get clothes so I can get to church . . ." I excused, but Darren already retreated and slammed the bedroom door to shut me out.

Without wasting another second, I buttoned my jeans, grabbed my socks and escaped the confinement of the bathroom. Then I hurried to church, where at least I'd be safe for the hour I was there.

When I returned to my car after mass, a text message on my phone awaited me. *I would've dropped everything for you if you told me you were going to commit suicide. And you can't give me a simple good morning?*

I thought he had been upset that I was going to church instead of spending time with him, but it was because I hadn't reacted to his threat the night before? And now I was being chastised for not saying good morning? I had to replay the interaction with him in my head, just to double check that I remembered everything right. I couldn't respond or defend myself to him when I could barely keep track of what we were even arguing about.

I figured this would continue when I returned home from church anyway.

When I pulled into the driveway an hour later, Darren's truck was missing from its usual parking spot. I didn't know where he'd gone, nor did I care. I saw through the game he was playing, and I was maddened by the way he toyed with my emotions. He knew what time I returned from church every Sunday and had intentionally left before then, to leave me like I'd left him for my sister's housewarming the day before and to make me wonder if he'd left me altogether. The joke was on him, though. I was glad and relieved to have solitude in my home for the one day I had off work, and I wouldn't have minded if he'd done me the favor of ending this charade once and for all.

As such, I didn't reach out to him, though I knew it was only a matter of time before he'd solicit a response from me.

Five hours later, he proved me right. *With a friend. Hope you're okay. I love you very much. My head's just been in a bad place for a couple weeks.*

I begged to differ about our definitions of love. And his head? It had been in a bad place for more like twenty-some years, but who's counting?

"I Will Survive"

I was driving between jobs one day when my vision suddenly went dark. It happened on a side street with no traffic, so I was able to slow and pull over to a stop without crashing into anything or anyone. When my sight returned a minute later, I proceeded to my next destination safely, but the incident had scared me enough to consult with Dr. George again. I'd been increasingly short of breath anyway, doing simple tasks like walking up a flight of stairs and vacuuming at work. That wasn't normal for someone as active as I'd always been.

In the comfort of Dr. George's cozy office, I slumped back into the familiar high-backed chair I favored of the two available. I looked at the familiar full face, slightly too long black hair, and matching goatee as he leaned back into his chair and opened conversation. "So what's going on?"

"Well, first of all, I'm sorry I haven't been back sooner. I know you wanted me to follow up after seeing all the specialists earlier this year, but the functional medicine doctor ended up leaving her office to start her own before we got very far with figuring out what's wrong with me. Then I was inundated with the combination of a big tax bill and all the medical bills from all the doctor's appointments and tests I'd already had, so I just stopped pursuing this." I paused my rambling to take a breath. I'd been getting winded when I talked too long. "And honestly, I needed a break from the poking and prodding. I was starting to feel like a pin cushion."

Dr. George chuckled. "How are you feeling now? As far as your symptoms, are they better or worse?"

I told him why I'd been compelled to call him and handed him copies of all the test results I'd received from the specialists he'd sent me to. After reviewing them, and asking specific questions about the different doctors' assessments, he asked, "Did you ever complete the sleep study?" He looked through the lab reports again, as if he'd missed it.

I cringed. "No. I don't see how sleep has anything to do with breathing or any of my other symptoms, so I didn't want to run up another big bill needlessly."

"I can understand that," Dr. George said, nodding, "but I really think you should have it done. There are a lot of correlations between interrupted sleep and all the symptoms you're having."

"That's what the functional medicine doctor said. She wanted me to use some sleeping app, but I don't have a smartphone," I said, intentionally leaving out Darren's refusal to let me borrow his iPhone for the task.

"Do you still have the order I gave you for the sleep study?"

"Yeah, it's in my planner. Just saving it for a rainy day!" I joked.

"Well, I think the rainy day is here," Dr. George replied, turning to the dreary afternoon outside his office window. "It is October!"

We laughed at our banter, and I begrudgingly made the appointment.

Dr. Soteira was a short average-weight doctor with a heavy accent I couldn't identify but that sounded Greek or Russian. He wore a long white coat and the same warm smile his nurse had given me when she'd taken my vitals. I felt very comfortable in the genuinely friendly atmosphere of the office. It was as plain and neutral as any other doctor's office, but there was something to be said about the positive energy here. I supposed it had to be that way for people to be calm enough to sleep there.

"It sounds like you have UARS—upper airway resistance syndrome," Dr. Soteira thought out loud after asking preliminary questions about my symptoms and reviewing the results of all tests the doctors before him had ordered. "It's rare, but my son has it. That's how I recognize it in you. Now, open up and say 'Aah'!"

He examined my throat, my eyes' response to light, pressed upon various points of my neck, then returned to his short stool. "You were born with an unusually narrow airway, which is why you're not getting enough oxygen. That explains the dizziness, blacking out, and low blood pressure. You said you feel like you hold your breath when you sleep?"

"Yes. I wake up at night gasping for air, and I get headaches when I haven't slept well. I'm guessing that's because my brain isn't getting enough oxygen. I've had a scratchy throat for a couple years straight now, as well, and I wonder if that has anything to do with my trouble breathing."

"It's all related. Your tongue relaxes and falls backward when you sleep." He stuck his tongue out of his mouth sideways and slumped back into his chair with his arms hanging limply off the side. I laughed as he sat back up and returned to doctor mode. "It's thick and big and blocks your airway. Then your lungs strain to breathe, causing the throat pain. Let me look again. Say 'Aah'!"

He pressed my tongue down with a large popsicle stick and looked down my throat with his tiny flashlight. "Your tonsils are like a baby's—so tiny!" he said in the same high-pitched tone one would talk to a baby in. Then he sat and rolled back on his little stool. "Removing them won't make a difference." He paused to think. "Your blood pressure is low too . . ."

"It's always been," I interjected. "I'm guessing that's why my hands and right arm go numb when I sleep?"

"Yes, and with your family history of diabetes, I'm concerned your feet will go next. Do you exercise?"

"Pretty much every day of my life since junior high! I walk about five miles every morning before work, sometimes after work too, but I try to jog if I feel up to it." It was my only way of escaping the house, and Darren, without leaving the property.

"Okay, then keep it up, as long as you can breathe comfortably while doing all that!" He moved his arms back and forth swiftly, as if running. He cracked me up. "I'm going to order a home sleep study for you. You'll take home a little box and put the sticky things on you. It will measure your oxygen and heart rate and brain activity while you sleep. We'll use the results to get pre-approval from your insurance for an overnight sleep study. Okay?"

"Yeah!" I replied, nodding enthusiastically. I was thrilled to have a doctor who thought he already knew what was wrong and was eager to medically prove the diagnosis. I should have listened to Dr. George when he told me to come here in January. He was always right!

"Now, what do you do for work, honey?"

"I have a house cleaning business."

"Business is good?"

"Too good! I have too many clients and never enough help!"

"Well, cleaning houses is no good for you."

He discussed the obvious ill effects of chemical exposure and explained the particularly harmful effects of dust inhalation. Dust is actually dead skin that flaked off people's bodies, so it's full of all the bacteria and viruses people pick up wherever they go. It made sense, then, that I had coughing fits in especially dusty homes. It was my body's way of protecting itself from infection.

Like Dr. Newport, he warned me to find another occupation, or to at least wear gloves and a mask to prevent ingestion of harmful toxins. I told him I'd done that for a while, but people looked at me strangely, like I had the plague or some infectious disease, and I didn't like the negative attention. He understood but urged me to reconsider.

In addition, Dr. Soteira advised me to stay away from fire pits, bonfires, wood-burning fireplaces, grills—basically anything that emitted smoke. I agreed, since I'd always been intolerant of smoke, especially second-hand cigarette smoke, but refrained from sharing that we heated our house with a wood-burning stove. We had a furnace, but wood was cheaper than propane, and I knew Darren would never assume the higher cost in consideration of my health. I also knew there was no way to communicate that truth without avoiding a lecture to influence me to do what I'd already decided to, so once again, I withheld to protect Darren's reputation.

We wrapped up the appointment then, with Dr. Soteira telling me where to obtain the home sleep study equipment.

As he walked me out, he said, "You need to eat some ham or something too! I normally have to tell people to lose weight, but I want you to get some meat on you!"

"I had ham last night," I said, "and three big pieces of rum cake!"

"Really?" He sounded like a little boy who'd been told a tall tale.

"Really!"

"Well, go home and eat more! I want you at least a hundred pounds when you come back!" He pointed at me and smiled.

Everyone assumed my small frame was a result of poor appetite or starvation. Only Ryder and Darren knew the truth about my binge-eating and excessive exercising to overcompensate for calories I couldn't resist.

I was as obsessed with food as I was about maintaining a slender physique, which is why the dramatic thinness of autoimmunity worked for me. I could eat what I wanted and still look great in a bikini (not that I ever wore one anymore). I thought of it as looking at the bright side of a bleak reality, but maybe I was sicker than I'd imagined.

All I knew was that my own husband had no idea how sick I was at all. He didn't ask about my appointments or how I felt day to day. He just didn't care. But I'd stopped caring about him at some point too. At least we finally agreed on something.

"Jar of Hearts"

As I was getting ready for bed one November night, loneliness pulled me straight down the rabbit hole. I stood in front of my bathroom mirror with hunched shoulders, too weak to lift my toothbrush to my mouth. My bottom lip quivered anyway, so it would have been of no use to try. The put-together, tough-girl exterior I put on was crumbling fast behind the closed door. I just didn't have the energy to live this life anymore.

It wasn't just Darren's usual mistreatment and anger bothering me. The holidays were approaching. Everywhere I went, families were decorating with lights, planning celebrations, and shopping for gifts for their loved ones. But who did I have other than Ryder? He wouldn't even be home to celebrate the holidays with me.

My mother had invited Ryder to her home for Christmas Eve. Grandma said I was welcome there too, despite being banished from the family for having a relationship with my dad. Apparently, it was disloyal to my abusive stepfather, who hadn't spoken to me since I'd attended my dad's ex-wife's funeral. The fucked-up logic boggled me just as much as the idea that I'd break bread with a man who'd abused me and continued to insult me to my son and other family members behind my back. I tried not to let it bother me, but it did, because Christmas should be spent with my son, my mother, and Grandma.

Jane and Denise only communicated with Darren anymore, so I wasn't even sure what their plans were. I guessed they had the same plans as usual—to gather at Jane's on Thanksgiving, and then again on Christmas Day. Darren hadn't said anything, though, so I scheduled myself to clean a couple offices on Thanksgiving, figuring if I had to work, I wouldn't have to face the pain of not being invited or the hurt feelings of exclusion I felt when I was with them.

I was excluded from holidays with my dad and siblings too. Aside from the Easter dinner they'd come to my house for on the same night I was confirmed in the Catholic church in 2016, I'd only been invited to one Christmas with them before, and it wasn't even on Christmas.

So who would miss me at Thanksgiving or Christmas? No one. I wasn't part of any family. I didn't belong to any group of friends who'd miss me. My own husband and son thought nothing of leaving me alone on a holiday. Invisible and insignificant to everyone, I might as well have been dead. Nobody would notice if I was gone anyway.

I threw down my toothbrush in frustration and put my fists over my eyes, as if trying to dam the overflow, but the tears saturated the large cuffs of my thick red robe anyway. Then I succumbed to my misery and collapsed onto the cold white ceramic tile floor. I sobbed into my knees as my mind replayed every insult, demeaning comment, aggressive action and inaction which supported my worthlessness. Most everyone I could think of had hurt me deeply, except for my grandma, who I didn't even see because she lived with my mother now.

I was every cliché used to describe someone's mental undoing— becoming unhinged, screws being loose, losing it (the "it" being the shit I was losing). I thought I'd built a solid wall of protection around myself, but the truths that had served as my armor had been dismantled by vicious lies that tore me down. I'm not even sure I knew what the truth was anymore because I was the common denominator in all the dysfunctional relationships in my life. I was the only one removed from every tribe I'd thought I belonged to, stripping me of my entire sense of safety and security. Exposed, crippled, and left to fend for myself, there was nothing left to protect whatever little pieces of me remained.

Darren came into the bathroom then, distracting me from my depressing thoughts. He sat on the edge of the tub with a sorrowful expression and extended his hands to me. "What's wrong, babe?"

All I could do was shake my head no. I didn't want to be with this hateful man who pretended to care, but I needed someone, and he was the only one there.

"Come on, babe," he urged.

I craved love, even if artificial. So, despite everything that had happened between us over the years, his presence in this particular moment was like dangling a hot meal in front of someone starving to death; I couldn't resist.

I crawled to him, situated myself between his legs, and leaned my head on one of his thighs. I'd hoped he'd pet my head like my great-grandma had done to soothe me when I was little, but he put his hands on my upper back instead. The physical touch soothed me just the same, which only made me cry harder because I didn't trust his affections.

Why couldn't he console and love me *all* the time? Why did he pick and choose when I was deserving of love? I thought parental and marital love were supposed to be unconditional, but that hadn't been my experience.

"I don't want to do this anymore." I sobbed harder when I heard myself speak my truth.

As if he hadn't understood what I'd said, Darren calmly whispered back, "I love you. It's you and me against the world, right?"

He lifted my chin with his index finger. My sad eyes met his seemingly empathetic expression. I wanted so badly to believe him, but he'd broken my heart too many times for me to subject myself to giving him another chance. So instead of responding with another lie, I said nothing.

Darren understood what I was saying with my silence, though. His face tensed. He huffed to emphasize his disgust with me, then dropped my chin and left with a slam of the door.

Alone again on the bathroom floor, I cried for what could have been and for the inability to endure what *was* for much longer. I couldn't love us both, and loving him was killing me.

He probably hoped I would kill myself. And if I were truly suicidal, I would have.

"I Won't Stop Running"

By mid-December, I'd completed both the in-home and overnight sleep studies, and Dr. Soteira had my results. I was eager to get a diagnosis, but my body was not as eager to function.

On the morning of my appointment, I awoke stiffer than usual. It took much more effort to sit up and stand, but I finally made my way to the bathroom, moving like a ninety-year-old lady. I couldn't help but notice my reflection as I walked past the large mirror. It was of a weak and sickly woman I didn't recognize. Dead eyes that used to exude fire now showed dark bags as proof of sleepless nights. Shoulders which used to demonstrate perfect posture now folded into a discouraged slump. *What happened to me?* I wondered. The answer was asleep in the other room.

I moved towards the toilet to pee. My fingers were so red and swollen, my hands so pained, I couldn't tear the toilet paper from the roll to wipe. I repeatedly attempted to grip the hanging end, but my fingers couldn't get a firm hold. Tears welled up in my eyes as I feared what would become of me if I couldn't take care of myself.

Despite my dysfunctional hands, I was able to wriggle on some sweatpants and a sweatshirt. I left for work knowing this was one of those days I shouldn't drive and that cleaning would be another feat altogether.

I headed east on the highway, directly into the bright morning sun. My sensitive eyes squinted at the assault. I blinked to get rid of the multicolored spots floating in my vision, then opened them widely a few seconds later to find myself two lanes over from where I'd been. I checked my mirrors to make sure I hadn't run anyone off the road and was thankful to see I was one of the few cars on the road at all. I released a deep breath and wondered how I'd fallen asleep so fast in the first place.

The next thing I knew, adrenaline had jolted me awake again, just in time to avoid the ditch between me and the oncoming traffic. I swerved to the right to get back in my lane and checked all my mirrors to make sure I hadn't affected anyone else's travel. Relieved I hadn't, I released a breath I'd been holding, then widened my eyes to force them to stay open. I opened the windows too, counting on the cool morning breeze to keep me awake.

Like a drunk driver who hadn't been caught, I was thankful to get to my two cleaning jobs, and then the doctor's office afterward, safely.

The sound of the door clicking closed when Dr. Soteira entered the room startled me awake. My legs were curled up in the gray metal chair, and my elbow on the arm of it propped up the hand which held my head. Just like in the car that morning, I had no recollection of falling asleep. I straightened myself up nonetheless, noticing I'd taken my boots off as well.

"Tired, huh? Or are you tired of being tired?" he joked as he sat on his short stool. I mustered half a smile for him before he continued.

"Well, honey, as I suspected, you have a sleep-related disorder called upper airway resistance syndrome. It's like having fibromyalgia and COPD at the same time. You're probably a light sleeper?"

"I've been a light sleeper since I was a kid," I told him, "but I only started having these symptoms the last couple of years."

"Many sleep disorders and autoimmune diseases lay dormant, sometimes for decades, until something traumatic wakes them up. That's why they're common among those who were abused as children or who are in abusive situations as adults," he clarified. "Like your autoimmunity, it's always been in you. You're just now exhibiting the symptoms."

"That makes sense, actually." I hadn't told him about my abusive childhood, nor my tumultuous marriage, both of which disallowed sleep. The slightest bumps in the night aroused me into hyper-alertness because I felt like I had to be on guard to fend off oncoming threats.

"What's happening is your brain sends signals to the nervous system to focus as much energy as possible into the lungs to keep you breathing, and your parasympathetic nervous system compensates by lowering energy required for your other organs to function, so they function at the bare minimum. That's what causes you so many problems," he explained.

"So it's the lack of oxygen causing all my heart problems too?" I deduced.

"Yes," he confirmed. "Your occasional bradycardia and arrhythmia are what make you feel tired and nauseous. The sore throat and chest pains are a result of your lungs being overworked to breathe, and waking up with headaches is also due to lack of oxygen during sleep. We have to be careful because you are at a forty to fifty percent risk of congestive heart failure."

That was a serious claim which immediately saddened me. I dropped my head and muttered, "My family doctor told me the two things I could be sure of in my life are diabetes and heart failure."

"Yes, we need to find a solution to make you better," he said. "You already have TMJ and grind your teeth, so a mouthpiece to help you breathe better during sleep isn't an option. CPAP is not well-tolerated by people with UARS, because your heightened senses will be bothered by the noise of the machine and interrupt your sleep even more than it already is. The best option is surgery to open your airway, but there's no room to do surgery *because* of your narrow airway. I even considered having your tonsils removed to make room, but your tonsils are so tiny, it wouldn't make a difference."

"So what do I do? Just live like this?" And let the stress actually kill me?

"You need oxygen, but your insurance company won't cover it. They won't cover any more tests to prove your need for it either, because of your weight. They think this is a fat person's disease. I will get you what you need, though, so don't worry. If I have to call those assholes myself . . ." he said as he stood to walk me out.

His off-the-cuff comment made me laugh, though I knew he would follow through on the promise. Dr. Soteira was intent on helping me, and I trusted him to do so. With the holidays so near, however, I doubted anything would be resolved until after the New Year. So I made a conscientious decision to stay active and continue eating clean foods, to give my muscles and lungs and entire body a fighting chance of better function.

Back at home, Darren asked about my appointment. I was surprised by his sudden concern for me. Maybe my near nervous breakdown moved him to rethink our relationship and his role in my life. Then I remembered it was only my ability to serve him with which he was concerned, though the pity a sick wife offered him sufficed. Or maybe he wanted to hear I had a terminal disease so he could be rid of me for good. My cynicism made me sound paranoid, but this was my unfortunate reality.

"I have an upper airway disease that basically minimizes my bodily functions so my body has enough energy left to breathe," I shared, then explained the resolutions I didn't qualify for. I left out the part about how common this was among abuse victims. I didn't need to deal with whatever defense or reaction he'd have when I was resolving myself to a more difficult existence and potentially premature death *because* of him.

I blamed him for this. He was the reason I was sick, and the reason I could possibly die before Ryder graduated and got married and went through all the life events I should be there for. Granted, he'd only finished the job my mother and stepfather had started. It was his abuse, however, that pushed my mind to push my body over that edge into irreversible, lifelong damage. I'd never forgive him for it.

So when he wrapped his arms around me in a seemingly loving gesture meant to console, my arms remained limp at my side. I wouldn't pretend everything was okay when it wasn't, nor would I return the slightest affection to a man who'd effected my ruin.

Insulted by the withholding of affection, Darren released me and went upstairs to bed. I should have been upset he was more concerned about his feelings of rejection as opposed to what I felt after my diagnosis, but I was strangely indifferent—glad almost. I didn't want his fake concern anyway. I'd been through enough.

"You Won't Be Satisfied"

On Christmas night, I was awakened by a sudden urge to vomit. I crept out of the master bed I'd slept in to keep peace on the holiday night and quietly made my way out to the grass off the porch just in time. Darren would have railed on me for waking him with sounds of gagging and puking in the house.

I never threw up. Ever. I hadn't eaten anything bad, but maybe the few glasses of Disaronno I'd chugged to get through the holiday had been too much for my underweight body, especially since I was just starting to drink alcohol again after years of abstinence. My head was pounding too, so a hangover made sense, though the mere two I'd had in my life hadn't felt as bad as this.

Freezing but burning up at the same time, I lingered in the snowy grass, looking up into the dark starry sky as I soaked the winter air into my skin and lungs. I didn't even mind the icy feel on my knees and legs. It felt good.

When I regained enough strength to stand, I headed towards the porch. Although clammy and dizzy, I managed to pull myself up the couple stairs, using the porch rail for support. I stripped down to my panties and clumsily fell into one of the antique wood chairs meant for decoration, allowing the arctic air to cool my overheated body. A few minutes later, I put my pajamas back on and settled on the loveseat inside, where I fell asleep.

When my eyes reopened, it was still pitch black. I must not have slept long. I was still sitting but slumped to the right with my head leaning on the puffy back cushion of the loveseat. The pain in my head hadn't ceased, so I instinctively put my hand to my forehead to rub it and simultaneously check my temperature. I was still burning up. I stumbled to the kitchen for water and ibuprofen, blinding myself with the light I switched on. I opened and shut my eyes repeatedly, to rid them of the blurs and spots I saw instead of the time I was trying to make out on the microwave. Predictably, it was 3 a.m.

I thought to force myself through my ten-thousand step walk in the basement, figuring the movement would get my blood flowing while I gave the ibuprofen time to kick in, but my muscles were as stiff as a cadaver and just breathing made me nauseous. I attempted to salvage what remained of my morning routine by making coffee, but after running outside to puke up the one sip I'd taken, I gave up. I poured hot water over the messes I'd made in the grass, knowing Darren would make me do that later if I didn't do it now, then I settled back on the sofa in a sweat.

My short, hard breaths told me I shouldn't even try to go to work, but, being self-employed and the only income earner in our household, I didn't have sick days to rely on to pay the bills for me. So, as miserable as I felt, I drifted off for another hour, got ready at a snail's pace, then set out for the day.

Every slight vibration of the car caused my head to pound harder. The little light from the sunrise was bothersome too. Having the heat and chill of a fever caused me constant discomfort, and switching from heat to air conditioning when the outside temperature was fifty below zero with the wind chill wasn't good for my car.

It wasn't until after I'd puked a few more times into the small wastebasket I snatched from my back seat that I surrendered to illness. I texted my cleaning crew to tell them they'd have to figure out the day without me and headed back home. I couldn't in good conscience work around our elderly clients in this condition anyway.

Too weak to remove the ski jacket, hat, and gloves I'd bundled up in, I sank back into the loveseat as I was and closed my eyes.

The sound of cabinets banging shut and dishes clinking awoke me a little later. The sharp pains in my head couldn't withstand the piercing sounds. I squinted in the bright light of the morning, unsurprised to see Darren was the culprit. He was standing at the kitchen counter with his back to me, preparing his bowl of Frosted Flakes. When he turned around to carry his bowl of cereal and banana to the couch, he was startled at the sight of me, causing the milk in his bowl to slosh back and forth.

"I thought you were at work!" he said with a raised voice and ridiculing tone I didn't appreciate. He proceeded to his usual post on the longer sofa facing me and set his bowl on the wide-cushioned arm as if it were a table.

If I'd felt better, I'd have called bullshit on him. The loveseat I sat on was positioned just to the side of the bottom of the stairway. So, unless he was blind, there was no way he could've missed me there when he walked down from the bedroom on his way to the bathroom and kitchen. I didn't have it in me to fight, though, nor did I want to wake Ryder—who was on Christmas break from school—with another argument.

"I'm so sick", I whispered as reason for my presence, then rushed to the bathroom just in time to throw up again. Sweating and out of breath, I pulled off my hat and scarf, before unzipping my coat on the way back to the comfort of the cold leather loveseat.

"I can already feel myself getting a sore throat!" Darren griped. "And now you're gonna get your germs all over everything." He got up, went back to the kitchen, poured his cereal down the drain, and practically threw his bowl in the sink. The sound of the crash caused my head to throb harder.

I cringed as Darren stomped back up the stairs to the master bedroom and slammed the door shut. After a lone tear slid down my cheek, mourning the vow to love in sickness and health, I closed my eyes for much-needed rest.

I didn't know how long I'd been asleep when I was startled awake again by Darren yelling, "I'm imprisoned in my own fucking bedroom! It's fucking bullshit!" I looked up to see his angry face glaring down at me with disapproval from the railing overlooking the living room. Then he returned to the bedroom, slamming the door shut behind him. Unmoved by his tantrum, I immediately dozed off.

Darren emerged from the bedroom at frequent intervals throughout the day, intentionally waking me with loud footsteps, slamming doors, and insults for offending him with my illness. He even started a fire in the wood-burning stove just feet away from the loveseat I slept on, without consideration for the fever already burning me up. It's like he wanted me to suffer. But I didn't say anything. I'd been suffering so long, a little more wouldn't make a difference.

When Darren left to go out drinking with a friend that night, Ryder came out of his room to check on me. He'd seen me sick before. He'd seen me struggle to push through whatever came my way. He'd never seen anything take me down like this, though. "You gonna be okay, Mom?"

Still slouched on the loveseat where I'd been all day, I looked at Ryder's worried face. He stood at the kitchen island looking at me helplessly, like he wanted to cure my ills but didn't know how.

"I don't know, kiddo," I whispered as loud as my raspy voice could muster. That was a loaded question, on so many levels.

I'll never know how I got through work the next day, but when I was done, I just wanted to go home and go to sleep. But when I walked in the door, Ryder burst into the "Happy Birthday" song. Darren joined in from where he lay on the couch.

I smiled weakly as I walked to the kitchen island and blew out the singular candle in the store-bought chocolate mousse dessert, thankful there weren't forty-three individual candles to remind me of my wasted youth.

"Open your present!" Ryder encouraged.

My eyelids were ready to close and call it a night, but I couldn't deny Ryder the excitement of opening my gift. "Will you help me?"

He obliged and pried open the large cardboard box leaning on the kitchen island. It was a portable stair-stepping machine I'd saved to my Amazon wish list.

"Thank you, guys!"

"I'm gonna put this together for you now, Mom," Ryder said like an eager little boy anxious to open a new toy. It was hard to believe he was already sixteen.

"Okay, kiddo," I said as I hunkered down on the floor with the pineapple upside down cake a customer had baked especially for my birthday. I'd have normally been concerned about the extra calorie intake, but I hadn't eaten much and I couldn't resist sweets. So I dug in while I watched Ryder remove all the stepper parts from the box. The irony of getting a stepper I was too weak to use to burn off the extra calories of a cake I knew I'd throw up anyway made me chuckle.

Darren got up from the couch and stood over Ryder as he assembled the stepper. I noticed Darren's arms and shoulders tense, then his teeth clench. I recognized his agitation and waited for the brunt of it.

With his hands on his jutted hips, he shook his head. "This is too fucking big," he finally said.

"It's fine, Dad!" Ryder said as he tightened some bolts onto the base.

"It's cheap as hell!" Darren grabbed a handle and shook it, which was an unfair assessment because Ryder hadn't tightened those bolts yet. "Do you know how much I paid for this piece of shit?"

"Darren, please," I begged.

"You're not using this on the wood floors," he mandated. "It'll ruin them."

Our wide-plank southern pine wood floors were separated at the seams, scratched by animal claws, and had been impounded with the fireplace poker when Ryder was a toddler. There was no way these floors could be ruined any more than they already were. I actually preferred the worn look of them.

"I only put this on my list so I could use it here in the living room at night," I pointed out, "because you said you don't like me on my computer or reading a book while you're watching TV."

"Yeah! Because we're watching TV to spend time together! But it's not spending time together if you're paying attention to something else!" Darren retorted.

"I just thought stepping on this next to the couch would give me something productive to do instead of just staring at the TV screen with you." I refrained from commentary about how he'd watch TV whether I was there or not, thereby disqualifying it as an activity we specifically engaged in as a couple, which was a farce in itself, because I didn't want to spend time with him at all!

"We could put a mat underneath it, Dad," Ryder suggested, trying to save me from a fight.

"No, it's *not* going on our wood floors."

"Well, our entire house has wood floors, Darren, except for the laundry room in the basement, and I'm not gonna use it down there!" I argued. I swore he was being obstinate just for the sake of asserting his dictatorship.

Challenging Darren made him angrier, and his opinion of the stepper's quality declined at the same rate. Suddenly, the welding wasn't done right, the structure was too weak to support my body weight, the bottom was uneven and unstable . . .

Ryder offered a solution for each negative comment, then attempted to prove the stepper's worthiness. "It's fine, Dad! See?" He pressed the entirety of his body weight into the resistant pressure to achieve just one step. I chuckled at the inequity of his efforts and results.

Darren squatted down and pressed a piece of the base. "What a fucking waste of money!" Just like the No Doubt CD years ago, the waste was my fault.

I'd had it. "If you don't want it in here, let's just put it back in the box and return it for a refund. Honestly. I have a whole list of things on Amazon I can get instead."

"I'm not going through all that to get a refund," Darren said.

"Amazon has a good return policy," I insisted. "They email the return shipping label, so all we have to do is put it back in the box and drop it off at a UPS store. Doesn't cost anything either. I'll even do it all, so you don't have to."

"You wanted this thing, and now you want to send it back? After what I spent on it?" he replied, seemingly arguing just to argue.

"You obviously don't want it here, and I'm not going to use it in the basement, so yeah! I'd rather get something else from my wish list that I *will* use."

"We're not returning it," he maintained.

Ryder and I gave each other that knowing look—we weren't going to win this one. We never did. So, with the slumped shoulders and sad face of defeat, Ryder dragged the heavy stepper down to the laundry room where it was banished, then hid away in his bedroom.

"Happy fucking birthday to me," I mumbled as I used a chair from the kitchen table to leverage myself up off the floor. Then I asked no one in particular, "Should I order pizza now?" My favorite had been the plan for my birthday dinner, though my queasy stomach wouldn't allow me the special treat, especially after eating all that cake.

"Whatever. I'll pick it up when it's ready," Darren said. Then he walked out, slamming the door behind him.

I watched as he walked into what used to be an entire second house until the pipes burst after he'd failed to sufficiently heat it one winter. It was gutted and turned into a work-shop he only went in to sit in his dad's old recliner, which had taken up residence in the corner of the main floor there. When Darren got mad, he'd go to the shop to sit in the chair and pout, presumably waiting for me to chase after and grovel and beg him to come back to the main house with me. His ploy for attention was ineffective, though. I stopped chasing him long ago.

I ordered the pizza instead and washed dishes to pass the time. When the pizza was ready for pick-up, Darren hadn't returned, so I gathered my wallet and keys.

"I'm leaving to get the pizza, kiddo!" I called out.

Ryder came out of his room and put his hand out. "I'll drive, Mom." I appreciated that at least Ryder cared about my condition, and I handed him the keys.

When we got in the car, Ryder looked at me and said, "I'm sorry Dad is acting like this on your birthday. You don't deserve it."

He was absolutely right. I didn't deserve it. But this was my life, and he didn't need to take responsibility for his father's mistreatment of me. "It's okay, Ryder." I laid my head back upon the headrest and tried not to let the dark barrenness of the country road lull me into sleep.

When we returned home, Darren came in and sat at the table with crossed arms. He was still brooding, so I put a couple of pieces of pizza on a plate and pushed the plate towards him. "Come on, Darren. I got this pizza for the two of you," I urged.

Darren shoved the plate back at me and stood up so abruptly that his chair knocked backward before returning to its upright position. Then I heard the sofa's leather crunch behind me.

Ryder and I looked at each other. Fortunately, we'd both learned to ignore Darren and live our lives despite him.

I made casual conversation to cover up the tension. "What are you up to for the rest of your Christmas break?"

Speaking with his mouth full, Ryder responded, "I don't know." Then we chatted about his friends' holiday happenings until he was finished eating.

"Wanna watch a movie together?" we heard Darren ask as we cleared off the table.

Was he serious? He'd berated me for being sick, banished my gift, refused to eat, and now, all of a sudden, we were going to play "happy family"? But what was I supposed to do, say no?

Ryder and I looked at each other. "Sure," I said, pacifying Darren for both of us. Then we pushed our chairs in and went to the living room.

Darren remained lying across the entire living room sofa and made no motion to move for one of us to sit with him. So Ryder sat on the loveseat—the only other seating option. I didn't want to sit so close to Ryder and risk him catching what I had, so I lay on the bare wooden floor in front of the TV stand and covered myself with a throw blanket from a nearby basket.

"Mom, you're not lying down there. Take the loveseat," Ryder insisted. "I'll go back in my room."

"No! I want you to stay with us for the movie," I said. Then I paused to give Darren an opportunity to move his feet or sit up, so one of us could sit on the larger sofa with him, but he didn't. So I reconciled myself to the floor after all. "I'm fine, really!"

Ryder struggled with his conscience for a moment but reluctantly remained. Despite being on the floor and being too tired to even make it through the opening credits of the movie, it made my heart happy to have my son near.

I awoke later in the pitch dark. The TV was off, and so were all the lights. Yet, I lay exactly as I'd fallen asleep. Nobody had bothered to put a pillow under my head or wake me to move me onto the loveseat. I had just been left lying there, on the floor, sick, on my birthday. I wasn't upset with Ryder, though. I was his mother, not his responsibility. I blamed Darren—for once again failing to treat me with basic human decency.

After I'd gone outside to vomit, I knelt in the snow-frosted grass and cried. I couldn't do this anymore. I was officially done.

"Spiderwebs"

After a week of what turned out to be some kind of flu or virus going through our area, I recovered just after the New Year of 2020 and just in time for Ryder's in-person interview with a representative from WyoTech—the technical school he hoped to attend after graduation next year. Most technical schools admitted everyone entrance, but WyoTech was selective. The school adhered to faith-based morals and values and, as such, required a family interview as part of the admission process. So, despite the deterioration of our marriage, Darren and I put on our show for Ryder, and he was accepted. The representative left our home with a deposit check to hold Ryder's spot in the Diesel Technology program, beginning mid-2021. Knowing Ryder's future was secured, I felt a certain peace. Everything else would fall into place as planned, specifically where Darren was concerned.

Since deciding our marriage was over, I avoided Darren altogether. I slept in the basement, left before he awoke, worked as late as I could, made dinner, then went back down to the basement to the too-early bedtime I'd adopted.

I didn't worry about Ryder. He'd never been fazed by me going back and forth between sleeping in the basement and the master bedroom over the years. He was rarely home anyway. Ever since he'd gotten his driver's license last year, he kept busy working two part-time jobs, and spent his free time and most nights at friends' houses, probably to escape the tension between me and Darren at home.

I did worry about Darren's reaction to my detachment, however. He lay on the couch day in and day out, watching me come and go but making no effort to interact. He was strangely unemotional and unreactive, which made me nervous he was brewing some malicious surprise attack on me, like the calm before a storm. I hoped he'd just finally given up on making me miserable instead. The only indicators of his mindset were emails and text messages sent while I slept at night, most of which I ignored.

On a February morning in 2020, the following email awaited me: *I love you and want to be with you, but I can't stop you from leaving. If I have to give you everything I own, I will. I am nothing without you and am about two seconds from ending my life. I don't want to be here without you.*

I shook my head as I closed my computer. He knew he'd lost his grip on me, and this latest heartfelt plea, laced with the threat of suicide, was just another desperate ploy to keep me. It wouldn't work, though. I had to get to work anyway.

Unbeknownst to Darren, I had a phone appointment with a divorce attorney later that afternoon, which I took in my car in the parking lot of the nearby medical center on my way home. This was my sixth time speaking to one, and hopefully my last.

"So what do you want to get out of this?" the female attorney asked after collecting basic information.

"Nothing. I just want my kid."

"Nothing?" She sounded surprised, though at her young age, she assumed wives wanted the house, alimony, custody of children, and whatever else they felt entitled to for their trouble.

"Nothing," I affirmed. "He can have everything—the house, the vehicles, the toys, the cows, all the money . . . I just want my kid."

"I get it, but you're entitled to certain things under Illinois law," she insisted.

"I understand that, but fighting over money or petty things isn't worth the stress or my health. Money can be earned. Things can be replaced. I just want out."

"That's how I felt about my ex-husband, but you can't let him get away without giving you what's rightfully yours, Dana!" I must have struck a nerve because the tone and volume of her voice elevated quickly. "You're at least entitled to half of the 401K he cashed out, half the home equity he spent, and also half of the equity still left in the home!"

"Believe me, it's not that I couldn't use the money, but he'll fight me on everything, and I don't want to make this any harder than it has to be. If he thinks he's screwing me, it'll be a lot easier and a lot faster for everyone involved."

"Dana, think about what you're saying! We're talking upwards of eighty thousand dollars here!" I liked her passion. I needed a fighter on my side. But I'd made up my mind.

"I've thought about it for fifteen years. There is no amount of money worth my freedom. I just want this to be over already." A lone tear dripped from my right eye down to the corner of my quivering lip.

"I hate when men fuck us over and get away with it!" she burst out. I was surprised she'd used a cuss word in a professional context, but I was more trusting of people who spoke their mind. "I get where you're coming from, though," she continued, "so I'm gonna give you some homework. First off, the cows have to go. You need to sell them or butcher them—just get rid of them. The house needs to be dealt with next. From what you told me about finances, you would be capable of taking on the mortgage yourself, but I highly recommend you just get rid of the house too. Do you have a place to go?"

"Yes. I started looking at places last month, and I've had a few offers to stay with people," I said. "But I don't want my son's life changed in any way, so I'd rather just keep the house until he's done with school. It'll only be another year or so."

"Okay, but then we need to get Darren's name off the house. If you think you can get his cooperation to sign off on the title and deed, then refinance so the house is only in your name. Then we can proceed. But promise me you'll leave if it becomes unsafe for you to stay."

"I've stayed this long. Surely I can stay a little longer."

"Okay, but don't be too brave. Guys like that go off the rails when they find out you're leaving," she warned. "When you get the house figured out, let me know and we'll move forward."

"I'll get on it right away!"

A long exhale released all the hesitations and fears I'd held onto all these years—doubt about whether I should divorce, what I needed to do to prepare, and how it would all play out. The only wild card was Darren.

I went home on a mission, but the desolate house distracted me from my tasks. Ryder was probably at work or at a friend's house. Darren, however, never went anywhere.

I went to see if he was in the bedroom. The open door told me he wasn't. I went to the window in my office then, to see if I'd missed lights on in the garage or second house when I came in, but I didn't even see Darren's truck out there. I turned away from the window and noticed a handwritten letter, on blue-lined yellow legal paper, waiting for me on my desk. Was this a Dear John letter? Had he found out about my phone consultation with the attorney and pridefully left me before I could leave him?

Dear Dana,

I know you don't want to be with me anymore, and I understand. I've been an asshole husband to you. I don't want to be, but I don't know how else to be either. I went to talk to my mom today, and I want you to know I am committed to you and to our marriage. I want this to work. I'll do anything you want me to—I'll stop drinking, I'll go get a normal job with benefits so you don't have to work so hard, I'll sell the cows and the whole farm if I have to. I just want to be with you because none of this matters without you. I thought I was making a good life for us, but if you're not happy, I'm willing to make the changes. I don't know if I want to travel everywhere you want to, and it won't be easy to live on a small property without my animals, but I will follow you wherever you need to go to be happy. It's you and me against the world, right? I promise I'll try to be better.

Love, Darren

To anyone else, this would be a heartwarming admission of love taken for granted, sprinkled with promises and hope for a happier future. But I'd heard it all before, and nothing ever changed. Not to mention there was still an eerie sense that he knew the details of my conversation with the attorney today. Had he put some kind of recorder in my vehicle? I'd suspected him of it in the past. It didn't really matter, though. Whatever he knew or didn't know would be known in due time anyway, giving me all the more reason to get to work on getting him to give me the house, or getting him out of it.

"I'm Stuck"

As if the universe were playing a cruel joke on me, the state of Illinois mandated a shelter-in-place in March 2020 to prevent spread of the deadly COVID-19 virus. Only essential workers, like medical professionals and agricultural employees, could continue working, which meant I'd be confined to the house with Darren. The courts were closing too, which meant no divorce either. Indefinitely.

The shelter-in-place did allow the general population to go to gas stations and big box stores like Walmart, which was all we had in the sticks anyway. We just had to wear masks, or some similar face covering, and maintain a respectable six-foot distance from others. I didn't need gas to drive nowhere, and I had no money to spend if I wasn't working, so I was stuck at the hell I called home, with the devil I'd been trying to distance myself from.

Since I'd already taken up residence in the basement, I decided to set it up like a make-shift apartment. I got lots of steps in carrying down my laptop, clothing, toiletries, phone and computer chargers, and whatever else I thought I needed on a daily basis. The couches and TV were already in place, and the extra refrigerator/freezer in the laundry room could keep food and drinks cold. I could use the laundry room sink to brush my teeth and sponge bathe. I'd only have to go up to the main floor to use the stove, microwave, or toilet.

I could have gone without the latter if Darren hadn't shut the water off to the basement toilet for the sole purpose of preventing my use of it.

What he didn't know was that I'd discovered I was light and flexible enough to boost myself onto the laundry room sink, so I peed in there instead. It was gross, but I wouldn't let Darren railroad me into going upstairs if I didn't have to. I only wanted to share space if it was while I was walking out the door.

While settling in the basement, my phone rang. It was Dr. Soteira. "Hey, Doc!" I sat on the sofa I used as a bed.

"Hello! I just wanted to call and make sure you aren't working. I worry about you getting this COVID virus!"

I appreciated his concern. Not too many doctors cared enough to call to check on their patients outside of scheduled appointments. "Not at the moment," I stalled, "but I'm hoping to get *some* of my clients to let me clean. If I don't work, I don't get paid, and if I don't have income, I can't pay my bills!"

"I know, honey, but a common cold can kill you!"

"I don't have a choice," I said. "I promise I'll be careful, though. I bought disposable gloves and hand sanitizer, but the masks are hard for me. I can't breathe with them on!"

"I imagine so! But it's very important you cover your mouth and nose if you leave the house. Were you able to pick up the CPAP machine I arranged for you?"

"Yes!" I'd gotten it just a week before. "The lady I spoke with there said it was the best machine available, and that you called in a favor to let me have it at no charge for three months?"

"We got nowhere with your insurance, and I couldn't let you go without something to help you breathe, especially if you got sick. They're saying COVID *causes* difficulty breathing, and we can't take the chance of your oxygen levels dropping too low," he said. "Now, remember, the CPAP may or may not help the UARS. But try sleeping with it, if you can, and let me know how it goes."

"I did try to sleep with it, but it was awful."

"What was the problem? Did you have trouble operating the machine?"

"No. They set me up with an automatic machine that adjusts to my breaths, and the lady took her time showing me how to use it. But the full-face mask she fitted me with is almost too tight. I can't breathe out of my nose once I strap the thing on. And then I get panicky because I can't breathe . . . It's the same feeling I've had when I've tried to put on a snorkel mask in the past, which is why I don't snorkel!"

"It sounds like a different mask might suit you better, but medical facilities are all shut down now."

"Yeah. But like you said, at least I have something just in case I do get sick. Also, a friend of mine got her aunt to sell me a practically new Inogen One—you know, one of those portable oxygen units? My friend's uncle recently passed, so they had no use for it anymore, and they let me have it for a fraction of the cost!"

"That's wonderful!" he said. I thought so too. Darren didn't, though. When I came home from picking it up, excited to share the blessing, he'd said he'd "bought plenty of dumb shit too".

"I know! It fits perfectly in this little backpack I bought to carry it in, so I can clean houses with it, or do things around my house . . ."

"I wish you didn't clean for work right now, honey. But I understand why you have to. Just be very, very careful. And if you do get sick, stay home. Don't go to the hospital, and stay away from doctor's offices and medical facilities. Because if you don't have COVID, you'll likely pick it up or get sick with something else," he warned.

"I will. And thank you again for all you've done for me," I said, then ended the call, thankful my healthcare was in such good hands.

I spent the rest of the day drumming up whatever work I could from the handful of customers brave enough to let me in their homes despite the virus and sheltering order. I figured if I was allowed to drive to Walmart, authorities wouldn't know to stop me if I went to a customer's house to clean instead.

You're welcome in my house! I'm more worried about getting you sick, my customer, Doug, replied when I asked if I could still clean Wednesday as planned. I'd met him at the BP gas station in town in late 2016, when he peeked at me from behind a pump and introduced himself. I already knew who he was, though; his sister-in-law was a realtor I'd befriended over a decade earlier and whose youngest son was good friends with Ryder. It was through his sister-in-law that Doug had learned of my health issues, and from whom I'd heard private details about Doug's life as well.

I'll be all right. Gotta work no matter what! I responded. *You know how it goes, being self-employed.*

Yeah, but these masks suck. You wearing one? Doug asked.

Would rather not. I can't breathe as it is!

Well, you don't need to wear one here!

Doug had built a sprawling ranch on twenty-five acres of land off the beaten path, so I presumed the odds of catching COVID there were slimmer than anywhere else I'd go. Neither he nor the one of his two adult sons who lived there were ever home anyway.

Appreciate it! I'll be okay, though. Hunkering down in my basement!

I lived in my basement for a while too. He was referring to the time leading up to his divorce.

Not ideal, but it suits me just fine considering the situation.

Do I need to come get you?

My racing heart screamed, *yes!* But my worried mind reminded me I had a jealous husband whom I'd suspected of reading my text messages in the recent past.

Awww . . . that's very sweet of you, but I'll have to decline for now. I hoped he interpreted the last two words as I intended.

I know you're still married. Just worried about you.

I appreciate that. Stay healthy, and I'll be over Wednesday. If I'm wearing a bandana over my face, don't shoot! :)

Doug didn't "lol" my reference to the Wild West, instead asking, *What's :) ?*

A smiley face! It's sideways so you have to turn your phone to see it, I guess. I don't have a smart phone with emojis :(That's a sad face . . . lol.

He sent back, :)

I smiled as I deleted the conversation from my phone, like I always did after we texted.

We'd been communicating more since his dogs had passed away a year or so before. I'd noticed his sensitivity then and thought it attractive for a man to allow himself to be seen in such a vulnerable state without worry of feeling emasculated. It was that same sensitivity which caused him to abruptly avoid me afterward. We'd been drawn to each other's empathy, drawn to each other, but he didn't want to seem like a creep who was luring me into his home under the guise of needing a housekeeper. But then one afternoon in 2019, when he showed up at his brother and sister-in-law's house and saw my car there, he came upstairs to where I was in the midst of cleaning a tub and, without a word, hugged me tightly. It was an awkward moment which I'd neither expected nor understood until Doug later admitted that he'd been asking his brother and sister-in-law about me, since he'd seen the dramatic change in my weight, and what they'd told him about my marriage and declining health concerned him. He kept tabs on me after that, continually asking his brother about anything he'd heard me share, until eventually Doug gathered the courage to ask *me* about my well-being instead. I appreciated his care and concern and wished I could reciprocate the feelings, but we remained friends out of respect for my marriage, regardless of how shitty it was.

Speaking of that shitty marriage, I needed to speak with my shitty husband. The work I'd been able to scrape together was nowhere near able to cover even a month of household expenses. I'd been secretly stashing money again, but the little I'd saved since paying that atrocious tax bill was meant to free me from this prison, not fund Darren's lazy ass through this pandemic.

I went upstairs and sat on the coffee table in the living room, being careful not to knock over Darren's can of "Sprite". I knew he'd been hiding alcohol in those green cans for a while now, and I didn't appreciate being lied to about it.

He stared at the TV, as if I wasn't a foot away. That pissed me off even more. "I'm not having much luck getting people to let me clean right now, so I need you to help me out. Menard's is hiring temporary employees, and you obviously have the time and physical ability, so I think you should apply," I said.

"I'm not pushing fucking carts for ten dollars an hour!" Darren growled. I was slightly amused at how asking him to work got his attention.

"Well, I'm not going to lose this house or live without lights because you want to watch TV all fucking day! Anyway, they're paying twenty-five dollars an hour for part-time positions." I stood and crossed my arms. I wasn't backing down on this.

"I'm not going to work for anyone doing menial shit like stocking shelves!"

"Not even for just a month or so, or however long this COVID thing lasts?" He ignored me with a tight-lipped frown and crossed arms, reminding me of a pouting toddler. I threw my arms up in frustration. "I don't think you understand that I work my ass off to make just enough money to pay our bills, and now that I won't be working much at all, we could seriously lose this place."

"Then you better get to it, Mama! I'm not gonna blow my entire season of mowing by working another job. I'm set to make eighty thousand this year!"

"Doing what? There's no way you'll make that much money mowing lawns!" I didn't care if he promised to make a million dollars. He was full of shit and needed to get off his ass and help me!

"I ran the numbers," he touted.

"Okay, numbers man, then explain to me why you claimed a fourteen-thousand-dollar loss for last year?"

"I had a lot of expenses you don't know about."

I rolled my eyes and huffed at his evasive response. "So when you start mowing and making eighty thousand a year, are you going to help pay the bills? Because I have yet to see any of this mowing money you claim to earn."

He said nothing, which told me everything. Darren wanted the esteem and respect of a high salary, only he didn't make one, nor would he share it if he did. His money was his money, to spend on things that gave the impression of someone who had money, so he could feel important. Well, he could feel important by himself. I sighed in disgust and walked back down to my basement.

If he didn't care about our finances, then I honestly didn't care either. Losing the house would be a great favor, actually. I wouldn't have to worry about him signing off on it, refinancing it, or selling it for the divorce. I had plenty of places for me and Ryder to stay anyway. It was Darren who'd be screwed, but he'd have screwed himself.

Since I couldn't influence Darren to help pay bills, and I couldn't change the fact that I was self-employed and mostly out of work because of a pandemic I had no control over, I released myself of the worry and pressure of it all. I worked enough to pay the mortgage, utilities and vehicle expenses, but not so much that I was as overworked and over-stressed as I had been over the last handful of years. As a result, I breathed easier and had more energy. I didn't get the tension headaches and migraines I'd learned to live with. My stomach didn't ache anymore. I felt better overall—almost normal!

By the end of April, the warmer weather and loosened shelter-in-place restrictions allowed some normalcy to return to our lives. I was back to cleaning for a majority of my customers, Ryder was partially back to school, and Darren got off the couch to go make that $80,000 I knew he wouldn't.

Darren was gone most of every day, including weekends. I saw very little of him, but it was hard to miss the shiny new rims on his truck. I even had a couple cleaning customers comment on how they'd seen Darren's new wheels as he drove through town, which invalidated the concerns I'd voiced about finances. If he was able to afford rims, then he was able to start paying some bills.

I spent an evening listing the household bills on a piece of notebook paper. I figured Darren should pay for half the mortgage and utilities, at the very least. Plus, it would demonstrate his ability to afford rent or a small mortgage after the divorce, in case he requested alimony.

I specified in the itemized list of bills that I would take full financial responsibility for Ryder's private school tuition, medical insurance, and all other living costs, as well as my car payment, vehicle insurance for mine and Ryder's vehicles, and all my business expenses. Not only did this come off as generous, it put me in a position of demonstrating to a judge that I was—and could continue to be—the sole custodian of Ryder in every way. Darren couldn't, and wouldn't, do the same.

Then, after Darren had gone to bed that night, I left the note on the kitchen counter for him to see when he awoke the next day.

I opened my laptop in the morning and saw an email from him. I took a deep breath and stretched my neck each way, anticipating emotional and physical tension. Then I read: *Please come back to me. I want you to be happy, but the negativity is too much. I'm hurting like hell inside. Have chest pains every night. I know you're a runner, but I'm tired of you leaving when times get tough. I'm gone working? Issues. I'm not making money? Issues. I drink? Issues. I don't drink? Issues. I say the wrong things. I don't say anything. This roller coaster needs to stop! I want you! I married you! I love you! You are my best friend. Listen to me now! Don't push me away! PS—I saw your proposal and it's more than fair. I am willing to talk about it.*

I rolled my eyes. This didn't even make sense. Come back where? Unfortunately, I hadn't left yet! And mimicking my emotions and physical symptoms as his own? Was he kidding? Presenting more heartfelt pleas in writing so it looked like *he* was the one begging for change? I'd wasted over twenty years of my life waiting for him to demonstrate his love and enact the promises he made, but *now*, when it was convenient for him to love me for the financial benefit, I was suddenly worthy of it all? No thanks. We were in this mess because I'd let him lure me with sweet words and a diamond ring, but it was my salary he loved—not me—and I wouldn't let him use me for money again.

This electronic relationship was pissing me off too. It was a cop-out. He wanted to come at me with bullshit but deny me the opportunity to call him out on it so he didn't have to come up with supporting evidence or another lie to refute my rebuttals. Or if I did dare to respond in writing, he'd use that as evidence against me, of what a mean person or terrible wife I was. Either way, if he really wanted to talk, all he had to do was knock on the basement door or catch me in the kitchen.

So I closed my laptop, went up to the kitchen, and asked my Amazon Echo to play music. I sang along to the Colbie Callait song it chose for me, as I prepared my caffeine fix for the day. Shortly after, Darren came downstairs looking grumpy as ever. I wanted to feel bad that the music might have woken him, but I didn't.

As he approached the kitchen, I saw his fists clench, and I could hear the huffs out of his nose. I backed away, but the counter at the kitchen sink stopped me. I leaned back and turned my head at the oncoming assault.

Darren pointed a finger barely an inch from my face and spit-screamed, "It's not me! It's you! You're the fucking problem!" Then he disappeared into the bathroom.

I immediately took my coffee and hid behind the basement door, where I secured the two-by-four piece of wood under the knob. Then I sat on the stairs in the dark, listening to him pound his feet down the hallway, and slam the door on his way out. His screeching tires signaled an "all clear" for me to emerge, but I remained a moment in silent fear. Then I released a breath I hadn't known I'd been holding. Funny how he could suffocate me without using his hands.

"All We Ever Do Is Say Goodbye"

*D*arren pestered me for weeks after, to finally talk about our marriage. I saw no point. There was nothing to say that hadn't been said a million times before, but I finally agreed because I was tired of beating a dead horse. We needed to just end this already.

It was a sunny early Wednesday afternoon in mid-May. I cut my work-day short so we could meet while Ryder was still in school. I never knew where Ryder was anymore, and I didn't want to risk him interrupting or overhearing whatever would be said or decided that day.

Darren was already lying on the couch in the living room when I walked in. He stared straight up at the ceiling instead of acknowledging my arrival, so I leaned back against the kitchen island with my arms crossed, waiting for him to initiate this conversation he'd insisted on having.

After a long minute, I'd already grown impatient. "So?"

Silence.

As usual, the burden of everything fell upon me. "We've never gotten along, Darren. Ever. You don't smile when you see me. You don't ever want to go anywhere or do anything with me. You intentionally pitted your family against me with lies. You bought rims for your truck when we didn't have money for bills. And let's be real—trust went to shit early on in our relationship. And you're still lying to me! I mean, I just found out you have two Facebook pages, after we'd agreed not to be on Facebook at all! So I'm done! I don't want to do this anymore!"

"I need a Facebook page for my lawn business!"

"I've managed to run a very successful cleaning business without one,

365

so I'm calling bullshit on your excuse. And that's the thing, Darren—there's always an excuse. After Merrick's wife threatened our son's life, we agreed to stay off social media. But here you are with not one, but two Facebook pages now! You lied!"

"Do you not want me to make money?" Darren yelled.

"Why does everything come down to money with you? I don't give a flying fuck about the money! I just want my husband to be honest with me for once! You could have come to me and said, 'Hey, I'm thinking I should have a Facebook page for my lawn business. Whaddya think?' And we could've discussed it. But you went and did it behind my back, probably thinking I'd never find out. So I'm sorry, but I feel betrayed. And it's not the first time, so I'm done!"

Darren remained silent and still. I took a deep breath and consciously calmed my approach. "Look, I don't wanna put Ryder through the torment of a nasty divorce. So let's remain amicable for the sake of getting Ryder through his last year of high school with his home life intact. He deserves that at the very least. Are you on board?"

"I don't wanna be friends," Darren said.

There was a long silence between us. I didn't know what to say, and he wouldn't relent.

Then he finally spoke. "You know, children of divorce tend to get involved with drugs and alcohol. I've been researching it."

I recognized the threat, but I wouldn't let the fear of it bully me into doing something I didn't want to do. "That's common knowledge, but it's our job as parents to handle this properly so he doesn't fall into a stereotypical situation."

"So you're okay with screwing him up? Good parenting, Dana!"

"You know damn well I'm not okay with 'screwing him up'! But shit— he's seen and heard enough to damage him already and he's somehow okay." *Thanks to me*, I thought.

"Well, watch what happens if you go through with divorcing me! I guarantee you he'll go down the wrong road!"

"I'm going to choose to be a good mother and parent our son so he doesn't make poor choices in response to life stresses. I can't make you do the same, but if you really love Ryder, you'll try. You might want to start with not being a drunk."

After another silent moment, Darren sniffled. Years of playing Darren's games had hardened me, though; I'd grown immune to the guilt, and I was tired of acquiescing to his fake emotions. As far as I was concerned, the fate of our marriage had been decided, and I had things to do. So without another word from either of us, I went to the basement.

While I was at work the next morning, Darren texted. *Just to confirm, we're "pretending" for our son for another year? I can't fucking do it!*

I knew what he was doing. He was baiting me into a written response as proof to others that I was the one ending our relationship, so he would be perceived as the victim of a loveless wife. But I was the true victim, and I wouldn't give him the satisfaction.

There was no further communication between us until I came up from the basement for my nightly pumpkin pudding dessert that night.

"So is this how it's going to be?" Darren asked nastily. I heard Ryder's bedroom door shut.

"For the love of God, Darren!"—I threw my arms up—"I'm exhausted by this!"

He lay on the couch with his arms crossed over his chest. His bottom lip quivered until tears dripped down his cheek. I stared at him, waiting to feel any compassion or sadness, but I felt absolutely nothing. I was stone cold. I didn't want to be, but I wouldn't be lured back in with false feelings. "I'm tired of trying to make something work that just doesn't, Darren. Please, just stop this already."

"This is why I can't talk to you!" he shouted with an exaggerated frown, reminiscent of a child claiming something was unfair. "You don't like when I text and email you, but when I try to talk to you, you attack me with your words!" Then he pounded up the stairs to isolate in the master bedroom.

The truth was an attack? Whatever. I couldn't expect a liar to handle the truth.

Glad to be rid of him for the night, I settled on the loveseat with my dessert. It was nice to sit in the living room and watch *his* TV for a change. Ryder even came out and watched a funny show with me, when he'd heard me laughing. It felt good to laugh again. And to hear my son laugh. That didn't happen often enough.

After Ryder and I went to bed, Darren stomped up and down the stairs, louder than usual. Then, every couple of hours through the night, he stomped around some more.

I lay on the basement sofa with the blankets pulled over my head, but the stomping sound made me hyper-vigilant. Like a rabbit who'd been spotted in the open, I remained still all night, eyes wide open, because I never knew whether he was just having a tantrum, or if his actions would escalate into a more severe punishment. I had to be ready for anything.

Finally, in the wee hours of morning, quiet fell upon the house, and I slept for a couple hours. When I awoke and checked my phone for the time, there was a text from Darren. *I no longer want to have sex with you. I don't enjoy it.*

Good! I'd no longer have to starfish with my eyes closed, imagining another man on top of me—Doug, specifically. I always worried I'd say his name by accident anyway.

"Can't Be Loved"

If you've checked out of our relationship already, please just tell me. I want you to be happy but I need to be as well. Would it be easier on you if I moved into the shop? I can't live in this bedroom for another year wondering if you'll ever come back to me. But if you're done, be warned I will have to cut you out completely. Just be upfront and tell me. Love you.

Was he serious? This was how I was waking up on Mother's Day? With another threat? *I thought we did this already, Darren. I'm not happy. You're not happy. It is what it is.* How many fucking times did I have to say it?!

Shortly after I sent my response from the basement, I heard loud sobbing from the master bedroom. Part of me saddened, because I never wanted to be the reason someone cried, but the tears were about twenty years too late. I got up off the couch, peed in the laundry room sink, then turned on the TV to tune Darren out while I walked.

When I finally went up to the kitchen to make my coffee, Darren came downstairs and placed an armful of what appeared to be Amazon packages on the coffee table. "Happy Mother's Day," he said dimly, offering one arm for a half hug.

I didn't expect the day to be happy, but I didn't want to ruin it right from the start either. So I leaned into the half hug and quickly pulled out. Then I walked into the living room. "What's all this? Stuff you need me to wrap for your mom?"

Darren sat on the couch. "No, my mom won't allow visitors because of COVID. These are for you."

"Oh!" I stood with an open mouth, unsure of how to take the kind gesture. I thought it was weird for him to give me gifts, considering we were sort of separated. Or was this bribery to return to my role as his dutiful wife? He'd called me a gold digger enough times for me to know he thought women just wanted money and things.

"You wanna open them before I leave to mow?" he ordered in the framework of a question.

"Sure." I sat on the edge of the coffee table and selected one of the packages from the bunch. It took some effort to tear into the thick, brown paper. When I finally did, I recognized items from my Amazon wish list.

"Thank you," I said politely, though I wondered how someone who hadn't paid a bill in four years could afford two expensive lipsticks. Another gift, sent in a white bubble wrap pouch, was a pair of gold-rimmed heart-shaped pink sunglasses. I'd always loved hearts and anything pink. I opened a small box next. "I don't remember putting this little frying pan on my list. It's nice, though!" I commented as I carried it to the kitchen to put it away. It was part of the set of organic cookware I used.

"I thought you could use it instead of the small pot you use to scramble your eggs every morning."

"I only use the pot because it's already out to boil water for my coffee," I explained. I was always explaining myself to him, I noted. I needed to stop that.

"Well, I'd rather you use the pan. It bothers me when you make your eggs in the pot."

I froze in the midst of reorganizing the pots and pans in their cabinet and looked back at Darren like I'd heard him wrong, but I knew I hadn't. "I'm sorry the way I make my eggs bothers you so much. They're fucking eggs, dude."

Darren snatched his jeans and shirt off the couch then and stormed to the bathroom. I calmly gathered the Amazon packaging to put in the fire pit, lacking any remorse for provoking his anger.

Darren rushed past me a minute later. When I didn't react, he turned to me and yelled, "You're never grateful for anything I do! I spend all my money on gifts for you, and you can't show me one fucking ounce of appreciation! I swear, I'm ... you're ..." He clenched his teeth, then finally blurted, "You're such a fucking cunt! I don't know why I'm still here!"

"I don't either, Darren," I said in a low monotone.

"THEN LEAVE ALREADY! IF YOU DON'T, I WILL!" he screamed and slammed the door behind him—the same door he'd accused me and Ryder of slamming to the point of requiring replacement. The door wasn't damaged from him trying to pry it open with a crowbar years before, when we'd locked his drunk ass out. He'd tried to strike me with that crowbar that night. I'd ducked just in time. But nothing was ever his fault. It was always mine or Ryder's.

Thinking about all the shit I'd taken from him over the years caused an overload of anger to erupt out of me. I swung the door open and screamed, "Maybe I will! I don't want to be married to you anyway!" Then I slammed the door as hard as he had. Tit for tat, motherfucker.

He whipped around and charged towards the door. I moved away from it, expecting him to barge in and harm me, but he stopped just outside the glass barrier. He pounded his finger against it, hollering, "I'll just go somewhere and SHOOT MYSELF! You and Ryder would be happier without me anyway!"

We would, actually. At least, I would. But Darren wouldn't follow through. He never did.

I watched him tear out of the driveway recklessly, hoping he hadn't run over one of our barn cats. The trailer on the back of his truck teetered as he took the turn onto the road too fast. I prayed he didn't return with the same haste.

Later that afternoon, I heard shouting outside. Familiar shouting. I moved away from my file cabinet to look out the window of my office. I saw Darren yelling in Ryder's face so fiercely, I swore I could see the spit spewing from his mouth. Ryder then positioned his body offensively and shoved Darren with his chest. I was proud to see Ryder holding his own! But when Darren pushed Ryder back with both hands, I decided to intervene. No one touched my son like that and got away with it.

I flew down the stairs and out the door, screaming, "*Get your hands off my son, you piece of shit!*" Then I threw my body between them.

"Mom," Ryder said very sternly, "just go." He put his arm out in front of me to block my interference. I stepped back unwillingly, in pain from the sharp gravel under my bare feet, then stepped in front of Darren when I regained my balance.

Darren reached around me and pointed his finger an inch from Ryder's face, "You owe me a fucking apology! You better apologize *right fucking now!*"

"LEAVE MY SON ALONE!" I screamed in Darren's face so loudly my throat felt scratchy. I threw both my arms out to protect Ryder, but when I looked behind me to assure him I wouldn't let anything happen to him, he was walking back to the house. I whipped my head back towards Darren.

"You don't even know what's goin' on!" he said. "But you always take his side, you fucking cunt!"

"I don't need to know what happened! You're a grown-ass man yelling at my kid! So, yes, I'm gonna defend him!"

Darren stormed towards his truck, throwing back the most hateful glare in place of the punch he'd probably have liked to throw in my face instead. I'd have punched back. I was infuriated.

"One day," I hollered, putting my index finger up as I briskly walked back toward the house. "I just wanted one fucking day of peace."

Ryder's bedroom door was shut when I went in, so I let *him* have the peace I'd been disallowed. There was nothing to say anyway. I didn't need to know what they'd argued about, nor what Darren felt he was owed an apology for. Ryder didn't deserve to be treated like that, especially by his father, and I didn't deserve any of this either.

I was in the kitchen washing dishes when Darren came in a short time later. Without a word, he went straight to bed. I was glad to be rid of him for the rest of the day.

I went to Ryder's room then, to see if I could salvage the day with him. He was sitting at his desk watching YouTube videos when I opened the door. "Hey, kiddo! You wanna watch a scary movie with me? I'm thinking pajamas, dessert . . ."

"No." Ryder sounded regretful. "I'm sorry, Mom. Maybe another time. Just not right now."

He was obviously affected by what had happened earlier, but I didn't want to reopen the wound. I also wouldn't let him feel bad for declining my invitation; it wasn't his fault his dad had ruined the day. "No worries, kiddo. I love you no matter what. You know that, though. But if you change your mind, you know where to find me!"

The upbeat facade I'd put on for Ryder faded into sadness the second I closed his bedroom door behind me, but I proceeded with my plan, hoping a horror film would scare the sadness out of me.

As I tucked myself into the basement couch later that evening, my phone buzzed. It was Doug.

Hope you had a happy Mother's Day!

I responded with a simple sideways smile, which was more than my face could have mustered up after the day I'd actually had.

The next morning, Darren came into the kitchen where I was making eggs in my new frying pan. He put his hand on my left shoulder and kissed me on the forehead.

I stepped sideways to avoid any more unwanted affection. "See? I'm using the frying pan you got me!"

"You need to stop eating eggs for breakfast. I'm selling our eggs to my lawn care customers from now on," he said. Then he left to mow.

I stood there dumbfounded, wishing I could beat him with this pan instead.

Suddenly, the Dr. Seuss book *Green Eggs and Ham* inspired my own rhyme: I have no eggs, I have no ham, but fucked in the head, that's what I am.

I chuckled to myself. At least I still had my sense of humor.

"Leave the Pieces"

O n May 29, 2020, Ryder left for a week-long four-wheeling trip with a friend's family.

"Have fun! Love you!" I called out as I waved goodbye from the porch with exaggerated enthusiasm.

I felt like I had to make up for Darren's intentional neglect that night. He'd refused to participate in Ryder's birthday dinner, because he felt slighted that Ryder wouldn't be home for *his* birthday six days later. It wasn't a milestone, nor did we have plans, but Darren wanted to make sure Ryder felt guilty nonetheless. So he went to bed early. He wouldn't even come down to bid our son farewell.

Ryder did feel bad too. He almost didn't even go on the trip. With some encouragement, and a promise to take one for the team in his absence, I eventually convinced him to go. But as soon as the vehicle he'd been picked up in drove out of sight, I went to the basement and put the long two-by-four under the knob. Then I lay in the quiet, nervously anticipating whatever was brewing two floors above. Fortunately, nothing happened, though my lost night's sleep may have been the intention all along.

The next morning, I was getting ready to leave for work when Darren came down the stairs. His decision to ignore Ryder's birthday was childish and unforgivable, so I ignored *him* instead of voicing my opinion about it all.

Darren approached me anyway and leaned in to kiss me. I jumped back, wondering what the hell would make him think I would let him!

"You can't even give me a 'Good morning' kiss now?"

I threw my arms up to the side. "Since when are we kissing again?"

"It doesn't matter," he said. "I'm leaving . . . even though I love you and want to try to make things work." He looked and sounded like Winnie the Pooh's friend Eeyore—sad and dejected, walking away with slumped shoulders and a head as down-turned as his spirit. Then he left for work.

A short time later, I was on my way to my first job of the day, when my phone vibrated. I ignored it, assuming it was Darren chastising me for not reacting to his hurt feelings. So when it buzzed again, I huffed in aggravation and grabbed up my phone. My tensed shoulders relaxed when I saw Doug's name on the caller ID instead.

Heading out of town for a week. How're things going with you?

Going. Wish I was "going" wherever you are, though! A week away sounds great right now!

Things not going so good?

Eh. I can't stay in that house with him much longer. I've been scoping out my options and have some places to go. Just not sure if Ryder will come with me. Plus, I don't want to impose on anyone. Not my style.

You're welcome to stay at my place. You can have the master and I'll move into the guest room. I'll try to keep my hands to myself . . .

I suddenly felt like a school-girl whose crush said he was sweet on her too! I couldn't flirt back, though. The last thing I needed right now was another man!

I actually talked to your dad about staying in his extra room, I responded, intentionally ignoring Doug's advance. I'd been cleaning for Doug's dad for several years, and often talked to him about my problems at home. *He said rent is cheap! Lol. And at least I know the old man has a gun! He'd defend me if Darren ever came looking for me there!*

Yeah, and he wouldn't hesitate to use it either! No, you come to my place. I'll protect you.

I knew he would too. He was a peaceful man but loyal to a fault. He'd never let anything happen to someone he cared about, and I ranked within that realm.

I couldn't string him along, though. As much as I wanted to see where things would lead, I wasn't available. Not legally, at least. So I changed the subject to avoid the flirtation. *Where are you going again?*

North. My oldest son and his wife invited me on their vacation. I'll get to spend the week at a cabin, fishing with my grandson. Looking forward to it.

Until he arrived at his destination a few hours later, Doug and I exchanged messages back and forth. The communication flowed easily and seamlessly. Neither of us had to pretend to be something we weren't to impress the other, because we'd already known and liked each other a few years. The conversation just made us realize how much more we had in common than we'd thought—politics, religion, finances, kids, marriage, and life in general. We literally agreed on everything!

And Doug was everything I could ever imagine wanting in a partner. He possessed a childlike naivete that made him pure and sweet, but with just enough irreverence to say (and hopefully do) naughty things to make me laugh, and the mind-set and integrity of a wise old sage. I knew I could love this man, and love a life with him, if we were ever able to entertain our feelings towards one another.

I had concerns about Doug's readiness for a relationship, however, since a family picture in which he and his two sons held his ex-wife sideways like the Queen of Sheba, had still hung above the fireplace in his living room, almost four years after the divorce. I wouldn't get involved with a man who was hung up on his ex. But when I'd cleaned Doug's house just the week before, I'd noticed that the picture was gone and photos from his wedding to his ex were piled in a corner of his foyer floor. He was finally over her.

I didn't get my hopes up, though. I'd never have a chance with a man like that. He wouldn't want the mess I was, and I had my situation at home to deal with anyway.

I wasn't even sure what the situation was, though! I'd been coming home from work to find Darren helping strangers pack their cars with items we'd been storing in what used to be an in-law house. Darren was obviously selling it all, which meant he needed money for something. I just couldn't figure out what. But when I came home from work to see my kickboxing bag being hauled away, I waited in the kitchen for Darren to explain.

"What's going on?" I leaned back onto the island with crossed arms and a scowl.

"Nothing! Why?" he said nonchalantly, filing several bills in his wallet.

"Nothing? This is the third time this week I've come home to you selling our stuff!"

"You keep telling me to clean out the garage and shop," he deflected. Then he laid on the couch and picked up the remote.

"Not recently!" I said, but the TV powering on cut me off. "What the fuck, Darren?!"

"I'm not going to sit here and argue with you, Dana."

"I'm not arguing with you! I just want you to answer my question honestly for once! You're selling items, some of which aren't yours, and I want to know why!"

"My money paid for them, so they're mine to sell."

"*Your* money?" I stopped short of giving him a piece of my mind because I saw a text message from Ryder pop up on my phone screen. "You're unbelievable. Ryder's texting me right now, wondering why you're selling his kayak. He saw it on Facebook Marketplace."

Darren lay there silently like he always did, with his arms crossed and a deep frown. I'd busted him, and he had no defense.

"I'll give you whatever you're asking for the kayak, since you obviously need the money so badly, but don't you dare sell it! I gave it to Ryder, and it's pretty shitty of you to try to sell it while he's away. Not to mention *I'm* the one who bought it in the first place!" Darren stared at the TV as if I hadn't spoken. "Hello?"

"What?"

"What do you mean 'What'? I want you to tell me you're not selling the fucking kayak!"

"I don't want your money."

"What do you care who gives you the money? You want three hundred dollars for it? I'll give you the three hundred dollars. It's bullshit, but don't you dare fucking sell it."

"Ryder doesn't even use it!"

"He has plans to kayak with friends next week! You'd know that if you talked to the kid once in a fucking while!" I went to my purse and pulled $300 out of my wallet. "There's your fucking money," I said as I set the bills on the kitchen island. Then I huffed and went to bed in the basement, even though it was still daylight out.

As I was silencing my phone for the night, a text came in from Doug. *Hi!*

A rogue smile came upon my lips.

Hi back! I responded.

What's for dinner? We often compared menus.

Had an argument with the husband for dinner instead of food.

Don't sweat it too much. Divorce isn't that bad. For a couple months it is, but then everything's okay.

It is what it is. Just waiting for courts to re-open so I can get on with my life! For now, sleep!

Sweet dreams!

:)

I released a long exhale and held my phone close to my chest. Then I closed my eyes and imagined a life with Doug—a man who treated me well, made me laugh, made me feel like I mattered, cared about my well-being, and most importantly, a man I respected. I knew it would never be. A girl could dream, though.

"Little Wonders"

I know you're not happy here. With me. And I think maybe you should move out. Find your happiness. I don't want you to, but this place was my dream, so it just makes sense for me to stay. As long as you keep paying the mortgage here and—

I huffed and shook my head in disbelief. I was standing in the middle of a busy grain scale office with people buzzing around me. The sound of corn kernels falling through a metal measuring device like bullets being shot out of an automatic weapon made it impossible to focus on anything but cleaning.

Darren knew I was working, so he couldn't possibly expect me to engage in a discussion about a major life decision that would impact our son's life and all our futures. And he'd be out of his mind to think I'd agree to move out and let him live there with *my* son on *my* dime. So after a few more texts pressuring me to engage or agree, and my texts back refusing both because I was at work, I stopped responding.

Although we barely interacted and tried to avoid each other altogether, I hoped to run into Darren when I got home. We obviously needed to have a conversation about our living arrangements and consequential budgetary agreements, especially if we were considering dividing households. We'd need to discuss all this in preparation for divorce anyway. I just wasn't going to do it through text messages, and certainly not at work.

Neither Darren nor Ryder's trucks were in the driveway when I pulled in at home that afternoon. I walked into the house with the mail, figuring I'd tend to some chores while I waited to talk to Darren, but a certain stillness that felt different than the normal quietude of an empty house made me pause and look around. I dismissed the sense something was off, chalking it up to the eerie quiet of being home alone, and proceeded upstairs to my office. At the top of the stairs, however, I noticed something out of the corner of my eye that made me glance into the master bedroom. The mattress—it was bare! Every pillow, sheet, and blanket was gone!

I went into the bedroom to investigate further. With a quick survey of the room, I saw the picture frames on the antique five-legged table had been placed face down. I knew I hadn't done that, so it must have been Darren. We hadn't been getting along for a while, though, so it didn't bother me.

I couldn't figure out where the bedding had disappeared to. We didn't own another king-sized bed, and I couldn't imagine Darren taking it all to the laundromat when we had our own machines in the basement. Then I remembered the text messages. I said I wouldn't leave, so had Darren left me? I went to his closet for confirmation. When I opened the bi-fold doors, the half-empty closet told me what he'd been too much of a coward to.

I closed Darren's closet and stood in the middle of the empty bedroom with a strange sense of calm. I should have been devastated. I should have cried. I should have gone in search of my husband to either beg his return or beg for answers. But I didn't. I'd already resolved myself to the end of our marriage. I was actually relieved. I'd been so worried I wouldn't be able to get him out of the house when I filed for divorce, which I hoped would be soon since the courts were finally re-opening.

Darren's mind changed as often as his mood, though. I suddenly worried that if he got it into his head that he wanted back in the house, I'd never be rid of him. So I went to my office and contacted the attorney and mortgage broker, expressing urgency to complete the paperwork for the refinance of the house in my name only. Then I went down to the kitchen to get something to drink. Still cool as a cucumber, I leaned back against the kitchen island and gulped straight from my carton of cashew milk.

The sound of the door bursting open and then bouncing off the immobile side of the French entry startled me. I whipped around to see Darren plow through with a scowl on his face. Like a man on a serious mission, he made a spectacle of stomping up the stairs, then back down right away with a couple of shirts. He didn't look my way. He just hurried out the door and straight into the old in-law house.

So he hadn't really moved out. He'd just moved out of the main house. And this little show was his way of telling me. I swore I was married to a five-year-old!

Just then, Ryder came home from work.

"Hey, kiddo!" I greeted him a little too cheerfully.

"Hey." He glanced at a bare wall on the way to the bathroom. I could tell by his quizzical expression that he noticed something missing from its usual place, so I looked there too. A picture was missing from where it usually hung on the wall. I looked around and noticed some other knick-knacks had disappeared as well.

I knew I had to tell Ryder his dad had moved out before he figured it out himself, or before Darren got to him with some story about how I'd kicked him out or whatever other lie could depict me as the villain. So as soon as I heard him come out of the bathroom, I walked to his room and leaned against one side of the door frame with my arms crossed.

Ryder looked at me expectantly, and I took that as my cue to begin speaking. "So, your dad moved out while I was at work today. To the shop, I guess."

"You know he's just doing this for attention. Just go get him," he responded nonchalantly, and then turned his attention back to his computer. "He'll change his mind in five minutes and be back anyway."

He was totally right, and I was glad he was unfazed by all the dysfunction around him, but I needed him to understand this was the final affront for me.

A dismal, "I can't," was all I could come up with.

Ryder looked at me as if he hadn't heard me correctly. But the apologetic look on my face verified what I'd said.

"Just go!" He stood and shut his bedroom door in my face. I knew he understood my reasons for letting his dad go, but I'd also broken my promise to him. So I let him be to process the situation, and I set out to do the same.

I went through the motions of a typical evening, thinking normalcy would help us both through this transition. Where I thought I'd feel some sadness or regret, I was glad to feel noticeably lighter. I could do as I pleased without ridicule or judgment, like peruse Amazon on my laptop, read, make what I wanted for dinner instead of worrying about where a certain meat fell in the rotation of options. I could even watch what I wanted, except the TV wouldn't turn on when I pressed the power button on the remote.

Where's the Fire Stick for the TV? I texted Darren.

Sorry, took it for the TV out here. I'll get another one for ya tomorrow. Also forgot my bananas. Can you put on porch tomorrow morning? Thanks. Then he admitted, *I bought a frozen pizza for dinner so borrowed the new pizza oven as well. That's all, though. Night.*

That was never all. But for the time being, I sat on the living room sofa like a queen who'd been restored to her throne, relishing every bite of my pumpkin pudding.

"You Broke Up with Me"

~~~~~~

When I returned home from work the next afternoon, I saw Darren's truck barrel up our gravel driveway recklessly. I swore he was going to kill one of the outdoor cats driving the way he did. Assuming he was just trying to get attention again, I leaned back against the kitchen island and continued sorting through the mail.

The next thing I knew, Darren barged into the house and up the stairs. Seconds later, he ran down the stairs and out the door, carrying his hand-gun case, which presumably held said hand-gun, then got back in his truck and tore down the driveway. When his truck turned too fast onto the road and sped off, I reflexively released the breath I'd been holding.

Darren had obviously seen me come home on the Ring video doorbell he'd installed outside our door and enacted this spectacle to intentionally scare me. He wanted to make sure I knew he had his gun and that I was defenseless. It was sick, disgusting, and outrageous, and exactly why I wanted out of this twisted marriage.

A little later, Ryder startled me when he walked in the house and slammed the door behind him. I heard him stomp down the hall to his bedroom, the same way Darren made sure everyone knew he was unhappy. I always prayed he wouldn't turn into his father.

"What's wrong?" I called out from my office.

"Oh, I don't know," Ryder replied snottily, as he returned to the living room, "maybe that you're divorcing Dad?"

I descended the stairs quickly. "Who told you we were getting divorced?"

"Dad."

"Well, we aren't living in the same house, which was his choice, by the way, but neither of us has filed for divorce as far as I know!"

"That's not what Dad said. He said you filed." Ryder threw me the same hateful look I'd seen on Darren's face too many times. Then he slammed the door on his way out, disallowing me any defense.

I felt hurt and betrayed by Ryder because he believed his liar of a father over me and also because he thought it acceptable to talk to me as disrespectfully as Darren did. After everything I'd done for that kid ... but my beef was with Darren. Ryder only knew what he saw in his primary male role model—avoidance, manipulation, passive-aggression, irresponsibility, inconsideration. Hopefully my sense, intellect, and more positive perspective would prevail in his personality at some point.

I sat on the stairs and dialed the piece of shit right away. "Where do you get off telling Ryder I filed for divorce?"

"I slipped. I'm only human," he excused in a sarcastic tone.

"Bullshit, Darren. You know damn well I didn't file for divorce. So unless *you* did, you just lied to our son. And you had no business having that conversation with him anyway! That's a conversation we should have with him together."

"It just came out," he said with that same remorseless sarcasm. "He asked me why I moved out, and I told him you wanted a divorce."

I had a sudden compulsion to reach through the phone and wring his fucking neck. "Listen to me. Don't you dare have any discussions with Ryder about anything regarding our marriage. He's seventeen. Let him be a teenager and enjoy his last year of high school without worrying about the shit show around here," I threatened, knowing full well I had no control over what Darren said or did.

"I'll tell my son whatever the fuck I want!"

"Are you trying to fuck him up?" I used his own words against him as he'd done to me so many times before.

"No, you are! This is all you, Dana! I'm not to blame for this!" He hung up before I could remind him he was the one who'd chosen to leave us in the middle of the day while we were at work. Coward.

I went back up to my office and distracted myself with computer work to calm down. Then I went about the evening as usual, cooking dinner and putting away laundry, hoping Ryder would return home so we could talk through his feelings about what was going on. When evening descended, I figured he might have opted to stay at a friend's house to avoid both me and Darren for a night.

I waited up anyway, just in case he did come home. Sometime after 9 p.m., I was in my office writing my cleaning crew's paychecks, when I heard the familiar sound of tires on our gravel driveway, and then the front door open and close. The bathroom door closed, and the shower turned on, then Ryder's bedroom door closed a bit later. I was that hurt Ryder was ignoring me, but he was obviously not ready to talk, so I let the issue go for now.

As I settled into bed myself, my phone buzzed. I checked it, thinking it might be Doug. Although I knew it best not to string him along, I missed hearing from him. His texts were fewer and far between lately. He was probably busy. Or maybe he realized how unavailable I really was and had moved on. The mature part of me hoped so, but the selfish part of me wanted him all to myself, even if I couldn't have him. Yet.

My face fell when I saw Darren's name on the caller ID instead: *This sucks. I keep thinking you're going to walk through the door. Not sure how much more I can take.*

Ryder was right. Darren really did think I was going to come and get him. He wanted me to beg him to come back! *Sorry. Not happening.* I boldly retorted. *I'm finally happy and disinterested in your feelings.*

I'm glad you're finding happiness. Just wish you could have with me. I just need to stop texting you, I know. But it's hard. Seeing you reminds me of what we had. You, Ryder and this house were my life and I liked it. I worked my ass off to get here and now I have to start all over.

I was his life? When was this? When I needed oxygen and he said he didn't have the money, but bought new wheels for his truck? No, I think I was his life when he put me out in the workforce with a lung disease during COVID, so he could use the virus as another excuse to lie on the sofa all day watching *Impractical Jokers*.

I was his lifeline, not his life. What he says "we had" was his control over me to ensure his life remained as he wanted it. But he was right about one thing—he would have to start all over. With someone else. Because I wouldn't be his means to an end anymore.

"Last Hurrah"

By the first of July, I was feeling a little depressed. Ryder was busy being a teenager, working and having fun with friends. I'd alienated myself from my own friends too long to have any. And I guessed Doug was too busy for me too. I hadn't realized how hard I'd fallen for him until I realized how much I was missing him.

Even Darren left me alone for a short time, until my phone buzzed almost immediately as I walked into the house from work one early afternoon. *DTF?*

That was an acronym for "down to fuck." I should have been repulsed. We hadn't been intimate with each other for months. Even then, I only gave in to appease him, lying on my back with O-shaped lips like an unemotional blow-up doll.

I was human, though. I longed to feel soft lips on mine, and a man's strong hands on my body. A certain man's hands, that is. I was crawling out of my skin just thinking about how badly I wanted Doug. I was mostly drawn to his kind heart and sensitivity, especially towards animals and children. I loved his deep-toned voice and the way he slapped his knee when he laughed. He spoke with gentle strength, soothing and commanding at the same time. He was respectable, morally rightful, and considerate . . .

He wasn't hard on the eyes either. Doug was very tall, with the belly of a man who liked a good meal. It showed security in who he was, that he wasn't trying to be anything other than genuine. He had wavy dark blond hair he wore just long enough to see the slight curl, and crystal blue eyes that sparkled in the light. When he smiled, his dimples showed, making him that much cuter.

So was I "down to fuck"? Yes. With Doug. Except we'd make love, because he wasn't the kind of man who used women for sexual pleasure. But I wouldn't let that happen, even if the opportunity presented itself. I didn't want to be the married woman who screwed around on her husband. Again.

Since I couldn't be with the man I wanted, I went to the second house to succumb to a man I wanted no part of. When Darren answered his door, I walked straight past him and up the stairs to his make-shift apartment, without saying a word. I wanted to get it over with before good sense changed my mind. Darren followed my lead. Once in his bedroom, we stripped down hurriedly. He lay upon the bed expectantly, and I climbed onto him.

I kissed him with desperate passion. Then we had sex. I was just as passionate in the act as when we kissed. I even achieved ultimate pleasure and continued on, until I looked down and saw that he wasn't the man I had a burning desire for. I panicked when I realized I'd just given myself to a man who'd dominated and unwillingly taken me in the past. I shouldn't have substituted him for Doug. I shouldn't even be here.

Suddenly disappointed in myself for betraying my feelings towards both men, I rolled off Darren and onto my back, tears of regret falling from my eyes.

Darren mistook my aggressive initiation as a demonstration of feelings for him, and assumed I was on my back awaiting him to take the power position. So he mounted me and pleasured himself. I lay still and allowed it. I don't even know why. I guess it was my self-inflicted punishment for giving him the wrong idea, though I turned my head to the side so I didn't have to see him smile down at me.

When Darren finished, he lay next to me and put his arm out to cuddle. I was repulsed, more by my own participation in this than his, so I jumped off the bed and grabbed my clothes off the floor. Darren squinted in confusion as I threw my shirt over my head. We weren't together, so I didn't feel I owed him any explanation. I just wanted to get out of there and pretend it never happened.

I ran out of Darren's house in just my shirt and panties, unconcerned about anyone seeing too much of me. Once in my house, I locked the door. Ryder wouldn't be home for a while, and I couldn't risk Darren coming in, wanting to justify the indiscretion or lure me into another. I just wanted to shower, to cleanse myself of the stain on my character, and to hide my shameful tears in the scalding hot water which fell upon me. I don't know if it was the haste with which I'd moved or the heat built up in the bathroom, but I struggled to breathe. My short breaths steadied into longer ones once upstairs in the master bedroom, where Ryder insisted I sleep now that I was head of the house.

Although the mid-afternoon sun shone brightly outside, my mood was gloomy and dark. I hated myself for what I'd done. I just wanted to go to sleep and end this god-awful day. So I covered my body with soft, warm pajamas, then crawled into the king-sized bed. The heavy down comforter held me as I wept, but it couldn't soothe the worry that I'd lose Doug completely if he ever found out what I'd done. I wouldn't expect him to understand, because I didn't understand it myself. I didn't deserve him anyway. Nobody could love someone as screwed up as I was. Not even me.

"Lose You to Love Me"

Have a good day baby! Darren texted me.

Baby? What the fuck! I hoped he hadn't mistaken sex and an invitation to a family dinner as anything more than what it was. But after being called "baby," I removed the diamond wedding band I'd kept on my ring finger and replaced it with a garnet heart ring which would remind me of my new commitment to love and respect myself, first and foremost. It was Independence Day after all!

When it was time to eat dinner, Darren walked into the house smiling. "Smells good, Mama!" I'd asked him to work with me to maintain our family unit for the sake of stability for Ryder, but this was too much. He was cooperating, though, so I smiled back and accepted his one-armed side hug, but only for a second.

"It'll be nice to have a home-cooked meal," he said as he sat at the kitchen table. I set a plate of food in front of him, then called out, "Come and get it, kiddo!"

Ryder sat at the table just as I set down the last plate of food. Then I took my seat across from him. I noticed his sour expression and wondered what was bugging him, but I dug into my meal instead of calling attention to it.

"How's your shitty apartment, Dad?" Ryder glared at Darren with contempt.

I nearly choked on my food.

"That's nice. See what you did, Dana?" Darren yelled as he flung his cob of corn onto his plate.

Ryder stood up from his chair and knocked it against the table angrily. Then he retreated to his bedroom and slammed the door. I just sat still and silent, wondering what the hell just happened.

"This is because you fucking filed for divorce!" Darren knocked his chair down to the floor as he rose from the table, then walked out the door.

"I *haven't* filed for divorce yet, you stupid fuck!" I yelled out after him. Then I sat back down to eat the holiday feast myself. Upset never deterred my healthy appetite, and I was tired of cooking uneaten meals.

A minute later, my phone buzzed. *Holding back tears after seeing your wedding ring off.*

There was always some sappy excuse for his misbehavior.

Yeah, it's been off for a while. My fingers swell when I'm under stress or it's cold. I have Raynaud's syndrome, remember? The ring was strangling my blood flow. Suddenly disappointed in myself for engaging, I retracted. *I've been explaining myself to you for years though and I'm over it.*

It's fine. I just saw you weren't wearing your rings and got sad.

Bullshit. He wanted me to put all three rings back on, profess my forever love to him, and then fall right back into our miserable dynamic. It wasn't going to happen.

Is there someone else? He texted before I could respond. That's what he really wanted to know.

Yeah, me.

The rest of the day was quiet. Then, just as I got into bed, my phone buzzed. *Night beautiful. Sleep well!*

His oblivion to reality was pissing me off. I closed my eyes and drifted off into my own fantasy world, in which Doug had sent me that message instead.

When I awoke the next morning and checked the time on my phone, there was yet another plea: *I regretted the moment I moved out here.*

I'm not doing this! YOU moved out. YOU told Ryder we're getting divorced. So we're getting divorced. You're happier. I'm happier. So please don't argue with me, stay out of my fucking house, and leave me the hell alone! I'm DONE!!

And I truly was. I was done with unhappiness and loneliness. I was done with the life Darren had forced upon me. It was time to start a new life, and I wanted that life with Doug.

Doug must have been reading my mind because he texted that same day. *What's for dinner tonight?*

I hadn't heard from him for a while, but it's like we were picking right back up where we'd left off. *Homemade barbecue chicken pizza . . . my favorite!*

We eat too much pizza around here. Probably not too healthy.

There's no such thing as too much pizza. And it's very healthy! There's dairy in the cheese. And veggies if you put them on there! Lol.

Doug and I talked and texted constantly after that. He texted when he had to pull over on the highway due to a swarm of bees in his van. He texted me before work in the morning to tell me where he was going. He texted in the middle of the night when he got up to pee, just to say hi. No matter what he messaged me, I got butterflies just seeing his name pop up on my phone. It wasn't because our relationship was new; we'd known each other almost four years now, and we'd genuinely clicked from the get-go. We were like-minded and could be ourselves without holding back. Oh, and Doug wasn't an asshole.

Then on July 30, I was at my first cleaning job of the day when Doug texted. *Do you think it's appropriate to kiss a girl during COVID? Asking for a friend.*

Doug could have any woman he wanted, but he wanted to kiss me? Of course, I wanted to kiss him too, but I didn't want to come off too eager!

Attempting to play it cool, I responded, *I guess it depends on the girl. But tell your "friend" I think it would be okay!*

My heart raced after I sent that text. I stood in the middle of a customer's bathroom, staring at my phone, anxiously awaiting a response. When Doug didn't respond right away, I got nervous that I'd misinterpreted the message. Had he really asked for a friend? I was so embarrassed for thinking he was coyly referring to me!

I waited and waited. Every minute that went by made me panic that much more. Finally, after almost an hour, Doug responded. *Meet me down by my house after work.*

Instantly relieved, I inhaled deeply and exhaled even longer. *Okay . . . I'll be waiting.*

I couldn't wait. I rushed to get through my unusually short workday, then sped down the back roads towards Doug's house.

Then I thought about what I was about to do. It felt wrong to kiss someone who wasn't my husband, and I was nervous Doug wouldn't like kissing me. I didn't even know if I was a good kisser! I was definitely out of practice, as I avoided Darren's touch whenever possible.

Overcome with anxiety, I couldn't breathe. My nerves were triggering my body's stress response. I lifted my chin to open my airway and strained for air. When that didn't help, I reached into the bag on my passenger's seat and grabbed a canister of portable oxygen. It was like an air compressor force-filling my lungs. I breathed in and out deeply. When my breathing was nearly restored, I saw Doug's name come up on my caller ID and got nervous again.

"Hello?" I tried not to sound like I was choking for air.

"Hi! I'm on O'Malley Road, right by my house. Where are you at?"

"Um . . ." I was so nervous I couldn't think straight. "I'm on your road. Not sure exactly where, but I'm close!" I saw Doug standing on the road just then and slammed on my brakes. He laughed as he watched me reverse to pull in behind his work van.

He met me at my car and opened the door for me. "Hi, sweetheart!" He smiled. There were those dimples! I was so nervous I only mustered a half-smile back.

Doug took me by my hand and helped me out of the car. I looked down shyly, avoiding contact with those crystal blues. They matched his light-colored jeans, which looked perfect with the plain white T-shirt he wore. He was a no-fuss guy. I liked that about him.

Doug put his arms around me then and held me close. Then he leaned me back against my car and lifted my chin with his fingers. He extended his long legs outward to lower himself to my level. I couldn't help but smirk when our eyes met. I might have fluttered my eyelashes a bit too.

Then he pressed his body against mine, leaned down, and moved in. I closed my eyes and parted my lips to give his tongue permission to enter. When it did, I felt tingling in other places I wanted him to discover. Movement in his groin told me he felt the same. The attraction between us was so overwhelming, insatiable thoughts of ravishing him right there had to be controlled.

As we moved our soft lips and wet tongues in and around with intense passion, cool raindrops began to fall. We simultaneously looked up at the sky, then looked back at each other and smiled. Rain represented new beginnings, and this was our new beginning—together.

"F*CK YOU, GOODBYE"

Ryder came home from school one mid-afternoon in August and went straight to his room. I walked down from my office to greet him. "Hey, kiddo! What do ya feel like for dinner?"

"Would you buy light bulbs for my bathroom?" he asked too seriously for the question.

"What?" I instinctively turned around and flipped the switch in the bathroom across the hall. No light. So I looked up where the light fixtures were. There were no bulbs inside them! I whipped my head back towards Ryder with a confused expression. Our eyes met, then he looked away.

"I'll get bulbs at the store tomorrow," I said, refraining from commenting about his dad's immaturity. There was no other explanation. Then I went upstairs to retrieve the bulbs from my bedroom light to put in his bathroom for the time being. Three bulbs were two too many for my sensitive eyes anyway.

As I unscrewed the bulbs, I noticed the ceiling fan chain was missing. I looked on the wide-plank wood floor to see if it had fallen, but it wasn't there. I looked around and saw it laying on the five-legged table near the bed. I knew I hadn't dismantled it, but I had one guess about who had.

Despite repeatedly asking Darren not to come into my house without permission, he came into the house regularly, just to make me aware he could and would. One afternoon, I'd found a pair of expensive, fancy-pocket jeans in the washing machine. They were neither mine nor Ryder's, and I'd never seen Darren wear anything like that. But when I checked the tag, they were Darren's size. He just wanted me to know he was dressing up

394

to go out, I guessed. Too bad I didn't care. I hoped he'd find someone to occupy his time and take his attention off me!

Then we had a mouse problem in the kitchen. We didn't leave food out, and I cleaned out all the cabinets, but when I checked the drawers, I found one full of half-eaten acorns. We didn't have acorn-producing trees on our property. Darren had access to acorns, though, when he mowed people's yards. That had been Darren's drawer too, where he'd kept his wallet and keys when he'd lived in the house. Once the acorns were removed, we never saw a mouse in the kitchen again.

Although minor annoyances, I worried about what else Darren might be doing in the house when Ryder and I weren't home, and how far he'd go to make me pay for not begging him to come back. Paranoia pushed me to the point of checking under my bed and between my sheets and blankets before going to sleep every night, just to make sure there wasn't a snake or scorpion awaiting me!

I finally had the gumption to set a boundary with him one night. *I think you need to ask your two friends with rental properties if they have a place for you to stay. I don't feel comfortable with you living here anymore.*

I'm not signing off on the house, then.

It was always tit for tat.

I'd promised Ryder we'd remain in the house at least through his senior year, but if Darren didn't sign off on the title and deed, we'd have to sell it and move. Darren would get the satisfaction of pointing out to Ryder that I'd broken another promise, and Ryder would resent me for doing so. Darren knew it too, which meant he knew he was in control. So whether I liked it or not, I had to play ball, unless I could figure out a way to blindside him.

I called the female attorney I'd been working with since before COVID, to see if there was any way to get the divorce before the house was refinanced, but she was behind on cases and wouldn't have time for mine for at least a few more months. As much as I liked her determination, I couldn't wait. So I asked a judge I knew for some references, and scheduled a consultation with the one attorney he said could get the job done fast.

The phone consultation with the new attorney took place a couple days later, mid-morning, when I knew Darren and Ryder wouldn't be home.

"So you're thinking about divorce?" the attorney, Tim, began.

I stood in my office, looking out the window at the calm, cloudless morning, feeling the same strange peace in my heart. "Not thinking. I want it done as soon as possible," I said, then informed him of the terms Darren and I had agreed to thus far and where I'd left off with the other attorney.

"When you've agreed on everything already, we call it a 'walk-in divorce'. However, I would only represent you, since you are the one retaining me to file. And as your attorney, I want to make sure you realize you're entitled to half of the 401K he spent and probably all of the equity currently in your home."

"You're not the first to tell me that, but this isn't about what I'm entitled to. I just want to be done. I don't care about money. I won't fight over things. I just want it to be over already."

Tim's sigh expressed his hesitation but also his understanding about my situation. "Okay. I can have the paperwork ready by this afternoon."

I wasn't used to things going my way, so it took me a second to realize what he'd said. "Really? That would be amazing! How soon until the divorce would be finalized, then?"

"About three weeks. The courts are still catching up from COVID," he replied.

"Then, yes! Please! I can bring full payment to your office in an hour. All cash." I couldn't risk Darren finding out about this on a bank or credit card statement before he was served with the papers. He'd surely sabotage the swiftness of the situation, by not answering the door to be served or something.

"People usually aren't this excited when I talk to them," Tim chuckled.

"Well, I'm not in a usual marriage. You can call it irreconcilable differences, but . . ." There wasn't any use talking about it anymore. It was about to end. "Thank you so much for doing this. You have no idea how much I appreciate your help."

For so many years, I'd wondered when I'd be ready, if it was the right thing to do, if Ryder would be okay. Ryder and I were doing great, though, and I'd never been so firm on a decision in my life. So exactly one hour later, I handed the wad of cash to the receptionist at Tim's office. I felt reinvigorated, like I'd taken a giant leap towards a finish line I didn't think existed.

The marital dissolution papers were emailed to me later that evening. I'd gotten Tim's approval to present the papers to Darren for signature myself to avoid the confrontational nature of official service by a deputy of the court. Plus, I didn't want Ryder to see this transpire, nor whatever show Darren would put on if he knew Ryder would be witness. So I texted Darren on the way home from work the next day. *Will you be home before 3 to go over some papers?*

Yep. Just got home. Pretty wiped out, but we can do that.

Cool. Be over in five minutes.

Just in case something went awry, I texted Doug. *It's happening. Going to Darren's with the papers now.*

Good luck :)

I took a few deep breaths before walking over. I was confident and clear-headed, but everything important to me—my son, my happiness, my freedom—depended on the signature of a man who'd taken the same from me. There was no telling how this would go.

"Come on up!" Darren said in a chipper tone when he answered his door. We walked through the shop area where he kept his four-wheeler, motorcycle, and the older bike he and Ryder were restoring.

The stairs going up to the apartment were in the back corner. I noticed shoes on a mat at the bottom of the stairway, so took my Converses off and left them with the other shoes.

"You don't have to take them off," he said.

"It's fine. I respect your house rules," I brown-nosed. It was never too early to prep someone for planned manipulation.

I waited until he proceeded up the stairs in front of me—a safety tactic I'd learned years ago in a real estate safety class. You never want to be cornered or blocked from fleeing your environment.

Once up the stairs, Darren sat on a light brown leather couch which used to be in our living room in the main house. I hadn't noticed it when I'd been here before, but I now wondered if he'd saved it for his own secret plan to leave. It didn't bother me, though. I didn't care so much that he'd left so much as I cared that he stayed gone.

I was still looking around at the slight improvements he'd made, when he motioned for me to sit on the couch with him. He'd painted the walls a medium khaki color, which looked nice against the raw wood side table and entertainment center he'd apparently built for the space. I recognized his half-assed carpentry skills, but I liked the rustic look of it all regardless.

"I'm good," I declined. I just wanted to get this over with and get the hell out of enemy territory. I knew he had guns up here. "So I had an attorney draw up a legal version of everything we've agreed to, as far as living arrangements and how we divided belongings and assets."

"Okay."

He wasn't very good at reading legal documents, so I proposed, "I figure we can read through these together, just to make sure everything is exactly as we agreed. That way, we can initial and sign as we go too. Does that work for you?"

"Yep." He grabbed a pen from above his ear. His preparedness was a good sign, though I wondered what had changed to make him so cooperative.

As I read the dozen pages to him, we each initialed where indicated. He didn't give me a fight on anything, nor should he have, because he was getting all of his income, money, vehicles, toys, and perfect credit, as well as being relieved entirely of any financial duty to me, Ryder, and the house. He knew he was screwing me and was happy about it. And so was I, because giving him the air of victory had been the plan all along.

When we reached the last page requiring signature, he hesitated. "I know you went over all this with me, but I feel like I'm not doing my due diligence unless I read through it all myself," he said. My heart stopped in a panic, but I acted cool.

"Of course. I'm hungry anyway, so I'll go grab a sandwich real quick and give you a few minutes to look things over. When you're done, text me, and we'll run over to the bank and get this notarized before they close."

"That works," he agreed. I placed all the papers down on the light oak coffee table. It looked just like his friend Ryan's old coffee table. I looked around and saw a few other things from Ryan and Tara's house. Then it occurred to me why he'd sold all the stuff we'd been storing here—he needed to make room to move in! He'd been planning to leave me at the same time I was planning to divorce him!

I returned to reality and realized I'd been standing there too long and too quiet. Darren stared at me curiously.

"Sorry, I zoned out for a second," I lied. "I'm going to go, so just let me know when you're ready to go get this notarized."

"Will do."

About ten minutes later, when I was just about done eating a fried egg sandwich, my phone buzzed. *Signed the last page.*

I closed my eyes and tilted my head back. I wanted to scream, "Thank you, Jesus," like Melissa Gorga often said on *The Real Housewives of New Jersey* but went out to meet Darren instead.

Ten minutes later, the papers were notarized. A half hour after that, I personally delivered them to the attorney's office. And by 9 a.m. the next morning, the divorce was filed. No contest. No custody battle. No alimony. In three weeks, I would appear in front of a judge with my attorney, and it would finally be over.

"Sorry Not Sorry"

awoke on September 9th, 2020, with a smile. It was D-Day. Divorce Day. Done Day. Dana Day. And if things kept going the way they were, Doug day.

After I stretched my arms over my head and extended my pointed toes, I noticed the sun shining through the dark shades. It felt symbolic of how I was coming out of my own dark place and into the light, like a butterfly emerging from its cocoon. In a matter of hours, I'd be free.

I took a rare day off work, so I could take my time getting ready. I specifically selected a very short and tight bright red dress with a sequined black strap across one shoulder, as my final "F.U." to Darren. With my long curly hair wildly draping over bare shoulders, I appeared bold, confident, and unapologetic—exactly the look I was going for.

After one last look in the mirror, I strutted down the stairs in my black strappy stilettos and walked out to my car. The thought of leaving this house as Darren's wife for the last time put a little more swag in my step too.

When I arrived at the attorney's office where we would Zoom with the judge, nervousness replaced my overconfidence. I suddenly felt completely uncomfortable in my red dress, so I put on the lightweight black trench coat I'd brought with me, hoping it would pass as a long blazer. Instead, I looked like a mistress going to surprise her married boyfriend at his office during lunch hour. It was better than going in looking like I'd gotten lost on the way to the strip club though, and maybe this look would come in handy when I saw Doug later anyway.

The receptionist led me into a conference room with a long oval table surrounded by oversized black leather office chairs. Tim came in just as I'd settled into one. "Ready?"

"Freddy!"

He sat next to me with his laptop and explained that the judge would ask simple questions to confirm the settlement agreement. I was to respond with a simple yes or no unless elaboration was requested. "Any questions before we proceed?"

"Nope! Let's do this!"

Tim opened his laptop and entered into the Zoom meeting. We appeared together in a little box on the screen, along with the judge, a court reporter, and ... Darren? He'd pled no-contest and waived the right to appear!

Tim saw me squirm on the edge of my seat, cut the video, and muted us to explain, "We sent him an email to inform him of the court date, and he asked to be present with us via Zoom. He does have that right."

"Okay," I said, but I was not at all okay with it. Darren liked to fuck things up for me. "But I want this done today. I don't want him dragging this into another court date." I stared at Tim to impress my seriousness. I'd be devastated if I was still married after this.

"Unless there are any surprises, you will leave here a single woman." I held my stare to judge his confidence level. He didn't waiver, so I decided to trust him and turned my attention back to the Zoom.

"I believe all parties are present, so I'll go ahead and start," the judge said when we reappeared on the screen, then proceeded to introduce himself, his court reporter, Darren, and then me and Tim. "How ya doin', Tim?"

The judge's personable demeanor relaxed me. He had the gray hair of someone old enough to have enough life and legal experience to properly assess the situations presented before him while also seeming humble and young enough to relate to the average Joe.

"Doing well, Judge! I represent the Petitioner today," Tim replied. Their friendly rapport implied a well-established professional association that made me even more confident in Tim's abilities.

"Good afternoon, ma'am," the judge addressed me.

"Good morning, Your Honor!" I greeted with a nod.

Then the judge directed his attention to Darren. "And you, sir, will you have legal counsel today, or are you joining us on your own accord?"

Darren pressed his lips together. "I just found out about this hearing a couple days ago, sir. And I was under the impression my wife's attorney represented both of us."

"An attorney can only represent one party in a hearing, and it appears the petitioner retained him to represent her interests. And because I am presiding over this matter, I cannot advise you or represent you in any way either." The judge picked up the papers before him and scrutinized them quickly. "Seeing as this is no-contest and all terms have been agreed to, will you be comfortable proceeding?"

"I guess," Darren said lamely, then rested his forehead on his hand.

"Very well! Let's proceed with the swearing in of the petitioner and respondent. Would you both please raise your right hand?" Darren and I did as the judge instructed. "Do you swear that the testimony you are about to give is the truth, the whole truth, and nothing but the truth?"

Darren said, "I do" at the same time I offered a simple, "Yes." He looked as displeased as ever, probably because he thought I'd use his verbiage and have some sentimental regret about how we'd vowed those words to each other before. I wouldn't make that mistake again, though.

Then the judge reviewed all of the agreements contained within the divorce decree to confirm our accordance with it all. I agreed, but Darren piped up, "I did agree to these terms, Your Honor, but since I don't have my own attorney, I'm not sure I'm getting my fair share." I tensed then.

The judge rifled through his papers and looked closely at one. "Again, sir, I cannot represent you in these proceedings. I do see here, however, that you have not had employment income since 2016 and are declining spousal support. Am I to understand that you, Dana, are the head of household where income is concerned?"

"Yes, Your Honor," I responded, though angry expletives were running through my head.

"And what do you do for a living?"

"I clean houses, Your Honor." I intentionally avoided calling it a "business," since such a status implied a higher income.

The judge asked for confirmation of my previous year's income, as had been provided to him in my tax returns. Then he turned his attention back to Darren. "And you claim to be disabled on your taxes?"

"Yes, Your Honor," Darren responded, bowing his head for pitiful effect. The lying bastard failed to tell the judge he'd been mowing lawns for two summers now and had even plowed snow last winter.

Just then, the judge moved his face closer to the camera on his computer. He seemed to be examining something. "Are you in your truck, sir?"

"Yes, Your Honor," Darren replied.

"Is that a work truck?"

"Yes, your honor," Darren had forgotten to lie.

The judge chuckled. "I've had people Zoom from their semi-trucks, offices, all kinds of places!" Then the judge moved close to the camera again and squinted. "What does that say on your shirt? Is that your last name? Do you have a lawn care business?"

Busted, bitch! I thought in victorious glory.

"Um, yes, your honor," Darren said. I tried really hard not to smirk despite the face mask I was required to wear.

"So you do have your own income by which to support yourself, then," the judge deduced. "My only concern would have been to ensure you could support yourself without spousal maintenance, but seeing as you are gainfully self-employed, we can proceed." Darren pressed his lips together in defeat.

It served him right. I'd have stayed married before giving that taker a dime of my hard-earned money.

After a few more confirmations, the judge ruled, "I hereby grant the dissolution of marriage presented before me by the petitioner." Then he hit his gavel on the sound block. It was finally over. I waited until Tim closed his laptop to react.

"You're single!" Tim proclaimed.

"Yay!" I clapped and smiled.

He nodded his head and laughed at my uninhibited joy. "We normally don't congratulate people after a divorce, but you seem really happy, so congratulations!"

"You have no idea! And thank you again for making this happen so quickly." I expressed my gratitude to everyone in that office on my way out, breaking up the usual solemnity of their duties with laughter at the little dance in my step.

When I returned to my car in the parking lot, I reminded myself that the divorce was only a legal division of assets. I still had to interact with Darren because I'd reluctantly agreed to allow him to live on the property until Ryder graduated from high school in eight months.

We had to cooperate in parenting Ryder too. The kid didn't even know I'd filed for divorce, never mind the hearing today. And I wouldn't put it past Darren to tell Ryder, so Ryder would know I'd betrayed him.

So although it was pointless to ask Darren for a favor after just divorcing him, I texted, *I don't think Ryder needs to know about this.*

I agree. And congratulations! Should be no more stress in your life. Enjoy.

I didn't believe him, but I couldn't ask for a more cooperative response. I just hoped his actions would follow for once.

I was eager to text Doug next. We'd agreed not to let anyone know we were together, nor go out together in public, until after the divorce, out of respect to Ryder and to preserve the good-girl reputation I held. I didn't want to look like the woman who cheated and divorced her husband to be with the guy she cheated with. Despite our feelings for each other, that's not what had happened.

So this divorce meant we could finally go out on actual dates instead of secretly meeting in isolated locations and hoping no one saw us together.

In the midst of typing to Doug, another text from Darren came through. *Hey, what if Ryder hears from someone else? Don't ya think it would be better to hear from us?*

He sounded like such a good parent when it was convenient for him. On the other hand, I was starting to look like a hypocrite. I crucified Darren for lying and keeping secrets, yet here I was, doing the same to Ryder. I could only defend myself with intention—mine was good, to protect Ryder and ease him through the life transitions we were facing; Darren's lies only protected selfish desires and poor decisions.

So I saw those words as the warning they were. Ryder wasn't going to hear about our divorce from some random person. He was going to hear it from whomever Darren told to ensure Ryder would find out! Then Ryder would know I'd lied.

I couldn't let that happen, and I knew it was best for Ryder to hear it from me. I just wanted a little time to think about how to approach him on this. Since he was in school and had a golf meet after, I figured it could wait for now. He wouldn't be home until 9 or 10 p.m. anyway, and I was eager to get to Doug.

It's done! I'm all yours! I texted my official boyfriend. *Hope you're almost done with work! I'll be waiting for you at your house so we can celebrate!* He sent me back a thumbs-up emoji. I'd recently purchased my first smartphone, so the days of sideways smileys were over.

A couple hours later, I heard Doug walking through his quiet house looking for me. When he walked into his bedroom, I was lying on his bed on my side with my head propped up. He stood in the doorway, in his dirty white T-shirt and blue jeans, taking in the sight of me.

"I have something for you, love," I said. I pulled a wrapped rectangular box from behind me and set it in front of me.

Doug came and sat on the end of the bed to open it. "What's this?"

"Well, I can't tell you, silly! You'll have to actually open it to find out!" I giggled. "It's just a little divorce day gift." I sat up on the bed next to him.

"I should be getting *you* something then!" Doug said as he opened the top of the box to reveal two T-shirts. He pulled one out and held it up. It was a white shirt with black letters that spelled "Clyde"—my nickname for him—except the "L" was a pistol. "This is great! Thanks, sweetheart!"

I pulled the other shirt out of the box and held it up against my chest. It said "Bonnie"—his nickname for me—and the 'O' was a red-lipped smooch. "We don't have to be on the run anymore, Clyde! We can be together now. For real." I dropped the shirt and threw my arms around his neck, and we kissed passionately.

I pulled back for a moment and looked into his eyes. There wasn't a doubt in my mind I had my guy—the right guy this time. "I have a feeling we're gonna get into a lot of trouble together," I said, smiling.

"Yes, we will, Bonnie. Yes, we will."

"Happy Now"

*T*he morning after the divorce, I heard Darren's tires squeal when he left for work too early in the morning. He truly didn't care who he affected with his anger, just as long as whomever he was angry with knew how he felt. And I did. I was fully aware. I paid no mind to him, however, and went on with my morning routine of walking and coffee, thankful for the normalcy after such a major life event.

A couple hours later, I'd just started cleaning at my first job of the day when I received a text message from my mother, whom I hadn't heard from in nearly a year.

Morning, Dane. Darren reached out to me and told me about the divorce. We had no idea! He said you really needed me and that I should get in touch to make sure you're okay. I can't imagine how you must be feeling. There are a lot of emotions involved when your life changes like that. I just want you to know Dad and I are here for you and Ryder, whatever you need. We told Darren the same. Love you, Mom.

That piece of shit was unbelievable. Darren knew how many years of heartache I'd endured to come to some peace with my mother gaslighting me about the abuses she and her narcissist husband had inflicted upon me. According to her, none of it had ever happened, and, like this text, she perpetuated the lie by putting on the facade of the normal, happy family we were nowhere near being. I mean, I hadn't seen or heard from her in almost a year!

So to reopen a door I'd spent years trying to close for the sake of my emotional and physical well-being was just cruel. Did Darren forget my

UARS was triggered by stress? That I was at risk of congestive heart failure? Or was he trying to get rid of me again without getting his hands dirty?

Darren hadn't forgotten anything. This was an intentional act meant to cause me physical distress, as well as provoke my gossipy mother to say something to Ryder about the divorce he knew nothing about.

Although my stilled heart was beating strongly now, thanks to the adrenaline of my fury, I could only deal with one toxic person at a time. So I responded to my mother and figured I'd deal with Darren later.

I'm sorry Darren involved you in this, but you don't need to worry about me and Ryder. We're fine. I was the one who filed for the divorce, not that you would know that, or anything else about my life. And I've been taking care of us for a long time, financially and emotionally, so we don't need anything from anyone. As far as Darren, have whatever relationship you want with him, but know he's just using you to manipulate me.

Later that afternoon, I pulled into the driveway at home, just behind Darren. The fury I'd felt earlier instantly rose again.

"That was a low blow, that shit with my mother this morning!" I yelled the second I emerged from my car. Darren was standing outside the open driver's side door of his truck.

He looked at me with upturned brows of innocence and said, "I was just saying goodbye."

I smiled and huffed in disbelief. "Of course you were. Because you love her so much." I walked towards the house. "I'm not stupid, you know. I see what you're doing. You're trying to hurt me and you want my mother to open her big mouth too and tell . . ."

"Well, we need to tell him we're divorced!" Darren hollered. I looked around in a panic to see if Ryder was outside or in the garage where he could have heard that, which had been exactly Darren's intention, I presumed. Thankfully, I didn't see him.

Darren hurried towards his house like a cockroach running for cover, and I yelled after him. "You want him to know so bad? Then come over here and let's tell him right now!" I challenged, but the coward slammed the door shut to avoid responsibility.

I went into my house, riled up and pissed off that Darren was still manipulating me. The only way to change our dynamic was to take his power away by telling the truth.

I peeked down the hall and saw Ryder's bedroom door shut, so I leaned against the kitchen island for a minute and took a deep breath to clear my head. I needed to think about how I would tell Ryder, though I knew I'd probably just cut straight to the point like I normally did.

Out of the corner of my eye, I saw movement out the window. Darren was back outside. I rushed out to the porch and called out, "You coming in to tell him with me?" I crossed my arms and jutted out a hip as I awaited response.

"It's all you!" Darren dismissed with a wave of his hand as he briskly walked back into his house.

"That's nice," I yelled loud enough for him to hear through his door. "Good parenting!"

Then I went back into my house, muttering, "Fucker," on the way. I went directly to Ryder's room this time and slowly opened the door. "Hey, can I talk to you for a second?" Hearing the difference with which I spoke to Ryder alarmed me for a second. I was switching gears as fast as Darren now!

Ryder was watching YouTube videos on his computer. "What?" His serious tone told me he didn't care for the disruption.

"I just want to tell you something real quick," I said, then sat on his black futon, which was folded up like a couch. He muted the video on his computer and looked back towards me.

"So . . . I'm just going to say it—your dad and I got divorced yesterday."

Ryder turned back to his computer screen and stared at it blankly. I waited patiently, knowing he needed time to process my words. After what seemed like forever, I whispered, "Say something, Ryder. Please."

"What do you want me to say?" He whipped his chair around and raised his voice. "I always thought I was lucky because everyone else's parents were divorced but mine weren't. And now . . ."

"Listen to me," I said. "All day today, you were fine. You had two parents who love you but live in separate houses on the same property. Now, in this very moment, you have knowledge that we are divorced, but nothing has changed. You still have two parents who love you and live apart. The only difference is what you allow yourself to believe about it, so don't make it into something it's not."

"Everything has changed!" Ryder threw his arms up and turned his chair back to his computer. "I know you two never got along, but you stayed together anyway. And now you're divorced!"

"Nothing has changed, Ryder," I calmly insisted. "A divorce is just a piece of paper saying who gets what, but the relationship isn't any different. Believe me, I wish it was, because you're right that your dad and I never got along. We have a chance to be happy now, though, so that's a good thing!"

"Yeah, divorce is great!" Ryder responded sarcastically, then jabbed, "If you never got along, then you should've thought twice before you had a kid!"

He might as well have stabbed me in the gut. That hurt. But if he wanted to have an honest conversation, I would go there with him. "I had you, Ryder, because I wanted to bring you into this world and be your mother. That is totally and completely separate from your dad and our marriage. I wanted you, I had you, I love you, and I gave you a good life. I did everything for you, including staying with your dad this long. And I'm still here and still doing everything you want me to do, so that's not fair."

"Well, it still sucks."

"I'm sorry, Ryder. I really am. But you and I have been happy here together since your dad moved out. You can't deny there's no tension, no fighting, no worrying about what he expects and what he doesn't allow . . . I know everything is going to be okay going forward, because it already is," I advised.

Ryder fell silent again. He knew I was right. Yet, this was like a sick loved one passing away. We'd all known it was coming, but you're never fully prepared for the emotions until it actually happens.

"I'll leave you be. Just know I love you. That will never change," I promised. I touched his shoulder before leaving him with his thoughts.

I went to the kitchen so I would be close by in case Ryder decided to talk more after all. While I waited, I texted Darren: *Our son has been informed. He's obviously very upset.*

Darren responded immediately. *Think it's good he hears it from us instead of other people. There really was no way of hiding it.*

Us? Of course he would take credit for my handling of the situation!

And of course he presented himself as some reasonable, mature parent again. I was so disgusted with him I couldn't even respond.

After preparing dinner for Ryder, he still hadn't emerged from his bedroom, so I went up to my office. I immediately noticed the mess of papers on my desk, as if my neat, ordered piles had been rifled through. My laptop, which I always kept open, was closed. Who had been in my office and what were they looking for? It couldn't have been Ryder; he never came upstairs, and he always respected my space. He would even stand in the living room and talk to me from down there. There was only one other person who had access to the house, and he had no right to be in it, nor go through my things. I was infuriated.

While I took deep breaths to calm myself before reacting, I checked emails. Of course, there was one from Darren, from earlier in the day. "Was trying to get everything out that was mine . . . Sorry I didn't ask to come in your house, but I've been very generous on what you get to keep while I'm stuck in this tiny piece of shit apartment paying half the mortgage."

Everything was his, according to him. Except for me. And I knew I wasn't done paying the price for it.

"Every Breath You Take"

Reacting to Darren made him aware he could still affect me, so I tried not to. But because he knew emotional stress caused me physical *distress*, being able to harm me without actually *doing* anything to me put him in a prime position of being able to hurt me without consequence. As a result, his contemptuous behaviors amped up.

He'd tear out of the driveway in the wee hours of the morning, screeching his tires loudly to wake me. The startle, which could cause heart failure, thankfully only caused me panic and chest pains instead. If we crossed paths outside, he glared at me with that hateful face only he could affect me with, which either annoyed me or made me anxious, depending on the day. The anxiety would make my heart race, and sometimes my hands would tremble.

If we drove past each other in the driveway, he'd veer as close to my car as he could without hitting it, though a white paint streak along one side of my black Kia evidenced what I presumed to be an intentional side swipe I hadn't been in the vehicle to witness. There were knuckle marks on the hood and trunk too. It was only a matter of time until he was drunk or mad enough to punch *me*, and I had no defense against him.

Avoidance was the only way I knew to protect myself. So every day after work, I'd wait for Ryder to come home, make him dinner, then leave for Doug's before Darren returned from mowing. Ryder had no idea where I disappeared to every evening, nor did he ask.

Perhaps it was guilt for leaving him, or for withholding information, but I started giving him little hints. I'd say I was going down to the "old man's house" in town, referring to Doug's father. I'd developed a good enough rapport with the old man, after cleaning his house for so many years, that I did sometimes go hang out with him. His house was the family hub, so people were always there playing cards, cooking food, or just visiting. Ryder knew that, since he'd been friends with Doug's nephew for a long time, so he thought nothing of it. In fact, he told me it was good to see me going out and having fun.

Then one night when I returned home from Doug's, Darren and Ryder came out of Ryder's bedroom, glaring at me as if I were the most repulsive and vile human being they'd ever laid eyes on. I froze in place, instantly fearful of what I'd done to provoke this scornful affront.

Darren advanced towards me. My sorrowful eyes held his stare, hoping for mercy. I turned my head slightly to avoid the potential physical assault I always expected.

"You're fucking unbelievable, you fucking whore!" he yelled as he stormed out. I closed my eyes and released a breath when the door slammed shut behind me.

I reopened my eyes seconds later to see Ryder standing at the doorway to the bathroom, still glaring at me hatefully, just like his dad. I tilted my head and scrunched my brows, as if asking for an explanation, but Ryder went in the bathroom instead and firmly shut the door behind him, symbolically shutting me out too.

My head dropped in regret, and for a moment I mourned the close relationship Ryder and I used to have. He'd taken on a more negative disposition since being exposed to Darren's apathetic attitudes the last four years—Darren's self-proclaimed disability having kept him couch-bound during our son's formative teen years, of course.

There was nothing I could do about it now, though, so I locked the deadbolt on the door, then went upstairs to get ready for bed. After flossing and brushing, and pulling my hair up into a high bun, I locked myself in the bedroom and curled up in the puffy, white down comforter, which failed to soothe me. I wished Doug were there to cuddle me and tell me everything would be okay. I always felt safe with him.

Wait, was that it? Was this about Doug? Doug and I hadn't wasted any time after the divorce to go out together. I even took him to one of

Ryder's golf meets, where senior players were honored before heading out on the course. I could tell by Ryder's grimace that he hadn't been too happy about seeing me with another man, never mind bringing the man around Darren. Ryder hadn't been around Doug enough, however, to be able to recognize him as his friend's uncle in the crowd. I think he worried more about being publicly humiliated by Darren's reaction anyway, but Darren remained in his golf cart next to the audio booth—glaring, of course. Doug and I left immediately after the preface to the meet, to relieve Ryder of his worry and avoid confrontation with my ex.

I'd also taken Doug to an outdoor music event at Ryder's school. We were sitting in lawn chairs with some drinks, enjoying the performance of a violinist playing pop music, when I saw the mother of a boy on the golf team take a picture of me and Doug with her phone. I acted like I hadn't seen her violation of my privacy but I knew in that instant the photo would get back to Darren, since they were friendly. She probably thought she'd caught me cheating, since few yet knew about the divorce.

Over the next few nights, Ryder was standoffish with me. He'd ensure I got home safely, but he clammed up when I attempted to chat before bed. Although it bothered me tremendously to be at odds with him, and curiosity to know what exactly had caused the discord nagged at my thoughts, I wasn't going to push the issue by bringing up the elephant in the room.

But the elephant trounced into the room anyway. "Are you dating that grandpa you're always hanging out with?" I had just walked in the door when Ryder met me with the question.

Doug was a grandpa, but I knew Ryder was referring to Doug's dad. I burst out laughing. "Oh my god, Ryder, no! I mean, he's funny as hell, and I like his company, but damn, kid!"

"Well, who's Clyde, then?"

My mouth fell open, but no words came out. How could he possibly know I referred to Doug as Clyde? *No one* knew that! Had he heard me say that name on the phone, or had he seen the name on my caller ID? I was careful not to leave my phone anywhere, in fear Darren might somehow get a hold of it and scroll through my messages, as I'd caught him doing in the past. Just in case, however, I'd put the name Clyde in place of Doug in my contacts to intentionally throw off anyone who might see a call or text from Doug coming in.

My back was figuratively up against a wall; I couldn't keep lying to my son. He would find out sooner or later anyway.

I exhaled out of my mouth before explaining, "Clyde's not the grandpa, hon. I *have* been hanging out with the grandpa and his family, and while I've been down there, I kinda got to know Doug a little better. And we kinda like each other. We've been spending a *lot* of time together, actually." My face looked like the cringing emoji on my new smartphone.

"Doug?" I watched his face as he put together his friend's family tree. "Oh!"

"Yeah," I confirmed. "That okay?"

"Yeah, that's cool," he said, "but I wouldn't bring him around here or around Dad!" Then he walked to the bathroom to get ready for bed.

Relieved to have Ryder's presumed consent, I continued doing what I was doing. Doug said he didn't want to let a day go by that he didn't see me anyway, and I couldn't bear to be away from him either.

I actually thought I was doing Darren and Ryder a favor by staying away from the house. It gave them the opportunity to spend time together without Ryder feeling like he was favoring one parent over the other. Whether they did spend that time together, I didn't know. I just made sure to return home between 10 and 11 p.m. so I could visit with Ryder before bed. It was a nice routine we got into. He even left the outside light on for me and waited up to make sure I got in safely.

One October night, however, total darkness awaited me when I pulled into the driveway at the usual time. The outside light wasn't on. Even Ryder's bedroom lights were off, which meant he'd gone to sleep without waiting up for me. Nothing had happened between us, so why this display of rejection?

My heart started beating at a panicked pace as I cautiously proceeded up the gravel drive, looking for any indication of what might have happened in my absence. That's when my headlights caught Darren sitting on the large boulder in the grass near the garage. I looked over at him as I slowly passed, trying to determine what he was up to. He just sat there with slumped shoulders, one hand on his thigh and the other holding a red solo cup, glaring at me with that hateful look. Suddenly I couldn't breathe. It's like his hands were around my neck, restricting air flow. They might as well have been. He looked like he wanted to kill me. I was terrified.

My chest heaved as I struggled to take in air. I managed to park my car, but at the other end of the garage from my normal spot. I wanted to be as far away from him as possible when I got out. Getting from the car to the house would be a whole other issue, but I couldn't sit too long and let him think his stalking intimidated me, nor could I give him more time to do anything more than scare me.

I took my taser out of my bag. It had been given to me by a concerned client who knew I lived on the outskirts of town with only my son and had no protection against an assailant. The taser looked like an old cell phone and could supposedly take down a five-hundred-pound person instantly. I slid the power switch to the "on" position, hoping to God it could prove its claim, then got out of the car.

Exposed and vulnerable in the pitch black of night, I walked towards the house swiftly. I purposely avoided looking in Darren's direction. I was afraid he'd see the worry in my face, though he obviously couldn't see anything in the dark.

Once in, I engaged the lock on the knob and the deadbolt above. Then I stood with my back against the wall for a moment, listening for any sound of movement outside. There was nothing but silence. I crept up the stairs to the master bedroom then and locked myself in.

As I slid into bed, I suddenly envisioned Darren shooting me through one of the bedroom windows. The combination of mistrust and fear over so many years had turned me into this delusional crazy person who always felt threatened. My paranoia wasn't too far-fetched, though. Darren could easily gauge my normal sleeping position from outside or from the window on the west side of his apartment, which faced my bedroom.

To ease my mind, I decided to lie with my head at the foot of the bed. I figured if he tried to shoot me, I'd rather sacrifice my legs than die from a bullet to the head. I laid on the opposite side of the bed from the window too, as far over as I could get without falling over the edge. With the taser in hand, I lay awake until my eyes finally gave in to sleep. Fortunately, the night passed without incident.

"It Hasn't Been Long Enough"

A week later, I was leaning against Ryder's door jamb, having my nightly visit with him before bed. He hadn't indicated why he'd shut off all the lights before I'd gotten home that night, but we were back on track now, and that's all that mattered.

All of a sudden, we heard pounding on our entry door. Ryder and I looked at each other apprehensively, frozen and muted by the interruption. Then he immediately rose from his desk chair, grabbed me at the sides of my shoulders, and forcibly moved my paralyzed body just inside his bedroom.

"Stay here," he ordered as he closed the door behind him. I realized too late I should've stopped him. He took his role as the man of the house seriously, but he was my son, and we had no idea who was out there and what they could want at this late hour. It was almost 11 p.m.

Feeling like I should do something, I felt around in my robe pockets for my phone. The least I could do was call 911. Empty pockets reminded me I'd left my phone on its charger upstairs, next to my taser.

Helpless and worried, I listened carefully to see if I could determine who was here and what was going on.

"Tell me right now! Who is it?" I heard Darren yell.

"No! You need to chill the fuck out!" Ryder yelled back.

"Give me a fucking name! I'm not leaving until I know who the fuck it is!"

"No! Go back to your fucking apartment, and leave us alone! I'm not fucking telling you anything anyway!"

From the opposite end of the house, I listened to Darren and Ryder hurl more expletives at each other, but no words which provided explanation for Darren's angry ambush. I could picture them shoving each other with puffed chests and wrestling with interlocked arms to assert dominance over the other, as they'd done in the past. I opted not to intervene, however, since Ryder sounded like he was holding his own.

I wondered what this was all about, though. Whose name did Darren want? What had they done, and why was Ryder protecting this person?

After a final "fuck you" screamed as loud as Darren could summon, I heard the sound of the door opening and slamming shut, then the deadbolt being engaged. Loud footsteps came down the hall towards Ryder's bedroom, and the door opened.

I breathed out in relief when I saw Ryder, and I relaxed even more when I saw he was physically unharmed. But his crinkled brows and offensive stature indicated major distress.

"What's going on?"

"Dad!" Ryder shouted, even though I stood two feet away. He sat in his desk chair and stared at his dark computer screen blankly. I recognized numbing when I saw it, because I'd done the same to avoid feeling the extreme emotions imposed upon me. I hoped I hadn't taught my son to detach from his feelings too, but I'd worry about that another time.

"What about him? What's his problem?"

"He needs to move," Ryder declared firmly. Then he spoke words I'll never forget: "I'd have never forgiven him if he'd stabbed you with that knife."

I inhaled sharply. "What are you talking about, Ryder? What knife?" My speech was as hurried as my heart rate now. I knew Darren wanted to hurt me, but a knife?

Ryder avoided my question. "He wanted to know who you were taking to Aunt Gia's wedding, but I didn't tell him! So just go to bed!"

"It's just a ceremony at a church! They're not even having a reception because of COVID! And how does he even know I'm taking a date?"

"Because I told him!" Ryder shouted, then closed his eyes and nodded his head shamefully. After a long pause, he reopened his eyes and said, "When you told me you were bringing Doug, I made the mistake of mentioning it to Dad, because I thought I could talk to him about how I wasn't ready for a stepdad and everything."

"Oh, Ryder," I consoled. "You didn't do anything wrong, kiddo."

We both hung our heads and remained quiet for a minute. He felt guilty for causing this whole mess, and I felt guilty for not being as attentive as I should have been to his feelings. I certainly didn't blame him for going to his dad though; a son should be able to go to his father for support and advice. He'd just forgotten he was walking a very fine line between Darren's instability and my safety.

"I didn't tell him, by the way—that it's Doug."

"I'm not even worried about that, Ryder. You don't need to protect me and Doug. It's not your fight. It shouldn't be anyone's fight. Your dad and I are divorced and free to—"

Ryder cut me off. "Just go! Please, Mom!" Tears welled up in his eyes. Then he put his fists against his temples. I knew there was nothing I could say or do to alleviate the conflict in his heart, but I didn't know how to walk away from my son either.

I knew better than to push the issue, though. He needed time to resolve his feelings on his own. "Okay, kiddo. I'll go. But just know I love you. No matter what. There isn't a thing in this world that could ever change that." I closed his bedroom door behind me and walked up to bed, where I lay awake awhile, crying softly for my son's hurt heart.

I lay awake awhile after that too, worried about what Ryder had said about the knife. I should've known I couldn't end a relationship with a narcissist like Darren. He wouldn't let me go until one of us was dead.

"Look What You Made Me Do"

When I checked my email inbox the next morning, everything made sense.

At 10:19 p.m. the night before, Darren wrote, *FYI I'm not okay with Ryder going to your sister's wedding with you and your boyfriend. If that happens, you better fucking believe I'm fighting for custody of him. I have over $30,000 saved and will spend it all on that!!!*

Whatever. He didn't have $30,000, and he couldn't tell me what I could and couldn't do.

The next email said, *I will follow you to that wedding and fuck it all up! Test me on this one! My mom will find whatever lawyer I need to get Ryder away from your crazy ass, and you will never see him again!*

He knew Ryder was my weak spot, but I wasn't the least bit worried. Ryder was old enough to have a say in where he lived, and he'd chosen to remain with me. He'd be eighteen years old in seven short months anyway, so it would be stupid for Darren to fight me for custody for whatever short time remained until Ryder was legally an adult.

No judge would give Darren full custody anyway. He'd been in jail more than once, had been arrested for DUI, fined for public disturbance, wrecked multiple vehicles, and couldn't prove income for the last four years. His friend, Ryan, had given him a job recently, but he hadn't been working long enough to prove stability.

On the other hand, I looked like an angel on paper—college degree, cross country coach at Ryder's private Catholic school, active parishioner and weekly mass attendee at my church, soup kitchen volunteer . . . Plus, I earned a solid income with which I'd been supporting us all on my own. I was a straight arrow with a solid reputation for being reliable and trustworthy, and I had a clean background check to prove it.

Still, his threats unnerved me. I breathed deeply, pushed my shoulder blades together to crack my back, then read the last of the emails. *I see what you're doing now. Very clever, pinning me against Ryder so I get upset at him. Guess what my next move is, then? Didn't know we were gonna play this way.*

I closed my computer. I wasn't going to waste my time and energy defending my good character to a drunk. I had to leave for work anyway.

As soon as I got in my car, I checked my voicemail like I always did, to see if any customers canceled or rescheduled before I went on my way. The low and barbarous tone of Darren's voice came over the Bluetooth audio instead. I stopped the car in the middle of the driveway to listen. "What nerve do you have bringing our son to your sister's fucking wedding with this guy? Are you fucking kidding me? Isn't it bad enough you hung pictures around?" Now I knew for certain Darren had been snooping in my office that day I'd found my desk in disarray and my laptop closed.

I had exactly three pictures of Doug in the house, and they were all in my personal space upstairs—in my office, at the top of the stairs just outside my bedroom, and on the five-legged table in my bedroom. The one at the top of the stairs had been specifically chosen to taunt Darren in case he did come into the house. I sang Meghan Thee Stallion's song "Savage" when I'd hung it too. It was a picture of Doug and I about to kiss. My head was tilted back, my long curly hair flowed down upon my bare shoulders, my eyes were closed, and my mouth was open just an inch from Doug's lips.

"Do you know what this is doing to him?" Darren's voice spiked as the voicemail continued. "And you're going to fucking introduce this guy to my fucking son? You gotta be shittin' me! It's only been a fucking month!" A month since the divorce had been finalized, I corrected in my head. Our marriage had been over for at least fifteen years—roughly the same amount of time Ryder and I had known Doug's family.

"I know when you guys met. I know who this fucking guy is. I fucking know everything!" No, he didn't. Otherwise he wouldn't have been pounding on my door last night to find out.

"Fuck with my head all you want, you fucking bitch, but don't fuck with my kid's head. I swear to God I'll take all my mom's money, all my fucking money, and sue fucking . . . get his fucking . . ." He grunted angrily. "Goddamn, you got me so fucking pissed off! I will sue for custody of his ass because you're never fucking home anyway, and I'll have every right because you're fucking bipolar. You got every other fucking issue under the sun too. Don't bring him to that fucking wedding, or I'll make sure you never see your son again!"

As I listened to the end of this newest threat, I realized Darren's anger wasn't about Ryder, Doug, or the wedding. He wouldn't accept me being with someone else because, in his mind, I was still his. He'd always been jealous. So these emails, this voicemail, and the knife, predicted this would turn into one of those "If I can't have you, no one can" situations. I wasn't safe, and neither was anyone around me, unless Darren was stopped.

Despite my promise to Ryder not to involve the police, I was starting to feel like I had to. Or did I? Darren wouldn't *really* murder me, would he? I mean, he'd pulled his arm back in a fist many times, but he'd never actually hit me. Even the knife was just a desperate threat, I thought. It wasn't abuse or domestic violence.

Darren was a drunk and a narcissist, violent at times but not abusive. He just liked to *threaten* physical violence to bully me into submission with fear. And it had always worked.

Unsure of what to do, I contacted my dad. Although our relationship was limited to "Merry Christmas" and "Happy birthday" texts, his career in law enforcement made him the best person to advise me about my legal options.

It's abuse, Dana, he texted. *And without a paper trail, there's no evidence of it. You have to file a police report so there's evidence!* After we'd gone back and forth about what domestic violence really was, my dad continued to press me to involve the police.

I understand, I replied. *But Ryder would never forgive me if he knew I went to the cops. And I won't risk that.*

Ryder is the child here, Dana, my dad pleaded. *You're the parent and you need to make the call to keep you both safe. Ryder will get over it.* He was right, I knew, but this wasn't the time to become the liar Darren told Ryder I was.

I worried more, however, about the consequences I'd face if Darren found out I went to the cops about him. He was already behaving more erratically than he had in the past, and he didn't take well to people outside our home knowing the truth about him. To the world, he was kind and helpful and funny. But Mr. Hyde was different with me, and this was getting serious. So as much as I hated to break another promise to Ryder, I went to the courthouse after work.

I was directed to a desk to fill out a petition for an emergency order of protection. Basic information first—name, address, phone number, date of incident, summary of occurrence. I stuck to the facts and kept it simple.

The next section defined abuse and required me to check boxes. I didn't expect to check anything, but I read the options anyway. Repeated communication by phone and email. Check. Following. Check. I'd seen him sitting at a street corner watching me as I left a house I'd cleaned. Keeping me under surveillance. Monitoring my comings and goings with the Ring doorbell qualified for that, so check. Intimidating. That night he'd sat on the rock. Check. Threatening. To take Ryder away. Check. Threatening physical force. Knife. Check.

I gulped at the thought of that last one. I'd been so distracted with my concern for Ryder that night, I hadn't fully grasped the gravity of what Darren had done. He knew I was scared of knives. When he'd still lived in the house with us, he kept a jagged-toothed switchblade in a little drawer in the coffee table, next to where he'd lay on the couch, so it was always within reach. Knowing it was there kept me in line, like a shock collar on a dog. But I'd never thought of it as abuse. I would have never allowed myself to be abused after a childhood full of it.

I frantically reread all the boxes I checked, just to make sure I'd checked the ones that truly applied to my situation. I didn't want to imply abuse where there was only fear of it. But again, I checked off the same boxes in my mind that I had with my pen.

So, according to the law, Darren was abusive. After all these years of calling him controlling and accusing him of mind-fucking me, I'd never realized Darren was actually abusing me. I dropped my head to let that sink into my saddened heart.

After a long moment of self-pity, I straightened myself up. With newfound vigor, I completed my petition and handed it to the administrator.

She directed me to go upstairs to the courtrooms, where I would await a hearing.

The stairs came up to the middle of the top floor, directly in front of the elevator. Two courtrooms were on opposite sides, a row of metal chairs lining the walls outside each. The beige paint covering the concrete block walls failed to hide the age of the building and gave a sterile feel to the otherwise emotionally charged environment.

A bailiff sat at a worn wooden desk at the entrance to one courtroom. He was an older gentleman dressed in black law enforcement garb, complete with a shiny star near the shoulder. He nodded his head to acknowledge me as I settled myself into a chair next to his desk.

There was a monitor in the center wall between the court rooms. I saw my last name towards the bottom of the list and suspected that was an indication of where I fell in the order of cases. I decided to pass the time playing Candy Crush Saga on my phone. It was always a good distraction from the seriousness in my life.

About an hour and a half later, the bailiff called my name. "Here!" I said, lifting my hand for him to see. Then I walked to the entrance of the courtroom where he stood.

"Right this way." The bailiff held the court room door open and motioned for me to sit at the plain wooden table immediately inside.

The courtroom looked like one would expect, minus the seating for onlookers. The female judge sat at an elevated level in the center, and there were two administrators seated at descending heights to the left and right of her. The court reporter sat in front of the bench, with her tiny typewriter at her tiny, well-manicured fingertips.

I could immediately sense the judge was a no-nonsense type. She had short black hair and small, thin-framed black glasses which matched her hair and her robe. She glanced at me with judgment I didn't expect, which made me even more nervous than I already was.

"The cause comes on for hearing on petition for order of protection. Petitioner personally present in court pro se. Respondent not personally present in court nor represented by counsel," the judge spoke for purposes of the audio recording taking place. "Are you prepared to give your sworn testimony?" she asked, looking at me over the top of her glasses.

"Yes, Your Honor," I replied.

"Please proceed."

I summarized the events of the night Darren had waited for me on the boulder, and then the night he'd come to the door, presumably with a knife.

"I don't see the need for an order of protection. Do you have further testimony?"

I was caught off guard by how cold and indifferent she was. I understood her need to be objective, but it was almost as if her time were being wasted with my fear to go home.

"Yes, Your Honor. I printed out the emails my ex-husband sent me before and after the altercation with our son, who is a minor. I also have a threatening voicemail message on my cell phone, if you'd allow me to play it for you."

"No. Just tell me what your ex-husband said which you perceived as a threat."

"I typed out the message word for word. May I read it aloud, Your Honor?"

"Permission granted."

I began to relay the awful voicemail Darren left me, but the judge cut me off before I got to the second sentence. "Is there any direct threat in the message?"

I felt like I was getting nowhere with her, and I allowed my frustration to speak for me, "I think coming to my door late at night with a knife qualifies, as does the language and tone in the message. Not to mention our minor son was in the middle of it!"

"I am not hearing any reason for an emergency order of protection in your testimony. Do you have any other evidence or accounts which would support your petition?" The impatience in her tone made me feel like a little girl begging to be believed.

No one had stood up for me when *I* was a little girl, though, so it was time to stand up for myself. "I can tell you all kinds of things that happened over the course of our twenty-four-year relationship that would prove my need for this protection, Your Honor," I responded snidely, matching her rudeness.

She made a slight show of ruffling papers around, then said, "I see no records or reports of any previous instances of domestic abuse. Therefore, based on the testimony presented, the Court denies the request for emergency relief." She hammered her gavel on the wooden block, dismissing me like everyone else I'd had the courage to tell the truth to before.

It had taken me years to summon up the courage to come here, so I couldn't accept that the system was going to turn its back on me merely because I'd been too scared to involve authorities before.

"But Your Honor," I pleaded, "I never reported any previous incidents because I was afraid of the consequences!" Tears fell from my eyes without restraint. I felt ashamed by the public display of raw emotion, but I hoped it would open her eyes to the depth of my fear.

"This is a court of law!" she said, raising her stern voice. "I will not tolerate anyone speaking out of turn! Case dismissed!"

The bailiff approached to escort me out. I looked up at him hopelessly, and I could see kindness in his eyes. He must be used to seeing this happen to helpless victims, I thought.

Outside the courtroom, the bailiff handed me a tissue from the box on his desk, then put his hand on my shoulder as I wiped my eyes with it. "It'll be okay, kid," he empathized.

"Thank you," I whispered, though leaving there as helpless and vulnerable as I'd walked in wasn't very reassuring. Just like when I *was* a kid, I was being sent right back into the lair of my abuser to fend for myself.

"Bulletproof"

The next night, I reached over Doug's naked body to grab my buzzing phone from his nightstand. *Happy Sweetest Day!* This was followed by the middle finger emoji. *Give your boyfriend a good blow job, you lying whore!*

My teeth clenched. "I have to go." I jumped off Doug's bed in a hurry to gather my clothes from the floor.

It had been a perfect Saturday night too. Despite Sweetest Day being considered a Hallmark holiday by many, because of its likeness to Valentine's Day, Doug had cut an out-of-town trip short to celebrate our first one together. We'd cooked dinner at his house, then we'd made love.

It was different than what I was used to. He was so gentle and careful with me, and more concerned with my consent and comfort than his physical pleasure, which just intensified my attraction to him and the whole experience altogether. I'd been glowing and happy, lying in bed talking with my sweet man, when that text had come in and ruined my mood.

"What's going on?" Doug moved onto his side and propped his head up with his hand.

"Darren," I stated—the name alone providing explanation enough for anything which caused me upset. I handed him my phone. "I don't know what his deal is, but something is going to happen, and I don't want Ryder to be home alone when Darren strikes."

Doug took his readers from his nightstand and put them on to read the text. "It just sounds like he's jealous. You don't think you're jumping to conclusions?"

"No! That text is an indicator of something worse to come tonight. I don't know how to explain it. I just know. Maybe it's a gut feeling? Experience with Darren's moods? Either way, I just know something is going down tonight, and I can't consciously be here with you while my kid is there by himself. It's almost ten o'clock anyway, and Ryder expects me by eleven," I said as I put my socks on.

Doug put boxer briefs on and walked me out to my car. "Be careful," he said, "and text me when you get there so I know you're safe."

"I will," I promised and drove away from heaven to submit myself to hell.

My anger subsided when I pulled into my driveway and saw a few of Ryder's friends' trucks there. The boys were gathered in the garage, tooling around.

"Hi, guys!" I said cheerfully when I got out of my car. The boys returned the greeting, then turned their attention back to whatever they were doing. Seeing them all reminded me of what was positive and good in this world.

Then I remembered what wasn't and glanced toward Darren's apartment. The bright outside lights of the garage made his place seem eerily dark. I didn't see the usual glow of the TV in the upstairs window either, but I suspected he was awake. He'd sent that text barely a half hour before.

This was all a set-up, wasn't it? He'd triggered my anger, so I'd rush home looking for the fight, doubly taking me away from the man I'd replaced him with. I'd look like a crazy person in front of Ryder and his friends when I confronted him, and he'd act like an innocent victim of my wrath, who'd been sleeping and had no idea what was going on. He'd manipulated me, and I'd played right into it. Shaking my head in disappointment, I headed into the house.

After putting on pajamas, I went to the kitchen for a snack. Ryder came in and went to his room, then came out with a handful of clothes. "What are you up to?" I asked.

"I'm staying at Maverick's tonight," he said on his way out the door.

Ryder hadn't slept over anywhere in a long time. I suspected it was because he didn't trust something wouldn't happen between me and Darren if left on the property alone. I secretly appreciated that too. But I wanted Ryder to live a normal teenage life, without the responsibility of babysitting his parents, so I was glad he was going despite my nervousness to be left alone, especially after that text.

"Okay, kiddo, have fun! I'll see you tomorrow!" I faked normalcy as I locked the door behind him.

Still standing at the door, I half-thought about going back to Doug's. I'd already taken my medications, though, and they made me too drowsy to drive. I glanced up at Darren's apartment again, looking for reassurance that I could get through the night unscathed. It was still dark, and there was no visible sign of trouble looming, so I dismissed my concerns and went to bed.

Just as I'd fallen asleep a short time later, shouting outside my bedroom windows woke me. I recognized the drunken ramblings of Darren's voice.

"Look at you, home alone on Sweetest Day! Where's your boyfriend, you fucking whore! Did you fuck him already? Or is he already tired of your crazy lying ass and fucking someone else now? I know you can hear me up there, you fucking cunt!"

This was no coincidence. His Ring doorbell notified his phone whenever it caught movement outside our house, so he knew Ryder had left and I was here alone.

I refused to engage with him, pulling the blankets over my head to drown out his ruckus. Though muffled, I could still hear the familiar nasty tone repeatedly calling me a fucking whore, a liar, a gold digger, a fucking bitch, and a fucking cunt. I'd heard the insults so often, I almost responded to them as if they were my name.

Despite the similitude of the shouting and name-calling to every other fit of drunken anger he'd ever subjected me to, something about this night still wasn't sitting right with me. I had no external reason for my gut feeling; things just felt off. So I whispered a quick prayer to my deceased father-in-law, Henrik. He'd been the only one who could ever reign Darren in. "Please bring peace upon this house. Please give Darren peace in his heart. Please protect me—"

I stopped mid-sentence. Darren had abruptly gone dead quiet. I pulled the blankets off my head and listened for any indication of his whereabouts, but I heard nothing. Then—

BANG! BANG! BANG!

The next thing I knew, I was huddled with my knees up to my chin, crying hysterically in a corner of the bedroom floor. I wasn't even sure how I'd gotten there from the bed, but I'd been conscious enough to grab my phone and get away from the windows. My trembling fingers struggled to dial 911.

"911, what's your emergency?"

"HELP ME! PLEASE HELP ME!" I screamed into the phone.

"What's the emergency?"

"He's outside my bedroom window! My ex-husband! And he's shooting a gun! Oh my god, please send someone right away! *Please!* I think he's gonna kill me!"

"Okay, ma'am, we're sending two squad cars right away," the operator promised. "What is your location?"

I gave my address in between cries for help and heard the operator dispatch county cops. They were at least half an hour away, and I feared I didn't have that much time. Darren could break the glass doors and come upstairs in no time. I could be dead in two minutes.

"What is your name, ma'am?" The operator asked calmly.

I told her, then begged, "Please hurry! *Please!* Oh my god, he's out there, and it's quiet, and I don't know where he is now! *I don't want to die!*"

"Ma'am, help is on the way. I'm going to stay on the phone with you until they get there, okay? I'm right here."

"I'm so scared. Please help me. Please!" I sobbed.

"I know," the operator consoled. "They're on their way."

I heard dispatch in the background.

"They're almost there. Where are you in your house exactly?"

"I'm in the master bedroom, in the corner by the door. He was shooting a gun while I was trying to go to sleep, so I got away from the bed and the windows." The quivering voice I spoke with didn't even sound like my own. When I realized it was, I cried harder. This couldn't possibly be real!

"Okay, Dana. It's going to be okay. They're almost there," the operator reported. "Can you tell me your ex-husband's current location?"

"I don't know! If he's not outside, he's probably back in his apartment in the small house behind the main one where I live." I felt so stupid for allowing him to stay here, but that didn't matter now. I just hoped this stunt of his got him in enough trouble to have him removed.

"Okay, Dana. You're going to be okay. They've arrived," the operator said. Suddenly, red and blue lights moved all around the walls. I exhaled out my mouth—I'd never felt so relieved.

"Oh my god, thank you! Thank you!"

"I'm going to stay on with you while they speak to your ex-husband. But you'll need to come out of the bedroom and let them in your house."

"Okay." I rose from the floor and cautiously opened the bedroom door.

The house was as pitch black as I'd left it, and I wanted it to remain that way. We had twenty-two windows, and you could easily see in at night if the lights were on. I proceeded straight ahead to the window in my office overlooking the second house and garage.

"I'm looking out the window now," I said. I could see six squad cars. "And they have him—my ex." I watched two cops escort Darren out of his house with his hands on his head. Darren wore ratty old cargo shorts and a white T-shirt with frayed edges where the sleeves had been torn off. His feet were bare, just like the night I'd bailed him out of jail for DUI. He wasn't laughing tonight, though.

They stopped at the hood of the squad car directly outside Darren's front door. One officer remained with him while two others entered his house. Darren didn't resist, though I hadn't expected him to. Compliance implied innocence.

Two officers walked toward my porch then.

"Okay, Dana," the operator instructed, "I'll need you to let the officers in now, to speak with you."

I was already halfway down my narrow wooden stairway and saw two officers shining flashlights through the glass doors. "I'm going to my door now." I flipped on the light over the kitchen table before opening the door for them. "Okay, they're in," I told the operator.

"Okay. I'm going to hang up now. You take care."

"Thank you," I said and ended the call.

A female deputy introduced herself while a young male deputy surveyed my living room and kitchen area.

"So what happened here tonight?" The female deputy pulled a small notebook and pen from her waist.

I relayed the events, beginning with the text message, and answered all her questions about the divorce and unusual living arrangement. I made sure to tell her about the knife incident, and I played the voicemail from that night too.

Another officer came into the house then. "Ma'am, is there anyone else who may have shown up here with a gun tonight? Perhaps someone you're seeing or someone you've upset?"

I was confused. "No, sir. I know for a fact it was my ex. I heard him. And this isn't the first time he's intimidated or threatened me."

"Well, he said it wasn't him. He said he just got home from a wedding."

"He wasn't at a wedding! I can provide witnesses that he was here at the house since about eleven a.m. slaughtering and processing our hogs! My son and a couple other people were here with them, and everyone left between nine-thirty and ten p.m. As a matter of fact, I saw him with my own eyes carrying cases of beer back to where they were doing the processing earlier. And when I got home about an hour ago, his car was here, and all his lights were out!"

"It's clear he's been drinking, but we can't arrest him for that because he's not operating a vehicle, and we have no evidence of gun shots. We inspected the grass around both houses and there are no shells," the officer reasoned.

"But he shot a gun outside my bedroom! You *have* to do something! This isn't even his house—the title and deed are in my name. He's not on them at all!"

"So there's no one else who might have been here tonight? He says it might have been someone you're currently dating?"

"NO! I am seeing someone, but he would never do that! Ever!"

"Do you have any video or security cameras or anything to provide proof of your statement, ma'am?"

"No," I responded, suddenly regretting that I hadn't yet fixed the video doorbell I'd installed above Darren's. Someone had dismantled mine the same day I'd put it up.

The three deputies exchanged glances as if communicating their suspicions to each other without spoken words. I sensed this wasn't going to end the way I wanted it to—with Darren being handcuffed and jailed.

Finally, the male officer spoke. "Well, here's the thing. We have no proof he shot a gun tonight, other than your word. He is drunk, but we can't arrest him for that because he's at his residence and he has a legal right to be here. So unless you are able to find some solid proof for us, we can't hold him or remove him from the property."

"Are you kidding me? This is *my* house, and I have a right to say who can be here and who can't! And I don't want him here after what he's done!" I started crying again in frustration.

"We understand, ma'am," the officer sympathized, "but our hands are tied."

"So you're just going to leave him here with me tonight?"

"Unfortunately, yes."

"Well, then, I guess *I'm* leaving!" I threw my hands up in the air and walked toward the stairway. The female deputy followed me upstairs and watched while I packed an overnight bag.

When we came back down, one of the officers asked. "Where will you be staying tonight?" I was going to Doug's, of course. Darren wouldn't suspect it, so I'd be safe there. Plus, I didn't want to put anyone I knew—or worse, their children—in the middle of Darren's violent tantrum. This was between me and him.

"And whose home is this, and what is their relation to you?"

I knew exactly how it sounded, so soon after the divorce, but I had to be honest, "It's my boyfriend's house." The officer looked up at me with a raised brow. I felt the judgment.

"All right, we'll follow you out," the officer said. I turned off the kitchen and porch lights and locked the door behind us.

The harsh white headlights of the six squad cars blinded me as I nervously made my way past Darren and towards my car. The lights served to counteract my medications too, by forcing wakefulness, though adrenaline had already done the same.

I dialed Doug as soon as I started the Kia. He answered right away.

"I'm on my way back," I said.

"Is everything okay?"

"No." I sniffled, on the verge of sobbing again.

He sensed my pain. "It's going to be okay, sweetheart. I'll be waiting."

Four squad cars escorted me away—two in front and two behind. Two stayed at the house to ensure Darren didn't follow. I was grateful for the forethought.

As I approached Doug's house on the desolate back road, my rearview mirror showed the last of the cops following me turn around to leave me. The exterior lights of the home were like a beacon of safety in the darkness. Doug was waiting outside his garage, as promised, with his arms crossed and wearing only the boxer briefs I'd left him in a couple hours before.

As soon as I pulled up, he opened my car door and offered his hand to help me out. I looked up at him with sorrowful, tear-filled eyes, but he didn't bother me with questions. He just wrapped his arms around me in a protective barrier, and rested his head upon mine.

I was safe now, so I closed my eyes and let the consistent beat of Doug's heart slow mine to the same steady calm. Then I took the cool fall air deep into my lungs and released the tension in my body with a long exhale.

Away from Darren, and the fear and chaos he imposed upon me, I could finally breathe.

"Breakdown More"

Back in Doug's bed, I was relaying the horrific events of the night when my phone buzzed. I broke off mid-sentence and instinctively held my breath.

"You okay, sweetheart?" Doug was lying on his side with his head propped up on his hand, watching the psychological trigger take its physical effect on my stiffened body as the phone continued buzzing. It was a call.

"No," I replied shakily. Straining for air, I sat up to decompress my lungs. After one very deep inhale, I looked at my phone. "Fuck!"

"Who is it? Darren?"

"No, Ryder!" My son never called me. Even text messages were rare and short. I frantically pressed the button to accept the call. "Hello?"

"What happened?" Ryder demanded. I sensed misplaced blame in his tone.

"How do you even know anything happened?" I asked, though I already knew the answer.

"What happened? What did you do?!" Ryder insisted with a forcefulness I didn't deserve.

"You mean, what did your *father* do, right?"

"WHAT HAPPENED?" He wasn't backing down.

"What happened is between your father and me. I'm guessing that's why you're calling? He called and tattled? He had no business involving you in this"—I paused to take another deep breath—"but if you want to know the truth, your father shouted like a crazy person outside my bedroom window after you left tonight, and then he shot a gun. Three times, Ryder.

And by the way, I'm okay." I purposely added that last part to remind Ryder that I'd been the victim tonight, not Darren, who was obviously trying to assume that position.

"Dad said it wasn't him."

"Your dad says a lot of things. And of course he's going to deny it! But it was him! I heard him shouting just before the shots were fired!"

"So you called the police?" His disapproving tone made it seem like an overreaction, which was insulting.

"Yes! I did! This isn't like all the other times he's gotten drunk and said or did stupid shit. He shot a gun! Do you have any idea how scared I was? And how serious that is? He could've killed me if he'd wanted to!"

"I don't believe you." He might as well have stabbed me in the gut.

"Why are you defending your dad?" I complained. "He waited until I was alone and shot a fucking gun outside my bedroom! That's not okay, Ryder! He crossed the line this time!"

"Whatever," Ryder murmured then hung up. I buried my face in my hands and cried. Darren had been waiting for the opportunity to turn Ryder against me, and he'd finally pulled the trigger on that too.

Doug knew how much I worried about Darren putting a permanent divide between me and Ryder. He also knew I was too tired and emotionally tapped out to handle the situation with Ryder on top of everything else tonight. "Ryder's going through a lot right now, love. And so are you. Give him time to calm down while you get some sleep, and we'll figure it out tomorrow."

I shook my head. I couldn't be at peace when my son and I were at odds. But I'd have to find a way, because emotions were too high to resolve anything right now. So I sniffled, wiped my nose with the top of my index finger, took another deep breath, and lay back down. Doug switched off the bedside lamp and held me tightly, until I eventually fell asleep.

When I opened my eyes very late the next morning, Doug was smiling down at me. I couldn't help but smile back. Despite all that had happened, it had been our first sleepover together. It hadn't been the planned event we'd anticipated, but having slept in his arms was thrill enough for me. So much so, it almost made me forget about the night before.

Almost. I worried about Ryder all day—about our relationship, whether or not he believed me, how he felt about what his dad did, or what I did, if he truly believed Darren over me. I didn't want to text or call him, though. This ordeal warranted a face-to-face discussion. However, I didn't feel safe going back to the house to see him until after dark, when odds were in my favor that Darren would be asleep or at least hunkered down for the night. So I waited until almost 11 p.m. to return home.

Tears welled up in my eyes when I pulled up to total darkness. The outside light was off. Ryder's bedroom lights were out. The light in my heart was out now too. I might have lost my son for good this time. Darren may have won.

"Call It What You Want"

*I*f I could prove Darren had shot that gun, Ryder would believe me and so would the cops. I leaned back against my kitchen counter with my morning coffee clutched tightly in both hands, wondering who might have seen or heard something.

The widow who lived next to us loved Darren. He and Ryder had been tremendous help to her around her house and farm after her husband passed. She'd never even believe Darren was capable of the things he did, let alone involve herself in our mess if she did, so I couldn't ask her.

Then there was Stacy. She'd felt like the sister I'd never had until Darren had moved back home in late 2007. Darren didn't like us being friends because Stacy wasn't shy about voicing her opinions against him, so I kept my distance from *her* to avoid argument with *him*. I'd even gone so far as to voice my *dislike* of her, to make Darren think he'd influenced my opinion to match his own, whenever he ranted about the disarray of her property or threatened to shoot her dogs for eating the cat food we left out on the porch for our barn cats.

So I felt like an ass texting her to ask a favor after all these years of disassociation, but I had no other options. This was my life on the line.

Hey, Stacy—Been awhile, I know. And I'm sorry to text you out of nowhere on a Monday morning while you're busy getting the kids out to school, but I wondered if you could help me out with something. We had a couple scuffles here last week. I'm sure the cops showing up in the middle of the night Saturday woke you all up, and I'm sorry about that too. But I wonder if you might have seen or heard anything before the cops came? I'm going to try to get an order of protection against Darren, and it would help me to have proof, like a witness at least. Just let me know. If you don't want to respond or get involved, I totally understand. You don't owe me anything. Just thought I'd ask.

She responded right away. *My husband and I knew he was up to something! Darren said some strange things when he was over here drinking with us not too long ago. Like he was planning to kill you or something! We figured he was just drunk and talking his usual crap, but when we heard the gunshots and then saw all the police over there that night, we realized he'd been serious about it all.*

I unconsciously held my breath. I'd often suspected that Darren wanted to harm me, but to hear that he openly discussed murdering me was downright chilling! *I don't know what to say to that. I appreciate your honesty, though. Things have always been bad between us, but the divorce has really pushed Darren over the edge. He's getting away with it all too! The cops didn't believe me. Ryder is siding with him. I need proof Darren did something before he actually follows through with hurting me!*

Stacy texted back, *Well, my husband and I were outside having a bonfire Saturday night and heard Darren shouting before the gunshots went off. I asked my husband to go over and check on you because I knew you were home. I'd seen both of your vehicles there earlier. He didn't want to deal with Darren, though. Then after we heard the shots, I begged him to go over to make sure you were okay, but he wouldn't, and we didn't want to go over together and leave our kids home alone with Darren on the loose with a gun. So I went in the house to call the cops. But by the time I did, they were already there.*

Stacy's witness was a major development. *I hate to ask, but would you be willing to testify what you just said in court, if it came down to it?*

My husband doesn't want me getting involved at all. I think he's concerned Darren will retaliate against us somehow. But I'm not afraid of Darren. That was the Stacy I knew! *I watched my mom go through years of mistreatment and abuse with a man. She wouldn't leave and now she's dead. I'm not going to lose you too.* Stacy went on to detail some of the abuses her mother had endured. I'd often thought my situation was unique, when really, it happened to people of all ages, in all walks of life. What really struck me, however, was the injustice for victims. Some died, some were harmed, some (like me) were just trying to get out alive, but our exes walked around in normal society without repercussions. It wasn't right and I wouldn't let him get away with this.

Reinvigorated with confidence, and on a mission to seek justice for all victims of domestic violence, I skipped work and was back in the courthouse later that morning, filling out another petition for an emergency order of protection.

When the bailiff called my name, I walked into the courtroom more confidently. No judge could deny my pleas for help after what had happened this time, I thought. My heart fell, however, when I saw the same heartless judge as before. She recognized me too and didn't even try to hide the annoyed expression on her face.

After being sworn in and asked to explain why I'd returned after being rejected the first time, I indignantly pressed, "My ex sent me a derogatory text message, involving a middle finger and telling me to give my boyfriend a blow job for Sweetest Day. Then he called me a lying whore—"

"A text message is not a sufficient reason for an order of protection. Do you have any other testimony or evidence to present to the Court?" the judge interrupted. The slight tilt of her head indicated I was wasting her time.

"Yes, Your Honor. My ex shot a gun outside my bedroom window."

She stopped pushing papers around and stared me dead in the eyes. I got her attention.

"What happened exactly?"

I gladly filled her in on the details of that night.

"Were there any witnesses?"

"Yes, Your Honor. The neighbors to the east heard the shouting and the fired shots. They said they thought about coming over to make sure I was okay, but they don't trust my ex, especially with a gun. They were about to call the police when they saw six squad cars arrive at my house."

"Are they willing to testify as witnesses to what they saw?"

"The wife will, Your Honor."

"Then you will want to bring her as a witness for your next court date, where I will make a final determination. The court will summon your ex-husband to be present in court with his defense on that date as well." She looked to me for acknowledgment, and I nodded my head to confirm I understood. "You will be allowed to bring as many witnesses as you feel will support your case. They should be able to testify to your ex-husband's character, to either of the two events on your petition, or any previous incidents which were not reported to the police or in a court of law. Do you understand your rights?"

"Yes, Your Honor," I responded with premature self-assurance, though no one had ever witnessed Darren do anything more than insult or demean me.

"Then the Court finds abuse does exist, and enters an emergency order of protection. The respondent may not have contact with the petitioner and is ordered to remain ten feet away from the main house of the residence, as well as the property in Verona owned by the boyfriend of the petitioner. Respondent is also ordered to turn over all firearms in possession." The gavel hit its block. I'd won this battle, but the war wasn't over.

Although Ryder had been giving me the silent treatment he'd learned from Darren, I decided to stay home that evening. I didn't want him to see Darren served with the summons to appear, and I wanted the opportunity to explain myself if he did.

As expected, a strange car pulled up around 6 p.m. while I was in the kitchen making one of Ryder's favorite meals for dinner. Ryder came to the kitchen and saw a man knock on Darren's door and then hand him some papers. When I looked to Ryder to gauge his impression of what he saw, he glared at me, then walked out towards the second house to see what was going on. I worried while I waited for him to return, knowing he was being fed more baseless lies about me and the events leading up to this. All I could do was hope Ryder would be open to hearing my side, but he didn't come back until late that night, long after I was in bed.

Ryder had been spending more time with Darren since the night of the gun shots, so it was no coincidence he was rejecting me the same way Darren always had. But it was cruel, and I was an emotional, dysfunctional mess over it. I cried while cleaning houses, cried in the car, cried at home in bed. I got irritable with Doug, and then he didn't take my calls nor respond to my texts for a whole day. I was completely distraught at the thought I'd lost him too.

So I was relieved when Doug finally texted the next day. *I'd like to see you tonight.*

I want to see you too, but I have a sports banquet to attend for the grade school, I responded. The school sometimes offered opportunities to work off tuition, so I volunteered time with the grade school cross-country team when I could, even though Ryder hadn't been on it since junior high.

Then I'll drive you. I need to see you.

Okay. I needed to see him too. I missed him. Going an entire day without contact was like flailing my arms hopelessly as I drowned in the waters of emotional distress. I needed Doug; I needed his support and love to get through this craziness with Darren, and his encouragement to get through this hiccup with Ryder.

Doug didn't need me, though. He was too old and put together to be with someone like me, who came with so much fresh baggage. He'd probably shut me out for that day so he could think about all the drama I brought into his otherwise private life, and he'd likely decided he needed to end our relationship. I should've seen it coming. I was no stranger to silence and abandonment.

When Doug pulled up to my house that evening, he didn't get out of his Jeep to open the passenger door, nor help me with the balloons and goodie bags I piled into his back seat. He was quiet. He didn't kiss me hello when I climbed in, nor did he hold my hand while he drove. He asked where he was taking me, then looked straight ahead at the road.

I stared at him, studying his face for any clue about why he'd wanted to see me, especially if he wasn't going to say anything. His face was blank, though, and it pained me that he didn't even glance my way. So I looked out the window, watching the rain pelt it before being blown away in the wind.

I was probably right about him wanting to end things. He just didn't know how to say it, and his sensitive heart didn't want to hurt me any more than I already was. I appreciated that about him, but I wished the mature part of me could tell him it was okay. I'd be devastated, but I understood completely and wouldn't blame him. He came from a world of sunshine and rainbows, and I just brought thunderstorms to paradise.

"Thanks for the ride," I said when he pulled up to the restaurant where the school event was being held. I took my time retrieving the goodie bags and balloons I'd volunteered to bring to give him one last opportunity to say whatever he wanted to say.

Just as I'd gathered everything and was about to close the door, he said, "Call or text me when you're ready to be picked up. I'll be at my friend's house nearby."

"Okay." I expected something more, but I shouldn't have expected anything from a man who'd tolerated so much in the little time we'd been together. I watched him drive away, feeling like my heart had gone with him. I had no desire to even attempt to put on the happy face people were used to.

Once in the restaurant, however, I lightened up a bit. It was hard not to when the junior high kids I sat with were cracking jokes about farts and making faces at some of the food being served.

When Doug returned to drive me home a couple short hours later, I was my normal talkative self, eager to tell him about the funny things the kids had said and done that night, what we'd eaten, and anything else I thought to mention. Doug still seemed preoccupied, though, so I eventually quieted to give him a last opportunity to say whatever he wanted to say to me before dropping me back at home. But he remained quiet, and quiet made me nervous.

I stared out the window into the dark night, absolutely certain Doug was done with me. How could I have thought he'd want any part of my chaotic life? I came off as positive and put together—that's what had attracted him to me—but that's not who I was. In truth, I was a mess! I guess I was a fraud for presenting as someone I wasn't, and now that Doug had realized he'd been duped, I wasn't worthy of his love any more than I was worthy of my own mother's, or Darren's, or even my own.

I just wanted to go home, back to my solitary life, and hide away. If I didn't go anywhere or see anyone, I wouldn't have to feel people's rejection. I held back tears, thinking about how I was victim of a life that made me impossible to love. It wasn't fair.

When Doug missed the turn onto the road that would take me to my house and turned south towards his house instead, I looked over at him. He maintained his stare into the dark night ahead, like a man on a mission, so I didn't say anything to interrupt it. Maybe he felt more comfortable talking to me in a place I couldn't run from or lock him out of. I admittedly had a tendency to escape painful situations.

When we were almost to his house, Doug pulled his Jeep over to the side of the road. His headlights barely lit up the trees bordering the one side, and the corn field opposite, but I recognized where we were. It was the site of our first kiss. I had no clue why we were here, though. I looked to him for explanation.

Doug turned on the overhead light, then fumbled with something in his coat pocket. He pulled out a small jewelry box and fumbled with it a couple more seconds before offering it to me. Was that what I thought it was? Frozen by this unexpected moment, I looked up at Doug, who finally met my brown eyes with an intense gaze of blue.

"Will you be my wife?" he whispered.

My heart pounded. My mind screamed, YES! But I didn't understand why this man loved me when no one else would. Even if he truly did, I knew I'd mess things up eventually. I always did. I couldn't be without him, though! I'd always been drawn to him, but after we'd kissed for the first time, I'd felt like that very cheesy line Tom Cruise delivered in the movie *Jerry Maguire*—Doug "completed" me. He was it.

Seemingly nervous because I hadn't responded, Doug exited the vehicle and came around to my side. He opened my door, took my hand, and led me out into the rainy night. Then he got down on one knee in the wet grass and opened the jewelry box.

A light inside the little box illuminated a diamond heart solitaire flanked by tiny round aquamarines (Doug's birthstone and also the color of his eyes). Not only had he remembered my obsession with hearts, the infinity-shaped white gold band symbolized the forever he promised, and the forever love I'd wished for my whole life.

There was no doubt in my mind I wanted to be Doug's wife, and nothing would make me prouder than calling him my husband. So I looked into his eyes and nodded yes.

We both smiled as he slid the engagement ring on my finger. It fit perfectly.

Then I stood on my tippy toes to kiss my fiancé. And just like the first time we'd kissed, we barely noticed the rain falling upon us.

"Who's Laughing Now"

The couple weeks leading up to the early November court date were quiet—no nasty text messages or emails, no middle fingers, no screeching tires in the morning. Even after going to my sister's wedding ceremony with Doug and Ryder, Darren remained unusually unresponsive to me moving on without him.

I guessed he'd noticed the Blink cameras I'd installed a couple days after the shooting. One pointed to the front of his small house, another recorded activity behind my house from where he shot his gun, and the last took video of the concrete area between the two houses and garage. So whenever Darren decided to veer off the straight and narrow path he was suddenly walking, I'd have solid proof against him.

On the off chance Darren would now behave, I printed all the emails he'd sent to me since moving out, scouring them for references to death, killing himself, not wanting to live without me, and any other threats he'd been stupid enough to put in writing to use in court as evidence of his ill intent. It was all I had, but I had enough to work with.

The day of the court hearing, my only concern was my engagement ring. If taking a date to a wedding brought a knife and gun to my door, there was no telling what Darren would do if he found out I was engaged, which is exactly why I hadn't told Ryder yet either. Although we were on good terms again, Ryder didn't need the additional burden of keeping a secret from his dad anyway. Our little family kept too many secrets already. So I turned my diamond in towards my palm when Ryder was around, and I did the same before heading into the courthouse.

444

After climbing the four flights of stairs inside the building, I immediately spotted Stacy sitting in one of the chairs against the wall outside the courtroom I'd become too familiar with. The chair beside her was free, so I headed her way.

"Hey," I greeted in a low voice. "Thanks so much for doing this for me." I quickly looked her over, trying to remember the last time I'd actually laid eyes on her. It had been years. The only difference I noticed was her pinkish-purplish-tinted hair, which meant she was the same bold Stacy I remembered from long ago.

"No problem," she said with poker-faced indifference. I took her standoffish demeanor personally, though I couldn't reasonably expect to pick up right where we'd left off after I'd essentially ghosted her.

I looked around the overcrowded area then and spotted Darren sitting on the opposite side of the stairway. Wearing a tan suit and tie, he looked like an upstanding member of society who'd been wrongly accused of the egregious claims made against him. I, on the other hand, looked like a twelve-year-old in my knee-length Hello Kitty joggers, black fitted tee, and red Hello Kitty hair bow.

What the hell had I been thinking when I got dressed this morning? I was a planner. I thought of everything! How could I have missed this one detail which would influence everyone's perception of me? I wished I could crawl into a hole and hide.

Just then, a rotund man—clad in a 1980s suit the color of baby shit and an oversized striped tie he should have thought twice about wearing—exited the elevator and approached Darren with a handshake. After a quick exchange, they disappeared into a nearby room.

"He got an attorney?" I asked no one in particular. I had a tendency to voice almost every thought that went through my head. Then I slouched in my chair, as panic replaced the last bit of self-assuredness I'd held on to.

I hadn't even thought about getting an attorney! I'd assumed I wouldn't need one! I expected to answer questions as I'd done twice before, and then present the evidence and witness I was told to bring. No one said anything about an attorney!

When Darren and his throwback lawyer came out of the conference room, I watched the attorney make his way to where Stacy and I sat. "Dana?"

He looked at us, trying to decipher which one of us was the plaintiff.

"Yes?" I piped up.

"Can I speak to you privately, please?" he bid, then turned immediately to walk back into the room he and Darren had just come out of.

I followed him and noticed Stacy right behind me. I hadn't expected her to follow, but I was glad to have her accompaniment. I'd been gaslighted by so many people that I felt validated when someone else could vouch for what I heard and saw.

In the private room, the attorney sat at a plain wood-laminate table, upon which he plopped a pile of papers from his briefcase. There were two chairs on the opposite side of the desk facing him, but Stacy and I chose to remain standing. He wasn't my attorney. He was the enemy, and I didn't intend to be in this room with him long.

"Let's just end this now," he said with cockiness. "You know you have no case against my client. Darren will agree to stay away from you, but he gets to keep his firearms." He leaned back in his chair, favoring one arm on the arm rest.

I'd dealt with his kind before—arrogant men who thought they could strong-arm this stupid little girl into submission. He expected me to say, "You're right! Let's just all go home!" Motherfucker.

I offered a polite do-over instead. "Excuse me?"

"You're not gonna win this trial, so cut your losses now and drop the case."

"No! Darren's been abusing me for years. I won't let him get away with it anymore!"

"You realize he'll lose his firearms if you go through with this," the attorney ass-backwardly tried to guilt me. *Yeah, and I'll lose my life if I don't!*

"Exactly!" Stacy said, jumping in to support me.

"Yeah, I don't want him to have his firearms. That's partly why we're here!"

"So you're refusing to cooperate with us?" The attorney minced my words.

"Refusing to cooperate?" I repeated so he could hear how ridiculous he sounded. "Darren shot a gun outside my bedroom window. So, no, he shouldn't have firearms, and I'm not dropping the case." I pressed my lips together firmly and huffed out of my nose.

"Okay, take your chances," the attorney warned to psyche me out. It didn't work, though. I was fired up now, and that fire restored my self-confidence. Darren and his attorney thought they could get their way by pushing this little girl around, but it wasn't happening today.

"Darren didn't give a fuck about his own kid when he signed the divorce papers, but he's worried about his guns?" I complained to Stacy when we returned to our seats. She looked at me inquisitively, so I elaborated. "Yeah, he didn't ask for custody or shared custody, didn't offer financial assistance with medical insurance, tuition, food, shelter, nothing! Didn't give a flying fuck about Ryder! But he gets an attorney for his guns?" I sighed in disgust and rolled my eyes at his misplaced priorities.

Fuming anger built within me until the bailiff called us into the courtroom.

Darren's attorney sat at the long wooden table furthest from the door, and Darren sat behind him in what looked like a church pew. The bailiff motioned for me to sit at the same table I had before, and Stacy sat behind me.

The stern female judge presided again, as expected. "Cause comes on for hearing. Petitioner personally present in court, pro se. Defendant personally present in court with Attorney Loki. Attorney Loki, were you able to come to an agreement with the petitioner?"

"No, Your Honor. The petitioner refused to cooperate," he exaggerated, "therefore we proceed with trial." I looked over my shoulder at Darren. He seemed quite pleased with his attorney's manipulative tactic to dissuade the judge against me with word choice.

"Is this correct?" the judge asked, addressing me.

"I opted to proceed with this trial, Your Honor," I clarified. "*That* is correct."

"Proceed with your case, then," the judge ordered. After a moment of awkward silence, the attorney and judge looked at me expectantly.

"I am not your attorney," the judge declared, "and I will not hold your hand through this proceeding."

I guessed I was supposed to say or do something, but I didn't know what. "I'm sorry, Your Honor," I said to stall.

Loki threw me an annoyed look, then looked up at the judge. "Your Honor?"

"You of all people should know when to listen and when to speak in court, Attorney Loki. Please wait until the Court addresses you."

If I weren't feeling defeated due to insufficient preparation, I would have taken great satisfaction in the tongue lashing he'd just received.

"Would the petitioner like to call a witness?" the judge nudged, raising her eyebrows towards Stacy behind me.

I perked back up, thankful for her prodding. "Yes, Your Honor. I'd like to call our neighbor, Stacy, to the stand."

Stacy walked up to the lone chair to the side of the judge's stand, which was positioned to face everyone in the room equally. The judge swore her in and then looked at me again. I was completely oblivious as to what to do, so I sat silently, awaiting instruction.

"I'm not going to walk you through every action in this trial! Will you please question your witness?" she demanded impatiently.

"Yes, Your Honor," I replied. I quickly thought of every court scene I'd seen on TV before addressing Stacy. "Can you tell me how long you've lived next door to me and Darren?"

"About fourteen years," Stacy said.

"And can you tell the Court what you witnessed the nights of October thirteenth and October seventeenth?"

Stacy summarized what she'd heard the night Darren had brought the knife to the house, and then the night he'd shot the gun off.

"Attorney Loki, would you like to cross-examine this witness?" the judge asked.

"Yes, Your Honor," Loki said as he struggled to raise his rotund body out of a chair he seemed to be stuck in.

"Proceed," the judge permitted.

"How did you know Dana was home on the nights in question?" Loki asked Stacy.

"Because she has two vehicles and they were both parked in their normal spots," Stacy explained. "We can see their garage and main house from our house. So when I heard Darren shouting on both nights, I looked over there because I was worried about Dana."

"Did you actually see Darren with the knife or gun on either night in question?" Attorney Loki asked.

"Well, no, I didn't *see* Darren with the knife, but I heard him screaming at the top of his lungs at their son, Ryder, and I didn't like the tone or language he was using. It was clear he was extremely angry," Stacy said. "And then that Saturday night, I heard Darren yelling outside Dana's house for about fifteen minutes before shots were fired."

"So you didn't actually see him with the gun, then?"

"No, but I've heard Darren yell like that before, so I know it was him. And the shots came right after."

Loki paused to confer with Darren, then proceeded. "Stacy, my client says you don't like him. Could that be the reason why you are testifying against him?"

"You're right! I don't like him!" Stacy chuckled. "He shot one of my dogs in the neck for no reason!"

Loki scrambled. "Your Honor, I'd like to strike that last statement from the record."

"You asked the question, Mr. Loki. So don't ask if you don't like the answer," the judge warned before siding with him. "But objection sustained—irrelevant to the matter at hand."

Stricken from record or not, no one could forget hearing that Darren had shot our neighbor's pet. Given the situation, it was completely relevant to the fact that he couldn't be trusted with a gun.

The judge proceeded. "Do you have any further questions for the witness, Mr. Loki?"

"No, Your Honor." He retreated with his tail between his legs.

"Witness excused," the judge said. "Does the Plaintiff have any more witnesses?"

"No, Your Honor," I answered. I'd reached out to my mother to testify to Darren's character, since she'd offered to help me with anything I needed after the divorce. She'd witnessed him grab my arm and yell at me at one of Ryder's early birthday parties. She expressed concern after seeing him spit-scream in Ryder's face when he was a toddler. He'd also shown up at her house drunk to pick up Ryder a while back. Unfortunately, my mother had opted not to testify for me, saying there was nothing she could possibly share that would help my case.

"Does the plaintiff wish to testify?" The judge nudged.

"No, Your Honor," I responded hesitantly. My testimony was valuable, but I'd already given my side of the story in the petition for the order of protection.

The judge saw the piles of papers I had in front of me. "Does the plaintiff wish to enter evidence? If so, please hand it to the bailiff and provide the Court with an explanation. Then tag it, please, and say the words, 'I enter document number . . .' into evidence," she instructed.

I couldn't tag and present every single one of these hundreds of emails, so I decided to choose the two that would have the greatest impact on my case. I flipped through the papers quickly to avoid testing the judge's patience any more than I already had.

"Yes, Your Honor," I stalled until I found one which would suffice. Then I tabbed the first document as exhibit one. It was an email dated February 19, 2020, in which Darren stated, *I am nothing without you and am about two seconds from ending my life, as I don't want to be here without you.* Someone who threatens to take his life shouldn't have a gun in his possession.

Attorney Loki asked to see the email, then the judge pressed me to move things along. "Are there any other exhibits you'd like to enter into evidence?"

I rifled through the emails once more, looking for a specific one I'd just recalled which would sway her more effectively than the first.

"Yes, Your Honor," I said more confidently when I found it, "I'd like to enter exhibit two, an email dated May twelfth, 2020, wherein the defendant states, 'It would be easier if one of us was just dead.'"

I slid the email into a plastic sleeve provided by the bailiff, and he handed it to the judge. Attorney Loki squirmed in his seat while the judge read the email. Finally, he couldn't contain himself. "Your Honor, may I review the exhibit, please?"

The judge handed it to the bailiff, and the bailiff handed it to Loki. He looked very uncomfortable as he read it, like he might shit his pants. I almost laughed when he turned back to Darren and whispered, "Did you really write this to her?"

Darren nodded his head with down-turned eyes. He never did think things through.

I looked back at Stacy with raised eyebrows, and she had the same look of shock on her face that Darren's attorney did. *We've got him!* I couldn't help but think.

After the email was returned to the bailiff and then to the judge, the defense was asked, "Do you have any evidence to enter herein?"

"No, Your Honor," Loki said.

"The court will take a short recess, then." Everyone dispersed.

Loki approached me outside the courtroom and asked for a private meeting. I looked at Stacy, considering whether I should bring her along again, but opted to go it alone since I'd presented enough evidence to nail Darren for his offenses.

"I'll be out here if you need me," Stacy reassured with raised brows.

"Thank you," I said, then followed Loki into an empty courtroom at the far end of the waiting area. We sat at a small table with four chairs.

"Will you agree to an injunctive order?" He pulled two papers out of his briefcase and set them on the table in front of me. I read them twice over to make sure I understood his proposal before responding.

The injunctive order was essentially an agreement not to harass, abuse, stalk, intimidate, interfere, or exploit the other. It also specified a no-contact rule, legally prohibiting either party from communicating in any way with the other. I thought it interesting that Darren had been the one to do these things to me, yet his attorney was presenting the agreement to me as if *I'd* been the perpetrator.

"I'm totally fine with this," I told Loki, "except that I email Darren an invoice every month for his part of the bills, and he leaves the payment on the kitchen counter. I'd prefer he didn't come into my house with the money, but I'm not putting myself in the position to go to jail for sending him an invoice either."

"We can fix that." He took the paper and wrote, "*The Petitioner shall continue to send the Respondent the monthly bills by email each month. The Respondent shall be allowed to leave his payment on the porch of the main house.*"

"That works!" It was what I'd come here for, so I signed it. The judge would rule on the guns anyway, and I presumed she would rule in my favor after Stacy's testimony about her dog. (The dog survived, by the way, after emergency surgery which I paid for out of complete horror and embarrassment of Darren's actions.)

Back in the courtroom, Loki submitted the agreement to the judge.

"Does the Plaintiff agree to dismiss the order of protection and enter the injunctive order in its place?"

"Yes, Your Honor," I responded. I knew Darren couldn't go no contact with me, so it was only a matter of time before he would break the rules and end up in jail, where he belonged.

"The Court will enter the agreement of the parties as an order of the Court and dismiss the emergency order of protection. The defendant is ordered to remove all firearms from the property, effective immediately."

I couldn't help but smile. Darren didn't like being told what to do, and he sure as hell wasn't going to allow any court to dictate his behavior either. So even though I left the courthouse no safer than I'd been before, I now had the ability to make him pay the consequences of what he'd do, which was justice enough for me.

Two days later, I came out to my car in the middle of the afternoon and found a note on my windshield. It read, *Please leave my mail in the mailbox.*

I'd been leaving his mail on his doorstep for months, but he wanted to make an issue of it now? No. What he wanted was for me to call the police for violating the injunctive order so he'd be carted off to jail. It would look like an overreaction when Ryder discovered his dad was arrested over a note about mail, and I'd lose my son again. I couldn't risk my relationship with Ryder so soon after getting back on track. So instead of notifying the authorities, I tucked the note in my planner. I'd learned long ago to always keep leverage in my back pocket, especially where Darren was concerned. And he never failed to hand it right to me.

"Better Days"

The Goo Goo Dolls song played on my Amazon Echo, adding even more of a melancholy overshadowing to the normally festive chore of putting up the Christmas tree and holiday decorations. So much so that I didn't pour the glass of Port wine while I sang along to Christmas music, as I'd done every year before. This year was different because it would be the last Thanksgiving and Christmas celebrated in our house.

When I was finished, rustic bells hung from the tree with plaid fabric ribbon, and red twig berry garland encircled the skinny but tall evergreen artifice. Snowflakes made of cinnamon sticks Ryder and I had made when he was little were strategically balanced onto the bendable limbs, and a cheery primitive snowman held onto the top with a red burlap bow I'd bought to match the quilted snowman tree skirt. Presents would cover it before long, but only for Ryder—another reminder of what remained after marital ruin.

The Christmas stockings were hung in their normal position along the garland twisted around the stair rail, minus one. Santa Claus and snowman figures were placed in their usual spot, except for the "dad" snowman in the wooden snowman family Jane and Henrik had handcrafted for us long ago. Henrik would be gone fifteen years this Christmas, I thought. Then I crossed myself and blew a kiss up to heaven.

The facade of Christmases past wouldn't fill the obvious void, but it gave the impression of stability for Ryder and helped prove to myself that life went on after divorce.

Ryder would spend the holidays as he always had—going to my mother's home for Christmas Eve, and then Jane's on Christmas Day. I

453

only asked to have Ryder Christmas morning, before I left for 9 a.m. mass. Ryder said Darren had agreed, probably thinking he'd won something over me, which was fine because I'd use my perceived sacrifice as negotiation leverage in the future if I had to.

So on Christmas morning, I went through my usual Christmas morning routine, overcompensating for Darren's absence. I dressed in holiday colors, choosing a sleeveless dark green blouse draped elegantly over black leggings. Then I applied the bright red lipstick I'd worn the year before, when Darren had told me I looked like a whore. A Christmas whore, I corrected, who baked monkey bread, played Christmas music, and couldn't wait to open presents with her kid.

When the scent of freshly baked Monkey bread finally lured Ryder out of bed, I jumped up and down like a little kid. "Can we open presents? Is it time yet? Can we? Can we?"

"Jeez! Relax, Mom!" He presented himself as cool, but I saw the smirk he tried to hide.

"Merry Christmas, kid." I wrapped my arms around him and squeezed. He just barely touched my back, but I didn't take offense. He'd grown less affectionate with age.

"All right!" I said as I pulled out a kitchen chair and placed it near the tree. "Have a seat, kid! It's all about you this year!" He smirked again and took his place on the make-shift throne.

I handed him one gift after another, waiting excitedly for him to open each. "Whad'ja get? Whad'ja get?" I joked in a high-pitched voice. We smiled and laughed. Nothing made me happier than seeing my kid happy, especially after all we'd been through.

When the last gift had been opened and we'd cleaned up the mess of ribbons and paper, I left for mass. I'd agreed to spend the day away from the house and not return until evening to give Darren and Ryder privacy to celebrate Christmas without the awkwardness of my presence. Doug and I were hosting his two sons, daughter-in-law, and grandson at his house anyway, and they were expected around lunchtime.

Before Doug's kids arrived, though, I started feeling dizzy. Then I felt cold and clammy. I couldn't see straight. In the midst of baking biscuits, I needed to lie down. Before I did, I measured my oxygen saturation and heart rate with the pulse oximeter a nurse had given me. As suspected, both rates were lower than normal. I ended up in bed with my portable oxygen machine, until Doug and his daughter-in-law awoke me to check if I was okay.

I wasn't. Although my stress-triggered symptoms had eased since the divorce and coupling up with Doug, being away from Ryder on Christmas didn't feel right. Neither did cooking and opening presents for kids who weren't mine. But things were different now, so I did what I always did and pushed through. I smiled despite my heartache, shortness of breath, and accompanying headache and played with Doug's grandson despite my exhaustion.

When they left, Doug tucked me back into bed and napped with me into early evening. We woke up a few hours later, realizing we were late to his family's gathering at his dad's house. Although my head still pounded, and harder than before, we rushed out the door.

On our way to Doug's dad's, I texted Ryder. *Whenever you're done with your dad, feel free to come down!*

I'm fine. Have fun.

I knew Ryder well enough to know something was wrong, and his bad moods were usually linked to Darren in some way.

"Check your cameras to see what's going on over there," Doug suggested when I shared my concern. I quickly pulled up the Blink app on my phone and spied on my house.

There were only a few recordings for the day. The first showed me leaving for mass just before 9 a.m. Around 11 a.m., Ryder walked off our porch and got into Darren's truck, and they drove off. The third recording was at 12:26 p.m. and showed Darren's truck pulling in the drive. He went into his house and Ryder came into ours. Then two minutes later, Darren left alone, and there'd been no more activity since. I checked the clock in a panic. It was almost 7 p.m. That meant Ryder had been alone all day—all *Christmas* Day!

Thankfully, Doug and I had driven to his dad's separately. So I wished everyone a happy holiday, then left for home, feeling like the worst mother ever.

My fucking ex had done this on purpose too. He wouldn't tell anyone he'd only spent an hour and a half with his son; he'd only share that Ryder had been left alone all day, because I'd abandoned him for Doug and his kids. I just hoped Ryder didn't see it that way. He tended to believe the bullshit stories his dad fed him. Hopefully Ryder knew I'd have been home in a heartbeat had I known he'd been left alone.

When I arrived at the house, I sat in my car for a moment to text Doug I'd arrived safely.

I'll be up to see you shortly, love. His response made me smile.

Movement in the rearview mirror caught my eye. The light in our kitchen allowed me to see through the pitch black of the winter evening and into the house, where Ryder was bent behind the Christmas tree. White lights immediately illuminated the kitchen and living room, so I got out of the car and went into the house.

As I entered through the door, I heard Ryder order, "Alexa, play Christmas music."

"Rockin' Around the Christmas Tree" sounded from the Amazon Echo, creating a festive atmosphere where jubilance had previously been discouraged.

So, even though my head was killing me, I put on my red-lipped smile and sang along with the Christmas carols.

I couldn't help but notice the quantity, quality, and expense of the gifts Ryder laid out on the kitchen table. It looked like he'd displayed them just for me to see. "You had a good Christmas, huh?" I asked.

"Yeah!" He seemed more chipper now that I was there. We talked about the different presents he'd received and from whom. Then he turned his attention to my gifts.

"Did you set up your new computer yet?" he asked, referring to the expensive laptop my mother and stepfather had given me for Christmas, as a show of what wonderful parents they were to an unappreciative daughter.

Although I'd put the laptop on my Amazon wish list, I intended to return it to them, since we weren't even on speaking terms. Ryder didn't need to hear that crap, though, so I surrendered my pride in lieu of my son's wish for me to keep the device. "No, but if you want to take it out of the box and help me get it going, that would be great!"

"Yeah, let's do it!" he agreed, and sat on the sofa to remove the laptop from its packaging. I poured myself a glass of wine I didn't need and plopped down next to him while he went through the set-up process on the screen.

"It's asking for a password." Ryder looked to me for a response.

"Um . . ."

"It'll be the password to unlock the computer, so keep it simple. Something you'll remember," Ryder advised.

"Okay, I got one, then." I said four numbers aloud. Ryder looked at me with scrunched brows, then typed the numbers into the set-up prompt.

"I know those numbers don't make sense to you, but they're kind of a big deal to me," I said, hinting for him to ask for elaboration. I took a sip of my wine while I waited for a curiosity he didn't have. "Look, I know you must have noticed the diamond ring on my finger by now. You're observant. And smart. And you know what this ring means."

With removing his focus from the laptop screen, Ryder responded, "Yeah . . . a little fast if you ask me, but . . ."

"I know. And I'm sorry for not telling you sooner. But I'm telling you now. And those four numbers are the date Doug and I are getting married next year. You okay with that?"

Ryder shrugged, then turned to face me. "Yeah. Just once, though. If you get divorced and get married again . . ."

"Ryder!" I scolded, just as the familiar headlights of Doug's Jeep came up the driveway. I got up to open the door for Doug while Ryder completed the set-up of the laptop.

Doug handed me a baggie with a few Advil inside. "Here you go, sweetheart. I brought it from my dad's." Then he blew hard into his fists to warm his hands from the cold.

It was good for Ryder to see how Doug treated me with care and consideration, I consciously noted. He'd never seen any man treat me well. "Thank you, babe!" I downed the medicine with the last of my moscato, then attempted to integrate Doug into the night. "Ryder and I were just setting up my new laptop!"

This was Doug's first time in the house with me and Ryder, so I knew we had to take baby steps with my kid. I had no expectations other than common courtesy for now, though I knew their common interests would make them great friends when Ryder was ready to open his heart to another man in my life. He just needed time, and Doug and I would be patient.

"What are these? Connectors?" Doug referred to a small pouch of rainbow-colored automotive wiring components on the kitchen table. I loved how adaptable he was, no matter what the situation.

"Yeah," Ryder responded flatly. His back was to Doug, so he didn't even see the item Doug was asking about.

"What are they for? Car audio?" Doug had an inquisitive nature. Plus, his positive mind set was oblivious to Ryder's adamant refusal to engage with him.

Ryder turned around then to see what Doug was asking about. "Yeah." Then he put the laptop on the coffee table and walked to where Doug stood at the kitchen table, to explain how he used the connectors to wire audio systems in vehicles. That led into electrical talk I didn't understand, but it was music to my ears to hear my kid and my guy having a conversation.

"Ryder's a genius with lighting and audio," I said. "He installs all that stuff in his friends' vehicles for them. You should see the LEDs in his room too!"

"Yeah, it's pretty cool," Ryder told Doug, heading into the back bedroom to give Doug a demonstration of the different color and light patterns the strips around the ceiling perimeter offered through remote control.

"That is cool!" Doug scanned the room and pointed at the wall-mounted entertainment center under Ryder's TV. "What kind of stereo is that?"

"JVC, and I've got the Bose speakers and subwoofer hooked up to my Bluetooth."

"It's my old stereo from junior high, but Ryder makes it sound like a club in here when he gets it going!" I joked. Ryder was only too eager to provide another show. After a few taps of his computer keyboard, the walls vibrated with every boom of the bass in the music he played. My head hurt, but my heart was happy.

I just wished my asshole ex were here to see his own plans blowing up in his face. Like the long-awaited sleepover he'd effected for me and Doug on Sweetest Day, Doug and Ryder bonding as a result of Darren's vengeful neglect was the best Christmas gift he could have ever given me.

"Good Riddance (Time of Your Life)"

Bought a house, Darren emailed, knowing I wouldn't risk my relationship with Ryder by reporting this violation of the no-contact order. *Closing around the end of January but will need to stay here until mid-February while I do some repairs there. Hope that's okay.*

Of course! I replied, presuming Darren wouldn't risk his relationship with Ryder either. *And congratulations!*

I thought I'd never get him off the property, so I was relieved to watch him emptying his small house over the next month. The more Darren took, the less he was around; and the less he was around, the more peace I felt at home. My heart broke for Ryder, though, who was watching his dad leave us for the final time.

It affected Ryder deeply, I knew. He became snippier. He stopped talking to me, perhaps feeling I was at fault for dismantling the life we'd known. I didn't mind taking the brunt of his feelings. I understood he was angry, and I was glad he was comfortable expressing his true emotions to me. That meant he knew he was safe with me—that no matter what he said or did, I would love him unconditionally and would never leave him. Still, I was frustrated that there was nothing I could do or say to soothe the rejection and abandonment he felt. I'd struggled with it in my own life, and had yet to know how to resolve it.

So when Darren's official moving day came, the day before Valentine's Day 2021, I opted to stay away. I didn't want Ryder to deal with any tension or argument that would result from conflict between me and Darren, nor did I want to make the friends who'd sided with Darren in the divorce feel awkward for helping him move. I had to work anyway.

I'd forgotten to turn off my Blink notifications, though, so my phone dinged every time one of the cameras sensed motion, which was all day. Eventually curiosity got the best of me, and I took a break from cleaning to sit in my car and watch some of the videos.

I thought watching Darren move would make me happy, that I'd feel some sense of victory. Instead, seeing the moving truck and the trailer being filled with furniture and boxes reminded me of the last time he'd packed his things in a box truck back in 2007. The difference was there would never be another last time. After twenty-five years of always coming back to each other, no matter how destructive our relationship was, this was it.

Unhealed wounds suddenly overwhelmed me, and I burst into tears. No matter what I did, what I bought him, or however else I tried to be the wife he'd expected me to be, I wasn't good enough. I wasn't worthy of his love despite tolerating years of verbal and emotional abuse, physical threat, infidelity, and financial devastation. I wasn't worthy of his time or attention, even though I'd submitted to his every whim and demand. I wasn't even worthy of kindness, despite having revolved my entire existence around him and allowing him to live the life he'd always dreamed of. No, I was a piece of garbage he'd just thrown out like a piece of junk mail that didn't matter.

My nature to overthink then wandered into doubts about Doug. Did he really love me, or did I serve some purpose to him too? Was I just a replacement for his ex-wife, who'd cheated on him and left him to marry the other man? Would it last, or would he eventually tire of me too? I knew better than to believe promises of forever, but I wanted that forever so badly my naivete sometimes got in the way of clear thought.

Then there were thoughts of Ryder, who hadn't been good enough for Darren either. "He's *your* son!" Darren would say to dissociate from him. "You two are just fine without me!" he rightfully asserted many times, intending to guilt us for ignoring his attention-seeking tantrums, though it was Darren who continuously removed himself from the family unit. "It's always the two of you against me!" He'd accuse, further dividing himself from us.

Darren had never wanted a family, though, so I couldn't be surprised he was leaving the one he'd made. But Ryder didn't deserve to be burdened with his dad's failings—nor mine, to be fair. I had been the one to bring him into this world to suffer with me to begin with.

When the coast was clear that night, I was anxious to get home. Doug accompanied me. He knew how concerned I was for Ryder and wanted to be at the house to support us both.

As we drove up the gravel drive, I scanned the grounds, like I was looking for something. The second-story window in the second house, which usually glowed from Darren's constant TV watching, was vacant and dark. The trucks and trailer which usually crowded the side drive between the big barn and chicken coop were gone. The place almost looked abandoned. It was eerie.

When I got out of the car, I looked around for what I still sensed was missing. Then I realized what it was—my triggers, my anxiety, my fears, the tension and worry that I'd done something wrong or something bad was going to happen. It wasn't that Darren was gone, but rather the effects of him. I had apparently grown attached to the trauma he'd put upon me, and now I felt empty. I wondered if Ryder felt the same.

Eager to get to my son, I rushed through the door, with Doug right behind me. We immediately froze when we saw the empty eating area. The kitchen table, which Darren had crafted for me from tree trunks and carefully chosen maple wood planks, was gone. Never mind he was legally prohibited from entering the house; he'd done so to prove the rules didn't apply to him, and, additionally, to affect Ryder. Only a selfish bastard could leave a boy and his mother without a table to eat meals upon together.

Ryder appeared out of the dead-quiet hallway. He saw me and Doug standing there, with the door wide open, staring at the empty space.

Like a well-trained soldier, he retreated to his bedroom and returned with the black folding table he'd borrowed from me a while back. He carried it to the center of the eating area, and slowly folded the four stick legs outward. Then he flipped it over to stand it upon its flimsy legs and centered it under the light fixture.

I remained still as I watched Ryder place our four white farmhouse-style wood chairs around it. I wasn't sure if he was trying to pacify his own anger, prevent me from unnecessary upset over family dinners that would never be, or if it was a strong show of how Darren couldn't affect us. Whatever the reason, Ryder's determination to withstand Darren's offense made me proud. In all these years with Darren, I'd demonstrated to Ryder how to rise above the bullshit and make the best of what we were left with. And now, in this very emotional moment, my son was showing me how to do the same.

I stood more resolutely then, matching Ryder's strength to move forward.

Doug placed his hand on my back, as if to guide me to sit at the table Ryder had just made for us. I looked up at him with a grateful smile, and took my first brave steps forward into our new life.

I went to the cupboard above the refrigerator, removed a red plastic tablecloth I'd used for parties, and spread it over the thinly cushioned top of the card table. Ryder helped me even it out and we all sat down.

Although no words were shared between us, I knew Ryder and I were thinking the same thing. Darren could deprive us of his love. He could strip us of our sense of who we were and what we could be. He could take away the table where we tried to sit as a family, and remove himself from our family altogether. But he couldn't destroy our family like he'd tried so hard to do.

Ryder and I were still here. We had each other. And now Doug. And a folding table. Standing on flimsy legs, but still standing.

We were resilient.

Afterward - "Still Breathing"

Although the plan was to put the house on the market in the summer, Darren's early move and rising home values made me anxious to have the house on the market in time for the equally anxious spring buyers who'd waited all winter for more inventory to choose from. Plus, Stacy and I had reconnected as friends and had decided to get our real estate broker's licenses together. We'd formed a real estate team at a local office, and my farm would attract the potential buyers we needed to kick-start business.

"Then let's get the house on the market," Ryder said after I mentioned all this during one of our nightly chats. He stood in front of the fireplace with his hands in the pockets of his jeans to keep warm.

I gulped the tomato soup in my mouth. "Really?"

"Yeah, it makes the most sense." Ryder was always very logical and matter-of-fact.

"You sure? I mean, I know I'm ready, but are you?"

"Yeah, this place needs too much work. Better to sell before something happens you can't afford to fix."

I thought he'd give me more resistance, since this was his childhood home, so I was thrilled to have his approval. I put the house on the market in mid-March, and it sold the next day, after receiving multiple offers well over the asking price.

Over the course of the next month, I took carfuls of belongings to Doug's. Although Ryder had agreed to the move, I thought it better to transition slowly. He'd already been through several major life changes in a short time. I had to be sensitive to that.

On the other hand, I was glad to finally move on. Like everything else, this farm had been one of Darren's wants. The only thing I wanted was to be rid of it.

By the time the movers came with their semi-truck at the end of April, the house was barren. Closets and cabinets were empty. No pictures or décor hung on the walls. Only the beds, sofas, and the large basement TV remained.

Doug spent the last night at the house with us, and after Ryder left for school, he took the beds apart and assisted the movers. I wasn't used to people doing things for me, so I tried to help.

"Just have your coffee, sweetheart," Doug insisted. "We'll take care of everything. It won't take us long anyway." I smiled as he caressed my upper arm, knowing he wanted me to take my time saying goodbye to this place.

So I stood at my kitchen sink in my gray pajama pants and lighter gray T-shirt, looking out the window to the back couple acres. The sun was shining, but I could feel the chilly spring air coming in through the open doors. I sipped my hot coffee to warm myself, noting this would be my last morning coffee here.

We'd had a lot of "lasts" during the past year. I didn't think they'd make me sad because I'd been so focused on ridding myself of this life, but this life made me who I was. It was Ryder's foundation. We couldn't deny the bad times, but we couldn't forget the memories made here either.

After the moving truck pulled away, Doug came to where I stood in the kitchen. He wiped a tear from my cheek, then bent down to look into my eyes. "You okay, love?"

I looked at his smiling face and couldn't help but smile back. He knew what I didn't have to say, and the empathy he communicated showed me love without words.

As Doug straightened back up, I set my empty cup on the counter. I wiped under my eyes with both hands and licked the salty tears from my lips. Then I looked back up at Doug with hopeful eyes and took a deep breath.

"Whenever you're ready, I'll be in the car," he said. Then he left me to my final goodbye.

Leaning back against the kitchen counter, I faced the living room. With everything removed, I barely recognized the place. It was like looking at someone you used to know, but not being able to match the memory of them to the person they are now. How could that be after seventeen years? Tears filled my eyes again.

I went upstairs to the master bedroom next to make sure we took everything. *Some of the worst moments of my life happened here*, I thought. Yet, I struggled to reconcile how a room that held my deepest, darkest secrets also seemed so detached and foreign to me now. I mean, my son had been stolen from me in this room! Darren had nearly killed me with a forceful punch in the bed that used to occupy this space. Just months earlier, Darren had shot his gun outside these windows! I'd thought I was going to die in this room that night. Had I numbed myself for so long I couldn't even remember how to feel in this house? Or had life become that turbulent that I was unfazed by the chaos? Either way, I didn't want to take my old life into my new one, and that new one was outside waiting for me.

So I shut the bedroom door, walked down the stairs, and solemnly closed the glass entry door. With one last look inside, I left all the broken promises, heartache, mistakes and regrets, with this unrecognizable old friend, and pressed the lock button.

Then I felt the cat rub herself on the back of my leg.

"Nut!" She was the last of our many barn cats to remain. Darren was supposed to have taken her, but here she still was, two months later.

I picked her up and snuggled her close to my face. She rubbed her head along my chin and cheeks eagerly. She'd always been so affectionate. I hated leaving her behind to fend for herself. Hopefully the new owners would love her as much as we did.

I climbed into the car with her for a longer goodbye. Doug reached over and pet her on the head. "Hi, Nut!" he greeted as she purred loudly. "You coming with us?"

My sad eyes popped open excitedly. "Can she?"

"Well, we're not going to leave her behind! Are we, Nut?" he coddled with a baby-talk voice. His love of animals made me smile. It was the first quality that had drawn me to him years before. "Ready?"

I closed the Jeep door and clicked my seat belt in the buckle. "Freddy!" I gave Nut a deep massage as Doug proceeded down the gravel drive, though I think I needed the soothing more than she did.

As I watched the farm fade away in the side mirror, I recalled the hopeful and naïve young woman who'd first carried her nine-month-old baby into that house. I'd tried so hard to make a good life for him here. All the parties, bonfires, farm animals, trees, and gardens . . . I'd just wanted to give Ryder the simplicity, peace, and happiness I never had as a child. A piece of me would always remain here, but that young woman was a distant memory, just like the life that had tried to break me down.

But I'd prevailed. I learned to decipher friends from enemies, and to protect and defend until the bitter end. I wore my battle scars proudly, as a reminder of where I'd been and what obstacles I'd had to overcome to get to where I was going. I'd risen above every challenge set before me and helped my son transform his own wounds into strength, wisdom, and maturity only life experience could provide. I was proud of the young man he'd become, and prouder of myself for holding on to the hope of love despite it all.

Love was all I'd ever wanted anyway. I'd thought I needed to earn it. I'd gone to great lengths to get it. When I hadn't, I'd thought I didn't deserve it. But when I'd finally realized my worth, I'd discovered love had been in me all along.

© Jenny Taylor Boudoir Photography

A survivor of child abuse and an abusive marriage, Dana Diaz has made it her mission to serve as a voice for victims of narcissistic abuse. Her experiences were the source of inspiration for *Gasping for Air*, her first book.

Dana lives with her husband in Illinois and is working on the prequel and sequel to *Gasping for Air*.

Learn more about Dana at www.danasdiaz.com